NORTHERN LIGHTS

NORTHERN LIGHTS

A Selection of New Writing from the American West

· ◆ ◆ ◆ ◆ ·

Edited by
Deborah Clow and Donald Snow

Vintage Books   *A Division of Random House, Inc.*   *New York*

A VINTAGE ORIGINAL, FIRST EDITION
NOVEMBER 1994

Foreword and compilation copyright © 1994 by Northern Lights
Introduction copyright © 1994 by Louise Erdrich

Library of Congress Cataloging-in-Publication Data
   Northern lights : a selection of new writing from the American West
   / edited by Deborah Clow and Donald Snow.—
     Vintage Original 1st ed.
        p.   cm.
     ISBN 0-679-75542-X
        1. West (U.S.)—Literary collections.   2. American literature—
   West (U.S.)
     I. Clow, Deborah.   II. Snow, Donald.   III. Northern lights.
   PS561.N67   19994
   810.8'0978—dc20   94-10196
                   CIP

Book Design by Robert C. Olsson

Manufactured in the United States of America
10   9   8   7   6   5   4   3   2

This book is dedicated to the memory of Carol Abrams
1950–1991

Ian,

Someday, we too will write about our time in our Grandfather's backyard.

Remember our Fall stroll through the sagebrush? Who could forget the Summer dust storm in Monument Valley? How about the time we froze our tails at Tuolumne Meadows?

We are lucky to have such a playground. I am lucky to have you.

Happy Birthday!

Ken
(1997)

CONTENTS

FOREWORD

For most of this century, the American West was a kind of national hobby. Unless you fished it, hunted it, vacationed in it, or got stationed in it, you probably thought about it much like that great *New Yorker* cover pictured it: an increasingly brown area somewhere beyond Cincinnati. Most didn't take its contributions to politics, art, or culture very seriously.

For people like our parents, who were born in the West, grew up here, went to school, married, and took jobs here, the West was never a hobby but a home. Most Westerners didn't realize that they were provincial. They didn't regard the East with bitter envy—the way America once regarded Europe—but perhaps felt slightly sorry for people who had to live amid such crowding. Westerners knew people loved to visit but didn't want to stay.

All of that has changed.

The West is now *the* place. Everybody's got a theory about it, everybody's got a crush on it, everybody wants a ranch in it, everybody wants to decorate with it. We binarians know that this, too, shall pass, perhaps in a nanosecond, but the die at any rate is cast. The West we grew up in is now a serious place making serious contributions to politics, art, culture, and fortunes in real estate, though not so serious that anyone needs to frown about it.

Northern Lights magazine publishes Westerners who write about the West. That is to say, they may be discussing marriage, divorce, habaneros, children, Hussein, horses, orgasms, beetle-kill, Dutch ovens, canoe trips, curling, Gifford Pinchot, viruses, Vietnam, assassination, acid rain, caffeine, or sports medicine, but they will invariably be discussing these somehow in relation to place. The place is the West. We stopped apologizing about this a long time ago.

People in the West see things differently than people anywhere else. It's a way of sensing things, a way of carrying the landscape inside, of moving through days the way rivers move through canyons and mountain valleys. This place casts its spell on the lives of those who inhabit it, and it is a serious and lasting spell. Perhaps every place on earth resonates with its own voice. The language that arises out of the landscapes of the West is as rich and splendidly textured as the place it describes. It is this voice that carries *Northern Lights*.

When Northern Lights Institute started the magazine in 1984, our board and staff had only the vaguest sense of what it could become. We expected to create a simple vehicle to publish the research findings of our nascent policy institute. But policy research is intrinsically boring, and places are intrinsically interesting, and the writers we managed to recruit were, anyway, far too absorbed in the experiments of their own lives to keep us very firmly wedded to policy in any conventional sense. If *Northern Lights* is a demonstration of anything, it is a demonstration of the power of place and nature in our lives.

Our greatest joy as the editors of the magazine and this anthology is the opportunity to publish new and emerging writers and artists. We are honored to have helped bring to readers' attention such writers as Rick Bass, Judy Blunt, John Daniel, Jeanne Dixon, Richard Manning, Ellen Meloy, Leslie Ryan, Mark Spragg, Jack Turner, Terry Tempest Williams, and many others. In a very literal sense, these are the voices of the New West.

Our debts of gratitude are enormous. First, we are grateful to the forty writers whose works appear in this book. Their generosity and good will allowed this anthology to be gathered. Next, we thank the many more writers and artists who have offered their hearts' work to *Northern Lights* magazine during its first ten years of publication.

Dan Whipple and Kathy Bogan, the magazine's original editor and designer, cut the trail we're still on. They gave the magazine its trademark, its central nervous system, its spice. Their vision, hard work, and clear thinking created *Northern Lights* and provided their home region with its enduring legacy.

Great writers demand great readers, and we have them. As a noncommercial magazine with practically no advertising, *Northern Lights* is a reader's trove. Our readers are very peculiar in one respect: they volunteer their financial contributions to the magazine, using a formula that more resembles support for public radio than conventional magazine subscribership. They know that if they don't contribute, we go off the air. The magic of that odd relationship has worked for most of the years *Northern Lights* has been alive.

We are also grateful to the Institute board members who saw the wisdom in making a magazine rather than a newsletter, and let the creature grow her own way after she was born. Med Bennett, Coleen Cabot, Betsy Coombs, Lucy Dayton, Barbara Dobos, Chase Hibbard, Huey Johnson, Robert Muth, Skip Oppenheimer, Janine Windy Boy Pease, Jack Pugh, Ken Pursley, Mary Lou Reed, Ann Roberts, Jon Roush, Peter Seligmann, Arnold Silverman, Pat Smith, John Fell Stevenson, John Thorson, Richard Trudell, Conley E. Ward, John Washakie, Dennis Wheeler, Charles F. Wilkinson, and Terry Tempest Williams have all shared in the struggle to make the magazine a success.

The many funders who have helped along the way are the hidden heroes of practically all the real work that gets done in the public interest. We are especially grateful to the George Frederick Jewett Foundation, the Cultural and Aesthetic Grants Program of the State of Montana, the Rockefeller Family Fund, the Charles Englehard Foundation, Patagonia, Inc., the William and Flora Hewlett Foundation, the Ford Foundation, Asarco, Inc., the Jessie Smith Noyes Foundation, the Wyoming Arts Council, and the Montana Arts Council.

Lynanne Otto, Bill Clarke, and Carol Abrams have held our tiny publishing business together over the years with loving management, a million envelopes, glue, and the most carefully tended circulation list in North America. Maeta Kaplan, Nancy Leifer and Richard Opper made critical contributions of labor and talent at critical times.

Finally, our thanks go to Jenna Laslocky, our visionary editor at Vintage Books. She shares our joy in this venture and knows she has a seat in the *Northern Lights* raft anytime. Renee Wayne Golden, our attorney, never gave up, and knows how to fish.

Deb Clow and Don Snow
Missoula, Montana
April 1994

INTRODUCTION

by LOUISE ERDRICH

"A good marriage," said Rainer Maria Rilke, "is that in which each appoints the other the guardian of his solitude." Most of us take our marriage to place for granted—though it involves our most fundamental survival here on earth. In this relationship, our task should be to protect the solitude, the basic integrity, of our vast and fragile partner. The question is—how are we to know what is right and proper? How are we to understand what a place needs? What sustains a world so complex and marvelous as ours?

Vigorously, by questioning, each from a private and determined ground, the writers in this collection wrestle with the problems and beauties of the American West. Our intricate, raw, and spacious ground is hurting. *We live surrounded by scars and loss*, writes Jack Turner. *This is my home, my home is a mess, and the damage is not random. It is caused by specific ideas and values, wounded by specific uses of language.* Reading just what specific language Jack Turner despises will give most of us a singular thrill of recognition, and all through his work, as through the body of this book, an energy of questions tumbles.

Who knows what place this is? An Inupiaq friend, Kuvlu, challenges Richard Nelson. *What's this got to do with cowboys and ranchers, anyway? And, holy cows on the hoof?* asks Edward Abbey. *Is a cowboy's work socially useful? No.* David Quammen asks the simple and essential question that must be asked when attempting to understand why it doesn't work to create desert isles of wilderness and call them national parks: *How big is big enough?* Terry Tempest Williams, in her penetrating and painful essay, asks simply of the incidence of breast cancer among her loved ones, *Is our family a cultural anomaly?* Answering that question requires this brave and honorable woman to examine personal and family history, and, eventually, the political history of her beloved home country.

A writer can also heal with questions of language. Leslie Ryan begins her personal essay with an extraordinary statement: *I have heard it said that storytelling starts with the body and ends with the body. . . . But as a woman I worry about this. For most women, the body, like the story, is not a simple thing. It's a battlefield. . . . I want a different story.* Women do tell different stories—fierce, medicinal, brainy. Linda Hogan's "Stories of Water" is a generous and lyrical expansion of thought. Gretel Ehrlich inquires wonderfully into the origin of design and the use of space. *If I built a house,* she says, *it would be part wild, part human, part beast.*

Jim Harrison seems to inhabit that very house, and writes, as always, out of a powerful thirst. A wise eccentric of passionate hungers, he describes the spiritual practice that attends the eating of bearmeat:

Eat it and dream, he says.

What story shall we dream?

The Native American people were living coherent lives, at one with their circumstances, when our people displaced them. . . . writes William Kittredge. That's about the best description of life anywhere that I can imagine—*coherent, at one with circumstances.* In one of this book's most moving passages, Frederick Turner relates the testimony of the great-granddaughter of a Wounded Knee survivor:

"To the wasicus," Marie Not Help Him said at length, "all this happened a long time ago. To the Lakota people this is still with us. We are still in mourning. I can still remember my great-grandfather holding me on his lap. I can still hear his voice telling me this and how hard his heart pounded when he would tell about the deaths of his family. I can feel his breath on my forehead, how it smelled of sage. It always reminded me of things growing."

Natural questions attend being and becoming at home in the world. Marilynne Robinson carefully considers Western myth and points out now with quiet irony that, *In our America the word "free" is likely to be followed by "trade" or "enterprise."* Debra Earling writes, from a tough Native American woman's heart, of individual and earth-linked power. *There you are,* she says, *standing on the wide prairie, knowing your feet touch your own grave.* The thought is desperately comforting, and Earling's dream of rage and purity stands here in striking contrast to Judy Blunt's bewildering memoir of what it was to grow up a ranch child, cut off from any true apprehension of tribal people, Gros Ventre or Cree, by her parents' hatreds. John Daniel uses an almost religious sense of language to describe what it truly means to clearcut in Weyerhaeuser's Northwest empire, and William DeBuys's airplane vision of the death of the Southwest is echoed by Jack Turner's horror at seeing Seattle from above. It is Ellen Meloy's gift to describe the hilariously awful regulated *"quality wilderness experience"* for river runners on a remote river in southern Utah. *Today's load is priests troubled by lapsed faith—pale, anxious, overweight fellows in the early stages of heatstroke.*

Gary Paul Nabhan gives us a visionary and religious look at the biological meaning of tumbleweeds that becomes a myth-deflating history of one of the staples of western kitsch—*tumbleweeds infest the most wounded places*—could be a song lyric but for its botanical truth. And over and over the marriage metaphor surfaces. Daniel Kemmis quotes Emma Goldman's description of a working marriage: *"Behind every marriage stands the life-long environment of the two sexes; an environment so different from each other that man and woman must remain strangers. Separated by an insurmountable wall of superstition, custom, and habit, marriage has not the potentiality of developing knowledge of, and respect for, each other, without which every union is doomed to failure."*

These writers, and others in this deep and generous collection, attempt to climb that insurmountable wall, to explain, to contend with this marriage, so easily denied and forgotten in cities—even though that is where nature is in effect piped straight in for massive consumption. Turn on a light in New York City and you're sucking energy from James Bay, destroying the habitat for animals upon which the Misstasini Cree have long depended for their lives. Turn on the water tap in Fargo and you're guzzling down a once-endless aquifer. Your refrigerator hums in Minneapolis, sustained by nuclear power from a Mississippi River island where dry-cask nuclear waste storage is cause for battle. Turn on a tap in Los Angeles . . .

Who knows what place this is?

The question has lodged in my mind. We depend fully on the earth and most of us give nothing back—the least we can do is inquire after the tallgrass or the city park, the river or the secretive mountain. To base our marital acts upon a fundamental respect requires that we each try to understand the other. The difference between clear-cutting a mountain's base and walking among its trees, or even selectively and intelligently logging them, is the difference between rape and making love—one an act of contempt, the other a way of addressing the essential mystery of the other person. Respecting what you love is very different from ultimately, wholly, possessing it. These writers give us a glimpse of what the world could be like if humans learned the knack of just touching the edge of wildness—not conquering, but learning to walk the serene hem.

What we've been fighting for isn't places but our souls, says C. L. Rawlins.

Exactly.

NORTHERN LIGHTS

LINDA HOGAN

❖ ❖ ❖ ❖ ❖

STORIES OF WATER

Earth is a water planet. It is a world of salt oceans, cloud forests, underground springs, and winding rivers. It has built arches and pillars, has burrowed a deepening way into caves. It has plunged into land and been lost to other places where the long slow dripping of moisture created glittering crystals and teeth of inner earth, and as ice it has taken the shape of large glaciers and ridden space.

The mountains where I live are young. Water still works them. With its freezing and thawing, earth gives way. Called home by gravity, slabs of stone crash heavily down to the canyon floor and we say, "The earth is alive, it shrugs the rocks off its tired shoulders."

In the canyon, springwater seeps out from stone walls, and we say, "Earth is weeping."

This canyon was created by a curling river that emptied itself into an inland sea a few miles down from here. The currents of that ancient sea lapped away at red stones, creating ledges and crannies that are now nesting places of birds. It formed stone bowls that hold what's left of every rain, pools of water reflecting the face of the moon. Lizards drink there.

The same water, freezing and thawing, contracts and expands the topsoil so that earth pushes stones upward, away from gravity. In spring when we go outside, new stones are scattered here and there. We say, Land has given birth.

And it does. Everywhere water travels, life follows. In a desert, only moments after a cloudburst, the terrain quickens; a plant flowers, an insect drinks moisture from its back and survives. Frogs rise up from beneath parched earth, mate, and return again to the cool underworld.

We have ceremonies to bring rain clouds to arid lands. We sing down the rain. We smell the ceremonies of life-giving rain, and hear thunder announce its presence, and the gray shafts of rain arrive from the distance. Then we celebrate the mud-filled rivers, the veins and arteries of our alive world. Seed crops send forth their first shoots. Reservoirs fill, and through some amazing alchemy, water is transformed, flowing through wires into homes, light at the touch of a finger.

There are stories of magic about seas, about the dense, dangerous swamps, the peat bog that caught fire and burned for two years, even the story of science that tells how fish began a precious journey from gill slit to amphibian, learning to survive at the elemental edge between water and air before they grew wings that lifted up the blue sky.

Or, they went another way, to our own inheritance of fragile skin.

Some years ago, I entered water's world, deep in the beautiful blue silence of the Caribbean. It was filled with slowly bending weeds and blue fish. It held me in its swaying grasp as thin yellow fish swam by. An octopus floated past like pink silk waving along a current of wind. Golden stars moved slowly, alive in caverns beside the black spines of sea urchins. I swam out farther in the cellular sea, through a school of barracuda who were all of one mind, all turning at the same sharp moment. A thousand small jellyfish surrounded me in the green light of water, floating by without so much as grazing my alien skin. It was a world apart from our world. I was taken in by it, taken almost away, surfacing to find no sight of shore, no memory of how I had arrived in this suspension of life.

As a girl, I went often to a small, almost invisible creek near our home to watch snails and birds that visited the water. But one year, it turned suddenly into a torrential river, roaring downhill full of stones and trees, taking earth down with it.

After the flood subsided, we looked at how earth was changed. Around us the rust-colored earth was covered with silt and broken trees. Parts of homes rose out of mud. A roof emerged from the water-torn side of a hill. A rocking chair sat on a mound of sand. Cattle were dead and bloated, stretched out on the silted new plains of earth. A red rooster was shining like copper in a sandy knoll. We saw our once familiar world through one of nature's cold eyes. We were small. We had no choice but to bend down before water's will; it was stronger than ours.

Recently, a man related to me his journey by canoe up the far northern waters to Hudson Bay. He and his friend, he said, had reached their destination and saw freshwater beluga whales playing beneath their canoe. Enchanted by the story, I wanted to pass through the mouth of that water in search of the white whales, wanted to see their smooth skin and limber motion, but as he talked on, the voyage he described was a crossing over of hell's river, a frightening journey of survival with mosquitoes so thick the veiled men could not open their nets even to eat, could barely see for the bloodthirsty swarms that clung to them. A single opening in a sleeve, a tear in a shirt, and they would have been overcome by the thick, hungry insects that torment caribou into their own migrations of escape. The days were hot. The nights were freezing. In one place the water receded and left them stranded in mud. Had they arrived an hour later in that muddy mooring, they would have been unable to reach firm ground at all.

In *Call Me Ishmael*, Charles Olson writes about the whaling quest that preceded Herman Melville's story of the white whale, *Moby-Dick*, by twenty years. Over a year after these whalers set out to sea, their ship was struck by a whale and sank. A week later, those few who survived, floating in a lifeboat, made the mistake of eating bread that had been soaked in ocean water, and the salt of it dehydrated them, causing their skin to split and blister. The only way to quench their thirst was to kill a turtle and drink its blood, and occasionally a flying fish would hit the sails of their small boat, fall inside, and be swallowed raw by the weak and hungry men:

> After a month on open sea they were gladdened by the sight of a small island which they took to be Dulcie but was Elizabeth Isle. Currents and storm had taken them a thousand miles off their course.
>
> They found water on the island after a futile search for it from rocks which they picked at, where moisture was, with their hatchets. It was discovered in a small spring in the sand at the extreme verge of ebbtide. They could gather it only at low water. The rest of the time the sea flowed over the spring to the depth of six feet.

Six feet under. The depth of a man's grave. What was it that drove them to the dead, paradoxical center of being surrounded by water and dying of thirst? And what was that more contemporary need for two men from the American privileged class to pit themselves against elements at Hudson Bay, rowing to within an inch of death's hand-hold? Melville himself, in spite of his writings, deserted his first whaling ship, was a mutineer on the second, and emerged mysteriously and without explanation from his third journey in Honolulu.

Perhaps they knew that water would carry them full circle face-to-face with themselves, or maybe they searched for a light stronger than that produced by barrels of sperm whale oil. The sea is a primal magnet, and maybe theirs were journeys into mystery and wilderness, a pull toward healing, toward a baptism in the enormous world of life, a coming together of land creatures with the holy waters of earth that carry not only ships and giant fish but our own hidden treasures. The dark inner seas seek us out like a song of ocean in a shell, and we turn back toward them, to our origins, our waters of birth.

Last summer, I traveled across Lake Superior to Isle Royale, an island most well known for its wolf and moose population. Between the mainland and the island, the boatman, who had lived in that region all his life, related this story: When he was a boy there was a shipwreck of the luxury liner *The American*. He watched as it disappeared beneath water's surface. He could hear the screams of people onboard. He and his father were part of the rescue effort, helping people into lifeboats and returning them to shore. The shock of watching such a disaster caused him to lose his memory. His first recollection, a few weeks later, was of a room in his home that was filled with sweet-smelling fruit. *The American* had carried a cargo of fresh fruits, and the water of Lake Superior was the precise temperature needed to preserve the fruit in the hull of the capsized boat. For months after that, divers descended into the clear blue water and returned with red berries still intact, apples that had been picked from mother trees and were carrying their seed, grapes and oranges, a new world, yes, with its sweet foods, and their saved seed pods of life, even bananas from the other America.

The last traces of older civilizations are beneath the water, broken down to almost nothing in the primordial oceans where mountains have become grains of sand.

Once, walking on a beach that in another life had been the rocky terrain of dry earth, I found a piece of smooth, gray clay. A line of blue glaze crossed it, but it looked like the clay had burst open, perhaps during firing, and in the center of that opening, a crystal was embedded. It was clear and faceted. It appeared to have been intentionally fired inside the clay. I treasured that tile, which I supposed to be from the ruined, fallen world of Atlantis. It was my share of hope that there was another, better, world than ours. Atlantis. Unlike a far heaven, unlike the fiery, molten core of hell, Atlantis, whether it existed or not, was a world we could believe in, a land like our own, a society whose fruits were a new, devastating technology, a country peopled with prophets and scientists, a world of lotus-eaters seeking beyond their own grasp, dreaming beyond their limits, and finding their ruin within those dreams.

* * *

But after all these stories, the most amazing tale of all belongs to water's own voice, telling a story of its unbroken orbit from itself to itself. Between earth and earth's atmosphere, the amount of water remains constant; there is never a drop more, never a drop less. This is a story of circular infinity, of a planet birthing itself. After I learned this, the clear raindrops began to break out of the sky, falling to the ground they had passed through before. I was overwhelmed with the beauty of rain's sparkling clarity, the clear flow of it, and how any of it, in our toxic world, ever renews itself in its journey through earth and sky.

A person related this story to me: They were traveling the Amazon River when they rounded a bend and saw a great tree filled with enormous pink blossoms. It was vibrant and alive in the green, wet jungle. As they drew near, they were amazed to see that the branches were filled not with flowers but with flamingos perching in the twisted branches. It was a marvelous vision, that story from the basin filled with silver-sided fish, blue frogs, and golden cats with silent paws, that place where rain falls and rises again to the sky, turning over inside clouds, flying above the emerald forests and falling.

To those of us who dwell in arid lands, this world with its bird-eating spiders, red lizards, and immense store of fruits and nuts seems supernatural. It carries the calling birds, the mating songs of frogs, the creaking insects. Rain's song lives there, and like everyone, I read daily that it is endangered. Half of the earth's animals live in the humid jungles, most of them yet to be named, and plants that have already transformed the history of modern, western medicine, plants used as treatments for leukemia and Parkinson's disease. A large percentage of the Costa Rican plants are thought to contain anticancer agents, and steroids were developed from Guatemalan yams. And these forests are the place our air is born, from a marriage of water and green-leafed, dripping plants. In their verdant density, they produce over a fourth of earth's oxygen.

We are only dreamers in such abandance as could feed our hungry world. Its soil is the living tissue of our earth. It is living membrane, these rain forests carried across the globe in the shape of toothpicks and fatted cattle that will feed sharp-toothed world-eaters who have never known such richness, such fertility. Inside this place, as deforestation continues, human beings, some of them still unknown to the outside world, are also being swallowed, though the papers don't mention the human losses. Since 1900, more than half of the tribal people of Brazil have become extinct. In the past ten years alone, as the Amazon Highway has been under construction, at least one new nation of people a year has been discovered.

Most of us cannot imagine such worlds as are nourished and created by our planet's water, but our treasures do not exist in water, or across it like for the seafaring people; the treasure is water itself. It means life to us, and survival. And while water is being exiled from the land it inhabits, it begins to take up residence elsewhere.

The journey of water is round, and its loss, too, moves in a circle, following us around the world as we lose something of such immense value that we do not yet even know its name.

Outside it is thawing. The creek is breaking apart. Water begins to seep out of the rock canyon above me. It has been around the world. It has lived beneath the lights of fireflies in bayous at night when mist laid itself about cypress trunks. It has been the Nile River, which is at this moment the smallest it has been in all recorded history. It has come from the rain forest that gave birth to our air. It brings with it the stories of where it's been. It reminds us that we are water people. Our salt bodies, like the great round of ocean, are pulled and held by the moon. We are creatures that belong here. This world is in our blood and bones, and our blood and bones are the earth.

Out from bare rock the water flows, from times before our time. The clouds flying overhead are rivers. Thunder breaks open and those rivers fall, like a sprinkling of baptismal water, giving itself back, everything a round river, in a circle, alive and moving.

Linda Hogan is a Chickasaw poet, novelist, and essayist. She is the author of several books of poetry and a collection of short fiction. Her novel Mean Spirit *received the Oklahoma Book Award for fiction, 1990, and the Mountains and Plains Booksellers Award. It was also one of three finalists for the Pulitzer prize in 1991. She is also the author of* Seeing Through the Sun, *which received the American Book Award from the Before Columbus Foundation and, most recently,* The Book of Medicines. *Hogan is the recipient of a National Endowment for the Arts grant, a Guggenheim fellowship, a Minnesota Arts Board Grant, a Colorado Writers Fellowship, and The Five Civilized Tribes Museum Playwriting Award. She is an associate professor at the University of Colorado.*

PART I

THAT AWESOME SPACE

BETH FERRIS

◆ ◆ ◆ ◆ ◆

LUNCH IN THE GARDEN

We have lived in these bodies
a long time;
they have been our boats and now
we are carried here,
all the abundance of summer
laid out on a white cloth.
Old friends under a roof of braided vines,
we take the garden's tender lettuces,
the fruits
and listen
to the whisper of leafy voices
telling us who we are:
women in middle age
crow's-feet around the eyes,
burnished and worn,
the sweet patina of the real
glowing on our skin.

So much has been worn
or eaten away
that we fall open
with the abandon of old-fashioned roses
that something else can emerge.
Our true selves, those secret
spirits we've kept veiled

even from our own eyes
take on invisible flesh—
fly out our mouths as we laugh.
Oh, none of us can see
the angels of our own lives.
Whether or not we believe
they are loose among the melons,
they lean over the rim
of the cobalt pitcher
lapping tomato juice with pink tongues.
Plump cherubs among the scattered plates,
they stretch out
dreamy and wide-hipped as nudes
from another century.
While we were busy with other things—
stuffing the compartments of our lives
full to bursting with books, shopping,
the lists we live by—
invisible wings fanned our faces.
Now, they grow tipsy
at our pleasure, toss grapes
into one another's mouths.
As we push back our plates and sink
into the lime pie,
our fat inner angels rise to the arbor
and look down on us
with the affectionate humor
of parents whose children
play together often.

Deep in the flickering shadows
they murmur
of all they have done to please us:
Lost in despair, illness, fatigue,
they drew the wind's silk over our foreheads,
turned our sad eyes

to the luxurious fall
of the last peony flower.
So often we did not see,
but this afternoon, they are proud.
For once, we got it right:
lunch in the garden, fragrant yellow lilies
gathered near the creek
and we don't ask too much
of ourselves or each other.
They take the time we have together
and slow it down
so the *tink* of glass
as we toast a friend's dead husband
travels through the shattered heart
and comes back healed.

◆

Beth Ferris is a poet living in the Rattlesnake Valley of Missoula, Montana, where she watches closely for angels in her garden.

RICHARD NELSON

◆ ◆ ◆ ◆ ◆

THE EMBRACE OF NAMES

I was born in Madison, Wisconsin—a place named for a politician who had never been there. The city is nested among four lakes—Wingra, Waubesa, Mendota, and Monona—names whispering the language of ghosts. Who among the living hears them?

When I was twenty-two years old, these whispers finally came alive for me, in the voices of hunters speaking names that rooted them deeply into the land. An aspiring cultural anthropologist, I had come to the arctic coast of Alaska to live with Inupiaq Eskimos. On a midsummer day, six of us were hunting walrus in a traditional sealskin-covered boat. We had traveled so far offshore that the flat expanse of land became a thin stain along the eastern horizon, then sank completely out of sight.

Sitting beside me was a man named Kuvlu, who had designated himself my benefactor and teacher (partly, I suppose, to keep me from dying on the tundra or sea ice and partly to savor the endless entertainment of my blunders). Kuvlu gestured toward the hard seam where water met sky. "Before the White Man came, Eskimos knew the world was round," he said. "The elders warned that if you went too far offshore it was hard coming home, because you'd have to paddle uphill." Later on, after we shot and butchered two walrus, a solid wall of fog swept in around us. For hours we groped blindly through congested ice floes, relying on one man's genius for dead reckoning to keep us headed toward land.

Then, suddenly, a clay bluff loomed ahead, like the prow of an oncoming ship. Kuvlu inspected the land for a moment, turned to the others and challenged: "Who knows what place this is?" To me it looked like everywhere else along this coast—the same high bank, same gray beach, same capping fringe of tundra grass, and a narrow ravine that seemed indistinguishable from a hundred others I'd seen on earlier hunting trips. To my amazement, Kuvlu's older brother had it immediately: "*Aqlagvik,*" he said with assurance, "Place to Hunt Grizzly Bears." I was incredulous. How could anyone know the country so well? But Kuvlu only smiled and nodded, as we turned to follow the shoreline home.

Over the next hour, Kuvlu recited the names of camps and abandoned settlements along the coast: *Nullagvik, Pauktugvik, Milliktagvik, Avgumman, Aqisaq, Imnaurat.* For a few, he offered translations: *Qilamittagvik:* "Place to Hunt Ducks with Ivory Bolas." *Mitqutailat:* "Arctic Terns." *Nannugvik:* "Place to Hunt Polar Bears." *Inuktuyuk:* "Man-Eater," a spring hunting camp used by those willing to overlook its ominous name. The fog cleared as we traveled north, and finally we saw the village—a scatter of weathered houses in a place called *Ulguniq,* "Where A Standing Thing Fell and Left Its Traces."

Reflecting on those times twenty-five years later, my mind whirls with Inupiaq names and the memories they bring: how each place looks, events that happened there, and stories I heard about it. *Qayaiqsigvik:* "Place Where a Kayak Was Accidentally Lost." *Pingusugruk:* "Big Pingok" (a hill thrust up by heaving permafrost). *Kangiich:* "Where Tributaries Join at the River's Headwaters." *Aluaqpak:* "Big Coal Outcrop." *Anaqtuuq:* "Many Droppings." *Qiqiqtasugruk:* "Big Island." *Umingmak:* "Musk Ox." Some names I remember without knowing what they mean: *Singauraq, Minnguqturuq, Aquliaqattat, Aqiagugnat, Kaulaaq, Ivisauraq, Amaktikrak* . . . and dozens more. Each one evokes for me a place set apart from all others and braided into the events that have made my life.

On my first caribou hunting trip, a man named Annaqaq gestured away from the frozen river where we stood. "Take your dog team to the top of that hill," he said. "We call it *Nasiqrugvik,* 'High Place Where You Look Out at the Land.' " I was confused by the name and by his instructions. Unaccustomed to the subtleties of a nearly flat tundra plain, I found the hill completely invisible. What would it mean, I wondered, if the people who carried its name disappeared like the ghosts of my Wisconsin birthplace? In a deep and vital way, *Nasiqrugvik* would vanish into a monotonous, undifferentiated terrain. And the earth would be diminished as a consequence.

During the years I spent with Inupiaq people, I was interested in place names because I loved the language and because they were vital as a map when I traveled alone by dog team or kayak. I never considered writing down the names, making them part of my work as an ethnographer; not until years later, when I began recording them as a way to establish people's tenure on their traditional homelands. I did this first with the Inupiaq and then with Koyukon Indians, who live in the forested interior of Alaska just below the Arctic Circle. Koyukon place names chart the landscape, and they color it with beauty and meaning, much in the way of Inupiaq names. I spent long evenings with Koyukon people in their village cabins, maps scattered across the floor, penciling down names, listening to stories that gave each place history and significance.

I also traveled widely in Koyukon country—hunting moose from camps along the rivers, searching for bear dens in the fall, following traplines through vast forested wildlands, fishing in the lakes and sloughs. In a small way, I experienced how the lives of the Koyukon were connected with places we discussed in our map sessions. And I was left with an array of names that are still lodged in my mind—not empty words but *names*, filled with memories, filled with the land's beauty, filled with stories from ancient times. What little I know of these things is at least a shadow of how the Koyukon people and their natural world are conjoined through names.

In the Koyukon tradition, many names tell you something about the places to which they belong—how the terrain looks, what animals or plants are found there, what was happened there in the near or distant past. These are names born from the land itself, as much a part of it as the spruce forests, the bedrock outcrops, and the twisting rivers. They are also rich in sound and sometimes aglow with spiritual power that renders the landscape sacred.

Let them speak for themselves: *Sis Dlila'*: "Black Bear Mountain." *Bidziyh Kohunaatltaanh Dinh*: "Where a Caribou Is Lying on Its Belly." *K'itsaan' Yee Hukuh*: "Big Grass Lake." *Ts'eydla*: "Black Spruce Hill." *Tin Lootleetna*: "Hanging Ice Place," a creek so named because dwindling flow in early winter leaves a hollow space under the ice, so an unsuspecting traveler could easily plunge through. *Dolbaatno'*: "River of Young Geese," where people hunt fledglings in midsummer, when the birds are big and fat but cannot fly. *Diniyh T'oh*: "Bearberry Place." *Oonyeeh Tilaah Dinh*: "Where the Blackfish Run in Season." *Gguh Tlitl't'o Tiya*: "Hill Named After the Nape of a Snowshoe Hare's Neck." *Tlookk'a Ts'ilyaan Dinh*: "Lake of the Fat Whitefish." *Dilbaagga Ts'oolneek Hu*: "Where Somebody Grabbed a Ptarmigan." *Toneets Ts'ibaa La'onh Dinh*: "Spruce-Covered Island in the Middle of the Lake." *Ts'atiyh Dinaa Dakk'onh Din*: "Where a Forest Fire Burned the Hill to the River." *Dotson' Kkokk'a Gheeyo Din*: "Where the Great Raven Traversed the Length of a Lake."

Each of these places is aswarm with stories. There is an invisible life in the landscape, one known only through the mind and memories of the Koyukon people. At a place called *Tsotlyeet* there is a one-room cabin, half hidden among birches and aspens, a cabin that would vanish entirely if left unused for a few decades. A stranger would think little of this place today, and nothing at all if the cabin were gone.

But *Tsotlyeet* is the place where one of my Koyukon teachers grew up—where he spent all the years of his childhood and early adult life. The surrounding woods and thickets, muskegs and lakes, creeks and rivers were the neighborhood for young William, and for his mother and father, his sisters and brothers. This is where he acquired his intimate knowledge of moose, bear, grouse, whitefish, wolverine, caribou, and the rest of the living community to which his family belonged. It is where William perfected his skills as a hunter and trapper. In later adulthood, he often stayed there with his wife, and in the forty-odd years since they settled in a nearby village, *Tsotlyeet* has remained the family hunting and trapping headquarters. This place is the nexus of William's life. It would be impossible to understand one apart from the other.

Yet sometime, perhaps not long from now, *Tsotlyeet* could cease to be a place. Without the Koyukon people and their collective memory, it would vanish from the significant world. And the same is true for literally thousands of other places, named and intimately known by Koyukon villagers.

One night I was poring over maps with William and his old friend Joe. During a break from our work, Joe looked at me, his eyes filled with sadness, and he spoke: "I'm really glad we're putting these names on the maps, because our kids don't know a lot of them." He thought quietly for a moment. "The names might get lost. And if I died, then that country would die with me."

By this time I knew the Koyukon homeland was saturated with names—the hills and mountains, the lakes and sloughs, the river bends and islands, the ridges and valleys; places where animals congregate; places where people fish or gather berries; places known for wind or calm or deep winter snow; places with trapping cabins, hunting camps, or burial sites; places of historical importance; places known from *Kk'adonts'idnee*, stories of the Distant Time, when animals and people shared one society and spoke a common language; places alive with sacredness, where the land listens and the earth underfoot can feel.

As Joe and William turned their attention back to the maps, my own thoughts slipped away, to imagine the entire North American continent in a time before living memory—this enormous sprawl of land, sheathed and cloaked and brilliantly arrayed with names. Names covering the terrain like an unbroken forest. Names that wove people profoundly into the landscape, and that infused landscape profoundly into the people who were its inhabitants. Names that gave a special kind of life to the terrain, as Joe and William knew so much better than I.

I imagined how these names had dwindled with the deaths of elders, beginning five hundred years ago; a steady impoverishment of names, as the Europeans spread west, knowing too little of the land and its people to realize what was being lost. The continent was plundered of its names, left desolate, emptied of mind and memory and meaning.

But all is not lost. Many Native American names survive, others are now being recorded, and some are finding their rightful places on maps. North America is also embellished with thousands of European place names, although many are opaque to the land itself, as if the earth were shaped into mountains and rivers as a way to commemorate the famous and the dead. There is no better example than Mt. McKinley, our continent's highest peak, named for a little-known politician who would later—coincidentally—become president. McKinley never laid eyes on the mountain, which Koyukon people know as *Deenaalee*, "The High One."

Our maps are littered with such names. One of my favorites is Goulding Harbor, on the southeast Alaska coast, which Captain Nathaniel Portlock named to honor, flatter, or court favor with the publisher of his book. And there's Mt. Hunter, named by a reporter for the *New York Commercial Advertiser* to honor the aunt who paid for his trip to Alaska. Furthermore, because of a mapmaker's error, the 14,573-foot peak enshrined with this name is nine miles away from the one for which it was intended.

I can think of few more worthy endeavors, few gestures that could better show our respect toward the environment that sustains us, than to remove this blight of numb, invading names. Where elders remain to teach us, we could resurrect original names and put them back where they belong. If all memory has vanished, we could find names through the land's own guidance and inspiration, as countless generations of inhabitants have done before us.

We could also follow the examples given by trappers, prospectors, lumberjacks, fishermen, homesteaders, and others who bequeathed to us names reflecting the land and its nexus with humanity. The wild country of Alaska is filled with wonderful examples. Some are purely descriptive: Dogtooth Bend, Flapjack Island, Splitrock Point, Islands of the Four Mountains, Skull Cliff, Naked Island, Ottertail Ridge, Coffee Can Lake, Three Tree Island, Ragged Cape, Bearnose Hill, Twoheaded Island, Bay of Pillars, and

White Thunder Ridge, named for the rumble of glaciers calving into an adjacent bay.

Many names carry useful information: Hell Roaring Creek, Moose Pasture Lake, Dog Salmon Creek, Over-the-Hill Portage, Rotten Fish Slough, Peril Strait, Walrus Island, Logjam Creek, Whalebone Cape, Caribou Snare Creek, 197½ Mile Creek, Crab Trap Cove, Fishless Creek, Sealion Rocks, Plenty Bear Creek.

There are also warnings for travelers: No Thoroughfare Bay, where extreme tides create terrific currents and reversing falls; Williwaw Point, named for its sudden and violent winds; Boiling Pinnacles, where tidal currents thrash over a shallow reef.

Others commemorate personal experiences or historic events: Slaughter Island, Easy Money Creek, Cow-and-Calf Moose Lake, Strangle Woman Creek, Threetime Mountain, Lost Temper Creek, Deadman Reach, Frozen Calf Mountain, No Grub Creek, Sore Finger Cove, Tired Pup Mountain, Broken Snowshoe Creek. And Saddler's Mistake, where an erstwhile navigator guided his ship into a swale joining two mountains, thinking it was the pass between neighboring islands.

The meanings of some, of course, are anybody's guess: Big Skookum Creek, Dull Ax Lake, Seven Egg Creek, Blue Mouse Cove, Helpmejack Lake, Zipper Creek, Mooseheart Mountain, Red Devil Creek, Bear Blanket Slough. And we can speculate about the whimsies that brought forth names like Seduction Tongue and Doctor Beaver Creek.

Look at the map for any state and you can find dozens of names like these, expressing every possible connection between humanity and earth. They are a powerful source of hope. Given time and a return to intimacy, we newcomers to this continent may yet learn to inhabit its myriad places, may yet become worthy of the gifts it offers us, may yet find the humility and grace of those who lived here for millennia before us, may yet learn to honor the land that nourishes us, gives flight to our imaginations, and pleasures our highest senses.

The names we choose, I believe, will be a fair measure of our success.

I am grateful to the people of Wainwright, Huslia, and Hughes, Alaska, for sharing their lives and traditions with me over the years; and to Eliza Jones and James Nageak for help with Koyukon and Inupiaq translations. I am solely responsible for inaccuracies and awkwardness of the place name translations. An anthropologist writes with the air of an expert but is seldom more than a raw apprentice, so I can only hope the elders will be patient with the inevitable errors and shortcomings in my work. Personal names used in this text are pseudonyms. Finally, because of typescript limitations, I have simplified the spelling of Inupiaq and Koyukon words; by doing so, I intend no disrespect for the beauty and complexity of these languages.

◆

Richard Nelson's books about relationships to the natural world among Eskimo and Athabaskan Indian people in Alaska include Hunters of the Northern Ice, Hunters of the Northern Forest, Shadow of the Hunter, *and* Make Prayers to the Raven. *He also wrote* The Island Within, *a personal exploration of nature and home on the northwest Pacific coast, which received the John Burroughs Award for nature writing. When he's not hiking, surfing, kayaking, fishing, hunting, watching wildlife, or camping with his partner, Nita Couchman, he works on a book about deer and their relationships to people in modern America.*

JON ROUSH

◆ ◆ ◆ ◆

SQUARE PLACES, ROUND WHOLES

One day a couple of years ago in Montana's Bitterroot Valley, a "domestic" bison decided it was time to head south. News reports tracked his progress. Yesterday he was seen in an irrigation ditch, today he was in someone's vegetable garden, and so on. Fences were a minor annoyance. When he did not find holes, he made them. Part Houdini, part linebacker, he let us pretend for a few days that our spaces were still wide open. If one bison could do it, why not a million? Why not one of those legendary herds that took days to pass a given point—grazing, wallowing, breeding their way across a boundless grassland? Someone finally caught the Bitterroot Bison before he reached the Divide, but it was fun while it lasted.

This winter, the state of Montana issued permits to hunt bison that strayed into Montana from Yellowstone National Park. State officials feared that the bison might carry bovine brucellosis, a virulent disease that causes cattle to abort. That Montana has been officially free from brucellosis for years is an important economic fact for cattlemen. Something had to be done. Not incidentally, the decision was applauded by hunters. The hunt was controversial wildlife management, but surefire box office. One December evening our television sets showed us a single bison entering stage right, pausing, staggering, falling dead. He had been picked off at thirty yards by a scope-sighted hunter. Wearing camouflage fatigues in the midst of reporters, officials, and protesters, this prime-time stalker seemed overdressed. He might have sensed some absurdity himself. He told the cameras that since the hunt was legal, it must be sport.

But for deep absurdity, consider the bison's point of view. He didn't even know he had crossed a boundary. Bison, like children and other natural creatures, do not bother with straight lines. They follow their interests along stream banks, around hills, from water to food to shade. That was how this Yellowstone bison was fooled. He did not have to swim any river or cross any ridge. He simply moseyed through the trees and across an open meadow. One minute he was in wilderness, the next—bam!—civilization. The absurdity that the bison did not understand, the absurdity that required his death, is the absurdity of laying straight lines on nature.

Yellowstone Park is square. It is square for the same reason that everything else surveyed in the Rockies is square. Our towns are laid out in square blocks, with a grid pattern of streets. Our sections are squares, one mile on a side. Our townships are squares, six sections on a side. Our states are rectangular, except for the squiggle that follows the Continental Divide to separate Idaho and Montana. Even the northern border of the United States, after looping lyrically along eastern rivers and lakes, leaves Lake of the Woods, Minnesota, to race straight as a falling rock across swamps, plains, and mountains to the Pacific.

On a map, straight lines look logical. They imply rationality and human control. The more wild the reality, the more important the reassurance of straight lines. It's easy to understand why nineteenth-century bureaucrats and politicians, more than a thousand miles from the scene, favored them.

Back East, surveyors had used a system of land description based on metes and bounds, in which boundaries are often described in reference to actual landmarks. The western system of sections and parts of sections is by contrast perfectly abstract. Instead of depicting an actual landscape on a map, the western surveyor's job was to take lines already drawn on the map and lay them on the land.

This abstract, cookie-cutter space conformed to the mind of nineteenth-century America. Once it had been ruled into interchangeable squares, the vast western space could be controlled from Washington and New York. It could be, and often was, bought and sold before the actual boundaries were even laid out. It was ready for the homestead acts. It was ready to expand, township by identical township, into an empire.

Besides the abstraction of space, the other step necessary for conquering the West was the abstraction of time. Instead of measuring time by the position of the sun, phase of the moon, or season, the settlers used clocks and calendars. Precise, uniform measures of time and space allowed the coordination of complex activities separated by great distances. Above all, they allowed the development of the railroads.

And strung across the lines were the railroad towns. They were mass-produced to house the hardworking souls who bought railroad land to live on while they built the town in which they remained to create railroad markets. In Montana, Wyoming, and Idaho, some railroad towns were virtual replicas of midwestern towns already built on the same line. For them, the grid pattern was as efficient as the corporate blueprints are to McDonald's.

Western towns were laid out for pure future, no past. To build a new community in the wilderness was an act of will among strangers. It was an act of will that could not afford to wait for organic growth. Boston had grown from within. Its meandering maze of streets was a fossil record of cow trails and colonial footpaths. Boston streets follow the ungeometric logic of real human community. But in the western towns that were to be the settlers' new homes, history began at zero. The newcomers might build courthouse, school, and church before anyone was buried in the cemetery.

When you look at those old posters depicting the street plans of western towns, you can almost believe that you are looking at an established community. The town may be young, but it already has achieved its most important historical mission, imposing manmade order on the wilderness. With so much accomplished already, this is a town with a future. A good place to bring up kids.

Usually those towns arrayed themselves along a straight and endless main street. It led from the prairie, through town, and back into the prairie. In town, it was the corridor of power, and when your eyes followed it out of town, you could see the horizon. You saw the town's future prospects were infinite. A good town to grow with. And in Casper, Billings, and Boise, the growth is still sprawling outward.

Such towns were built on the graves of bison herds and the Indians who relied on the bison for food, shelter, and clothing. In 1840, a few palisaded forts dotted an immense wilderness. Their anxious inhabitants walled out the wild. But by 1890, the towns declared victory. Without boundaries, they faded complacently into the surrounding landscape. And by the turn of the century, farms and ranches were subduing that landscape, too, with straight fence lines and the patterned order of cultivated fields.

That was why people started talking about national parks. It was time, some said, to wall the wild *in*, to protect it from the incursions of civilization. That way, the busy townspeople could be aware of wilderness, visit it, even revere it, without letting it interfere with business. So they put the bison in square parks and the Indians on square reservations.

But it did not end there. Bison carry brucellosis out of one park. Grizzlies lumber out of another and eat calves. Indian tribes claim water rights. At the same time, pollsters consistently find that our townspeople want more parks, more pristine water and air, more wilderness. The borders do not hold.

A hundred years ago, we would have known what to do about those stray bison. We would have rubbed out the whole herd in a weekend. Now we hesitate, uncertain. Blame nostalgia for some of the hesitation, wisdom for the rest. We have learned some humility. And we feel something missing from the compartmentalized spaces in which we have caged ourselves.

A fully civilized life includes more than law and order. It includes mystery, energy, diversity, surprise, and beauty—the qualities that make natural space nourishing and occasionally dangerous. The rigid fragmentation of western space has walled us away from essential parts of our own being.

◆

John Roush is President of The Wilderness Society. Before that, he was a rancher and consultant in Montana, Chairman of the Board of the Nature Conservancy, and the first Chairman of the Board of the Northern Lights Institute. He is a raconteur, bon vivant, and all-around good egg.

GRETEL EHRLICH

◆ ◆ ◆ ◆ ◆

LETTERS TO AN ARCHITECT

Make a model
Of this element, this force. Transfer it
Into a barbarism as its image.
—Wallace Stevens

Sunday

Dear Steve,

I dreamed you gave me a wooden globe. It was polished and smooth except for one patch of hacked-at breaks and draws with a high, reddish plain floating out from it, and a baby blue trailer house precariously perched on one of the hills. The place on the globe was Wyoming, the trailer house, where I lived.

I'm writing now because I have questions about how an architect places us properly on earth. In what ways do you contribute to a physical and philosophical order? How do you bring us into intimacy with the ground, with the society that lives on it?

Yesterday I came on a grackle's nest suspended in the forked branch of a currant bush. Ingeniously placed, it used the running water from ground predators. A nest is a cup of space and represents the transformation of the natural stochastic order to the social one. When you build a house aren't you capturing space, encircling a raw chunk of air and ground with walls through which you draw water, enclose lives? One of the German root words for *building* is derived from a word which means "to be," and the Japanese character "to live" can also mean "nest."

Since we're biological, not just culture mongers, I give you this: the first house is the uterus, or else the neck. One species of frog incubates in the throat of the father, and when the tadpoles are big enough, they swim from the "midtown tunnel" of the neck into the great pond. The cranial cavity, the whole body is a housing of sorts, and in turn we're all natural builders. I like the efficient way one genus of ant does things: they use their bodies architectonically, functioning doubly as doors and doorkeepers. Flattened in front with enlarged heads, they fit the entrance to the anthill with a carpenter's precision. They're color-coded to match the soil and savvy enough to allow entrance when secret knocks and smells are emitted.

What I'm getting at is this: too often we trivialize nature and dismiss our part in the animal kingdom. I say this partly because there aren't many buildings here and when I look out my window I see towering cottonwoods and bold nests. Some of the best builders are weaverbirds, termites, beavers, and bees. Yet the whole progress of civilization has moved away from the natural world, and too often nature and culture are thought of as being antithetical.

Human habitat has become all padding and armor: carpets, curtains, ornament—in such thicknesses as to protect us from weather, rawness, feeling. Now a wall represents the evolution not of imagination and skill but of self-imposed ignorance. Everywhere I go I see houses, schools, hospitals built with windows that can't be opened. How can a child understand life processes if he or she is sealed away from seasons and weather? The new parts of our cities are mirrored, self-referential faces. How can we see into the soul of a building when it has no eyes? Finally (I'm coming to the end of this extended complaint), we build with unforgiving materials which can't absorb human sweat or hold warmth, or the resonance of sobbing, singing, or laughter. Who wants to make love on the wrong side of mirrored glass?

Tuesday

Dear Steve,

The real trouble, the root trouble is our rigid conception of interior versus exterior, inside versus outside. These divisions are so flimsy as to not exist. Isn't there a commingling everywhere? We breathe air into our bodies and exhale again. Pollution travels through climax forests. We ingest the bodies of other beings into our own. We eat the stems and blossoms of plants and drink runoff from snowpack and glaciers. And aren't we food too? And aren't there wild birds in big American cities? Still we equate "inside" with a static sort of security, a maintenance dose of control, a solid defense against the commotions of nature, against the plurality of ourselves. *Outside* has come to signify everything that is not "us"—everything inimical.

But space is not a stable entity. A building is only an illusion of motionlessness. Death teaches us that molecules jump in and out of skins. Life breeds on change.

Here's what the Italian writer Italo Calvino says about this issue (from *Invisible Cities*):

> The traveller roams all around and has nothing but doubts: he is unable to distinguish the features of the city, the features he keeps distinct in his mind also mingle. He infers this: if all existence in all moments is all of itself, Zoe is the place of indivisible existence. But why does this city exist? What line separated the inside from the outside, the rumble of wheels from the howl of wolves?

Thursday

Dear Steve,

I've been wondering about the origin of design, which led me to think about formlessness. The Buddhist Heart Sutra says, "Form is emptiness and emptiness is form." Why, then, do we build against space, hide behind decor? As if it were something solid.

Twelve thousand years ago the first inhabitants of the North American continent lived in caves. They made beds of bark and grass and cisterns lined with flat rock for the storage of food. The Mogollon were among the first peoples to build freestanding structures. These were circular pit dwellings, like those built in Japan in the first century A.D., with conical roofs supported by a center post. Yet, not far from these roundhouses, another southwestern people, the Hohokam, began making freestanding buildings that were rectangular. The walls were made of cut brush and plastered with mud. Why the difference? Was it the site, the materials, or a figment of mind? Soon pots and baskets appeared in the cultures, tooled and dyed and glazed with an intricate mesh of geometric lines. Were these signs or were they freestanding ideas that accrued a form? In Canyon de Chelly and Mesa Verde, fine stonemasons erected their palace-cities against sandstone walls high up in the cliffs. I try and try to duplicate that squiggle of mind which opted for buildings rather than conformity. In Plato's allegorical cave the mind was said to progress from dark imprisonment toward light, toward what Plato called "the good." What made us leave the cave? And if everywhere we look asymmetry abounds in nature, what makes us favor symmetrical shapes? Are they the signature or signpost of human order?

Last week I drove through the Hole-in-the-Wall country west of Kaycee, Wyoming. I hiked up into the Outlaw Cave of Butch Cassidy fame. It's a deep niche a third of the way up a steep incline and, like the grackle's nest, uses Powder River as a moat. I could still see the lintels where a doorway had been and the cedar post with rawhide wraps where they'd strapped bunk beds in place. Some rustlers wintered there, pasturing their stolen horses on a south-facing slope around a sharp bend in the river. Inside the cave I noticed some graffiti on the smoke-blackened wall toward the rear. It read: "Plato was here."

Sunday

Dear Steve,

This afternoon, juniper shadows on the mountain look like venetian blinds, and the melting snow, caught in the crevices from the last storm, glints like wet sheets. I remember you telling me what Louis Kahn said about cities: "A city is a place where a small boy, as he walks through it, may see something that will tell him what he wants to do his whole life."

Wyoming has no true cities. Every hundred miles or so there's a small town. Some, like Moneta, Arminto, Emblem, Morton, and Bill, boast populations as minuscule as five or ten. A boomtown I drove through in the eastern part of the state consists of two trailer houses. One is the cafe–post office, the other is the school. Some Wyoming towns are a brief miscellany of log buildings whose central focus is the bar. When you walk in, everyone is sure to turn and stare at you. Others have shoals of untended pickups, rusting balers, and new backhoes behind which lurk a grocery store and a town hall.

Elsewhere, the environments Americans have fashioned for themselves are aswim in paradox. Being both pragmatists and idealists, we've adopted all kinds of high-minded utopian ideas, from the Greek revivalist to the International style, but upended them so completely they now stand for opposite ideals. Walter Gropius's antibourgeois, socialist housing has been transformed into the icy, machined skyscrapers in which the corporate *crème de la crème* hold court; the Greek columned portico, which Jefferson loved because it symbolized human uprightness and dignity within the Greek polis, appeared on the mansions of slave owners and came to symbolize their beleaguered era.

Wyoming has no architectural legacy except for the trapper's cabin and homesteader's shack: dark, smoky, often windowless, and papered with the classifieds from the weekly newspaper. Yet I like to think that those who landed here during Wyoming's territorial days had been exposed to the ideals of Jefferson and Thoreau. Both men distrusted cities, but Thoreau was disdainful of most social gatherings while Jefferson promoted a local participatory democracy in which each person had a farmable plot and an active citizenship to go with it. They sought out the opposite kinds of freedom. Thoreau's had to do with personal privacy, unencumbered by football games and town meetings, while Jefferson's implied a busyness— citizens having a voice in every proceeding.

Wyoming attracted people of both minds. The first trappers

and cattlemen, like Osborne Russell and Henry Lovell, thrived on the expanse and solitude of the state. They claimed territory the way geographers would—on the basis of water, vegetation, the contour of the land, not by the Jeffersonian grid.

The Mormons stretched Jefferson's fair-mindedness into a socialistic regime under the guidance of Brigham Young. Each "colonist" was allotted a town plot, arranged on streets of specific length and width, while farmland and the pasturing of livestock remained communal. The ward church dominated the town and was constructed according to standardized blueprints.

The word *building* is both a noun and a verb and implies two contradictory things Americans love: security and movement. We want a firm tie to a place but to remain footloose and fancy free. Native Americans rolled up their skins and followed the game through the seasons (now they go on the powwow circuit in smoky-colored vans); trappers and mountain men commuted between cities like St. Louis and the Tetons, the Wind Rivers, the Absaroka Mountains. Even now, cowboys and sheepherders move from job to job, ranch to ranch, and it's no wonder so many of the manmade structures here have a temporary feel.

But back to politics. It's one thing to construct shelter and quite another to announce with the grandness of one's architecture a hierarchical intention. Take medieval Europe, for example, whose first cities were built out of fear. They started as stone walls behind which herdsmen and their families huddled and fought off invaders. Temporary walls became permanent. People built houses behind them, and itinerant merchants set up shop there. Then the priests came and the governors, and the buildings they erected became physical signs of their authority. You can go anywhere in Europe and see how they did this. Castles and churches were built on hills. Everyone else had to use their dirty water.

Sunday again

Dear Steve,

I met a Navajo hand trembler once. She lived in a remote corner of the reservation in a cinder-block house adjacent to the hogan where her husband had died. The new house had a dirt floor, no running water, a few kitchen chairs, a ten-foot standing loom, a TV, and Kentucky Fried Chicken boxes stacked against one wall. A hand trembler works with medicine men to diagnose illness. She goes into a trance and her hands lift in front of her body and shake until she "sees" the disease in the patient's body. She can also locate missing or stolen articles. She found a friend's camera box on a part of the reservation she had never visited. It was behind a rock near the road between Window Rock and Ganado.

I mention this because of the intimacy with the landscape it represents. Possession of place, then, is not merely a monetary transaction. Navajos envision their land as a female body whose mountains are skulls, hearts, breasts; whose waters are veins and blood vessels; whose vegetation is hair, fur dress; through which the cornstalk rises—a spine and a penis.

The Ainu, the indigenous peoples of the northern Japanese island of Hokkaido, see themselves as coresidents with the animals who live there and the animal spirits called *kamui*. They think of their island as a great carpet separated into "fields." Here, ecologies and spirit groups are located. Headwaters where salmon spawn are power places, and the sacred window of every one-room Ainu house faces upstream. Because rivers are such important sources of food, each tributary is given a name, gender, and spiritual significance. Bears were numerous and thought to be humans in disguise. The chief of the bear clan is said to live "in the heart of the mountains and to own them." He sends emissaries—bears—to Ainu villages as gifts of meat so the Ainu won't have to go hunting. Even the ocean is divided into separate fishing ecologies: There's a gray whale field, a red snapper field, an eel field. For the Ainu, place is who they are; a field is a force, a generosity, a friend.

Wednesday

Dear Steve,

What if we discovered that buildings were made of trees and shrubs? To move a house would entail digging very deep, excavating through whorled root chambers. If not pruned, the buildings continue to grow. New York, for example, has long been let go. Now tree cutting is prohibited. Thirty-story buildings topple. They lie at oblique angles, and from the air, the new ones look like silvery snail tracks. People use deadfall as bridges. New buildings—seedlings— are slim, green, snaky, and grow up thickly around the old ones. When the sharp winds blow off the Hudson River, the whole city tilts east, and South Ferry, at the tip of Manhattan, bends back like brushed bangs.

If I built a house, it would be part wild, part human, part beast. The central axis of the house would be a stream trickling through the main room, and continuing through a series of gardens and *shoins* or studies. A rock wall carved with petroglyphs would serve as the load-bearing wall of the house. A dense forest of aspens or bamboo would obscure the entrance, then grow right into the house, thinning out until the space became the room. Walls, ceilings, and floors would be made of local things: Greybull sandstone, Precambrian granite, lodgepole pine, cottonwood, willow branches braided with sage. Floor levels would change with function or view, as the basins of waterfalls do, catching pools of activity, then spilling them again. Rooms would rarely have common walls. Covered verandas or corridors would take you to bedrooms, bathrooms, studios. On the way to these places, an alcove might invite you to sit and look at a hill where swifts and eagles nest, or a door might slide open onto a garden you hadn't suspected was there. These passageways would lift you up or down, alter your pace, your sense of yourself at the time. The part of the main room where you cook might have a granite boulder bursting through the wall, faceted with glass. Polished granite slabs would serve as counters, and outside the window next to where you eat, the stream—a reminder of movement and life—empties into a populous frog pond. The whole shape of the house follows the contour of the land. What we think of as rambling is really the way it speaks.

Friday

Dear Steve,

Frank Lloyd Wright said, "Architects are no longer tied to Greek space, but are free to enter the space of Einstein." I think of the Einsteinian architect as being airborne, pulling a sword from a scabbard and carving little half moons of space, then piercing them together with cornstalks and hinges of light. We're only now beginning to comprehend that space is *something*, not nothing, that, in fact, it is dense with life, it contains the broth of being, a minestrone chock-full of twin quarks, mesons, protons, strong and weak forces fluctuating.

Louis Kahn used to ask, "What does this building want to become?" There's a German word, *lebensraum*, which means "vital space, the space required for life, growth, and activity." Isn't that what a good building should be? Site, orientation, scale, use of materials—aren't these an architect's koans? A Buddhist lama I know said, "You cannot feel the earth unless you feel space. The more you feel space, the more you feel the earth."

Though traditional Japanese houses were standardized by the seventeenth century, I've always thought quantum physicists would like them. There is an overall unity and an indeterminacy at the same time. There is, from room to room, a flexibility of function. There are no rigid dividing lines between inside and out—the flimsiness of the walls ensures that, as well as the Japanese fondness for gardens. There's a unique regard for the inherent qualities of materials used: wood, straw, rock, paper. The architectural scale is a human scale, and, like the human body, the fragility of materials used makes perishability implicit. The classical Japanese house carries a spiritual equivalent. It teaches the art of living. It says, "The exposure of my structural bones is also your skeleton; my simplicity implies a transcendence of confused states of mind; to banish the division between inside and out is to do away with dualistic thought; shelter can be both a ceremonial response to nature and a form of nakedness; enclosure is space."

Saturday

Dear Steve,

I walked today. I had this idea about walking to the headwaters of the river near my house. It's connected to what I've been writing to you because what I'm interested in is *source*. Local resources, resourcefulness, the beginnings and origins of things.

After slogging through deep snow for some hours, I found the spot where the water first comes out of the ground. A rock had tumbled into the small crevice, and an inch above that was a mossy dome with an elk track imprinted on it. Water squeezed out around the rock. I leaned down to drink. "This place is umbilical, *sipapu*, a conception point," I thought as I swallowed. Then I followed the river home.

To make buildings that link us intimately to earth and space and help us live, we have to drink at the headwaters of thought. I knew a sheepherder who could taste samples of water and tell which spring they had come from. In the same way, an architect must drink the site, a building must taste of its source, don't you think?

Enough of my thoughts on the subject. What are yours?

Your friend,
Gretel

◆

Gretel Ehrlich was born in Santa Barbara, California, in 1946 and was educated at Bennington College and UCLA Film School. She moved to Wyoming in 1976. Her books include: The Solace of Open Spaces, Drinking Dry Clouds, Heart Mountain, Islands, the Universe, Home, *and, most recently,* A Match to the Heart. *Her work has appeared in* Harpers, The Atlantic, The New York Times, Antaeus, *and* Outside. *She was the recipient of an NEA Creative Writing Fellowship in 1981; a Whiting Foundation Award in 1986; and a Guggenheim Fellowship in 1987. The American Academy of Arts and Letters honored her with a Harold B. Vurcell Award for Distinguished Prose in 1986. She now divides her time between the central coast of California and northern Wyoming.*

PART II

MYTH

LINDA WEASEL HEAD

◆ ◆ ◆ ◆ ◆

THE STONE WOMAN

A young woman climbed
Into a green and blue stone.
Coyote threw her into the river
    right in the middle
    of winter.
        All she heard
            was clinking ice
        All she saw
            was brown bottle
        All she felt
            were jagged edges
            that cut her fingers
        All she tasted
            was her own dry lips
            thirsty for water
        All she smelled
            was thick piss
            that clung to her hair
        She remembered
            she had children
            somewhere.
Rolled downstream
By fast melting snows, she tumbled,
Stumbled out an old woman.
Her stone broken.

◆

Linda Weasel Head, a Salish Native, graduated from the University of Montana in 1989. She lives and teaches Grade 5 on the Blood Reserve and spends much of her time writing, a process that she compares to giving birth—"a lot of love, sweat, and pure energy." She has created many stories and poems—some good, some bad—and hopes you will accept them for what they have grown up to be.

WILLIAM KITTREDGE

◆ ◆ ◆ ◆ ◆

THE POLITICS OF STORYTELLING

*Plot in fiction helps us overcome the anxiety caused by
the loss of the "sacred masterplot" that organizes and
explains the world. Our lives are ceaselessly intertwined
with narrative, with the stories that we tell or hear told,
those that we dream or imagine or would like to tell, all
of which are reworked in that story of our own lives that
we narrate to ourselves in an episodic, somewhat semi-
conscious, but virtually uninterrupted monologue. We
live immersed in narrative . . .*

Peter Brooks, *Reading for the Plot*

*As they are told and retold, stories have the function of
wrestling with the ultimately inexplicable chaos of reality
around us. They give it form, and in shaping and re-
shaping the form, they help us gain control over it.*

Alan Jabbour, *The National Folklife Center*

The poet C. K. Williams came to Missoula some years ago and
spoke of "narrative dysfunction" as a prime part of mental illness in
our time. Many of us, he said, lose track of the story of ourselves,
the story which tells us who we are supposed to be and how we are
supposed to act.

It isn't any fun, and doesn't just happen to people, it happens
to entire societies. Stories are places to live, inside the imagination.
We know a lot of them, and we're in trouble when we don't know

which one is ours. Or when the one we inhabit doesn't work anymore, and we stick with it anyway.

We live in stories. What we are is stories. We do things because of what is called character, and our character is formed by the stories we learn to live in. Late in the night we listen to our own breathing in the dark, and rework our stories. We do it again the next morning, and all day long, before the looking glass of ourselves, reinventing reasons for our lives. Other than such storytelling there is no reason to things.

Aristotle talks of "recognitions," which can be thought of as moments of insight or flashes of understanding in which we see through to coherencies in the world. We are all continually seeking after such experiences. It's the most commonplace thing human beings do after breathing. We are like detectives, each of us trying to make sense and define what we take to be the right life. It is the primary, most incessant business of our lives.

We figure and find stories, which can be thought of as maps or paradigms in which we see our purposes defined; then the world drifts and our maps don't work anymore, our paradigms and stories fail, and we have to reinvent our understandings, and our reasons for doing things. Useful stories, I think, are radical in that they help us see freshly. They are like mirrors, in which we see ourselves reflected. That's what stories are for, to help us see for ourselves as we go about the continual business of reimagining ourselves.

If we ignore the changing world, and stick to some story too long, we are likely to find ourselves in a great wreck. It's happening all over the West, right now, as so many of our neighbors attempt to live out rules derived from old models of society which simply reconfirm their prejudices.

They see what they want to see. Which is some consolation. But it is not consolation we need. We need direction.

The interior West is no longer a faraway land. Our great emptiness is filling with people, and we are experiencing a time of profound transition, which can be thought of as the second colonization. Many are being reduced to the tourist business, in which locals feature as servants, hunting guides, and motel maids, or local color. People want to enclose our lives in theirs, as decor.

The Native American people were living coherent lives, at one with their circumstances, when our people displaced them, leaving them mostly disenfranchised and cut off from possibility in our society, their reservations like little beleaguered nations battling to survive in our larger one as we continue wrecking the traditional resources of their cultures. The result, for them, is anomie, nothing to hang on to, powerlessness. We are shamed and look away, and do little to help.

So it is deeply ironic that the Native Americans are being joined in their disenfranchisement by loggers and miners and ranchers, and the towns which depend on them. Our ancestors came to the West and made homes for themselves, where they could live independent lives. Because of their sacrifices, we in the dominant society think we own the West, we think they earned it for us. But, as we know, nobody owns anything absolutely, except their sense of who they are.

One Sunday, while living in the heart of the French Quarter of New Orleans a year ago February, Annick Smith and I were out walking in the rain when we realized we were hearing the echoes of someone singing, a vivid unaccompanied voice in the narrow street, maybe three blocks away when I first heard her, a black woman with her eyes closed and face open to the fullest as her voice rose and fell to *Glory, Glory, Halleluia*.

She shone in the gray light. I almost couldn't look, and wondered if she cared what anybody thought as I dropped two folded paper dollars into the coffee can at her feet. She didn't look at me at all.

Semitropical plants were draped along the lacy ironwork balconies above the broken sidewalk, nature in a place where everything was carpentered. My shuttered door was one in a wall of shuttered doors which stretched on toward Bourbon Street, each painted thick, deep green. The light seemed to rebound from the walls, illuminating the wet bricks.

I can still hear that woman. Her life looked to be endlessly more difficult than mine. Her courage and passion were evident in singing even if it was a street-shuck for money, and I envied her. I felt like weeping, for myself, and I was afraid of it, like something in my body might break.

There I was, living nearby to some of the best eating and drinking and music in the world, in a place where I never heard so many people—black, white, Creole, Cajun—laughing so much of the time, and I was awash with sadness.

Maybe it was because I had never lived so close to so much violence, which was the other side of things. During Mardi Gras, on Rampart Street, a little more than three blocks from our door, some lost tourist was shot every night, killed and robbed, mainly for drug money. Every week or so there was a school yard killing, a kid assassinating another kid with a handgun, settling scores.

The perpetrators in these crimes were most often young men from the so-called projects, publicly owned housing for the poor. Those young men were alienated and angry because they saw correctly that their situation in society was hopeless—they were essentially uneducated, their schools were war zones, and their chances of finding jobs, much less meaningful and respected work, were nil. A friend who grew up in New Orleans said, "They've got no place to go. There's no ladder up, no ladder out. They're left with nothing but selfishness. It's the second lesson you learn on the streets." The first lesson, according to my friend, is that nothing, nobody, is bullet proof.

It might be useful for us in the West to consider the ways in which the projects in New Orleans, in their capacity to generate hopelessness, are much like so many of our failing towns and our Indian reservations. It might be instructive to consider the rage that is generated by such disenfranchisement, and think of the ways it looks when it gets to the streets of our cities. It might be instructive to look closely at recent events in Los Angeles.

It starts with broken promises. In the West, people came thinking they had been promised something, at least freedom and opportunity, and the possibility of inventing a new, fruitful life. That was the official mythology. When that story didn't come true, the results were alienation, and anomie, just like in the projects, just like in LA.

When people are excluded from what their society has defined for them as the main rewards of life, when they sense that they are absolutely out of the loop, as a lot of Americans do, in the rural outback, and in the deep heartlands of the cities, they sometimes turn to heedless anger.

A lot of people on our streets are staring back at us (the enfranchised) with hatred which we all know to be at least partways justifiable. Some among them, we can see, might kill us for our selfishness. Fewer and fewer of them are willing to stand singing in the rain, waiting for a few dollars to accumulate in the tin cans at their feet.

Many of us live with a sense that there is something deeply and fundamentally wrong in our society. Many of us feel our culture has lost track of the reasons why one thing is more significant than another. We are fearful and driven to forget the most basic generosities. We anesthetize ourselves with selfishness. It's not, we say, our fault.

Many of us live insulated, as I do much of the time. In New Orleans I like to walk down a couple of blocks to the Bombay Club and disassociate my sensibilities with one and then another huge, perfect martini. In Las Vegas I like to stay at the brilliantly named Mirage, amid those orchids and white tigers. What I don't like to do is walk the streets and look the other side of my society in the eye.

I want to think I deserve what I get. I don't want to consider how vastly I am overrewarded. I don't want to consider the injustices around me. I don't want any encounters with the disenfranchised. I want to say it is not my fault.

But it is, it's mine, and ours. We'd better figure out ways to spread some equity around if we want to go on living in a society which is at least semifunctional. It's a fundamental responsibility, to ourselves.

We inhabit a complex culture that is intimately connected to societies all over the world, vividly wealthy while increasingly polarized between rich and poor, increasingly multiethnic and multiracial, predominately urban, sexually ambiguous, ironic, self-reflexive, drug-crazed, dangerous, and resounding with discordant energies, a selfish, inhumane society without a coherent myth to inhabit, a society coming unglued, a democracy that is failing. Its citizens do not believe in it anymore, they don't vote, they withdraw from the processes of governing themselves. On C-SPAN, all day long, you will see the other end of that same society, privileged, long-faced citizens trying to figure out what to do about our trouble without forgoing their privileges. You will see a society without much idea of how to proceed.

I want to inhabit a story in which the animals all lie down with one another, everybody satisfied, children playing on sandy beaches by a stream, in the warm shade of the willows, the flash of salmon in the pools. Children of your own as you see them. How do we understand our kingdom?

It is easy to see the world is luminous with significances. We want them to be part of the story of our lives, the most important characters after ourselves. We yearn to live in a coherent place we can name, where we can feel safe. We want that place to exist like a friend, somebody we can know. What we need most urgently, in both the West and all over America, is a fresh dream of who we are, which will tell us how we should act, a set of stories to reassure us in our sense that we deserve to be loved. We want the story of our society to have a sensible plot. We want it to go somewhere, we want it to mean something.

We must define some stories about taking care of what we've got, which is to say life and our lives. They will be stories in which our home is sacred, stories about making use of the place where we live without ruining it, stories which tell us to stay humane amid our confusions.

We must define a story which encourages us to understand

that the living world cannot be replicated. We hear pipe dreams about cities in space, but it is clearly impossible to replicate the infinite complexities of the world in which we have evolved. Wreck it and we will have lost ourselves, and that is craziness. We are animals evolved to live in the interpenetrating energies and subjectivities of all the life there is so far as we know, which coats the rock of earth like moss. We cannot live without connection, both psychic and physical. We begin to die of pointlessness when we are isolated, even if some of us can hang on for a long time while connected to nothing beyond our imaginations.

We need to inhabit stories that encourage us to pay close attention, that will encourage us toward acts of the imagination which in turn will drive us to the arts of empathy, for one another, and the world. We need stories that will encourage us to understand that we are part of everything, that the world exists under our skins, and destroying it is a way of killing ourselves. We need stories that will drive us to care for one another and the world. We need stories that will drive us to take action.

We need stories that tell us reasons why taking care, why compassion and the humane treatment of our fellows is more important—and interesting—than feathering our own nests as we go on accumulating property and power. Our lilacs bloom, abuzz with honeybees and hummingbirds. We can still find ways to live in some approximation of home-child heaven. There is no single, simple story that will define paradise for us, and there never will be. As we know, the world will not stand still; energies and processes are what is actual, complexity is actual.

On summer mornings I can walk down Higgins Avenue to the Farmer's Market by the old Great Northern Depot in Missoula, and buy baby carrots and white daisies, zinnias, snow peas, new corn, gladiolus, irises, and chard. In my simpleminded way I love the old men selling long-stemmed roses, and the hippie mothers who are becoming farm wives. I try to imagine their secrets.

When I buy, I like to deal with the Hmong, refugees from the highlands of Laos. They have been in Montana since the end of hostilities in Vietnam. They were relocated courtesy of the CIA, their cohorts in the narcotics trade, at least that's the story we were told. I wonder if their old people are crazy with grief for lost villages. Maybe they are, or maybe they were glad to escape.

On the wall above the place where I write there is a bedspread embroidered by a Hmong woman, imaginary animals on a field of tropical green, a royal red elephant with black ears, a turtle with a yellow and blue and red checkered shell, a black rabbit, an orange monkey on a branch, a parrot, a peacock, and a green prehistoric creature with white horns. It is the work of a woman transported a long way from her homeland, who stayed tough enough to dream up another story. It gives me heart.

◆

William Kittredge teaches creative writing at the University of Montana. He is the author of The Van Gogh Field, We Are Not in This Together, Hole in the Sky, *and* Owning it All, *as well as the forthcoming* White People in Paradise. *With Annick Smith, he edited* The Last Best Place: A Montana Anthology.

MARILYNNE ROBINSON

◆ ◆ ◆ ◆ ◆

HEARING SILENCE:

Western Myth Reconsidered

I am the last person in the world to assume that words like *myth*, or *Western*, or *American* can be used with precision. Still, they have their place. I have spent a good deal of time reading about European history and institutions, and I am utterly convinced that the habit of speaking of American culture as if it were essentially continuous with European culture is a source of much error. The difference, I think, results from the great confluence of peoples which so particularly characterizes our history. Our forebears were for the most part not from the strata of society which embody official cultures, or whose manners, dialects, or sympathies would have been made rigid by the belief that they were pure, approved, or correct. There is no reason to expect such streams of influence to remain unmodified. One might expect them to combine and recombine, until their separate sources become untraceable. To speak as we now do of minority cultures seems to foster the assumption that the dominant culture is, in all significant respects, white and Northern European. I do not assume this. It seems to me ethnocentric if not ethnomaniacal to think one culture (as if turbulent Northern Europe could be called one culture) could smother out all competitors for influence. When one uses the word *American*, one takes the risk of being understood in that narrow sense. The dangers of the word *Western* are the same. Tendentious definitions have the attraction of simplicity.

I know my use of these words is not systematic. But then, systems are most successful in dealing with problems that have been simplified to accommodate them. Language is not well adapted to reality. It becomes less so when its limitations are forgotten.

I consider myths to be complex narratives in which human cultures stabilize and encode their deepest ambivalences. They give a form to contradiction which has the appearance of resolution. When Greek gods favor or bully Greek heroes, free will and destiny interact as if they were more or less compatible. That is the point Socrates missed when he ridiculed the Homeric gods' behavior. He had little positive interest in free will or destiny, if it is fair to judge by the *Republic*. So the myths did not address an ambivalence that engaged him.

Myth is never plausible narrative. It asks for another kind of assent. To anyone for whom it does not strike an important equipoise, it seems absurd. The myth of the Fall makes it possible to think of humankind and the world as at the same time intrinsically good and intrinsically evil. Those to whom this vision is not compelling grumble about the apple and the snake.

I speculate that the attraction of the mind to myth comes from a sense that experience really is more complex than we can articulate by any ordinary means, or more than momentarily, emblematically. We know from physics that contrary things can be true at the same time, and we seem also to know this intuitively. I would suggest that the power of myth lies in the fact that it arrests ambivalence. I would suggest also that myths are coined continuously, usually in very small denominations, and that lesser myths are related to greater ones as a penny is related to a gold mine. Conceding all differences, they are describable in essentially similar terms. That is to say, I believe real myths appear and have their power, everywhere, even among us.

Contemporary cultures are put together out of all sorts of things— advertising campaigns, junk entertainment, the certitudes of the academies, machines with crude brains in them, floods of dubious information. We know we have not evolved as our material circumstances have elaborated themselves. We live like cargo cultists, among artifacts whose origins we could not begin to describe. Many of them seem to us to possess an uncanny value. Others we find ominous. We imagine we are passively conditioned by these things, dehumanized, but I think it is as likely that we prowl the landscape awestruck by the totems we have set up, sure that our wills are in the power of magicians, more or less in the manner of our remotest ancestors. The great joke of the human situation is that we do not know and can never know what the world is in itself, where it stops and we begin. I have read that American satellites did not pick up the hole in the ozone layer because their instruments are designed to discount extreme data. This seems to me to epitomize us, in a way. Americans consider it only reasonable to discard information that does not confirm our assumptions. This accounts for much of our peculiar immunity to experience and history, not to mention information itself. Our brilliant machines permit us to make characteristic mistakes on a grander scale. This is only to say that we are as trapped in our humanity as anyone ever was.

So it seems to me worth the experiment to say American myths work like other myths do by transforming ambivalence into a kind of equilibrium. My object is simply to set what we do back into a human context. It is only because we—cargo cultists that we are—have deified our props and machines that we can imagine our doings and thinkings are impinged upon by other than human forces.

The West was the last theater of the oldest ambivalence in American culture, from the point of view of the European settlement here. This is only to say that the West was an event in the life of the whole country, an astonishingly apt metaphor for a historic doubt as to the compatibility of freedom and civilization. That in itself made the West certain to be the locus of powerful myth. I think we have now outlived that ambivalence, simply because neither freedom nor civilization continues to have much hold on our imagination. In our America the word *free* is likely to be followed by *trade* or *enterprise*. We attribute this to the circumstances of our creation, on no grounds except that if we can blame the Founders, what we do is excused and allowed, almost compelled. Jefferson foresaw this decline, grimly. But who, outside Prague, reads Jefferson?

It would be fortunate if we could provide, at this juncture in history, a conception of freedom somewhat more capacious and congenial to the human spirit, but all we seem to come up with is the map to a wilderness we have never crossed. If people persist long enough in paying money they do not have for sustenance they cannot find, at last they will be free. Stand in the street for four hours trying to sell a broken umbrella, and you, too, will taste the elixir of freedom. No wonder the newly liberated so readily pour their hopes into other vessels.

But freedom was once a beautiful idea, and so was civilization, and the dread associated with them both was not always strong enough to reduce the tension between them to our present dreary stalemate. The West as myth could not survive without that tension. To the very great extent that it was the work of the national and world imagination, it has not survived.

And of course there was and is a real West. I grew up in it, in lumber towns. Anything Western—pearl-button shirts, electric guitars, knotty-pine paneling, Morris couches with Indian blankets thrown over them—*any*thing Western seemed like raw provincialism. Once there was a school assembly for an old man who played a long, gleaming, tremulous saw with a fiddle bow. We were told we must listen closely, because it was becoming rare that one heard such a thing. But the old man was cross and distracted. He knew he did not have our attention. I remember the first sentence in the first history lesson to be presented to my dawning literacy: England is our mother country.

At my grandparents' ranch old men sat around the dinner table and laughed about disasters they had survived. Old dogs hunted in their sleep. Trout and venison, huckleberries, flour in talcy pillows, a gate on a chain weighted with a cowbell. A barn as silver as feathers lying along a hillside like a bird with a broken wing, the prettiest example I have ever seen of true Western ramshackle. Yet it seemed to me that everything I knew about the West I learned from the movies. The West was the hero of so many movies.

The West is where they make nuclear weapons and test them. I have read about the nuclear wastes being shipped into Idaho from the East Coast and from Taiwan, about British bombs exploded in Nevada. Anyone can interpret. The stuff is so dangerous only space and distance can isolate it, even provisionally. How convenient that there is the West to take the brunt of calamity. It is true of all the poorer and emptier places in the world that they have poverty to sell, and space, and also a political weakness that assures these commodities can be enjoyed by their purchasers without disruption. I have read that a Korean corporation has bought the right to log in Siberia, and that it is devastating great forests with marvelous efficiency, because no government in that part of the world can exert any control over it. Weakness and poverty can release a great deal of wealth, into a very few hands.

Perhaps it has become the economic role of the American West to be poor and empty, and also politically weak. The less economically tenable life in the West becomes, the more it is de-populated, the more it will be plundered. The suitability of a place for use as a toxic dump is inversely proportionate to the number of delegates it sends to Congress. The attractiveness of waste storage as an economic option varies directly with the level of poverty. The cost of exploitation of resources drops with the cost of wages, and with the political pressure brought against environmental standards in areas of poverty; therefore, the economic stimulus to exploitation rises as populations contract. I hear sometimes the idea that if the West could be largely depopulated, its environment could be re-stored. On the contrary, it will become more and more a province and a dependency, and it will suffer every abuse such regions suffer. If there is to be a West in any tolerable sense of the word, then there must be Westerners, that is, people who make lives here.

To the extent that the region was ever protected by associations with hope or heroism, there is little left to appeal to. We know now that the paintings that showed these mountains or these prairies bathed in theological light were not naive but deluded, though they are, in fact, from time to time, bathed in what must resemble a theological light. Increasingly, the West is thought of as no more than the scene of a great crime, where the country's worst tendencies have had their freest expression. Perversely, the more aware we seem to be that this is a holy land to the Native Americans, the more inclined we are to view it and treat it as a desecrated place. I have read that the reservations are being offered money to accept nuclear waste, on the theory, I suppose, that a little more cynicism will never be noticed.

Most of what I have seen in the way of academic history of the West confirms these attitudes, as if it were doing something brave, going *against* a current. We all know that certain versions of history are urged upon us now, as if to take another view were to excuse the crimes of the past. It is salvation being preached—believe as I believe and your sins will be washed away. But look at the world we make: while we anatomize General Custer yet again, tuberculosis and alcoholism, poverty and suicide hasten his old work of destruction, worse every day of *our* generation's ascendancy. If he were to come back among us, how would we prove to General Custer that his war had not resumed after a lull, and with smaller risk to his side than he would have considered honorable? We could tell him we now say "Native American." But it might take more than that to convince him.

We are merciless in our judgment of history—to the extent that what we talk about should be called history—but in many ways we do worse than the generations before us. It seems reasonable to me to wonder if we are misspending our energy. If the new version of history were truth, then it would be necessary to accept it, without raising questions about the motive behind its telling and the effect it will have on its hearers. But it is, transparently, myth, and so such questions are appropriate.

In 1801, Thomas Jefferson appealed to Congress to ease

naturalization laws in these terms: "And shall we refuse the unhappy fugitives from distress that hospitality which the savages of the wilderness extended to our fathers arriving in this land? Shall oppressed humanity find no asylum on this globe?" This is myth, too. We know that many of the original European settlers were not fugitives, and that the indigenous people were not always hospitable. A Virginian would have been especially aware of this. Because his words have so little to do with fact, it is interesting to see what is established in Jefferson's narrative.

First, he wants the United States to be a land of refuge. His version of our origins establishes refuge seeking as the quality Americans will have in common—not, say, religion or language, as would have been usual in the period. Compare J. G. Fichte's contemporaneous *Addresses to the German Nation*. Second, he makes the salutary point that the land does not really belong to the white settlers, even in anticipating and preparing the arrival of more white settlers. Third, rather than representing the country as won through warfare from the indigenous people or from England, as a revolutionary leader might be expected to do, he tells his hearers that they are in America because of the graciousness of those to whom the land indeed belonged. Jefferson had great respect for Native Americans, and he was disturbed by the way they were being dealt with. At the same time, he thought of large-scale European immigration as a way of ending the labor shortage that made slavery viable, and he despised slavery. His myth creates an image of reconciliation among interests that would not be reconciled.

Our new and improved version of the myth of settlement has blond beasts with hegemony in their eyes indulging the appetites of conquest. Jefferson's refugees, with war or famine or persecution behind them, unvalued or unwelcome where they came from, have more to do with the truth, as events evolved. The immigration that followed 1848 was not a scheme to establish Irish dominance in the New World. It was without question the policy of the American government to settle the territories with farmers, to put an end to the prewar struggles for territory and influence between North and South that had led, as Lincoln argued, to the Mexican War. Lincoln,

Marx, Harriet Beecher Stowe, and others remarked on the powerful sympathy of European working people for the cause of the North. Their immigration was ideally suited to finally suppressing the slave economy and stabilizing the government. And it is remarkable the degree to which the Civil War did come to an end, and a great savings in blood and sorrow. On the other hand, the settlement policy led to the brutal dispossession of the indigenous population. It was a situation in which, one way or another, injury would be suffered, wrong would be done.

The new version of the story of settlement sounds like some musty old race myth about exultant Aryans sweeping down from the steppes. There are more than a few people who would rather imagine themselves descended from an army of all-conquering Europe than from a swarm of folk desperate for work or a plot of ground or a change of luck. But we know as a matter of common sense that there is no truth in that story, and we should be grateful on aesthetic grounds that there is not. A myth of origins serves to characterize a culture. It is arrived at by projecting backward from some present time, some present regime or enthusiasm that wishes to authorize or stabilize itself with the implication that it is inevitable. Origins are "discovered" in the collective memory or lore, as the moment in which the nature of the society can first be glimpsed. Caesar Augustus commissioned the *Aeneid*. Americans chose Plymouth rather than Jamestown as the settlers' definitive moment of contact with the New World—and this is interesting in light of the great influence of Virginians in the early period. If we say now that our origins were simply, merely, brutal, does that mean we assume we must always be brutal? Does it excuse us from other expectations? Do we want to be excused? Why else have we contrived this myth? Do we not assume, in other contexts, that the image we give people of themselves will affect their behavior? This Wagnerian drama of hegemony is powerfully, arbitrarily, associated with the West, and it has stigmatized the West, to the benefit of nothing and no one.

Reading James Galvin's book *The Meadow*, I was movingly reminded of the West of my memory. It occurred to me how intrinsic a part silence is of Western culture and experience, and how vulnerable they are to misinterpretation for that reason. It is truer of silence than of any speech that if you do not understand it, no one can explain it. In this silence, I think, something of the old aesthetic of freedom survives, something of the old individualism.

It seems to me Westerners subscribe to the notion of another order of goodness, one which consists largely in resisting the most available definitions of goodness. It seems to me they wish to proceed from an individual ethic rather than a social norm, to be self-consistent rather than merely reliable. I think they seek space and latitude through strategies of indirection.

I would suggest furthermore that fecklessness of a kind is built into the Western personality, as a form of moral and physical courage. It is a nod to human frailty, without which, after all, courage would be meaningless. And it is the sign and seal of a kind of orneriness that recognizes in self-interest yet another form of coercion. I would venture to say, too, that Westerners are quietists by nature. In some large part, they are descended from self-exiled people, who dealt with their quarrels with society by walking away from them. So they are less inclined than others to look to society for guidance or remedy. I think they tend to consider the brain an organ of delectation. They are of all people most likely to know things to which aesthetic pleasures attach, things to do with geology, astronomy, the ways of animals. Southerners are unsurpassed for humor and anecdote, but Westerners beat anyone at the remarkable, and they own the style of serious pleasure in which they confide it.

If this sounds like a version of Western myth, the Westerner as stoic Anglo-Saxon, then let us look at that word *Anglo-Saxon*. In a context like this one it is a charged word, an indictment. We spend an enormous amount of time saying American culture is richly compounded of a great variety of cultures, and then we go on to speak of it collectively as a great dull fool with hardly a human trait. Obviously both these things cannot be true at once. So we are back again in the regions of myth. This supposed dullness and rapacity are laid to the charge of a dominant culture which is called Anglo-Saxon. It would certainly be more precise to call it English or British, since Anglo-Saxons, descendants of the immigration from Germany, are only one demographic band of the British population and the British settlement here. For example, Jefferson's origins were Welsh, not Anglo-Saxon.

But we admire the British for just those traits we find absent or repugnant in the "Anglo-Saxon." We think the British are stoical, yes, but also modest and mild and decent and tolerant and immune to materialism. So what an embarrassment it would be to call the dominant culture English, although it would be, historically, less inexact. The term *Anglo-Saxon* is, in effect, an invention, an identity no one has to claim. If the function of myth is to encode ambivalence, to allow a culture to maintain at least two incompatible ideas in some sort of stable relation with each other, then this is probably a good example of myth. Americans are still so profoundly in awe of what they take to be their cultural origins that they cannot really criticize them, and must create a sort of dummy to absorb their resentments. The myth of the Anglo-Saxon pretends to revile what it, in fact, protects, which is the culture we take to have made the first and deepest impress on us. So once again, moral and critical energy is expended without result, and that may be the point. Myth seems inclined to promote stasis.

Let us consider that strange icon, the cowboy. To a degree that is striking in a society as nontraditional as this one, his appearance alludes to his history. He is surely remarkable as a male image in American culture in that he is permitted outright ornamentation, without utility or politeness to excuse it. He can wear bracelets, buckles, and boots as intricate as court finery, and shirts embroidered with flowers. Nineteenth-century French writers remark on the *dandyisme* of the Indians, how beautifully their braves and great men attired themselves. Certainly Mexicans seem much more at ease with male adornment than Northern Europeans. The ranch, the rodeo, the lariat—clearly influence from that side was vast. So perhaps, as icon, "Anglo-Saxon" is precisely what the cowboy is not. Perhaps he represents a unique cultural syncretism, and is the true inheritor of just those influences whose suppression we all regret. Maybe we do well to like the look of him.

I note that so great an authority as John Wesley Hardin observes a distinction between cowboys and cowmen. This is a kind of distinction much older than this culture. Laborers were spoken of or to as children, employers as adults, everywhere in Europe. The word *cowboy* signified a very degraded kind of worker, a child, or an adult good for nothing else, who followed a cow all day, making sure it grazed where it should. Needless to say, *cowgirl* is equally venerable.

In the West, the cowboy acquired a horse and a weapon, traditional accoutrements of the privileged classes. He became associated with space and movement, his life resembling the lives of the indigenous people who followed the buffalo. It is interesting that it is the cowboy and not the cowman who became the world's hero, since he never ceased to be, in the economic terms of his time, an itinerant, a casual laborer. Karl Marx, his older contemporary, ponders the use of the word *hands* to describe factory workers, saying the term indicates the degree to which their humanity was denied. *Ranch hand* is as free from stigma as *cowboy*.

What if the cowboy is the image of the worker in glory? What if his rise coincided with the rise of democracy, not accidentally but because for the first time, and also the last time, the imagination of the world found the lives of such men worth mythifying and romanticizing? What if the new contempt in which we hold him empties the myth of its positive value because we participate in the abandonment of democracy as an ideal? What if we have remade him as an agent of capitalist hegemony because we cannot believe people ever did admire propertyless men who sold life and limb for a dollar a day?

Oh, I know, the cowboy is male. But in the time of his flourishing there were women, like Elizabeth Barrett, Harriet Beecher Stowe, and Jane Addams, who enjoyed influence and respect vastly greater than we concede to any woman, dead or living. The absence of the female hero is our doing, not his.

The cowboy is associated with violence. So is the dragon. Heroics in every culture tend to revolve around episodes of violence, so one must exercise caution in drawing conclusions. The cowboy emerged after the Civil War, when there were hundreds of thousands of young men in the country not unaccustomed to shooting at other young men. It seems very probable that levels of violence would have been higher everywhere, simply as a psychological consequence of warfare on such a scale. And of course the War did not settle anything. It merely confirmed the significance of Lincoln's remark to the people of the South—"There are more of us than there are of you." Under such circumstances, violence might be expected.

Then there is the matter of the larger context. Given the insistence of many commentators on the Europeanism of this strand of the culture, I suppose it is inevitable that comparisons with Europe itself would seem irrelevant. But settlement in America coincided with a long series of catastrophic wars in Europe, which took tens of millions of lives, and which contributed mightily to our population. In 1871, when the West was wild, the French government besieged, starved, bombarded, and defeated the city of Paris, with vast loss of life. One must ask, wild compared with what? Grief, waste, shame— history. Americans act as though they should have been immune to these things. They also act as if they invented them.

My point is simply that what happened here need not at all be attributed to conditions special to this place. It seems racist to me to say that the conflict between settlers and indigenous people on this continent had particular virulence or inevitability because it occurred between what we call races. One need only look at what Englishmen did to Englishmen in Australia, or what Frenchmen did to Frenchmen in the Vendée. Many of the Scots who came here were driven off their tribal lands by Scots landowners. Many who did not find their way here died of poverty and illness. Surely no one would question the rightness of accepting Jefferson's poor fugitives. Yet it made us a population fiercely marked by history, in our various ways. How violent might such a people be, given the human tendency to do as one is done by? Is American violence *American* violence, or something we have brought with us, as an aspect of the kinds of experience that have brought us here? By the standards of the nineteenth century, America was not particularly violent. Of course the history of the nineteenth century reads like a psychotic nightmare. I share the opinion that we have become comparatively violent in this century, though to make such a judgment, one is dependent on statistics and definitions. Hitler's and Stalin's governments reported low rates of crime. Criminal regimes usually do.

To cast the tendency toward violence back in time is to make it, once again, a part of our myth of origins. Because we were violent in that past, we are and will be violent. We are predisposed that way as, say, the French and the British are not. But if they were up to appalling things then, too, how have they escaped this predisposition? Either they have not escaped it, in which case we are not especially violent, or the nineteenth century has nothing inevitable to do with what happens in the present. If that is true, our violence has another origin, and we should look for it, rather than blame cowboys. It is so characteristic of us to exercise our capacity for dudgeon, in the very course of evading responsibility.

Consider the classic moment of Western mythic violence, the showdown. This was reenacted obsessively in the 1950s and '60s, as I recall, in films and television. It is hard now to remember what an austere ritual it was: Two men approached each other from opposite ends of an empty street, stopped at a good distance from each other, and held their hands out from their holsters. The point was to determine who was "fastest." The hero had to be very fast, because the ethics of the situation forbade him to reach for his gun until his adversary reached for his. The hero was always successful. There was always something melancholy in his success because he was not at heart a violent man, or because he had wearied of violence but could not escape it. The adversary might be an old friend, or someone in whom he saw his own youth.

What historical basis any of this could have had, I cannot imagine. Any custom generally similar to it would, it seems to me, have been about as lethal as a game of catch. To pull a heavy old revolver out of a leather holster and fire it without taking time to aim—this seems to me an unlikely way to go about killing anyone. Compare European dueling, in which the pistol was carried in the hand, the combatants stood at fairly close range, and a signal was given to fire.

No doubt the showdown was a rarefied version of any number of real and imagined events involving guns and grudges and mayhem, or its near occasion. The very abstract form it took is particularly interesting because it would not have reflected innocence. Whether its origins were in the period after the Civil War or in the period after World War II and during Korea, the decades represented in the films and the decades that embraced the experience of the audience were certainly the two periods in American history when the population had been most broadly and deeply affected by violence. It is interesting that convention refined the showdown into a ritualized moment that made violence so small a part of it. By comparison, in the Eastwood period, violence became the whole of the event. While the old hero could not use his weapon until it became an act of self-defense, the new hero—I think it is coy to call him an antihero—deals death qualmlessly, businesslike as a pyrotechnician brought in for the Fourth of July.

The old showdown Westerns resembled revenge tragedy, the Elizabethan and Jacobean form in which rage or honor drove the hero to carry out a murder, at the extreme peril of his soul. I speculate that the conflict there was between chivalric culture—in which the nobility were a law unto themselves—and centralized national culture. In the sixteenth and seventeenth centuries, and again on the Western frontier, the prestige and influence of civilization and religion must have seemed about to become altogether ascendant, to supersede old codes and to disallow kinds of courage and skill they had celebrated. But the Renaissance plays are about the nightmare aspects of violence, full of bafflement, duplicity, and dread. The Western showdown was, by comparison, a rather frank, sunlit affair, a discrete act that did not litter the stage with corpses or ruin the innocent and the guilty together. It was myth, clearly, having to do instead, I think, with the legitimation of social order. Again in the background of the myth is the recent experience of catastrophic war.

The skills and virtues celebrated in wartime are intolerable in times of peace. Perhaps the myth of the pacification of the frontier rehearsed the emotional and psychological readjustment of the population to the norms of peace.

Western heroes mediated between the ungovernable souls beyond the frontier and the flow of civilization crossing the continent. Civilization was dull or corrupt or cowardly or pretentious, but it was inevitable. The hero identified with it for his own reasons, but for deep and obvious reasons, having to do with personal style, he belonged with the outlaws. In the myth, every concession is made to the way of life being suppressed. Romantic lawlessness is honorably met and defeated on its own ground. Westerns are always elegiac. Their world is always bringing itself to an end. It is not hard to imagine that the culture transacted a good deal of important business in its obsessive return to this imagined moment. Then the moment vanished.

The one thing true about any myth is that among those who are its host population it has the status of belief—not consciously held opinion but settled assumption, with a penumbra of related assumption spreading away on every side. There is nothing harder than to know what it is we assume. I think as a culture we have ceased to encode our myths in narrative as that word is traditionally understood. Now they shield themselves from our skepticism by taking on the appearance of scientific or political or economic discourse, and they flourish, neither shaped by the expectation that they should be large and resonant and astonishing nor self-limited as traditional myths have been because they invoke the very silences they break. What are we? Why are we here? What is being asked of us? A central myth of ours, if it were rendered as narrative, would sound like this: One is born and in passage through childhood suffers some grave harm. Subsequent good fortune is meaningless because of this injury, while subsequent misfortune is highly significant as the consequence of this injury. The work of one's life is to discover and name the harm one has suffered.

New myths do arise, and they have consequences. Cultures change. The way of thinking I just described is essentially new but recognizably ours, and it carries us further yet from all other cultures we admire, perhaps from all other cultures. It is a sort of latter-day, bungled Freudianism with the idea of sublimation stripped away (an implied demand, a compensation, a distraction) and the link broken between the pain of life, and adulthood, and civilization. It is a myth which allows us to keep ourselves before our eyes as the first claimant, in extreme cases the only claimant, upon our pity and indulgence. This entails indifference to certain values celebrated in older myth, for example, dignity, self-possession, magnanimity, compassion, loyalty, humor, courage, selflessness, reverence expressed as gratitude for one's experience of the goodness of life, reverence expressed as awe in the face of the pain and mystery of life.

I suppose it is obvious that I consider this a mean little myth, far worse than most it presumes to displace. Try to imagine it translated into statuary or painted on temple walls, or illuminating its texts. Again, it is a myth of origins that establishes the human personality as small and victimized, fixed in childhood unless—and here is the paradox, I suppose—one recovers one's childhood. In this world of sorrow, this world we make, in which every index of grief among the young shows a dramatic upward curve, we ourselves are the children with whom we are compassionate. Once again, valuable energies are misappropriated.

The Freudian father was overthrown in order to be internalized, and the process created the adult personality. Our myth disqualifies literal and virtual parents, not only by assuming that they in essential ways have failed but also by dismissing them as appropriate models of adulthood. It devalues adulthood as an attainment, as a work of character or imagination, and makes it merely conditional upon the circumstances of childhood.

I think there is probably a sort of fractal relation between the effect of the myth in terms of the individual and the fact of the urge to displace myth in the larger culture. We don't want to have parents, and we don't want to be parents. We reject the socializing effect of shared narratives as delusion and imposition. I am probably too aware that the past is fearsome, profoundly unsavory. But look at the world *we* make. It has never ceased to be true that the great human problem is to deal with the terrible side of human nature. We must certainly look at history with any compassion it deserves, in the hope that history will find some way to forgive us. Assuming, of course, that we allow it time and leisure to remember us.

According to one old story, God wrote, in stone, Honor your mother. Think what a mother would likely have been in those days, a child herself, a minor wife or a concubine, a little straggler with nothing to show for herself but her babies. But God demanded honor for her, in the same terse code that he demanded it for Himself. Not on condition of, or in the measure of, any kind of deserving. Honor her. This commandment must have required great exertions of compassion and imagination in multitudes of cases. It must have compelled the discovery of much oblique and difficult value where, without it, only fault would have been found.

Two things are true. Everyone deserves profound respect, and no one deserves it. To understand the claim anyone has on our respect requires compassion and imagination, attentiveness and discipline. And this brings me back to the subject of the West, and its myth, and its silence.

From my memory and my experience, I conclude that the true, abiding myth of the West is that there is an intense, continuous, and typically wordless conversation between attentive people and the landscape they inhabit, and that this can be the major business of a very rich life. I suspect that Western individualism is created by the assumption that anyone may be engaged in this conversation, and therefore he or she should be treated with a certain tact and respect. This contemplative aspect of Western life is recognizably a descendant of what we misname transcendentalism, the moral-philosophic-aesthetic enthusiasm which flourished in the period that established the West as a presence in the national imagination, and that otherwise expressed itself in utopianism and abolitionism, poetry, philosophy, and otherwise. In the West as nowhere else I have felt I was among people who appreciated, in the aesthetic sense, moment by moment, altogether and in detail, the place where they were. I have noticed how patient, and generous, they were with silence. I think it is a silence Thoreau would recognize, one that retains his own inflection. This is not something the larger culture is much inclined to value. To claim so much spiritual space, to have so little impulse to allow others access to it, these are now read as signs of pathology. With all the talk there is of tolerating a variety of cultures, it is inevitable that those characterized by disfavored traits, like reserve and stoicism, should be subjected to moral disapprobation. As if the larger culture had entirely resolved the question of the proper conduct of life.

Whenever I am asked to talk about the West, my first impulse is always to express deep gratitude, and my second impulse is to express it again, because it has preserved this spacious quiet, like a secret told to me, which I keep because I cannot find words to tell it. I cannot imagine my life without it. What if, at its core, beneath all that the world can perceive or impose, the essence of Western life is ascetic and contemplative? What if our mingled lives have produced here a habit of meditation on the immanent and the actual, like nothing else, so unself-regarding that it need not promise any reward, not enlightenment nor refinement nor prosperity nor peace nor health nor salvation? And what if we cast it off as a provincialism, or betray it to the impulse to interpret only in terms that vulgarize and devalue—our most reliable impulse in this strange time? Then, I think, the West would be gone. We would be left only with landscape.

◆

Marilynne Robinson, the author of Housekeeping *and* Mother Country, *lives in Ames, Iowa; she teaches at the Iowa Writer's Workshop in Iowa City.*

RICHARD MANNING

◆ ◆ ◆ ◆ ◆

THE FAILURE OF LITERATURE

Nature does not make a particularly good story. Yet we so much need our stories that we mine them from nature like gold: We dig the ore, cull to the bit that suits us or is pretty and flashy, and haul it off for display, leaving the most of what is nature like tailings on the ground.

To some extent this is a benign and sustainable exploitation. I may give you a poem built from a tree, but my poem leaves the tree to stand and carry on. My poem is not a logger, but we forget that our stories shape us, and we are loggers. In the end, this caricaturizing of nature to gain stories is simply exploitation.

Nature does not make a good story because nature is far more than we can imagine. It has no beginning or end. It does not hinge on development of character. There is no progress, nor good and evil, much as we need it to be otherwise. Nature just is, a notion that we and our stories are by nature ill-equipped to understand.

I could illustrate my argument with the whole anthropomorphic stream that is popular culture's grasp of nature, a view that finds its reductio ad absurdum in such as the Disney films. Yet attacking these examples does nothing to state the larger sweep of this issue. These stories are trivial and unnecessary, but many of our stories are not. Many of our stories imagine and therefore allow our existence, especially those of a particular sort, those that help us deal with nature's harshest reality, our consciousness of our own deaths. The failings of these stories are the hardest to face.

Such a story is Norman Maclean's final work: *Young Men and*

Fire. As a story it deserves its popularity, finely wrought, complex, and profound as it is. It deserves its place as a best-seller. As literature, it succeeds, but as an account of nature it is myopic and negligently incomplete, a failing I raise with no small amount of fear.

This fear is no device for argument, but something I mean. No matter how correct my attack on this story might be, perhaps it is better unsaid. In this matter of facing death, we are better off with faulty stories when weighed against the alternative. In their absence, we are left to face this thing alone.

Besides, living where I live in Missoula, Montana, I do not take this matter of criticizing Norman Maclean lightly, no matter what his subject. This is a town of writers, and he was our gray eminence. The very places he wrote about with profound affection hold my affections. Here he is an object of great respect.

Worse, here his character is known. Were he alive, this essay would be a hazardous enterprise in that he was a curmudgeonly son of a bitch. Were he alive to read this, I well could imagine his Volkswagen careening up my dirt road so that he could issue me a caning. He is dead, however, so it is safe enough to write this.

It must be written, because just across this dirt road of mine lies a ridge of trees that is a mess. Just beyond this ridge is another in the same condition, and just beyond that is the Fish Creek drainage that Maclean wrote about in the "Black Ghost" section of *Young Men and Fire*. It is also a mess, although the Forest Service has begun to do something about that by setting it afire. It's getting better now.

The sorry state of these ridges has very little to do with logging, although logging has had its effect here. The hills drained by Maclean's Big Blackfoot River, the setting of his story "A River Runs Through It," have been so severely logged that erosion has destroyed the fishing there. Most of the western end of the state is just that bad, so bad that when Robert Redford wished to make a film of Maclean's home grounds, he had to film it elsewhere.

Arguably, though, a greater destruction has been worked by the other role of the U.S. Forest Service: the fighting of fire. The attitudes toward wildfire that organize Maclean's last story are responsible for turning much of western Montana into a "biological desert." The quotation marks in that last sentence have a specific referent in that the phrase was last spoken to me by Laird Robinson, who was Watson to Maclean's Holmes in *Young Men and Fire*. Robinson was and still is career Forest Service. This and his position as a main character in a best-selling book provide an instructive irony, the full measure of which takes some telling.

On that ridge across from my dirt road, probably just now as I write this, there is a lion. This is a pretty safe assumption, because these days in this region, there is a lion in just about every niche that will hold one. The ridge, proximity to humans notwithstanding, is such a niche.

There is further evidence of a lion's presence. Last summer, five of my neighbor's six goats became prey within two weeks. My neighbors called the state animal control people, and they used hounds to tree two lions: an adult female and a juvenile. On the theory that the juvenile was an inept hunter and so taking goats instead of deer, they drugged it and transferred it to a more remote area. They left the adult in a tree in sight of my house, and there have been no troubles among the goats since. I assume the lion lives there still; the deer numbers have stayed agreeably moderate in our little valley.

The leaving of that female lion was an act of tolerance not without some peril. She may kill livestock—many lions do; she may even kill humans. A couple of years ago another lion killed a child just outside Missoula. Last summer a woman who lives near my house walked backward all the miles home from her daily jog in the mountains. She was followed by an intently focused lioness crouched to pounce. The jogger had stumbled on the lion's cubs.

Yet in the face of all this, there is a general tolerance here for the lions. It is understood they provide the balancing hand of death in a system that would be overrun by deer in their absence. They are evidence of the presence of nature's whole and working hand, and so we do not kill them. Some of us even like them.

I mention all this only because of the contrast the lion provides to the case of the wolf. During the earlier part of this century, the gray wolf was deliberately exterminated from the West. Our government hired people to do most of this, although ranchers provided a certain amount of help. Only recently we have begun to understand the stupidity of this act, and so have started actions to reintroduce wolves in the wilderness areas of the West that still might support them, areas such as my neighborhood. It has become one of our hottest political issues.

I have attended hearings complete with sign-carrying demonstrators with Stetson hats, potbellies, and a roll of chew in their jaws. My favorite sign was one that labeled the wolf the Saddam Hussein of the animal world. These same ranchers have promised to shoot any wolves reintroduced in Montana, Wyoming, and Idaho. For good measure, they have promised to shoot any bureaucrats who reintroduce them.

Meanwhile, at Yellowstone National Park, in what has become the nation's premiere petting zoo for large ungulates, it is a tough winter. Come spring, the starving elks will drop by the hundreds. This is ground zero for wolf reintroduction on the theory that these great predators will reestablish something of a natural balance in a place that is supposed to be natural.

If there is to be reintroduction of wolves, an issue that the government is finally supposed to decide later this year, it will be an act of political courage and will be imposed at enormous political costs. It has been and will be a hell of a fight. Unlike the lion, there is no tolerance for the wolf. Its killing is alleged by the ranchers to be "cruel" and "sadistic," whatever that means.

Yet the prey studies done around Glacier National Park on the Canadian border, a place where there already are wolves, show that wolves and lions are remarkably similar in their habits. Both eat mostly white-tailed deer. Both occasionally prey on livestock. If the lion has an advantage, it lies in stealth and efficiency. Wolves compensate for their relative clumsiness by organization. They are social hunters. This allows them to take larger prey like elk, which is why lions don't do the job in Yellowstone, but as far as livestock is concerned, the effect of lions and wolves is much the same.

As far as humans are concerned, it is different. Lions do kill humans, but there has never been a documented attack by a healthy wolf on humans. Still I have never heard the wolf haters issue a single peep in protest of the lion. I think this has something to do with the stories that we tell.

The wolf is working against several thousand years of terrible press, while the lion, at least in European cultures, is simply pretty. The wolf is the heavy of Western mythology, ranking up there as a symbol of evil with Satan, witches, and fire.

Only this month, my wife mentioned wolves to our four-year-old niece, and the child hid under the chair. She had seen the wolves in Disney's *Beauty and the Beast* and understood them to be "mean."

All of this would be only harmless storytelling if we didn't so need the wolves now, need them to restore balance in this ecosystem and need them to teach us of the creative power of death in nature. Now the political decision to support wolves must swim against the stream of our stories.

When bureaucrats last spoke of these matters in a small town in central Idaho, one man there promised he would bring his shotgun and "shoot them in the back" if they ever returned spouting such nonsense. To investigate what officials took seriously as a death threat, the federal government sent Laird Robinson to the scene. That's his job these days; he is the agency's lead official in the Northern Rockies for dealing with wolves and the public.

I have known Laird for many years, yet the last time we talked, there was a whole new spin on the meeting. *Young Men and Fire* reads very much like the best of novels, so speaking with one of its main characters is a bit like sitting down for coffee with Huck Finn. The story has changed him, or at least changed him in my eyes.

Maclean, who as a young man worked for the Forest Service, described his relationship with Robinson in his book:

It is a great privilege to possess the friendship of a young man who is as good or better than you at what you intended to be when you were his age just before you changed directions—all the way from the woods to the classroom. It is as if old age fortuitously had enriched your life by letting you live two lives, the life you finally chose to live and a working copy of the one you started out to live.

Knowing the respect Maclean is accorded, I imagine this charge so publicly made has forever changed Laird's life, and he says this is so. He tells long, affectionate stories of the writer, of the years they spent together, and of the sad, long days of his dying. He speaks of him like a father. He likes the book.

But knowing all of this I still expected a blunt answer from Laird to my blunt and key question: "Laird, was he wrong about fire?"

Maclean was wrong about fire.

The prosecution of this charge hinges heavily on what I mean by *wrong*.

Young Men and Fire is accurate enough in its main. It is a detailed retelling of the Mann Gulch wildfire that blew up near Helena, Montana, on August 5, 1949. By the standards of the day, it was a big fire, ultimately about 4,500 acres. Subsequent drought cycles have eroded those standards. Now a big fire is like the 250,000-acre blaze in 1988 that burned just a few miles from Mann Gulch.

What made this fire one of considerable note is that twelve of the fifteen men who went to fight the fire died there. The book is nothing so much as a grieving of each of their deaths, especially as they relate to each of ours and particularly as they relate to Norman Maclean's. The book was the work of the last fourteen years of his life, and he leaves no doubt he understands where it and he are headed.

Despite its epic goal, though, Maclean himself set for the book a rigid standard of truth, and (if it is possible under such circumstances) detachment.

"There's nothing wrong with romanticism, except that sometimes it isn't enough," Maclean wrote.

The book is wholly true to the first clause of that sentence, and that is just the problem. Throughout, the fire is demonized. It is evil. It is a monster. It is death generalized to the point that by the end of the book it is transformed to nuclear fire, in that "it looked much like an atomic explosion in Nevada on its cancerous way to Utah."

Ultimately, the story is cast in religious metaphor, the struggle between good and evil as prosecuted by young men. This should come as no great surprise from an author for whom even fly-fishing is a religion.

Maclean does venture beyond his romanticism, just as he promises, but only in a limited sense. That is, his science is very much the science of the 1950s, which is to say it is technology or hubris. His science is aimed at the stated goal of the day, that every forest fire be extinguished by ten o'clock the next morning. If there was a failure at Mann Gulch, it was a failure to grasp the proper techniques for achieving this goal.

Challenging the goal itself would be seeing fire as something other than evil, and Maclean was simply not capable of doing that. This is where he got it wrong, wrong by his own standards and wrong by the standards of some of the very people he relied upon to tell his tale.

The forests of the Northern Rockies have been severely damaged because of nearly a century of fire fighting. That is, the forests of this region evolved since the Ice Age in the presence of fire. Some were swept by fire as frequently as every seven years.

Slowly, we are coming to understand that fire is not evil but necessary. In its absence, at least in this region, trees grow too thickly and become diseased. Certain species supplant others, and the forests change to something that the natural systems are not prepared to defend. Even more trees die than under a natural regime, and those dead trees accumulate in the forests as fuels. Today the fires are not the 4,500 acres of Mann Gulch days, they run to 250,000 acres, and there is no putting some of them out, no matter how we try.

Fire-fighting heroics aside, the West ought to burn, and we

ought to have the political will to burn it. If we don't, the trees will die, the fuels will accumulate, the drought will come, and the West will burn anyway, only hotter. Fire, like the wolf, performs the role of predator, a sort of megapredator that balances the hand of life with death.

The core of this view is not hypothesis but rather an understanding general among the scientists who deal with wildfire. It is, in fact, official policy of the Forest Service, recorded as the "prescribed" fire policy. Bud Moore, a character in Maclean's book, had a hand in developing it. Robinson says Bud spent a good deal of time trying to convince Maclean that fire was not evil, but it wouldn't take. Instead Maclean would go to Robinson and complain that Bud was way off base.

"Norman couldn't comprehend prescribed fire. The word *fire* to him was synonymous with destruction," Robinson told me. Try as they might, he and Moore could not budge him from this view.

So it happens that Maclean's stubbornly held and antique view presents itself in a national best-seller. And so the public consciousness of nature feeds on something other than nature. This is where our literature collides with our science, or, more to the point, our consciousness collides with our consciousness.

In a sense, I am being too prudish about all of this, insisting on a notion of environmental correctness, which is to say, warping a damn fine story to suit my political ends. I am an environmentalist, and I believe that allowing fire is sound public policy. In many ways what passes between Norman and me is a political disagreement.

In this snit, I am missing the point, which is that Norman is dead. When he wrote the book, he was an old man, and as I write this I am not. When I am, you can bet I will myself be describing the hand of death in far more lurid terms.

There is a 60,000-year-old Neanderthal grave in Iraq in which the deceased is buried with flowers. Nature evolved consciousness for humans, and we used it first it seems to realize our mortality. From this we first derived religion and second derived literature. All of literature exists because we understand our mortality, so why should I now set a different standard for Norman Maclean?

But then our consciousness also begat our science, and from this we derived our tinkering with nature, and we are guided in our tinkering by the stories we tell. How now will we deal with our stories when our nature so needs its fires and its wolves?

We are a species endowed with a unique survival tool in our consciousness. We think of this tool as evident in our cleverness, and so it is, but also it is evident in our literature. Consciousness gives us a finely honed hatred of death, which manifests itself as a will to live. Nature values survival. To fulfill the mandate of our consciousness, we must see death as evil. Nature must see death only as death. This is why nature makes a lousy story.

For me, there are now two Laird Robinsons. In that his story has been appropriated for literature, he has been given a second life. Only a few of us know his real life; several hundred thousand already know the character. How that must strike him now even more than the rest of us, especially as he does his work. He is engaged in the creation of public policy. When he is finished with his current assignment dealing with wolves, he wants to angle for a new one. He wants to help the public understand the importance of the natural role of fire.

By then, public consciousness will have embraced even more the Laird of literature, the Laird of the world where fire is evil. Perhaps by then his alter ego will have grown larger than he is. I wonder how it feels to meet yourself in a public meeting as the opposition in the conflict between art and science?

◆

Richard Manning's books include Last Stand *and* A Good House. *He is also at work on a book that considers the possibilities of the resurrection of the American grasslands, to be published in 1995. His work has appeared in* Audubon, High Country News, The New York Times, Outside, E, *and* Backpacker, *as well as* Northern Lights. *He lives in Montana.*

PART III

WHOSE SPACE THIS IS

JOHN DANIEL

NAMING THE NEW ONE

They came from mountains and plains
to see the new one, the smooth-skin,
who stood on shaking hind legs
and stared, his eyes struck with light.

"He'll sleep cold," Bear grunted,
and walked away. Bigfoot
was already gone, scared,
and Hummingbird had things to do.

As the others walked and crawled
and flew by, the new one pointed
and hurled a sound at each of them,
louder and louder in his harsh joy.

"Those paws are no good," said Gopher.

"Call him *Wildmouth*," said Deer.
"Does he have ears?"

"He'll learn a song, maybe," said Owl.

Long after the new one stumbled away
they heard him crashing the brush,
still trailing his strange calls.

"Doesn't see where he's going,"
Cougar said.

"Well," said Coyote,
"we'll always know when he's *coming*."

He acted brave, but he was nervous.
"Let's watch him for a while.
There's plenty of room. When he finds
his place, then we'll name him."

◆

John Daniel, author of this poem, as well as the essay "Cuttings," which appears later in this collection, is also the author of The Trail Home, *a collection of nature essays, and of two books of poetry:* Common Ground *and* All Things Touched By Wind. *He is poetry editor for* Wilderness *magazine. This year Daniel is the Dutch Henry Wilderness Writing Resident on the Rogue River in southern Oregon, a position so wonderful, he refuses to talk about it. He has lived in the West for 28 of his 46 years and he hopes to settle down soon.*

DAVID QUAMMEN

◆ ◆ ◆ ◆

THE NEWMARK WARNING:

Why Our National Parks are Resembling Desert Isles

Abstract: *The red fox is missing from Bryce Canyon National Park because Bryce Canyon is too much like an island, and that island is simply too small.*

The red fox is missing from Bryce Canyon National Park. It hasn't been seen there, in that protected enclave of Utah desert, for twenty-seven years. The red fox is a small, quiet species, *Vulpes vulpes*, but the small, quiet fact of its absence seems to be part of a much larger and more ominous scientific mystery.

The pronghorn antelope and the beaver are also missing from Bryce Canyon. So is the northern flying squirrel. Crater Lake National Park, up in southwestern Oregon, has its own set of puzzling ecological absences. The river otter is missing, not seen since 1945. But fur hunters didn't kill it off, nor did poisoned waters. The river otter of Crater Lake vanished subtly, and evidently for reasons more abstract than human malice, malfeasance, or greed. So did the ermine, the mink, the spotted skunk, and the gray fox of Crater Lake, all of them gone for the past forty years. Zion National Park has a gap where its badger should be. Another gap, at Zion, once but no longer filled by the black bear. Mount Rainier National Park is bereft of wolverines and lynx, though both species were present ninety years ago, when the park was established. Yosemite, like Bryce Canyon, has lost its entire population of red fox.

There are no villains for us to hiss in this particular mystery. It isn't a morality tale about poaching, polluting, benighted notions of predator control, or the ineptitude of Park Service management. The local extinction of all these various species of mammals seems related, instead, to a complex ecological phenomenon that is no less dramatic, no less dire, for being elaborately indirect.

One scientist, Tom Lovejoy of the Smithsonian Institution, calls it "ecosystem decay." Our parks have been shedding species the way a lump of uranium sheds alpha particles.

For gathering the facts about this seemingly unaccountable species loss from America's national parks, and for making sense of those facts scientifically, great credit is due to a young ecologist named William D. Newmark. Newmark made the subject his business for a doctoral project at the University of Michigan, and the dissertation he submitted in 1986 may be one of the more famous unpublished documents of modern ecology. Bootleg copies began making the rounds; my own print of Newmark's dissertation is a Xerox of a Xerox of a Xerox that reached me through channels I couldn't retrace. Then, early last year, Newmark published the core of his work as an article in the journal *Nature*. Filling less than three pages, the *Nature* piece represents just what every publish-or-perish journal article should be but so seldom is: a concise blip of useful, provocative information for which other workers were already hungering. Newmark's title: "A Land-bridge Island Perspective on Mammalian Extinctions in Western North American Parks."

The red fox is missing from Bryce Canyon National Park, Newmark speculates, because Bryce Canyon is too much like an island, and that island is simply too small.

How big is big enough? is a question of mortal import to ecologists and conservation planners. How big must a population of some particular species be for that species to have good prospects of survival? (Three lonely California condors are clearly too few to have much chance of perpetuating the species in the wild—genetic impoverishment and the vagaries of luck would weigh heavily against them, even if nothing else did. But what about two hundred grizzly bears? If only forty of those two hundred are fertile females, is that number sufficient to carry the species past problems of inbreeding and natural catastrophe?) And how big an area is required—how much suitable habitat—to support at least that critical size of population? (Is New York's Central Park big enough to host a viable population of raccoons? Do the rectilinear borders of Yellowstone leave enough space for a *permanent* population of grizzlies?) Since a world emptied of other species is a world of dreariness and doom, and since that's precisely the condition our own world is headed toward, the question *How big is big enough?* carries mortal import for the rest of us too. That question lies behind the Newmark study.

Closely related to it is another: *What is the nature of the interconnection between species diversity and area?*

For more than sixty years, ecologists have recognized that the size of an area of wild habitat correlates strongly with the number of plant and animal species to be found in that area. This old truth, derived empirically from a handful of independent surveys, is known as the species/area correlation. Back in 1921 a Swedish plant ecologist named Olof Arrhenius published a paper straightforwardly titled "Species and Area," still cited as one of the landmarks in this long scientific journey. Based on his own investigation of species diversity within certain delimited plots, Arrhenius concluded that "the number of species increases continuously as the area increases." Arrhenius had surveyed plant communities on certain islands around Stockholm. His conclusion was not nearly so obvious, so logically manifest, as it might seem.

What's logically manifest is that the sheer numerousness of *individual* plants and animals should be greater in a large area of undisturbed land than in a small area. The possibility that diversity should also be greater—that there should be more *different species* as well as more total individuals—is something else again, a contingent fact dependent not on logic but on the intricate realities of how plants and animals interact. The species/area correlation is no more an obvious a priori truth than the fact that a bowling ball dropped off the Leaning Tower will gain speed at about thirty-two feet per second per second. Like gravity, the species/area correlation is just a reality of the particular world we happen to know. In 1957 that correlation was confirmed by Philip Darlington, from a study of reptiles and amphibians of the West Indies.

Darlington was less cautious than Arrhenius, going so far as to extract from his data a neat mathematical ratio. As the size of the piece of landscape decreased by a factor of ten, Darlington noted, the number of species found there decreased by a factor of two. On a Caribbean island of roughly 40,000 square miles, for instance, Darlington found roughly 80 species of reptiles and amphibians; on an island of 4,000 square miles, he found roughly 40 species; on an island of 400 square miles, he implied bravely, he'd expect to find about 20 species. The important thing about Darlington's work is not that neat ratio but the more general confirmation of a strong positive species/area correlation. And the intriguing thing about Darlington's work is that, like Arrhenius's, it was done on islands.

This was more than coincidence. Island habitats were especially useful for studies of species diversity within delimited plots—from the beginning of those studies and ever after—because islands by definition *are* delimited plots.

In 1967, Roger MacArthur and Edward Wilson published a small book called *Theory of Island Biogeography*, which has held a mesmeric influence over this corner of ecological research (arguably, over almost *all* ecological research) for twenty years. MacArthur died young, Wilson shifted his interest toward sociobiology, but their theory still presides like an Aztec deity, challenged constantly by apostates and heretics but never ignored. It's a complicated theory, and the criticisms against it are even more complicated, but we can limit ourselves here to three points for which the MacArthur-Wilson work is especially notable. First, its empirical foundation was the species/area correlation, as that had been charted by Arrhenius and Darlington and others (including Wilson himself, studying ant species of Melanesia). Second, this theory posited that the number of species on any island tends to move toward an equilibrium level, at which extinctions are balanced off by new colonizations. Third, and most important, MacArthur and Wilson with this little book brought island biogeography back to the mainland.

"Insularity is moreover a universal feature of biogeography," they wrote. "Many of the principles graphically displayed in the Galápagos Islands and other remote archipelagoes apply in lesser or greater degree to all natural habitats." Caves, streams, tide pools, patches of taiga where it breaks up into tundra—all these fragments of habitat stand ecologically isolated in much the same way as an island. Therefore, like an island, they might show certain special patterns in the way that species arrive, persist, change, disappear. "The same principles apply, and will apply to an accelerating extent in the future, to formerly continuous natural habitats now being broken up by the encroachment of civilization," MacArthur and Wilson added presciently.

William Newmark may have been in third or fourth grade back then, but these two adult strangers had given him his dissertation topic.

Scientists sort the world's islands into two types: oceanic and land-bridge. Not only do these two types derive from different geologic origins, they also show very different ecological histories. An oceanic island, like Oahu, has raised itself up off the sea bottom, generally as a steaming pile of vented lava, and therefore necessarily it began its island existence totally empty of living species. Long after the lava cooled, wayward plants and animals began to arrive. A land-bridge island, like Santa Catalina, is one separated from the mainland by just a narrow, shallow channel. It once *was* part of the mainland, a peninsula or small spit, until geologic subsidence or rising sea level insularized it. Such a land-bridge island began its island existence with a relatively full share of the mainland ecosystem; all the terrestrial animals of the continent had been free to come and go, and to carry plant seeds back and forth with them. But when the waters rose, that free traffic stopped, and suddenly a rich ecosystem was confined within skimpy borders. Inexorably, the species/area correlation would have begun to reestablish itself, pushing the species number downward. Area had been drastically delimited; biological diversity would be reduced as a consequence.

Imagine a particular piece of wild habitat, roughly the size of an American county. This plot of land is rich in species, undisturbed by humanity, and connected to a vast continental expanse of similar habitat. The plot is frequented, let's say, by elephants and tigers and rhinos and orang-utans, maybe two or three species of deer, two or three species of monkey. It's covered with tropical forest, say, and attached to the greater Malaysian peninsula. But an ice age is ending, so the sea level begins to rise. Soon the plot is an island. You might call it Bali.

There's not enough room for a viable population of elephants, so for that reason alone the Bali elephant goes extinct. The tiger and the rhino and the orang-utan disappear too. Some of the monkey and deer species vanish. Bali with its small area just can't support so much diversity. The disappearance of those large animals occurs rather fast, possibly even within decades. But more changes are to come.

Maybe there is a species of frog, native to this plot, whose reproductive strategy entails laying its eggs in the muddy puddles formed by the footprints of rhino along the banks of a clear stream from which the rhino were accustomed to drink. This frog is not adapted for laying its eggs in the stream itself, say; only those muddy stillwater puddles will do. Say that the tadpoles of that frog eat mosquito larvae. Say that the mosquito species in question carries a certain protozoan disease. Say that one of the (so far) surviving species of monkey is susceptible to that disease. Say that the same monkey, a fruit eater, plays a necessary role in the reproductive cycle of a certain species of fig tree. Say that a species of leaf-cutter ant depends on that species of tree. Say that a certain lizard feeds on those ants. Say that the same lizard feeds also, occasionally but not often, upon a particular species of social wasp. Say that the wasp competes with a hummingbird species for ideal nesting sites of the type they both require, small hollows safe in the heights of trees. Now consider some of the delayed repercussions of rising sea level: Because the rhino has disappeared, so does the frog; the mosquito population explodes, inflicting an unusual severity of disease on the monkey; the monkey population falls so low that, during one dry year when none of the tree species bear fruit, it goes extinct; the fig tree has lost its reproductive assistant, and so, one hundred years later, the last member of that fig species dies without having left offspring; meanwhile the leaf-cutter ants have declined and, with them, so has the lizard; eventually the ants vanish, but the lizard barely hangs on; with the lizard population depressed, the wasps have exploded, filling every good nesting site on the island; so the hummingbird goes extinct.

These creatures and interrelations are hypothetical, not the actual particulars from Bali. But they represent more than a Rube Goldberg fantasy. This is the way real ecosystems fit together—and the way, sometimes, they fall apart. Slowly, over more decades and centuries, the species/area correlation asserts itself, until finally a new equilibrium is established. The place we've called Bali is still a remote, undisturbed (by humans) tropical island. Ecologically, though, it's not what it was.

Now imagine the same plot again, but give it a temperate forest and populate that forest with wolverine, river otter, mountain lion, mink, brush rabbit, grizzly bear, red fox. Give this plot legal protection from human disturbance. But let the waters of civilization rise on all sides. Turn it into an island. Call it Yosemite.

"If nature reserves are considered to be similar to land-bridge islands, because most are slowly becoming isolated from their surroundings by habitat disturbance outside the reserves," wrote William Newmark in *Nature*, "several predictions follow." First among these is that the number of extinctions within each reserve should be larger than the number of colonizations by new species. Second, the number of extinctions should be inversely proportional to land area: The bigger the reserve, the fewer extinctions. Third, the number of extinctions should be directly related to reserve age. In other words, both the passage of time since isolation and the smallness of the isolated area should correlate positively with the rate of extinctions. Newmark looked at forty-two separate cases of extinction of mammal species in fourteen North American parks. He carefully disregarded those extinctions caused by direct human activities. The sad and significant message from his study is that all the predictions came true.

Newmark concluded, "The natural post-establishment loss of mammalian species in western North American national parks indicates that virtually all western North American national parks were too small to maintain the mammalian faunal assemblage found at time of park establishment."

It seems that Bryce Canyon is not big enough for the red fox. That Zion is not big enough for the badger. As the waters keep rising, as species/area ratios waver, adjust, slide toward some equilibrium level, only more passing time will reveal whether Olympic National Park is large enough for the mountain beaver, or Arches for the piñon mouse, or whether Grand Canyon can indefinitely support its population of ringtail cat. Of course these places aren't literally islands. Some folks will even tell you, contrary to William Newmark, that all this chatter about insularity has no relevance to our mainland national parks. In one sense they are right. Don't send to know for whom the bell tolls.

◆

David Quammen is the author of six books, fiction and non-fiction, and a passel of magazine articles. For the last thirteen years he has written a monthly column on natural science for Outside *magazine. His forthcoming book,* The Song of the Dodo, *concerns global patterns of the evolution and extinction of species, and the way those patterns are illuminated by the study of islands. In the course of researching it, he has traveled to Madagascar, New Guinea, Guam, Mauritius, the Galá-pagos, Krakatoa, Sulawesi, Tasmania, the central Amazon, Komodo, and Wyoming.*

JERRY MCGAHAN

◆ ◆ ◆ ◆ ◆

WAXWING

Before the Nature Conservancy there was Harry Early Thunder.

He was born and buried just outside Wind Flats. Harry Early Thunder's high school track record for the 440 and 880 still reigned, established for forty years the name of Wind Flats in the book of track records for Class C schools or whatever they were called then. After Harry, the book had to recognize a reservation town where the inhabitants ranged in age from thirteen to eighty, depending on whether you drew a line around the post office, the church, and a bar named Lorelei (known locally as Frankie's) or made a dogleg jag to take in the dozen or so shacks over the hill on Takseen Creek.

Harry broke those records when he was only a freshman; he quit school before the next year was up so as to find something better than staring out windows. He worked for two years at Ben Hatler's and put up more hay for every hour worked than two men did before or since, and did it without any complaint. He became the unstinting force for another's ambition until Ben saw the oldest of his three daughters watching Harry. Harry was stripped to the waist pitching hay from the loft, and Ben, seeing what she saw, Harry's body moving like trees in the wind, gave the Indian his walking papers right there, went up the ladder, and sent Harry down the road, watched him go still without hearing any question or protest.

Somewhere between Ben Hatler's hayloft and Frankie's floor, where Harry spent the next three years, someone had invited into that callused hand a bottle of Silver City apricot brandy, which put him on all fours, where he stayed off and on until that day in February when the bird hit the glass and he heard it and knew what it was. In those days he was sleeping in a tar-paper shack behind the church in a hovel of old newspapers and sacks of insulation, curled like a snail with his knees to his chest. He shivered and dreamed and craved the syrup fire and its slurry drift until in one night's dreams a buckskin-colored bird fit itself in the palm of his hand. It was on its back freshly dead. He turned it a little with one finger and found flecks like blood on each wing but it was not blood, hard instead but bright as wet blood, and he knew—still dreaming—something was going to happen. It was the first time in his life he had ever expected anything to happen. He kept watch, even when he was on all fours in the Lorelei, so when it happened he already knew what it was. The flock of twittering winter birds came off an ash tree in front of the church, and the gusting wind flung them across the street, where one struck the glass and fell into the road. Harry got to his feet and went out to see what he knew was already there. He never went into Frankie's again.

The bird never spoiled. It did not change except to harden. He kept it wrapped in rabbit fur, tucked in a hole in the sill log of the cabin he built across Pelican Marsh. He drank water, nothing else, ate sparingly but well enough on rabbits and muskrat and apples in the winter and biscuit-root, camas, berries, and jerky in the summer. Harry worked every waking hour, roved from one crew to another. He combined for a half-dozen dryland wheat farmers, fought fire, and built trails for the CCC, and at night and on weekends he trapped, skinned, and stretched furs, wrapped every earned dollar in red neckerchiefs, and hid them under the bowls of magpie nests in the hawthorns around the marsh. He retrieved them one by one whenever another farmer pulled up stakes in the cedar-break country to the south, paid the back taxes and bought the land, burnt the house and barn, the chicken coop and outhouse, and left the place to what it would be. He kept one neckerchief for tax notices and paid them all at the same time when they came due.

One day he went to the courthouse in Sanders and said he wanted to finish it.

"Finish what?" the treasurer said. It was Delores Scherberg, the banker's wife.

"Payin'. I want it done." He unfolded the tax notices, smoothed each crumpled sheet atop the other.

"They're already paid," she said. "It doesn't come due now till November."

"No, I don't want it due again. I bought it. I want it bought done. It's bought land, free now. I want it bought enough so it never needs to be bought again." Never before had he said as many words at one time to another person.

She laughed. "You can't do that. The taxes are due once a year. They always will be. You own the property. It's yours, all right, but you've always got to pay taxes."

"No," he said, "not anybody's. But I'm doing what needs to be done to get it loose again. I'm doing what you say so that it won't belong to anyone again."

"You do what you want," she said curtly. Harry watched her cheeks shake. "But taxes are due every year."

"I want it done." He went on with the same imperturbable evenness. "You tell me how much and I give it to you. No one ever says they own that again. Forever. How much?"

"Forever?" She was amazed. "Forever," she said again. She turned her head away and back again, sighed condescendingly. "When you die it goes to whoever you will it to, or the state takes it, keeps it or puts it on the market, but what it'll do most likely is go to your next of kin."

"I have no kin except that—what's out there. How much is it now to have that done?"

"There is nothing you can do to have it done." Delores Scherberg slapped the counter with one hand. "No one owns anything after they're dead anyway. It goes to your next of kin or the state or to whoever buys it, and then they own it and they pay the taxes right here and that's all there is to it and I'm not going to talk about it anymore. Take your money and come back in November." Harry stared at her red, twitching face. She went on: "That's all there is to it. There's nothing you can do to keep somebody from owning it, and when they do, they pay their taxes. Period." She slammed her hand down again.

In one soft, very sudden motion Harry pressed the back of her hand with the end of his forefinger. "No one owns any land." He said this with terrific softness. "You have said this yourself. They die. It stays. Still you say it is owned. I say this, all right, it is owned. Then I will buy it for what you say, that owning. I have the money and I will do that."

"Get out of here." She tore her hand out from beneath his finger.

Harry Early Thunder's expression altered none whatsoever. He folded the tax notices one at a time, fit them into the neckerchief with the money, knotted it there, and slid it to invisibility beneath his shirt. He waited a moment and then he turned and went out.

◆

Jerry McGahan is a beekeeper and lives with his wife and three daughters on the Flathead Indian Reservation near Arlee, Montana.

DEBRA EARLING

◆ ◆ ◆ ◆ ◆

THOMAS KICKING WOMAN:

Holding the Fire

Maybe I haven't been making myself clear to you. Maybe there is no way we can make ourselves clear to each other, otherwise, you wouldn't be running from my brother and he wouldn't be trying so hard to please everybody but himself. And we wouldn't be hiding on this hill with your heart beating like a rabbit's. There is no surface to what I want to say to you, Louise. Understanding sleeps below the surface and is hard for us to catch as a fish is hard to catch in deep standing water. We start thinking when we see something, when it looks close to us, we can have it. But things are always changing. You have to remember that the power to be so close to the weeds, so close to the sage and the cheat that even the dirt doesn't measure our footprints, is the same power that is always changing.

And it will change on you too. It has changed on me. The power not to be seen, the power to be invisible is like a warrior who fights in two camps but is claimed by neither. To be invisible on the land, to be one with the grass and the dirt was once a good gift we held. But when the white man came, this fight became a power that could shift away from us. Many days now you are not seen when you want to be seen and then seen when you wish to remain invisible. One day you will be passed over because the whites and maybe even the Indians won't see you at all. It is happening now. It is happening to our people. It is not because we don't have leaders in these bad times. It is because we don't see them. We choose not to see them. The power has changed on us and we have lost the ability to keep up.

There are some Indians here who say that I am Blackfeet because my father is Blackfeet, because my name is Blackfeet. They cannot see that I have lived on this reservation all my life, that my mother is Flathead, that all I know comes from the land I know here. They cannot see me for what I am. They see a name that I have made my own through living. But they do not see me. That is the danger of not being seen. We can only be accepted when we are seen. But we are Indians, and because we are Indians, I know we will always need the ability not to be seen sometimes. Indians have always recognized that in all power there is danger.

Charlie is just down the hill, and he is coming closer. Even if he had a hundred dogs that could sniff the blood in our necks or chase the scent of our crotches, he would not find us. See. In this short grass he cannot see us. In the white August grass where we sit dark as the black man, he cannot spot us. Because deep down I think he doesn't want to catch you. He doesn't want to drag you back to the white school. On the surface, Charlie thinks that what is best is what the white man wants.

It is confusing, I know, this talk of power. What can make a man blind to a bull elk sniffing the blood in his wrists? I have seen white hunters near Thompson Falls walking through trees with their rifles drawn while all around them the elk are so thick the shadows of their horns touch the ground like branches. The power has changed for Charlie, and he has lost the ability to see what it is he really wants. He is lost here on the land.

There was a time not too long ago when the power was lost to all of our people for a terrible, bad time. When we as a people stood blinking in the blindness of a great fear. We could have lived for years on this reservation with our power growing. We could have kept the peace and acted too. We could have saved a nation, a brother looking for help. When Chief Joseph came up here from his home in the Wallowa. Running. We would not let him stay. Even though many of our own people rode up with him under the protective arm of his vision, we turned away. We would not help him for fear we would harm ourselves. We lost our power to see the right way, to help others. We turned ourselves away from the needs of ourselves. You have heard Coyote stories of Coyote shitting on himself. We laugh at Coyote because we can see what's going on there. Coyote falling in love with his own shit. Well, that is what we did. We fell in love with our own shit, the only difference is we're not laughing.

There were women with Chief Joseph, women who had walked so far in moccasined feet that their tough soles broke open to rock, to cold ground, to miles of running with small children, with old women and men no longer warriors. All of them hungry as winter. They had come to stand out on empty, open ground, on miles of prairie in daylight. The sun was so bright, shadows were dull beneath sagebrush and dark beneath the eyes of all these people who had not slept for days. No tree to hide in, no bush to claim comfort. Only this rugged stretch of prairie-bitten weeds. And they stood there on the land with their children crying at their skirts, with their old men bowing to a wind so high they could hear the voices of their dead calling.

Imagine the sound of a hundred horses' hooves running on dry ground so hard the sound becomes your heart beating thunder. Imagine you have nothing to defend yourself with, maybe a small stone you can dig out of the earth with your fingers, an old rusted gun that can easily backfire on you. Nothing to lift up against your enemy but your empty hands, your voice lost to wind. Imagine watching your breath, the company of your dying tribe's breath lifting up white to meet the hill where the white soldiers are coming from. Imagine the white soldiers are coming with swords so cold your tongue will stick to the blades. Their bullets will swipe the cold air beneath your running feet and sting your children down like bees. You will see only sky without trees, no mountains. You will hear no sound of water when the bullets drop you, when the bullets bury in your tender hips, when the bullets sing through your hearts and cut through the hands you hold over your children.

There you are, standing on the wide prairie, knowing your

feet touch your own grave. And this must be the end, I know you must be thinking, standing out there on the land.

When the medicine man begins moving. Walking at first, going nowhere, as if the white soldiers don't matter, as if he were only walking. And then he is turning on his heel and each time he turns, the tips of his heels are turning blue, his body lights a fire, a blue flame you can't be sure you're seeing, only believe. Believe, when the flame turns him to powder, a powder so blue you think you are seeing sky. And he crouches down low as a snake in shallow grass and begins to suck from the ground, not a dry cloud or a spirit wind whirling, but to suck so hard the hollows of his cheeks turn inside out and his penis presses up through his loincloth, to suck a mud-wet cloud that spins up to sun, leaving behind a stinging shimmer of mica, a glaze that covers the people, covers them, like lightning for a moment, covers darkness.

◆

Debra Earling is a member of the Confederated Salish & Kootenai Tribes of the Flathead Reservation. She teaches at the University of Montana.

FREDERICK TURNER

◆ ◆ ◆ ◆ ◆

WOUNDED KNEE III

I

Not long after we had blundered into these shores the question arose as to whether we could assimilate the new lands and their natives. To be sure, there was something remarkably arrogant in this, since by the close of the first century of exploration, we had hardly so much as a map to show us accurately the contours of America, whether it was shaped like the nipple of Paradise, as Columbus believed, whether it hooked somehow onto the fabled Far East; nor any idea how many natives there might be awaiting our discovery within the continent's shadowy and unimagined interior. A tiny expeditionary force from the Old World, we were confined to reservations of white civilization on the coasts, trying there to survive starvation, mutinies, and the attacks of those natives we had so far dispossessed. Even so, it is possible to discern in the early Spanish, French, and English documents a shared assumption that one day all of America would be ours. And that meant we had a native problem: What would we do with them?

The native point of view was precisely the opposite: What would they do with these whites? Some believed we would eventually just go away. In the prophecies of some Southwestern tribes, for example, the white man was fated to disappear at last, ghostly, evanescent, like those who had once wandered through their lands, vanishing in a shimmer of heat and dust: the Coronado expedition, the whites called this.

Three centuries later it was apparent that it was we who had known better after all, having in the intervening years so successfully imposed ourselves on America that we had overspread it, however thinly, and owned title to all but a few scraps where the natives existed on sufferance. In 1890 the Census Bureau reported the disappearance of that line between white civilization and wilderness that from the beginning had really defined what America was. Now the frontier would pass into memory along with the buffalo and the passenger pigeon, and as the final act in this process there was the opening to white settlement in this same year of 11 million acres of the Great Sioux Reservation in South Dakota.

The Sioux cession was equally significant as fact and symbol. More than the Iroquois, more than the stubborn Seminoles or the far-flung, elusive Navajo, the Sioux were to white Americans marplots and troublemakers whose lands lay squarely in the westward path of progress. In 1862, the Santee Sioux had arisen in Minnesota and effectively cleared the state of white inhabitants. Four years later on the Bozeman Trail in Wyoming, the western Sioux had wiped out Captain Fetterman and his entire eighty-man command. Two years after that the government agreed at Ft. Laramie to abandon the Bozeman Trail and its forts and to "give" the Sioux all of South Dakota west of the Missouri for their exclusive use, plus hunting rights in southeastern Montana—a humiliating capitulation as many whites saw it. And then there had been the Custer disaster, which had spoiled the nation's centennial celebration.

That did it. Howls went up in Congress and almost everywhere else for vindictive punishment of the Sioux, and hardly had the dust from the Little Bighorn settled when commissioners backed by a huge armed force arrived on the Great Sioux Reservation to threaten and bribe the Sioux into giving up the Black Hills, their Montana hunting range, and about a third of the Great Sioux Reservation— all this in violation of the Ft. Laramie treaty, which required consent of three-fourths of the adult Sioux males to make any changes in its provisions. In their successful resistance the Sioux had succeeded also in focusing the attention of a nation on them, and that nation was no longer in the mood for gradual measures. William Tecumseh

Sherman, who had been placed in charge of the Plains campaigns, spoke for the majority when he said that the Indians would "all have to be killed or maintained as a species of pauper." By the time of the opening to white settlement of those 11 million acres of Sioux land, Sherman's vision had been fulfilled everywhere in America and nowhere more fully than on the Sioux reservations where the once haughty Lakota (as they called themselves) were in truth a species of pauper, utterly dependent on the uncertain flow of their treaty annuities, bereft of the buffalo, forbidden their religious practices, their tribal and band structures destroyed, and even the remaining lands slated for dismemberment into individual allotments as per the provisions of the Dawes Severalty Act. As the commissioner of Indian affairs put it in July 1889, "The settled policy of the government is to break up the reservations, destroy tribal relations, settle Indians upon their own homesteads, incorporate them into the national life. . . . The American Indian is to become the Indian American." This was assimilation, late-nineteenth-century version, but it would not be too difficult to see it as a plan for cultural extermination.

That was certainly the way the Lakota saw it. They had suffered defeats in the past—in skirmishes with the Pawnee, the Crow—and they had suffered the harsh vicissitudes of nomadic life on the Great Plains—hunting mishaps, scarcity of game, winters so savage even the camp dogs were snow-blinded and crows froze in flight and fell dead against the sides of the lodges. Yet their winter counts, the oral histories of the bands that reminded them of these things, told them also that they had survived everything, had endured with honor. History was a source of hope and encouragement then. Now history seemed to be coming to an end under the rule of these implacable *wasicus* (whites), who, it would seem, would be satisfied with nothing less than the disappearance of the people:

1881   **Site g.leska kte'pi**
       Spotted Tail/they kill
       (Spotted Tail, chief at Rosebud Reservation, is
       killed.)

1882   **C'a c'ega k'i'la c'ica'wa ic'i'kte**
Drum/he carries on his back/his son/a/he kills
himself
(Drum on the Back's son shoots himself.)

1884   **T'at 'a'ka Ska t'awi'cu kikte'**
Buffalo-Bull/White/his wife/he kills his own
(White Buffalo Bull kills his wife.)

1888   **Wo' p 'ahta yuble'capi**
Bundles/they are opened and exposed
(Reservation policemen stop the practice of med-
icine.)

1889   **O'g.le Sa t'ak 'si'tku wa ic'i'kte**
Shirt/Red/his younger sister/a/she hanged herself
(Red Shirt's younger sister hangs herself.)

**—Entries from the winter count of Ben Kindle of the
Oglala Sioux. Translated by Martha Warren Beckwith.**

Not surprisingly, deprived thus of their history and of hope,
the Lakota got caught up in the Ghost Dance fever that swept through
so many Western tribes in 1889–90, for the prophecy of the new
religion said that history was not at an end, that indeed the past
was returning in the spring of 1891. At that time the dead Indians
would return along with the buffalo, and the *wasicus* would choke
to death on the land they had been so greedy to possess. A new
earth would roll over the old one the *wasicus* had profaned, and
history would recommence its round. A desperate hope, to be sure,
as Sitting Bull acknowledged when he asked what difference it made
whether the new religion was true or not. We have nothing else to
hope for, he said.

1890   **Si T'a'ka kte'pi**
Big Foot/they kill
(Big Foot and his band massacred at Wounded
Knee.)

II

"Stop here," Dale Looks Twice directed me. We were on BIA route 27, where it curves through the site of the Wounded Knee massacre of December 29, 1890, and on our way to the town of Pine Ridge, where Looks Twice would interview a descendant of one of the massacre's victims. Looks Twice was collecting such interviews to be broadcast over the Lakota-language radio station for the centenary ceremonies just a month hence. On this bright and windy day of high skies and mare's tails no creature moved up there on the hill where the soldiers' Hotchkiss guns had sat. Only the grasses waved like hair, and behind the poor, thin arch that marks the entrance to the mass grave a bit of bunting fluttered from a post.

I had been here several times in the past, including just after Wounded Knee II in 1973 when the American Indian Movement under Russell Means and Dennis Banks had occupied the site in a seventy-day standoff with federal officials, but I had never had a native guide. For a white this was a mixed advantage as Looks Twice pointed out where the cannons and companies had been positioned, where Chief Big Foot's tent had been and the lodges of the Ghost Dancers. "Over here," he said, pointing left, "is the ravine where the people tried to escape when the firing began." Very few did so as the soldiers rode them down and shot them, the bodies of women, children, and babies being found three and four miles from the encampment.

At the time, the massacre had been misrepresented as a battle and misunderstood as the consequence of an Indian uprising. In fact, it was the wholly avoidable conclusion to the Ghost Dance revitalization movement. Sitting Bull's murder on December 15, 1890, precipitated the concatenation of events that led to this place where I now sat with Dale Looks Twice: In the wake of the murder there had been the frightened flight of the Ghost Dancers under Big Foot into the Badlands; the massing of the troops on the reservation; the Ghost Dancers' decision to try to make it some two hundred miles south to Red Cloud's people at Pine Ridge; their interception and forced encampment here at Wounded Knee Creek. The next morning, the disarming of the Indian men, the struggle over a rifle, a shot, and then the massacre in which Custer's old unit, the Seventh Cavalry, had figured with a terrible prominence.

Marie Not Help Him's great-grandfather had left seven of his family on that field. At her trailer home parked not many yards from the chapel to which the massacre's few, torn survivors had been brought to live or die, a small delegation of Latter-day Saints worked the rutted streets of the court, the pages of their tracts assaulted by the irreligious wind. Inside, I counted eight family members coming and going, sorting laundry and folding it, cooking breakfast. But once Not Help Him leaned into a reclining lounge chair and took Looks Twice's microphone in hand they disappeared.

Then commenced the tragic litany, delivered in an incantatory way, the speaker's head turned toward the window, beyond which lay the communal desolation of the reservation, the recited words taking us back to that hill, the creek flats, the ravine that wound west toward a vain hope of escape. But now the old events, so often rehearsed, debated, and embalmed in white historiography, began to dilate with the quality of life undergone as they issued from the lips of this stout woman who absently held a microphone in hand:

The flight of the dancers "and many who weren't even Ghost Dancers." The murder of Sitting Bull and the mutilation of his corpse. The decision of Big Foot and his council to try to reach Red Cloud at Pine Ridge. The weather on that two-week flight so severe the breaths of humans and horses instantly froze on the blankets of the women and children: "Many of them didn't have moccasins but had their feet bound up with bits of blanket. They didn't have gloves. Their faces were all frostbitten." The interception of the people at Porcupine Butte, less than twenty miles from their destination. Their forced encampment at Wounded Knee: "All during the night the people could hear the ammunition wagons arriving. All during the night the military was interrogating the men, trying to find out which ones had been at Little Bighorn. They could hear the soldiers drinking and the sounds of orders being given. At one point some of the soldiers came over to Big Foot's tent and asked him to come out and fight."

In the morning, the order for the men to produce their guns: "They wanted to see if they were Henrys or other guns that had been taken at Little Bighorn." Yellow Bird, the man generally identified with the first shot, "was deaf and couldn't understand the orders. He held his gun up and said, 'I have never turned this gun against any man, but I have used it to feed my family. And now I must give it up?' " In the struggle that ensued, "the gun discharged, but our people say Yellow Bird's finger was never on the trigger, that both his hands were on the stock."

On the third day after the massacre, the burial of the people in a trench atop the hill: "The soldiers jumped up and down on the bodies so they could fit more into the trench. Some of the people buried there were still alive. There was a young man, who was sixteen or seventeen. He was wounded and frozen, and as he lay there he cried out. But they just threw him in. There were some babies still alive who were thrown in there."

When she had finished her cheeks were shining with tears. Even Looks Twice, who had heard the story many times, sat stunned by the force of her narrative, his recorder spooling on in silence. "To the *wasicus*," Marie Not Help Him said at length, "all this happened a long time ago. To the Lakota people this is still with us. We are still in mourning. I can still remember my great-grandfather holding me on his lap. I can still hear his voice telling me this and how hard his heart pounded when he would tell about the deaths of his family. I can feel his breath on my forehead, how it smelled of sage. It always reminded me of things growing."

I I I

Pinky Clifford wanted me to understand that the ceremonies today (December 28) and tomorrow were not a matter of a few months' planning but had been pointed toward for four ritual years. A mixed-blood Oglala who had been serving as treasurer of the Wounded Knee Centennial Commission, she was coordinating last-minute details from her store a couple of miles from the massacre site, which even now the Big Foot Memorial riders were approaching at the end of their two-week pilgrimage. In making the observances stretch over the symbolic four-year period the commssion had clearly wanted to impress the people with the cultural significance of the event. But as Clifford and I drove over to the site so that she could see to the delivery of hay for the riders' horses, she remarked that not all the people were interested, and that even some of those who were had disagreed about what the event signified and how it ought to be observed. Some felt the period of ritual mourning should not be ended because the American government still had not apologized for the massacre and had recently merely expressed a formal regret. Others objected to the presence of the (white) media at the ceremonies. And there was great disagreement about what ought to happen subsequently at the site, some believing it ought to be incorporated into the National Park System, others feeling the tribe itself ought to develop it as a tourist attraction, and still others feeling that the land as it is constitutes the best memorial. Even the very earth of the site itself (at which we had now arrived) was disputed, a plat of it looking like a nightmare of white-dominated history: Here within a relatively restricted area of the reservation are tribally owned lands; allotted lands; deeded lands of three distinct varieties; and sections whose ownership has for years been a matter of legal dispute. So, whatever is planned for the future of the site is certain to raise historical antagonisms developed over the past century and more.

Yet in a way metaphorical of Lakota culture's peculiar and tenacious survival against very great odds, the ceremonies of the twenty-eighth and twenty-ninth were held—and impressively so—though even the weather seemed to conspire against them. On this day it was minus three degrees at noon and dropping, with a stiff wind out of the northeast. Still, a brave gathering of vehicles was already at the site, and more were arriving by the minute. A sullen sun made the snowy hills a steely gray, and the few grasses that poked through were a sickly yellow. The wind sent wraiths of snow across the road and spinning upward in small clouds from the earth. Exhaust from tailpipes whipped away as if shot from gun barrels. Most of the gatherers waited in their vehicles, but on the hill a few people wrapped in blankets or parkas stamped about near the mass grave, beating their arms against their bodies. Below in the road tribal police cars flashed their lights, and TV and movie cameras were set up and facing east, awaiting the arrival of the riders.

They appeared at 1:30, coming over a hill a mile off, a string of swiftly moving gray dots in the blowing snow. As they came down the road they coalesced into a dense dun cloud of riders, horses, and breath, while above them fluttered feathered lances and wind-shredded flags. They swept down the highway and then into the site itself, the horses snorting and clotted with rime, and made a great prayer circle in the midst of which stood four medicine men, including Zach Bear Shield, who lives behind the hill and has been ritually feeding the spirits of the dead for more than twenty years. When the circle had been closed at last, then the riders' high tremolo cry went up into the snow-swirled skies, and the medicine men began the prayers that would enclose and sanctify an event in the people's history. If white America had forgotten Wounded Knee, and if even many of the Lakota themselves had succumbed to the long pressure to put it behind them as "history"—that dead thing—it was clear that there were many others who had remembered and who had seized upon the event as a way of reminding the people of who they are, where they came from.

When the prayers were finished and the medicine men had left the circle, then the riders took their horses down behind the hill into the portable corrals there as word made its muffled way through the watchers that because of the intense cold the ceremonies would be continued at the Wounded Knee District School down the road in Manderson. Here there were to be the testimonies of the riders who had retraced the dodges of Big Foot's people a hundred years ago, when the country had been full of soldiers hunting them.

In the barnlike, high-ceilinged gym more than fifty of the riders stood about in front of the stage, still in their heavy range wear, their faces haggard, cheeks and noses bitten with frost, eyes glazed with distance, fatigue, and something more the nonparticipants would never quite know. More than an hour into their testimonies I could still smell the cold emanating from their blankets, parkas, hoods, and chaps as if it had been the spirit of the old event itself that had permeated these people during the two wintry weeks they had spent in the emptiness of the north country, which now they had brought inside, but which no amount of forced heating could alleviate. Wounded Knee I was almost palpably present inside the brightly painted cinder-block walls, a brooding, bleak, unappeasable presence, and I think even the *wasicu* journalists, their cameras and recorders flashing and whirring, shivered a bit under it.

Wounded Knee II was present also. When Ben Nighthorse Campbell, congressman from Colorado, addressed the audience, he remarked on the tremendous difference he saw between this event and one held in 1976 to commemorate the centennial of the Little Bighorn. Then, he said, law enforcement officials had been so nervous there might be an "uprising" on the battlefield grounds that "there were almost more marshals than there were Indians," and when Campbell and some others had returned from the field to their cars, they had found the feds taking license numbers. Quite a change, he said, referring to the Wounded Knee ceremonies, and as he was drawing the comparison my eyes were on a big, striking-looking man sitting in the bleachers, his braids wrapped in fur. A small circle of emptiness surrounded him, as though he possessed a sort of negative *wakan* (power). He appeared not to be listening to the congressman's remarks, but whatever Russell Means was thinking about at that moment, there could be no question that he and his organization had been the major reason for the anxiety of those lawmen at the Little Bighorn in 1976. Before AIM there had been no Indian "uprisings" since the Ghost Dance, and just as the Ghost Dance had aroused white fears wildly incongruous with the nature of the phenomenon itself, AIM had conjured up in our time the ghost of the armed savage on the warpath, and Means had been transmogrified into the avatar of Sitting Bull. If there were federal law enforcement officials here, they were very much undercover, and even the tribal police hung discreetly about the edges of the gathering, mingling there in a guardedly friendly fashion. No one, it was clear, wanted Wounded Knee IV, and in the long wake of the takeover of 1973 everyone remained vividly aware of the possibilities.

When I had been here in the summer of 1973, the smoke was still in the air and Pine Ridge was a stunned and very dangerous place. It no longer had any of that feel to it, and yet the month previous when I had talked with people in Rapid City, and on the Pine Ridge, Rosebud, and Cheyenne River reservations about the upcoming centenary observances, virtually all of them had brought up Wounded Knee II. The comment of Victor Douville, a Brulé on the Rosebud reservation, was typical. He said that AIM was really a thing of the past, especially on the Lakota reservations, "but they certainly made everyone aware of what the conditions were here, and they instilled pride in the younger people. In this they did well, and as a piece of political advertising, I'll have to say it [the takeover] was a masterstroke." Pinky Clifford told me that in the planning of these ceremonies there had been a determined effort to keep them from becoming a political platform for any group, and to an extent that effort seemed to have been successful. And yet Wounded Knee II was surely a presence here, and if it was not as much so as the massacre itself, still the character of these ceremonies seemed powerfully conditioned by the events of 1973. It was not only the remarks of Ben Nighthorse Campbell that reminded you of this, nor those of some of the riders who expressed hostility to the *wasicus* who had perpetrated the massacre and their successors who persistently misrepresented it. It was also—and more essentially—that Means, Dennis Banks, Clyde Bellecourt, and the others of AIM had brought the idea of the redress of historic grievances to the reservations, and it was likely here to stay. Wounded Knee III had been planned as a spiritual event, but no one could keep Wounded Knee II out of it. Means might be sitting by himself in the bleachers, but he was there, and everyone knew it. When the testimonies of the riders had been concluded, I sat down next to him at the feast of boiled buffalo and tripe served the assembled.

This was easy enough to manage because at the long portable table as in the bleachers there was space around him. At first, he took no notice of me, being then at work on an earnest, fuzzy-haired liberal out from the East Coast to hawk his new Indian magazine. The young man had asked Means for a literary contribution, and now Means was stating his conditions in terms the young man was trying hard to digest. When Means had finished, the editor was looking at a potentially serious boil in his budget.

Then it was my turn, Means asking the nature of my errand. When I mentioned the name of the magazine that had sent me here, Means repeated it twice, giving it a vicious twist, then spooned up a mouthful of the tripe and appeared to contemplate his next remark. I could see the young man across the table regarding me with what I took as a mixture of commiseration and relief.

"Well," Means finally said, "I guess we should be grateful any time the lordly white man takes notice of us." He turned back to the editor, asking if he had seen *Dances with Wolves*, which had recently been playing in Rapid City to around-the-block lines. Another illustration, Means was saying, of the white man's generous attentions. "I guess we should be happy to be portrayed as colorful primitives, as savages." But even he could no longer sustain his ironic tone. "An abomination!" he broke out, and then went into a detailed inventory of the film's faults.

That evening as I waited in the crowd exiting the gym I saw him again, holding up an AIM T-shirt that was for sale, regarding it speculatively as if he had never seen such an item before. Behind me, also waiting to exit, two girl members of the far-flung Wannabe tribe voiced disappointment at the way things had turned out, for they had wanted to sleep overnight in the gym and evidently weren't going to. "I thought," said one, "this was gonna be, you know, a real powwow where we'd all get together, in our sleeping bags, you know, and just kind of mellow out."

IV

A century ago, when the firing at Wounded Knee finally ceased and the soldiers had left the field to the dead, the wounded, and the dying, there had been a brief hush before a blizzard swooped in, blanketing the victims and warping the bodies into the attitudes of the last, winking rigors. December 29, 1990, brought that natural event forcefully to mind: At 8:00 A.M. it was minus twenty-one in Gordon, Nebraska, where I had spent the night. In another of the Dale Looks Twice's interviews, Claudia Iron Hawk had said it was from Gordon that the whiskey seller had come out to service the troops the night before the massacre. Others, including Mari Sandoz, say the man was from Rushville. But it was surely in Gordon that the troubles began that culminated in the takeover of Wounded Knee in 1973, for here the winter before a Lakota named Raymond Yellow Thunder had been found dead, grotesquely propped up inside a truck in a used car lot. The authorities' casual dismissal of the matter had brought Means and more than a thousand AIM people down into Gordon in the movement's first real show of force.

This event was in the back of my mind as I rode in the wrecker that was hauling my utterly frozen rental car to the Co-Op garage on Main Street. Foremost in my mind, of course, was whether these friendly, obliging mechanics could get the car thawed in time for me to make the Wiping of the Tears ceremony at the grave site, scheduled to begin in about an hour. They had said they would do their best, and in the unhealthy air of the garage I could see they were: blowers, ether injections, the works. As they went about this task they never asked what I was doing in their country, and after one of them went out, then returned from a service call, I was glad they hadn't. I overheard him telling his partners about the call: "He said to me, 'Hey, you guys are pretty randy. Are you this way with everyone?' So, I says to him, 'No, only with Indians.' "

That brought forward in mind what I had heard of Gordon's Indian attitude, and as I watched this same man diligently trying to get me on the road again, I had occasion to recall also a comment of Belva Hollow Horn when I had talked with her about the centenary ceremonies. All the bordering towns, she claimed, were so hostile to Indians it was difficult to so much as go into them for gas and groceries. "Gordon, Alliance, Rushville, Chadron—they look at you like you're from outer space. There's so much fear and ignorance." She doubted any whites from those towns would come up for the ceremonies. "Probably," she said, "it'll just be the Indians and the media with maybe a few politicians thrown in." She had followed this with a laugh, but it was a laugh as bitter as today's weather.

Probably there was a goodly measure of that fear and ignorance inside this garage where American white men were helping a stranger who looked like themselves; and standing uselessly around, my hands in my pockets, I could let my mind range even further back to another day I had spent in Gordon, a hot, still Fourth of July years before. Then, in company with Caroline Sandoz Pifer, one of Mari Sandoz's sisters, I had encountered a big Lakota man at this very garage who had told me of a powwow being held that day up on the reservation. Afterward, I had reminded Mrs. Pifer that on a Fourth of July a century before Red Cloud and fifteen hundred of his men had ridden into the nearby town of Chadron for the festivities, and that her father—alone among the whites—had gone up into their encampment to spend the day with them. "Goodness me!" Mrs. Pifer had exclaimed. "If fifteen hundred Sioux were to show up in Chadron now, they'd scare every white clear out of the country!" An hour later, riding the empty roads north toward the reservation thirty miles distant, I had to wonder how much really had changed in the century since the whites in this country had hollered for the military to stop the Ghost Dancers. And I was still mulling this over when I arrived at the massacre site to find that the ceremonies were just beginning. My mechanic friends in Gordon had indeed done their best.

The crowd at the grave site was much smaller than that which had greeted the returning Big Foot riders the day before. Mingling with the huddled group, I learned that some descendants of the victims had objected to the public nature of the occasion and so had arranged for the medicine men to conduct the end-of-mourning ritual privately. Those who had elected to participate in this public version were now being escorted by the medicine men from the small Catholic church atop the hill to the trench the white gravediggers had hacked out of the frozen earth after the blizzard had cleared and into which their relations had been so unceremoniously dumped. Though some whites continue to dispute that Lakota oral version of the brutal details of the burial, photographic evidence shows too plainly the stripped and looted bodies stacked like cord-wood at the trench and also the proudly posed figures of the grave-diggers. Black, bent figures against the gray and white of the sky and snow, the descendants now moved singly to the trench, left ritual offerings, and departed slowly, their vehicles trundling down the hill in little clouds of exhaust and snow, taillights winking. Behind, on the hilltop, observers and media people hopped painfully about, waiting for deliverance. Means was there, fur-capped and mufflered to his flashing black eyes. "This is nothing to us," he said to no one in particular, referring to the weather. "We're used to this."

Inside the cab of a truck parked in front of the church an official spoke into a microphone looped through a partly opened window, announcing that as yesterday the ceremonies would be adjourned to the gym. He said there would be a recounting of the history of the event, followed by a reading of the names of some of the more than three hundred who had died here. The governor would be there to speak of reconciliation, though Senator Inouye would not be present, as had been advertised. And then, he said, there would be another feast to which all were welcome.

When the church doors were clapped closed and the last herd of cars and pickups had filed down onto the road to the school at Manderson, there were left only a five-person French film crew and myself. The crew was debating its next move: There were other ceremonial events scheduled this afternoon at Kyle and Pine Ridge, and so which to cover? Inside the chain-link fence that guards the grave the plates of food left in offering to the spirits had already hardened like death itself, and garlands of plastic flowers vibrated stiffly in the wind on their wire stems. The creek flats below that yesterday had been filled by the riders had been smoothed by the blowing snow. Beyond them lay the ravine, and beyond that the dark, naked forms of the trees along Wounded Knee Creek. It was simply too cold to stand there any longer, meditating on the Ghost Dancers, on the frozen body of Big Foot, who, with his twisted, upraised hands, seemed to be struggling to ask one final question. But I had that image for company late that evening as I headed through the bitter blackness of the Badlands, back toward Rapid City and American civilization.

◆

Frederick Turner is the author of six volumes of nonfiction that explore various aspects of the American experience, including his study of the metaphysics of discovery and conquest, Beyond Geography; *a biography of John Muir,* Rediscovering America; *and a collection of essays on the American West,* Of Chiles, Cacti, and Fighting Cocks. *He lives in Santa Fe, New Mexico.*

JACK TURNER

◆ ◆ ◆ ◆ ◆

ECONOMIC NATURE

The conservation movement is, at the very least, an assertion that these interactions between man and land are too important to be left to chance, even that sacred variety of chance known as economic law.
— Aldo Leopold, *The Conservation Ethic*

I

We live surrounded by scars and loss. Each of us carries around a list of particular offenses against our place: a clear-cut, an overgrazed meadow, a road, a dam. Some we grudgingly accept as necessary, others we judge mistakes. The mistakes haunt us like demons, the demons spawn avenging spirits, and the presence of demons and spirits makes a place our home. It is not accidental that *home* and *haunt* share deep roots in Old Norse, that we speak of the home of an animal as its haunt, or that *haunt* can mean both a place of regular habitation and a place marked by the presence of spirits. Like scars, the spirits are reminders—traces by which the past remains present.

Forty years ago big cutthroats cruised the Gros Ventre River of Jackson Hole, Wyoming. Now, in late summer, dust blows up the riverbed. It's as dry as an arroyo in Death Valley, a dead river drained by ranchers. Each autumn much of Jackson Lake, the jewel of the Grand Teton National Park, is a mudflat baking in the sun, its waters drained to irrigate potatoes. Without good snowfalls each winter the lake could disappear and with it the big browns and with those browns Hopkins's "rose moles all in stripple upon trout that swim . . ." The western border of Yellowstone National Park can be seen from outer space, a straight line cut through a once fine forest by decades of clear-cutting. From the summits of my mountains I see to the west a mosaic of farms scarring the rounded hills and valleys, as though someone has taken a razor to the face of a beautiful woman. Farther west the sockeye salmon no longer come home from the sea, and I believe their absence wounds our rivers.

These wounds and scars are not random. We attribute the damage to particular people or corporations or to generalities like industrialization, technology and Christianity. But we tend to ignore the vast unity that made *these* particular wounds possible. This unity lies in the resource economies of the West: forestry, grazing, mineral extraction, and vast hydrologic systems that support agriculture. Healing those wounds requires altering these economies, their theories, practices, and, most deeply and importantly, their descriptions of the world, for at the most fundamental level the West has been wounded by particular uses of language.

Modern economics began in postfeudal Europe with the social forces and intellectual traditions we call the Enlightenment. On one level, its roots are a collection of texts. Men in England, France, and Germany wrote books, our Founders read the books and in turn wrote letters, memoranda, legislation, and a constitution, thus creating a modern civil order of public and private sectors. Most of the problems facing my home today stem from that duality: water rights, the private use of public resources, public access through private lands, the reintroduction of wolves into Yellowstone National Park, wilderness legislation, the private cost of grazing permits on public lands, military overflights, nuclear testing, the disposal of toxic waste, county zoning ordinances—the list is long. We are so absorbed by these tensions, and the means to resolve them, that we fail to notice that our maladies share a common thread—the use of the world conceived of as a collection of resources.

Everyone agrees the use of public and private resources is out of kilter, but here agreement ends. This loss of agreement is the key to our difficulties, not, for instance, the cost of grazing fees.

A civil society is marked by barely conscious consensus on beliefs, values, and ideals; on what constitutes legitimate authority, on what symbols are important, on what problems need resolution, and on limits to the permissible. I think of this consensus as a shared vision of the good. Historically, our shared vision of the good derived from shared experience and interests in a shared place. In the West, these "sharings" have vanished, so we share no vision of the good—especially about economic practices. One of the many reasons for this is the realization by some people that our current economic practices are creating an unlivable planet.

The decline in consensus also erodes trust. Trust is like glue—it holds things together. When trust erodes, personal relations, the family, communities, nations delaminate. To live with this erosion is to experience modernity.[1] The modern heirs of the Enlightenment believe material progress is worth the loss of shared experience, place, community, and trust. Others are less sanguine. But in the absence of alternatives the feeling of dilemma becomes paramount: Most of us in the West feel stuck.

Daniel Kemmis's fine book *Community and the Politics of Place* traces some of the West's current dilemmas to the often conflicting visions of Jefferson and Madison, and no doubt some of our dilemmas can be discussed productively in this context.[2] But I think the problems lie deeper. After all, Jefferson and Madison derived their ideas from the works of Enlightenment figures, especially John Locke and Adam Smith, whose thought was a mixture of classical science, instrumental reason, and Christian revelation.

The vigor of the Wise Use movements derives from an accurate assessment: The social order they believe in *requires* Christian revelation, classical science—pre-Darwin, pre–particle physics, pre–Kuhn, and a model of reason as the maximization of utility. The accuracy of this assessment, in turn, disturbs both liberals and conservatives who wish to preserve the ideals of the Enlightenment while jettisoning the Christian and outdated scientific foundations upon which those ideals rest. Unfortunately, that reduces social theory to economics. As John Dunn concluded twenty-five years ago in his *The Political Philosophy of John Locke:* " 'Lockean' liberals of the contemporary United States are more intimately than they realize the heirs of the equalitarian promise of Calvinism. If the religious purpose and sanction of the calling were to be removed from Locke's theory, the purpose of individual human life and of social life would both be exhaustively defined by the goal of the maximization of utility."[3] That's where we are now. Instead of a shared vision of the good we have a collection of property rights and utility calculations.

Since I am a Buddhist, I do not restrict equality to human beings, nor do I justify it by Christian revelation. I do not see any reason to restrict *common* (as in "the common good") or *community* to groups of human beings. Other citizens of the West have different understandings and justifications of these key political terms, so part of the solution to the West's dilemmas involves language.

Between Newton and the present, the languages of physical theory changed, and our conception of reality has changed with them. Unfortunately, the languages of our social, political, and economic theories have endured despite achieving mature formulation before widespread industrialization, the rise of technology, severe overpopulation, the explosion of scientific knowledge, and globalization of economies. These events altered our social life without altering our theories about our social life. Since a theory is merely a description of the world, a new set of agreements about the West requires some new descriptions of the world and our proper place in it.

Against this background, environmentalism, in the broadest sense, is a new description of the world. The first imaginings of this nascent movement have created what *Newsweek* has called "the war for the West." Public lands attorney Karen Budd says, "The war is about philosophy," and she's right.[4] The fight is over intellectual resources not physical resources. Environmentalists fight to reduce the authority of certain descriptions—*private property*—and extend the authority of other descriptions—*ecosystem*. It is the language of pilgrims who entered the wilderness and found not Him but the Wild.

These new forces have occupied the border of our minds—

strange figures claiming high moral ground, like Sioux along the ridges of the Missouri. It's unsettling. Folks employed in the traditional economies are circling the wagons of old values and beliefs. Their tone and posture are defensive, as they must be for those who, hurled into the future, adamantly face the past.

II

The pioneers who settled the West imposed their descriptions on a place of wilderness and savages. The great debates of Jefferson, Madison, Hamilton, and Adams were moral debates, filled with Enlightenment ethics, revelation, science, political theory, and economic theory. The pioneers brought their ideas west, creating a moral and rational order in a new land. The moral and the rational were connected by economics.

The government's great surveys redescribed the Western landscape. In 1784 the federal government adopted a system of rectangular surveying first used by the French for their national survey. The result was a mathematical grid: six-mile squares, one-mile squares.[5] Unfold your topo map and there they are, little squares everywhere. Fly over a town or city and you will see people living in a matrix resembling a computer chip. The grid also produced rectangular farms, national parks, counties, Indian reservations, and states, none of which has any relation to the biological order of life.

The grid delighted the pioneers though; they believed a rationalized landscape is a good landscape. It is a physical expression of order and control—the aim of their morality. And of course the grid was sold—the selling of the grid was the primary reason for its existence. This shifted the locus of the sacred from place to private property. As John Adams said, "Property must be sacred or liberty cannot exist." So the grid was sold to farmers, ranchers, and businessmen, and the places long sacred to the indigenous population simply vanished behind the grid, behind lines arrogantly drawn on paper. With the places gone, the sense of place vanished too, just disappeared.

The sale didn't work out quite as planned. Some land was sold, often for as little as $1.25 an acre, other lands passed "free" to those who worked them, and some land was occupied before it was surveyed. What was not sold became public land, or was reserved to imprison the remnants of the indigenous population. Much of it was simply given to commercial interests.

The railroads alone received a total of 233.0 million acres. For comparison, consider that Yellowstone National Park occupies 2.3 million acres. Then compare this 233.0 million acres with the 79.0 million acres of our entire National Park System, which includes our parks, the national monuments, historic sites, historic parks, memorials, military parks, battlefields, cemeteries, recreational areas, lakeshores, seashores, parkways, scenic trails, and rivers, in the lower United States *and* in Alaska. Then compare it with the 91.0 million acres in the National Wilderness Preservation System. Then meditate on this: 59 percent of our wilderness areas are smaller than Disney World.

Agriculture, another moral achievement, forever destroyed the autonomy of the land. Jefferson wrote that "those who labor in the earth are the chosen people of God, if ever He had a chosen people, whose breasts He has made His peculiar deposit for substantial and genuine virtue. It is the focus in which he keeps alive that sacred fire, which otherwise might escape from the face of the earth."[6]

God's chosen perceive it good to move water around with irrigation systems; they perceive it good to introduce foreign species of plants and animals; they perceive it good to destroy all that is injurious to their flocks and gardens. In short, they perceive as good that which is good for farmers and ranchers.

The Federalists were less convinced of the inherent goodness of farmers. After all, farmers had burned women at the stake in New England, and, in other parts of the world, still boiled and ate their enemies. It would perhaps be wiser, Madison thought, to depend on a federal system of checks and balances. Madison's idea for this was taken from Adam Smith's economic theories. Just as the free market would transform the pursuit of economic self-interest into the common good, so a federal structure of government would transform the pursuit of political self-interest into the common good. Unfortunately, the pursuit of self-interest merely produced more self-interest, an endless spiral that we now recognize as simple greed.

In short, the social order of the American West was a mash of splendid ideals and pervasive blindness—a rationalized landscape settled by Christians holding private property as sacred and practicing agriculture and commerce under the paternal eye of the federal government. Eventually, of course, these forces proved unequal in power and effect.

Things change. Governmental regulations, commercial greed, and the expanding urban population gobbled up family farms, ranches, and communities, and left in their place industrial agriculture, large tracts of empty land held by banks, suburbs, and malls. Now only 2 to 4 percent of Wyoming jobs depend on agriculture, and the cowboy is the butt of humor.

Things change. The little squares got smaller and smaller as the scale of the social order changed. First there was the section, then the acre, then the hundred-foot lot, then wall-to-wall town houses, then the condo. Last year the town of Jackson, Wyoming, contemplated building three-hundred-square-foot housing—about the size of a zoo cage. Much of the population lives in tiny rented squares, and the ownership of sacred property is an old dream. The moral force of private property, conceived as owning land, usually large amounts of land, has dropped accordingly, and for most of the population the problems surrounding large holdings of private land are inconsequential. Asking citizens to lament the government's incursion into private property rights increasingly obliges them to feel sorry for the rich, an obligation that insults their sense of justice.

Things change. The federal system of balances consistently stalls and sabotages federal legislation, making hay of federalism. Every time Congress meets it is pressured to gut the Clean Air Act or the Environmental Protection Agency. Despite widespread regional and national support, twenty years after the passage of the Endangered Species Act there are still no wolves in Yellowstone.

Many environmentalists believe that commercial interests will gut the Endangered Species Act.

Things change. Even the mathematical grid is under attack. The idea that our social units should be defined by mathematical squares projected upon the Earth from arbitrary points in space appears increasingly silly. One result is the interest in bioregionalism, the view that drainage, flora, fauna, landforms, and the spirit of a place should influence culture and social structure, define its boundaries, and ensure that evolutionary processes and biological diversity persist.

Things change. A new generation of historians have redescribed our past, deflating the West's myths with rigorous analysis of our imperialism, genocide, exploitation, and abuse, of our vast hierarchies of wealth and poverty, of the collusion of the rich and the government—especially over water, of the ingrained ignorance of most farmers, ranchers, and capitalists toward the land, and, finally, of how our old histories veiled the whole mess with nods to Republican and Jeffersonian ideals. Anyone who bothers to read the works of Donald Worster, Dee Brown, Patricia Nelson Limerick, and Richard White will lose forever the comfortable myths of pioneer and cowboy. [7]

Few, I believe, would deny these changes, yet in our public discourse of hearings and meetings and newspaper editorials we continue to trade in ideas appropriate to a small, homogeneous population of Christian agriculturists occupying large units of land. We continue to believe that politicians represent people, that private property assures liberty, and that agriculture, commerce, and federal balances confer dignity and respect on the West and its people. Since this is illusion it is not surprising that we feel stuck.

Only one widely shared value remains unchanged—money—and this explains our propensity to use business and economics, rather than moral debate and legislation, to settle our differences. When the "world" shrinks into a rationalized grid stuffed with resources, greed goes pandemic.

Many conservation and preservation groups now disdain moral persuasion, and many have simply given up on government regulation. Instead, they purchase what they can afford or argue that the market should be used to preserve everything from the ozone layer to biodiversity. They offer rewards to ranchers who allow wolves to den on their property, they buy trout streams, they pay blackmail so the rich will not violate undeveloped lands. They defend endangered species and rain forests on economic grounds. Instead of seeing modern economics as the problem, they see it as the solution.

The collapse of persuasion creates a social order wherein economic language (and its extensions in law) exhaustively describes our world, hence *becomes* our world. Moral, aesthetic, cultural, and spiritual orders are then merely subjective tastes of no social importance. It is no wonder civility has declined. For me this new economic conservation "ethic" reeks of cynicism—as though having failed to persuade and woo your love you suddenly switched to cash. The new economic conservationists think they are being rational; I think they treat Mother Nature as a whorehouse.

Ironically, the Enlightenment and civil society were designed to rescue us from such moral vacuums. The Enlightenment taught that human beings need not bow to a force beyond themselves, either Church or King. Now we are asked to bow to markets and incentives. Shall we bow to the new king? Can the moral concerns of the West be resolved by economics? Can new incentives for recycling, waste disposal, and more efficient resource use end the environmental crisis? Can market mechanisms restore the quality of public lands? Does victory lie in pollution permits, tax incentives, and new mufflers? Will green capitalism preserve biodiversity? Will money heal the wounds of the West?

One group that answers these questions in the affirmative is New Resource Economics. It welcomes the moral vacuum and fills it with markets and incentives. As economic theory it deserves scrutiny by economists. I am not an economist but a mountaineer and desert rat. Nonetheless, I shall have my say even though the word *economics* makes me hiss like *The Hobbit*'s Gollum: I hates it, I hates it, I hates it *forever*. For I believe classical economic theory, and all the theories it presupposes, is destroying the magic ring of life.

III

In the winter of 1992 I flew to Seattle at the generous invitation of the Foundation for Research on Economics and the Environment to attend a conference held to acquaint environmental writers with the ideas of New Resource Economics. The conference was held amid a mise-en-scène of assurance and power—subdued, isolated buildings, lovely meals, good wine. I felt like a barbarian invited to Rome to confirm its splendor.

The best presentations were careful, devastating analyses of the inefficiency and incompetence of the U.S. Forest Service. In sharp contrast were other presentations with vague waves at the preferred vocabulary of self-interest, incentives, market, liberty. These exuded an air of *you see!* as though the realm of social possibility was limited to two choices: sylvan socialism or New Resource Economics. Fingers were pointed at economic planning, especially Soviet-style planning, but no one addressed the obvious success of large-scale planning by our most powerful corporations, much less the corporate socialism of Japan, Inc. Art, emotion, and biophilia were absent. A sense of humor about economics and economists was absent. They were Eric Hoffer's true believers, folks who have seen the light and are frustrated and angry that others fail to see their light.

Not only did I fail to see the light but I failed to understand what was new about New Resource Economics. The theory applies ideas about markets that are now more than two hundred years old. After a while I had the feeling of watching the morally challenged tinker with notions rapidly disappearing over the horizon of history, and it was pure bathos to watch them attempt to upgrade one antiquated idea into another antiquated idea.

Having just flown over the devastated forests east of Seattle, I screamed—"See the fate of the Earth, the rape of the land!"—but they responded calmly with talk of incentives and benefits and inefficiency.

Finally I understood. The conference had a hidden agenda: to persuade environmental writers to describe nature with an economic vocabulary. They had a theory, and like everyone with a theory they attempted to colonize with their theoretical vocabulary, thus eliminating other ways of describing the world.

The conference literature reeked of colonization. Vernon L. Smith's paper "Economic Principles in the Emergence of Human-kind" described magic, ritual, and foraging patterns in hunter-gath-erer cultures with terms like *opportunity cost, effort prices,* and *accumulated human capital.*[8] An excerpt from Michael Rothchild's *Bionomics: Economy as Ecosystem* extended economic vocabulary to ecosystems and animal behavior. A niche became an organism's "profession," its habitat and food "basic resources," its relations to habitat a part of the "economy of nature."[9]

In *Reforming the Forest Service,* Randal O'Toole claimed that "although the language used by ecologists differs from that of econ-omists, it frequently translates into identical concepts. Where econ-omists discuss efficiency, decentralization, and incentives, ecologists discuss the maximum power principle, diversity, and feedback loops." O'Toole claimed that "these very different terms have iden-tical meanings" and concluded that "ecological systems are really economic systems, and economic systems are really ecological sys-tems."[10]

The redescription of everything with economic language is characteristic of those who sit in the shade of the Chicago school of economics. Thus Richard Posner's *The Economic Aspects of Law* colonizes legal issues with economic vocabulary. Here is Posner on children: "The baby shortage and black market are the result of legal restrictions that prevent the market from operating as freely in the sale of babies as of other goods. This suggests as a possible reform simply eliminating the restriction." John Bunker, Benjamin Barnes, and Frederick Mosteller's *Costs, Risks, and Benefits of Surgery* does the same for medical practice.[11]

Indeed, all areas of our social life have been redescribed in economic language. If you like the theory in one area, you will probably like it everywhere. Nor is economic redescription limited to social issues. Here is Robert Nozick, in *The Examined Life,* applying economic language to the question of why we might love our spouse:

Repeated trading with a fixed partner with special resources might make it rational to develop in yourself
specialized assets for trading with that partner (and sim-
ilarly on the partner's part toward you); and this special-
ization gives some assurance that you will continue to
trade with the party (since the invested resources would
be worth much less in exchanges with a third party).
Moreover, to shape yourself and specialize so as to better
fit and trade with that partner, and therefore to do so less
well with others, you will want some commitment and
guarantee that the party will continue to trade with you,
a guarantee that goes beyond the party's own speciali-
zation to fit you.[12]

In a footnote to this passage, Nozick says, "This paragraph was
suggested by the mode of economic analysis found in Oliver Wil-
liamson, *The Economic Institutions of Capitalism.*"

Why stop with love? Here is sex redescribed in a manner that
makes even me pine for Madonna. In *The New World of Economics*
by McKenzie and Tullock, sex becomes a calculated rational exchange:

It follows that the quantity of sex demanded is an inverse
function of price. . . . The reason for this relationship
is simply that the rational individual will consume sex
up to the point that the marginal benefits equal the marginal costs. . . . If the price of sex rises relative to other
goods, the consumer will "rationally" choose to consume
more of the other goods and less sex.[13]

So, many men are bores, and what to do? Why bother with
arguments, why not just giggle? Unfortunately, too much is at stake
to giggle.

If we are to preserve a semblance of democracy in the West,
we must become crystal clear about how economists colonize with
their language.

To start, look at an example of redescription by a theory you disapprove of. Consider, for instance, psychobabble.

"What did you do today?"

"I cleaned my desk."

"Ah yes, being *anal compulsive* again."

"No, it was just a mess."

"No need to be *defensive*."

"I'm not being *defensive*, I'm just disagreeing with you."

"Yes, but you disagree with me because you have an *unresolved conflict* with your father."

"No, I always got along well with Dad."

"Of course you believe that, but the conflict was *unconscious*."

"There was no conflict!"

"I am not your father! Please don't *cathect* your speech with *projected aggression*."

Ad infinitum. Ad nauseam.

Resource, market, benefits, rational, property, self-interest function the same way as *anal compulsive, defensive, unresolved conflict, unconscious, cathect,* and *projected aggression.* They are terms a particular theory uses to describe the world. By accepting its descriptions, you support and extend the theory. You could decide not to use the theory at all; you could decide the theory is fine in its home territory but you don't want it extended into other territories. But if we don't want the fate of our forests decided by bar graphs, we need to cease talking about forests as measurable resources. That does not require you to stop talking to your investment banker about the bar graphs in the analysis of your portfolio.

Economists and scientists have conned us into speaking of trees as "resources," wilderness as a "management unit," and picas gathering grass for the winter because of "incentives." In accepting their descriptions we allow a set of experts to define our concerns in economic terms. This predetermines the range of possible responses. Often we cannot even raise the issues important to us since the language used excluded our issues from the discussion. To accept this con emasculates not only radical alternatives but all alternatives. Every vocabulary shapes the world to fit a paradigm. If you don't want nature reduced to economics, then *refuse to use its language*.

The process of theoretical redescription is called colonization because it privileges one description of the world and excludes another. When the Sioux say the Black Hills are *sacred land*, they find that *sacred land* does not appear in the language of property law. There is no office in which to file a claim for sacred land. If they file suit, they discover that the Supreme Court will not protect religious practices in a particular place; the Court tends to protect religious belief (a very Protestant view of religion).

Language is power. Control people's language and you won't need an army to win the war for the West. There will be nothing to debate. If we are conned into describing the life of the Earth and our home in terms of benefits, resources, self-interest, models, and budgets, then democracy will be dead.

What to do? I have five suggestions.

First, refuse to talk that way. It's like smoking or eating lard. Just say no and point out that your concerns cannot be expressed in that language.

Second, develop a talent for lighthearted humor using economic language. Here Thoreau is a prophet. Henry knew a great deal about economics. He read Locke and his followers in both his junior and senior years at Harvard; he was acquainted with the ideas of Smith, Ricardo, Say, and Franklin; he helped run his family's pencil business at a time when making pencils in New England was competitive and undergoing rapid technological change. Indeed, he made important contributions to that technology.

But in *Walden* (remember, the first chapter is titled "Economy"), Henry flips economic language on its head. His *trade* turns out to be with the Celestial Empire; his *enterprises* are inspecting snow storms and sunrises; he *sinks his capital* into hearing the wind; he *keeps his accounts* by keeping a writer's journal; and he gleefully carries the cost of rye meal out to four decimal places: $1.0475. Nothing is fixed, all is metaphor, even economics.[14]

Third, become so intimate with the process of economic description that you *experience* what's wrong with it. Since economics is a world of resources—physical resources, cultural resources, recreational resources, visual resources, human resources—our wonderfully diverse, joyful world must be reduced to resources. This involves abstraction, translation, and a value.

Thus time is abstracted from experience and rendered mechanical (the clock) so it can be measured. Space is abstracted from place and becomes property—measurable land. Work is abstracted from life and becomes labor. Trees are abstracted from place and become board feet. Wild rivers are abstracted from place and become acre feet. Beauty is abstracted from place and becomes a scene whose value is measured by polls. By abstraction everything is reduced to a measurable unit. This makes it usable—a resource.

Economics reduces everything to a unit of measurement because it requires everything to be commensurate—"capable of being measured by a common standard"—its standard. The variety of these calculable units is great—board feet, time, tons, hours, et cetera, but all these units can be translated into a common value similar to the way different languages can be translated. In both cases something common is required. In linguistic translation it is meaning; in economic translations it is money—not the change in your pocket but the stuff that blips on computer screens and bounces off satellite dishes from Germany to Japan in less than a second. An hour's labor is worth a certain amount of money; so are three hundred board feet of redwood.

Once everything is abstracted into commensurate units and common value, economic theory is useful. If one kind of unit (computer chips) grows in value faster than another kind of unit (board feet), economic theory says translate board feet into money into computer chips. In ordinary English: Clear-cut the last redwoods for cash and buy Intel stock.

If you want to use economics to make a decision about whether to clear-cut a forest or preserve its scenic beauty and recreation value, then not only must you use a common standard by which they can be compared but the decision can't be determined by values internal to timber resources, visual resources, and recreational resources. No, you must also weight these values against the value of computer chips. If you don't like deciding the fate of whitebark pines by weighing the future of Intel, then you probably won't like economics.

Refuse these three moves—the abstraction of things into resources, their commensurability in translatable units, and the choice of money as the value of the units—and economic theory is useless.

Once you understand the process you can begin looking for examples. For instance, Randal O'Toole, in *Reforming the Forest Service*, describes wilderness as a *unique resource* and walking in the mountains as a *wilderness experience* using a *recreational resource* that generates benefits—cash and jobs. These benefits are compared with other possible uses of the resource, say grazing and logging, that generate other benefits. These benefits can be compared. This provides a *rational basis* for *budget maximization*.[15] Your walk in the Tetons becomes, by redescription, an economic event. This may be the dream of the eco-nerd, but for the rest of us it is a nightmare, and we need to wake up.

The fourth thing you can do to subvert economic language is to realize that nothing of great value to you is either abstract or commensurate. To see this start with your hand. The workers' compensation office can tell you the value of your hand in dollars. Feel the dissonance? Consider your daughter. An insurance company or litigation lawyer can tell you the value of your daughter in dollars. Become friendly with the dissonance. What is your home place worth in dollars? What is your lover's hair worth? A stream? A species? Wolves in Yellowstone? Carefully imagine each redescribed in economic language. Then apply cost-benefit analysis. Sink into the resulting feeling of sickness, a feeling familiar from any forest sale or predator control proposal. It is the sickness of being forced to use a language that ignores what matters in your heart.

Fifth, realize that describing life, the completely—individual—unique—here—now—alive—*this*, with abstractions is especially dissonant. Consider the "resources" used in a biology class. The founder of experimental physiology, Claude Bernard, said of the man of science, "He no longer hears the cry of animals, he no longer sees the blood that flows, he sees only his idea and perceives only organisms concealing problems which he intends to solve."[16] He sees only the idea that will give him something to do in the world. Meanwhile the screams of animals in laboratory experiments are described away as "high-pitched vocalizations."

In *Divorce Among the Gulls*, William Jordan, an entomologist who writes beautiful essays, describes his graduate education and the ghastly (his word) treatment of animals it required:

> Fifteen years ago I saw several of my peers close down their laboratory for the evening, and as they cleaned up after the day's experimentation they found that three or four mice were left over. The next experiments were not scheduled for several weeks, and *it wasn't worth the cost and effort to keep the mice alive until then.* My friends simply threw the extras into a blender, ground them up, and washed them down the sink. This was called the Bloody Mary solution. Several days ago I talked with another old peer from my university days, and she informs me that the new, humane method for discarding extra mice in her lab is to seal them in a plastic bag and put it in the freezer. (my italics)[17]

Economics treats life as trash. The screaming animals, the dead coyotes, the Bloody Mary mice, the stumps, the dead rivers are all connected by these processes of abstraction, commensurability, and financial value. There is no logical necessity for us to describe the world this way. The Chumash didn't do it. When we were young we didn't do it. And we need to reach a point where we don't do it now either.

We need to find another way of describing the world and our experience in it. Leave this pernicious, mean-spirited way of talking behind. One of my heroes said he could imagine no finer life than to arise each morning and walk all day toward an unknown goal forever. Bashō said this is our life. So go for a walk and clear the mind of this junk. Climb right up a ridge, over the talus and through the whitebark pine, through all those charming little grouse whortleberries, and right on into the blue sky of Gary Snyder's *Mountains and Rivers Without End*:

the blue sky

the blue sky

The Blue Sky

is the land of

OLD MAN MEDICINE BUDDHA

where the eagle

that flies out of sight,

flies.[18]

I V

Traveling to the conference last winter, I found the approach to Seattle from the east to be infinitely sad. Looking down at those once beautiful mountains and forests, so shaved and mowed down they look like sores, I realized I did not care if the land below was public land or private land, if the desecration was efficient or inefficient, cost beneficial, subsidized or not, or whether the lumber products were sent to Japan or used to build homes in Seattle. I was no longer interested in that way of looking at the world. I have died to that world. I am a barbarian in the original sense of the Greek word—one who has trouble with the language of civilization. I belong to that strange tribe now occupying borders of the Mind— the Greeks called them the Unintelligibles. And I resolved to follow a path that honors the unintelligible. I have followed many such paths during the past thirty-five years; they always led into rich and joyful experience and provided me with the finest days of my life. So, slowly and reluctantly, I am burning bridges to the past, all the while noticing, as if in penance, that the ideas and abilities of a trained pedant follow me close as a shadow.

Two famous passages from an obscure journal by the philosopher Nelson Goodman often occupy my mind:

> For me, there is no way which is the way the world is; and so of course no description can capture it. But there are many ways the world is, and every true description captures one of them.

> If I ask about the world, you can offer to tell me how it is under one or more frames of reference; but if I insist that you tell me how it is apart from all frames, what can you say? We are confined to ways of describing whatever is described. Our universe, so to speak, consists of these ways rather than of a world or of worlds.[19]

The only universe we can know is a universe of descriptions. If we find we live in a moral vacuum, and if we believe this is due in part to economic language, then we are obligated to create alternatives to economic language. Old ways of seeing do not change because of evidence; they change because a new language captures the imagination. The progressive branches of environmentalism—defined by an implacable insistence on biodiversity, wilderness, and the replacement of our current social grid with bioregions—have been sloughing off old ideas and creating one of many possible new languages.

Emerson started the tradition of dumping his Unitarian vocabulary and writing *Nature* in language that put the sacred back into nature. Thoreau altered that vocabulary further and captured our imagination. It proceeds with the labor of poets, deep ecologists, and conservation biologists. The process is not limited to radical environmentalism, however; it includes many who are only partially sympathetic to the radical cause. It is furthered when Michael Pollan reminds us, in *Second Nature*, that science has proposed some new descriptions of trees as the lungs of the Earth.[20] It continues in *The*

Economic Pursuit of Quality, when Thomas Michael Power suggests how *economy* can be extended beyond commerce.[21] It is enforced when Charles F. Wilkinson, in *The Eagle Bird*, suggests changes in the language of law that would honor our surrender to the beauty of the world and of emotion.[22]

Imagine extending the *common* in *common good* to what is common to all life—the air, the atmosphere, the water, the processes of evolution and diversity, the commonality of all organisms in their common heritage. Imagine extending *community* to include all the life-forms of the place that is your home. Imagine returning *accounting* to its original sense: *to be accountable*. What does it mean to be accountable, to whom, and to what purpose? What's "a good deal" with the Universe? Imagine an economics of need. Instead of asking What is this forest worth? ask What does this forest need? and What does this river need?

Consider Lewis Hyde's beautiful example of an Amish quilt sale:

> A length of rope stretched around the farm yard full of household goods. A little sign explained that it was a private auction, in which only members of the Amish community were allowed to bid. Though goods changed hands, none left the community. And none could be inflated in value. If sold on the open market, an old Amish quilt might be too valuable for a young Amish couple to sleep under, but inside that simple fence it would always hold its value on a winter night.[23]

Hold its value on a winter night. What's happening here?

It's as simple as that simple fence: A group of people has decided to place aspects of their shared experience above economic values determined by the open market. They don't ignore economic value, there is still a price, there is bidding and competition, but it is restrained by a consensus of appreciation a wider market would ignore.

Although this is a religious community, the power of the example does not turn on religion; although it is an agricultural community, it does not turn on agriculture. It turns on two things: shared experience and shared place—the politics of locale. Like the Bill of Rights the rope creates a limit with standards and values shared by the community. We need to imagine an immense fugue of variations on that simple fence, each creating a new world.

These imaginings will be the labor of poets and thinkers and artists. It is a good and worthy labor, every bit as hard as digging ditches. Their primary task, it seems to me, is to extend those qualities we feel and value most deeply in ourselves, the source of our moralities and spiritual practices, into what we call the world. Many will find that source is empty, drained like the great aquifers that water our greed. Others will discover the link between their integrity and the integrity of an ecosystem, between their dignity and the dignity of a tree, between their humiliation and the humiliation of an animal, between the trust of kin and the trust of the Earth, between their desire for autonomy and the autonomy all beings desire, between their passions and the wild processes that sustain all life.

Extend these moral and spiritual sources into nature and the spirits of your place will *speak* as they have always spoken—through art, myth, dreams, dance, literature, poetry, craft. Open the door and they will transform your mind—instantly. When children are raised with spotted owl stories, visit spotted owls, make paintings of spotted owls, dance the dance of spotted owls, see spotted owls in dreams, and leave at puberty to seek the gaze of spotted owls, then spotted owls will speak to us, transformed by mind into *Our-Form-of-Life-at-the-Place-of-Spotted-Owls*.

Then we won't have to worry about clear-cutting spotted owl habitat. When wildfires articulate their needs we will not drown them in chemicals. When wild rivers speak they will not be dammed, and the salmon will come home from the sea.

Dig in someplace—like a great fir driving roots deep into a rocky ridge to weather the storms that are inseparable from the shape of its roots. Allow the spirits of your chosen place to speak through you. Say their names. Say Moose Ponds, Teewinot, Pingora, Gros

Ventre, Stewart Draw, Lost Rivers. Speak of individuals—the pine martin that lives in the Dumpster, the lycopodium on the north ridge of the Grand Teton. Force the spirits of your place to be heard. Be hopeful. Language changes, and imagination is on our side. In a thousand years our most sacred objects will be illuminated floras, vast taxonomies of insects, and a repertoire of songs we shall sing to whales.

I am writing this essay on a picnic table beside Deer Creek in the Escalante country. It is April and still cool. Around me lies last year's growth, old sedges and grasses in lovely shades of umber and sienna. Beside me stands an ancient Fremont cottonwood. At the tips of its most extended and fragile branches, bright against a cobalt sky, are the crisp green buds of spring.

1. See Anthony Giddens, *The Consequences of Modernity* (Stanford: Stanford University Press, 1990). Trust doesn't disappear, but its focus moves from kin and community to abstract systems, especially money and a culture of experts. Attempting to reestablish "community" under conditions of modernity is not something that can be decided. This is the weakness of the Jeffersonian revival that includes everyone from Wendell Berry to Wise Use. Traditional forms of life are dying and they will continue to die. Soon they will be gone.

2. Daniel Kemmis, *Community and the Politics of Place* (Norman: University of Oklahoma Press, 1990).

3. John Dunn, *The Political Philosophy of John Locke* (New York: Cambridge University Press, 1983).

4. Florence Williams, "Sagebrush Rebellion II," *High Country News*, Vol. 24, no. 3, February 24, 1992.

5. Paul Shepard, *Man in the Landscape: A Historic View of the Esthetics of Nature* (College Station: Texas A&M University Press, 1991).

6. Quoted in Kemmis, *Community and the Politics of Place.*

7. Donald Worster, *Under Western Skies: Nature and History in the American West* (New York: Oxford University Press, 1992); Dee Brown, *Bury My Heart at Wounded Knee* (New York: Henry Holt & Co., 1971); Patricia Nelson Limerick, *The Legacy of Conquest: The Unbroken Past of the American West* (New York: W. W. Norton, 1987); Richard White, *It's Your Misfortune and None of My Own* (Norman: University of Oklahoma Press, 1993).

8. Opening address at the 1991 Mont Pelerin Society meeting, Big Sky, Montana.

9. Michael Rothchild, *Bionomics: Economy as Ecosystem* (New York: Henry Holt & Company, 1992).

10. Randal O'Toole, *Reforming the Forest Service* (Washington, D.C.: Island Press, 1988).

11. These examples are taken from Kenneth Lux's delightful *Adam Smith's Mistake* (Boston: Shambhala, 1990).

12. Robert Nozick, *The Examined Life* (New York: Simon and Schuster, 1990).

13. Quoted in Lux, *Adam Smith's Mistake*.

14. Quoted in Neil Evernden, *The Natural Alien* (Toronto: University of Toronto Press, 1993).

15. O'Toole, *Reforming the Forest Service*.

16. TO COME

17. William Jordan, *Divorce Among The Gulls: An Uncommon Look at Human Nature* (San Francisco: North Point Press, 1991).

18. Gary Snyder, *No Nature: New and Selected Poems* (New York: Pantheon, 1992).

19. Nelson Goodman, "The Way the World Is," *The Review of Metaphysics*, 14 (1960).

20. Michael Pollan, *Second Nature* (New York: Atlantic Monthly Press, 1991).

21. Thomas Michael Power, *The Economic Pursuit of Quality* (Armonk, New York: M.E. Sharp, Inc., 1988).

22. Charles F. Wilkinson, *The Eagle Bird: Mapping a New West* (New York: Pantheon, 1992).

23. Quoted in Lux, *Adam Smith's Mistake*.

Jack Turner has been climbing mountains for thirty-three years and has traveled extensively in Nepal, India, Pakistan, China, Tibet, Bhutan, and Peru. He taught philosophy at the University of Illinois and for the past fifteen years he has lived in Grand Teton National Park, where he is chief guide for the Exum Guide Service and School of Mountaineering. He is also the author of a collection of essays entitled The Abstract Wild.

EDWARD ABBEY

◆ ◆ ◆ ◆ ◆

SOMETHING ABOUT MAC, COWS, POKER, RANCHERS, COWBOYS, SEX, AND POWER . . . AND ALMOST NOTHING ABOUT AMERICAN LIT

Okay. I'm going to give a little talk here about cowboys, ranchers, beef industry. I used to be a welfare worker. Politics, and literature, if I get around to it. Some of the things I'm going to say tonight might possibly be construed as critical.

Like most professional writers, there's nothing I enjoy more than talking about writing, about books. It's a helluva lot easier to talk about books than to write them. Almost anything's easier than writing—sitting down to write or standing up to write. Legal pads. This is my word processor, and an old ballpoint pen somewhere.

I came here promising to talk about books and writing, about literature (mostly American lit, which is my field of play). And I will talk about it, if I get around to it. But I'd like to lead into my subject by saying just a few words first about cowboys.

The cowboy. The rancher. The Western mythology. And our most sacred form of public welfare. That is, the beef industry in our eleven Western states. I was a public welfare caseworker once, for about a year, in curious places like Hoboken, Albuquerque, Las Vegas. I've also lived in the American Southwest since 1947, when I began my student life at the University of New Mexico. I worked many seasons for the National Park Service. I worked a couple of summers as a hired hand on a couple of ranches. And I've wandered the open range as a nomad and explorer for nearly four decades now. So, I think I know something about cowboys, ranchers, beef cattle, sentimentality, and public robbery.

When I first came West to live, as a student at New Mexico, I was only twenty years old and just out of the army. I thought, like most simpleminded Easterners, that the cowboy was a kind of mythic hero. I idolized those scrawny little red-nosed hired hands, in their tight jeans and their funny boots and their snap-button shirts and their comical hats.

Like most new arrivals in the West I could imagine nothing more romantic than becoming a cowboy. Nothing more glorious than owning my own little genuine working cattle outfit. About the only thing better, I thought, was to be a big league baseball player. I never dreamed that I'd eventually sink to writing books for a living. Unluckily for me—coming from an Appalachian hillbilly background with a poor choice of parents—I didn't have much money. My father was a small-time logger. He ran a one-man sawmill on a submarginal sidehill farm. There wasn't any money in our family— no inheritance you could run ten thousand cattle on. I had no trust fund to back me up. No Hollywood movie deals to finance the land acquisition program. I lived for many years on what was called in those days the G.I. Bill, which paid about a hundred and fifty dollars a month while I went to school. I made that last as long as I could— five or six years.

The best I could do in 1947 and '48 was buy a thirdhand Chevy sedan (a '41) and roam the West, mostly the Southwest, on holidays and weekends and summers. Living on the land, though never off it. However, I had a roommate at the University of New Mexico. I'll just call him Mac here. I don't want him to come looking for me. Mac came from a little town in southwest New Mexico, where his father ran a feed store. Mackie was a fair bronc rider himself, anxious to get into the cattle-growing business. And he had some money, even then as a student. He had enough money to buy a little cinder-block house and about forty acres in the Sandia Mountains east of Albuquerque, near a little town we called Landfill. Mackie fenced these forty acres, built a corral, kept a few horses there, including an occasional genuine bronco (mostly for fun and practice).

I don't remember exactly how Mackie and I became friends in the first place. I was majoring in classical philosophy. He was majoring in screwworm management. But we got to know each other through the mutual pursuit of a pair of nearly inseparable Kappa Kappa Gamma girls. Or is it Kappa Gamma Gamma? Gamma Gamma Kappa? Something like that.

Anyhow, Mac and I somehow became pretty good friends. I lived with him in his little cinder-block house. Helped him meet the mortgage payments. Helped him meet the girls. We were both rather crude, shy, ugly, obnoxious . . . like most college boys.

My friend Mac also owned a 1947 black Lincoln convertible. One of those old types with the big grill in the front, something like what we used to call a cowcatcher on a locomotive. Only his was chrome plated, of course.

We used to race to classes in the morning, driving the twenty miles from his house to the university campus in never more than fifteen minutes. Usually Mac was too hungover to drive, so I'd operate the car. Clutching the wheel while Mac sat beside me waving his big .44. Taking potshots at the jackrabbits and the road signs and the billboards and the beer bottles in the ditch. Trying to wake up. Trying to wake up in time for his 10:00 class in brand inspection. Hoof-and-mouth disease.

I'm sorry to say that my friend Mac was a little bit gun happy. I can't stand that type myself. Most of his forty acres was in tumbleweed. He had a good crop of tumbleweed. He fenced in about half an acre of it with chicken wire and stocked that little pasture with white rabbits. He used that as the target range. Not what you'd call sporting, I suppose, but we did eat the rabbits. And sometimes, I'm sorry to say, we even went deer hunting with handguns. Mackie with his revolver, and I had a chrome-plated .45 Colt automatic that I had liberated from the U.S. Army over in Italy. Surplus government property.

I was once a military policeman, believe it or not, for about a year.

On one of our deer-hunting expeditions, I was sitting on a log in a big clearing in the woods, thinking about Plato and Aristotle, Kappa Kappa Gamma girls. I didn't really care much whether we got a deer that day or not. It was a couple of days before opening, anyway. The whole procedure was probably illegal as hell. Mac was out in the woods somewhere cutting around this clearing. I was sitting on this log, thinking, when I suddenly saw a chip of bark fly away from the log all by itself, about a foot away. Then I heard the blast of Mac's revolver—that big old .44 that he'd probably liberated from his father. Then I heard him laugh. He could laugh like a horse.

"That's not very funny, Mackie," I said, as he came out of the woods grinning at me.

"Now, don't whine and complain, Ed," he says. "You want to be a real hunter like me, you gotta learn to stay awake."

As a matter of fact, we never did get a deer with handguns.

Anyway, that's when I first had my little doubts about Mackie. And the cowboy type in general. But, I still loved him. Worshiped him, in fact. I was still in the grip of the Western myth. Anybody said a word to me against cowboys, I'd jump down his throat with my spurs on. Especially if Mac was standing nearby. He was a pretty big guy, and he loved violence. Sometimes I'd try to ride those broncs that he brought in now and then, trying to prove that I could be a cowboy, too. Trying to prove it more to myself than to him. I'd be on this crazy, crackpot horse, going up and down and left and right. Hanging on to the saddle horn with both hands. And Mac would sit on the corral fence throwing beer bottles at us and laughing. Every time I got thrown off, Mac would say, "Now get right back on there, Ed. Quick, quick. Don't spoil 'im. Don't let him get away with anything like that."

It took me a long time to realize I didn't have to do that kind of work.

Then there were the poker games. We both thought we were pretty good poker players. And we really liked the game. As I've said elsewhere, there's something about winning at poker that restores my faith in the innate goodness of my fellow man. When I lose, of course, I have doubts.

Mac was good at poker, too. Better than I was, really, as long as he could stay sober. But usually he'd keep drinking, and within a couple of hours he'd be too drunk and get careless and start losing money. In our two-handed practice games at his house, I'd play slow and cautious and usually get pretty far ahead. After Mac got into his third or fourth glass of bourbon. One evening, after he'd just received another remittance check from his father, I suppose, I took him for nearly seventy-five dollars, which was an awful lot of money in 1949. But I lost it all a few minutes later, when Mac proved on the final bet of the night that he could break a cinder block over his head. As I said, he was big and strong and violent.

One Friday afternoon, Mac and I got dressed up in our very best clothes—really snappy. We climbed in the Lincoln and drove down to Roswell, New Mexico—about two hundred miles away by road, then. It took us at least two hours to get there; Mac had heard about a weekly private poker game down there in what we called Little Texas. A regular little Friday night game among all the banker-rancher types there, with a lot of money involved. Mac thought it was time for him and me to break into the big time. Real poker. Since we only had about a hundred dollars in cash between us that day, we figured we ought to look as respectable as possible—which was the main reason we'd got dressed up. We also knew we'd have to talk our way into that game. Probably have to butt our way in.

I was wearing my high school graduation suit. A kind of gangster suit with padded shoulders. And Mac was wearing his brand-new gabardine cattleman's suit with a vest, tie, his pointy-toed boots, a great big silver-gray Stetson. A beautiful outfit. When he got all dressed up like that, he looked something like Randolph Scott with a hard-on for the world.

Of course, we planned to cheat a little bit. That's why we picked a game two hundred miles from Albuquerque. We really thought we were that good. We'd worked out some signals, of course. Signals for a cinch hand, aces wired, flush, straight, and so forth. None of it really made much sense, but we meant to try. Mac was about twenty-two years old then; I was twenty-one. We were young, impetuous, and stupid.

So, we got to Roswell. We checked into an old hotel in the middle of town, registering under false names. We got a nice, big corner room on the second floor, with corner windows overlooking the street. It was an old-fashioned hotel—the kind they use for wino apartment houses now. A nice place. Transom window over the door—you know, the kind of window that opens for ventilation. There was no clothes closet in the room. Instead of a clothes closet, there was what's called a clothes tree, which some of you may not be familiar with. Just a big pole, usually five or six feet high, with little pegs or branches sticking out to hang clothes or clothes hangers on. And the fire escape was a coil of rope on the windowsill. Old-fashioned, small-town, Western hotel.

We ate supper in the hotel restaurant and looked over the local crowd (they paid no attention to us). Then we made our way to the local Elks' club, where this game was supposed to be taking place. The place was full of strangers, of course, but Mac had a lot of confidence. He was a native New Mexican. He talked our way in. As I remember, it cost us each twenty-five dollars just to buy into that game—that's the kind of game it was, a lot of money in those days.

Mac was smoking a cigar, of course, trying to look forty-five instead of twenty-two. He carried a half-empty bottle of Jim Beam, which he diluted carefully with Coca-Cola. It was about fifteen proof. There were five or six men sitting around a table. Big men in the usual big hats and leather vests. They dealt awfully fast. I knew we were playing with pretty slick operators when the stranger who was dealing dealt me a pat hand the second time around. Three kings and a pair of aces! And this was draw poker—straight draw. A mighty powerful hand; a full house. I whipped my glasses back and almost loosened my necktie (our signal for the cinch hand). But then I hesitated and remembered something my father had told me about pat hands from strangers. My father tried to teach me and my brothers how to play poker. We'd work all week for the old man, piling slabs in that busy little sawmill of his. He paid us about a dollar a day. Payday was Saturday night. He'd pay us in cash and then take most of it back from us in a poker game.

Anyway, I remembered him warning us about pat hands from strangers dealing. It occurred to me that this might be a setup. Though I hated to do it, I had this hunch—so I discarded one of the kings. I kept two pair: kings and aces. I drew a queen, no help at all. So there I was with two pair of kings and aces, and a queen. No help. But the guy sitting beside me on the showdown ended up with three queens instead of that fourth queen he was planning on. And Mac won the pot. Mac won the pot with a club flush. Those other two crooks, you see, they hadn't planned on that.

About two or three hours later we slipped out of the game separately; one at a time. First Mac (I made sure he left before he got drunk), and then me, claiming some excuse or other, promising to come back. We met in the bar back at our hotel, counted our winnings, and by gosh we were about two hundred dollars ahead (equivalent to about a thousand bucks, now).

We had a few drinks to celebrate. 'Course, our first thought was, "We'd better get out of this town." But, no, we had to have a drink to celebrate. Then another and another. Before we knew it, it was past midnight and we were still sitting in that bar. As I said, we'd promised to return to that poker game, and Mac by this time was drunk enough to want to do it. But I managed to talk him out of it; I knew he was now too drunk to play well. We'd lose everything. Still, we were pretty nervous. A little afraid. Afraid those other guys would come looking for us. Afraid they may have thought we were cheating. And, worst of all, Mac had forgotten to bring his .44. He was naked! Unarmed! I don't know how he'd forgotten such an essential item. I guess we'd left in a big hurry.

We talked about just leaving town. But, then, about that time some old wino bum came into the bar and slopped around for a while talking to people. Finally he came to us, and here he had a little Beretta automatic for sale with two loaded clips. So Mac bought it. Bought this little set for fifteen dollars.

"I always wanted a Beretta," Mac explained. Everybody should have a Beretta. A nice little pistol you can stick in your jacket pocket.

Feeling a little safer, then, Mac and I went up to our room. As a matter of fact, I did have my .45 automatic with me. Concealed, of course, in my jacket pocket. But I didn't tell Mac I had it. I didn't want him waving that thing around in a strange town where he could get us into real trouble. So, we went up to our room. Closed the transom window so nobody could pull down on us while we were in bed. Locked and barricaded the door with a chair under the knob. Then got ready for a peaceful night.

I dropped my old oversize suit on the floor. But Mac, who was always sort of a dandy and very proud of his new gabardine cattleman's suit, very carefully took it off and hung it on clothes hangers and hung these clothes hangers on this clothes tree. He put his big hat on top of the clothes tree. Then we went to bed, turned out the lights, and Mac put his new Beretta under the pillow, of course. Loaded, certainly. I had my army .45 nearby on the floor in my jacket pocket. We were both pretty tired and drunk by that time. So, despite our fears, we soon fell asleep, to be awakened maybe an hour later by an awful crashing and banging right next door. Somebody shouting. We both woke up, sat up, and looked around.

The room was pretty dark, but there was a little light coming in from the window. And by the window was the outline of the figure of a cowboy who had got in somehow. Both of us reached for our guns and unloaded about four shots. And then Mac said, "Wait a minute!

"Wait a minute, Ed. Hold it, hold it." He turned on the bedside lamp, and, sure enough, we'd just blasted about eleven holes through his new suit. Through the coat, the vest, the pants, front and back. And, of course, through the front hotel window.

Well, we got dressed real quick. There was some yelling and running around outside in the hallway. We got dressed real quick, and Mac put on his new suit with the hole in the rear. Mac looked like he'd been ambushed by a SWAT squad or the FBI.

As I said, there were a lot of people running around in the halls doing a lot of useless yelling. We hitched one end of the fire escape to the leg of the bed and threw the running end out the window and slid down the rope. We snuck around the corner to the Lincoln and got the hell out of Roswell, New Mexico.

Net winnings, about a hundred dollars for me and about twenty-five for Mac, considering his extra expenses.

Getting away clean with the winnings—that always is the hardest part of a poker game, or craps, or eight ball, or sex, or public lectures, or any other good game.

Incidents like that could have made us compañeros, bosom buddies forever. But, unfortunately, Mackie and his Kappa Kappa Gamma girl fell in love, for chrissake! She was a horse lover. She fell in love with Mac's horses. In fact, like me, she was still in love with the cowboy mythology. She also loved Mackie's hat and boots and saddle and rope and so on. Damn near everything but Mac himself, so far as I could tell. Then they got married and threw me out of the house. Mac was also in love. He was in love with his girlfriend's money. She came from a pretty wealthy family in the Midwest, and Mac had his eyes on a certain ranch down near Silver City, New Mexico.

She was a Midwesterner who loved the cowboy cult. He was a cowboy who loved that Midwestern money. So they were made for each other. Maybe still married to each other, who knows.

On their wedding day, I was best man. I gave the bride my chrome-plated army .45 automatic for a wedding present. Knowing what I knew about Mac, I figured she might need it someday.

I should have married my Kappa Kappa Gamma girl, too. She came from a meatpacking family in Illinois. If I'd had brains enough to marry that sweet young woman, I'd now be a Cudahy or Hormel vice president in charge of sausages, living in some huge house on the hill outside of Kansas City or St. Louis or Chicago. I'd be miserable, but I'd be rich. And vice versa.

But I didn't. I blew it. I became, instead, a philosophical part-time seasonal Forest Ranger fire fighter and fire lookout, making about three hundred dollars a month during fire season and about thirty-five dollars a week during the winters (unemployment insurance).

I sank into the life of a beatnik in the '50s. Then I became a hippie in the '60s. And a writer. Beer cans and wine jugs. Love affairs and marriages all the way down.

To digress for a moment, back to my central topic . . . Cowboys and ranchers, dead horses and sacred cows. It begins to look like I may never get around to American literature, but it can wait.

In the thirty-six or thirty-seven years since rooming with my friend Mac, I've met and known dozens of cowboys, quite a few ranchers, including some damn decent people. In fact, most of them—the ones I knew personally—were very good people. They're not bad. Like people everywhere, the individuals, as individuals, are always a lot nicer, a lot better, a lot more human, than the class to which they belong.

I've got a theory about institutions. My theory is that institutions—big, powerful institutions—are always far worse than the people they represent. Jimmy Carter said he would give us a government as good as the people. But it's impossible. You will never have a government as good as the people, because government represents the worst, not the best, of our human nature, as a rule. This is true of all big power institutions. Power attracts and power corrupts. Power attracts the worst people and corrupts the best people, like power over nature, brings out the boss in all of us. It tends always toward evil.

When the U.S. Army put an MP's armband on my left arm and that .45 automatic on my hip, I became at once an obnoxious, intolerable punk. A bully. They also gave me a motorcycle, and that really completed my ruin.

It seems to me that if you put, say, a captain's bars on the shoulders of an ordinary, decent man, he tends to become another petty tyrant. Make him a general or a commissar or a dictator, and he may destroy half the world before we get him. Centralized power is evil. Domination of many by few is evil. Hierarchy, good organization, is what makes that possible. An army is nothing but a well-organized lynch mob. A government is a giant social machine, composed of human components. Put men in a machine, put them under the discipline of law, the fear of punishment, and they will commit crimes so vast and horrible that no ordinary, decent individual would either have the power to do on his own or probably even think of doing on his own—except in his sickest fantasies or worst nightmares.

That power over other people is the seduction and the beauty of the social machine. We give up our freedom of thought and action to this machine, and in return we gain freedom from personal responsibility.

"I was only following orders," said Adolf Eichmann when on trial in Jerusalem. Yes, indeed, he was. He was a nice husband and father. He loved his children, he loved classical music. And Lieutenant Calley in Vietnam—an ordinary, nice guy. And the pilot of the *Enola Gay* on his return from Hiroshima.

"We had our job to do," these people say, "so we did it."

How do you gain a free and easy conscience? It's easy. Avoid moral conflict. Stay on the side of power. Learn to take orders. Cultivate the habit of obedience. Surrender your innate humanity, and become a working part. Become replaceable, interchangeable, carefree, and subhuman.

Well, that's my theory of power institutions in the modern world. By "modern world," of course, I mean about the last five or six thousand years of human history. Since about the time of the invention of agriculture, cities, social hierarchy, and the pyramids of Egypt.

"The most amazing thing about the pyramids of Egypt," said Thoreau, "is that enough people could be found degraded enough to build them, when they should have taken that ambitious booby, the Pharaoh, and drowned him in the Nile."

I agree with Thoreau.

And I believe in democracy—real democracy. Rule by the people. And I think we ought to try it sometime. I believe in community sovereignty as an ideal to work toward. I believe in decentralized power. Decentralization of power in every form: military, political, economic, maybe even moral and intellectual. I like to call myself a libertarian, with a small *l*, and a democrat, with a very small *d*. I also call myself an anarchist sometimes, but that just leads to a lot of difficult questions. Or a Jeffersonian Democrat, or an Agrarian Egalitarian. I guess I'm completely out of it this year. I really believe in *égalité, fraternité, liberté*. No wonder those East Coast literati won't review my books, the sons of bitches. I'll probably never make it into the club.

Very well, what's this got to do with cowboys and ranchers, anyway? And, holy cows on the hoof.

You may have guessed by now that I'm thinking of criticizing the cattle industry. And you are correct. I've been thinking about cows and sheep for many years now. Getting more and more disgusted with the whole business. Now that I've finally been invited to give a speech up north here in the heart of cowboy country, this seems like the perfect time and place to say it.

To wit. The Western cattleman is a welfare parasite. The Western cattlemen have been getting a free ride on the public lands for a long time now. Over a century. And I think it's time we phased it out. I'm in favor of putting the public lands livestock grazers out of business.

How? you ask. And maybe a few of you might ask, Why? Those are good questions, which I'm happy to answer.

I'll tackle the why first. Because, first of all—and most important, perhaps—we don't need the public lands beef industry. Even beef lovers don't need it. According to most government information (Bureau of Land Management, Forest Service, Department of Agriculture), only 3 to 4 percent of our beef, our red meat, comes from the eleven Western states. By those eleven I mean Montana, Nevada, Utah, Colorado, New Mexico, Arizona, Idaho, Wyoming, eastern Idaho, eastern Washington, and west Texas. Most of our beef—at least 90 percent or more—comes from the East. Particularly the Southeast—the states of Mississippi, Georgia, Alabama, South Carolina, and especially Florida. From private land. From taxpaying property owners. And even New England produces a lot of beef cattle. According to some of the sources I've read, there are more beef cattle raised in the little state of Vermont than in the entire state of Montana. For very good reason: Back east, you can support a cow on maybe half an acre. Out here, it takes anywhere from twenty-five to fifty acres. Down in the red rock country of Utah, the rule of thumb is one section—a square mile—per cow.

Well, you'd need a lot of territory, too, if a staple of your diet was lichens on rock.

Even in Appalachia there are supposed to be more beef cattle grazing on the reclaimed strip mines of Pennsylvania, West Virginia, North Carolina, Kentucky, and Tennessee than in Idaho or Wyoming, or the whole desert Southwest. According to these government figures and other books and articles I've read on the subject—and they're probably true—eliminating the cattle industry in the American West should not raise supermarket beef prices by more than 3 or 4 percent. Furthermore, we'd save probably more money than that in taxes alone. And all the money we now have to pay for the various subsidies to these public lands cattlemen. I mean, things like so-called range improvement, tree chaining, sagebrush clearing, mesquite poisoning, disease control, predator control, fencing, wells, stock ponds, roads, range management, and a big part of the salaries of those who work for government agencies like the BLM. And you could probably also count in a great deal of the salaries of our overpaid, underworked university professors who are engaged in range management research and all the other lines of agriculture.

We do not need the Western beef industry. We'd be better off without it.

Which brings me to the second part of my answer to the question why. Why get rid of this public lands beef industry?

Because, the cattle have done, and are doing, much damage to our public lands, our national forests and our state lands and the BLM-administered lands and our wildlife preserves in many cases, and even some of our national parks and monuments. In Capitol Reef National Park down in Utah, for example, grazing is still allowed. In fact, I think it's recently been extended for another ten years, and the Utah politicians are trying to make that permanent. They probably won't get away with it. But there's at least one case where cattle are still tramping about in a national park. These beef cattle have devastated our rangelands.

Overgrazing, I think, is much too weak a term; most of the West, and especially the Southwest, is what you might call cow-burnt. Our public lands are infested with domestic cattle. Almost anywhere and everywhere you go in the American West, you will find herds—*herds*—of these ugly, clumsy, shambling, stupid, bawl-ing, bellowing, stinking, fly-covered, shit-smeared, disease-spreading brutes. They are a pest and a plague. They pollute our springs and streams and rivers. They crowd and overcrowd our canyons and valleys and meadows and forests. They graze off the native bluestem and grama and bunch grasses. They trample down the native forbs and shrubs and cacti in the Southwest. They spread the exotic chick grass and the Russian thistle and the crested wheat grass. *Weeds*.

Even when these cattle are not physically present, you'll see the dung and the flies and the mud and the dust and the general destruction. If you don't see it, you'll smell it. The whole American West stinks of cattle. Along every flowing stream, around every seep and spring and water hole and well, you'll also find acres and acres of what range management specialists call sacrifice areas. *Sacrifice* is another understatement. Places where the earth is so denuded of forage—except maybe for some cacti or maybe a little tumble-weed or maybe a few mutilated trees like mesquite, juniper, or hack-berry.

I'm not going to bombard you with a lot of graphs and statistics, which don't make much impression on intelligent people anyway. I appeal, instead, to your five senses and your common sense and to common knowledge. Anyone who goes beyond the town limits of almost any Western town can see for himself that the land is overgrazed. Badly overgrazed in the Southwest, my territory. That there are too many cows and horses and sheep out there. Of course, cattlemen themselves would never publicly confess to overgrazing, any more than Dracula would publicly confess to a fondness for blood. Cattlemen are interested parties. They do not and they will not give reliable testimony—most of them. They have too much at stake; especially their Cadillacs and their airplanes and their Lear jets and their ranch resale profits and their capital gains. I'm talking about the majority—especially the corporation ranchers here.

Money. Money matters. *Money*'s another word for power. Power over nature and human nature. Money gives you the power to .command the labor of others; to control the decisions of bureaucrats. To determine the votes of politicians.

And power, as I said before, is a form of intense personal gratification that appeals to the worst members of the human race, and to the worst in each of us. I know from experience.

Overgrazing is certainly worse in some areas than others. I'm not personally familiar with the degree of the problem here in the Northwest, by which I mean Montana, Wyoming, Idaho, eastern Oregon and Washington. But in the thirty-eight years I've lived in the Southwest, I've had ample opportunity to see what cattle have done to west Texas, New Mexico, Arizona, Utah, Nevada, parts of the Mojave Desert in California. I won't even try to describe what's going on in Mexico.

A common sight down there in the Southwest is a cow stumbling around through canyons and desert with stems of prickly pear or cholla cactus stuck to its muzzle.

Cattlemen like to claim that their cows do not compete with our deer. Deer are browsers, cows are grazers. That's true. But when the range is overgrazed, when the grass is gone (as it often is for whole seasons at a time), then the cattle become browsers, too, out of necessity. In the Southwest, cattle commonly feed on mesquite, cliff rose, cactus, acacia, or any other shrub or tree they find bio-degradable. And to that extent, they do compete with deer. And they tend to drive out the other and better wildlife, like elk, or bighorn sheep, or pronghorn antelope, and so on.

How much damage have cattle done to the Western range-lands? Well, remember, this has been going on since the 1870s,

1880s. There's plenty of data and documentation of the changes which this massive cattle grazing has made in the erosion of the land, the character of the land, the character of the vegetation. A lot of streams and rivers which used to flow on the surface all year round are now intermittent, or underground, because of overgrazing and rapid runoff. Anyway, the documentation is available for anyone who wants to really research this subject, or who will not believe the evidence of his own senses.

Most of you already know—I think it's common knowledge— that the public lands are overgrazed. The BLM knows it; the U.S. Forest Service knows it. The Goverment Accounting Office knows it.

Our public lands have been overgrazed for a century. Overgrazing means eventual ruin, just like strip mining or clear-cutting or the contamination of a river. Much of the Southwest already looks like Mexico or southern Italy or North Africa: a cow-burnt wasteland. As we destroy our land, we also destroy the basis of agricultural economy and the basis of all life. If we keep it up, we'll generally and gradually degrade American life to the status of life in places like Mexico or southern Italy or Libya or Egypt.

I promised not to bore you with numbers, but I do want to cite one set of statistics which is pretty clear and significant.

When the BLM was required by Congress, about ten years ago, to give a report on its stewardship of our rangelands (the property of all Americans, remember), the bureaucrats confessed, "Seventeen percent of [its] administered land was in good condition; fifty percent in fair condition; twenty-eight percent in poor condition; five percent in bad condition."

More important, maybe, they reported that only 19 percent of the rangelands were improving, while 65 percent were static, and 16 percent getting worse. This information comes from the BLM— the Bureau of Livestock and Mining.

If the BLM says that, we can safely assume that range conditions are really much worse. And as we all know, the Forest Service is just as much under the domination of industrial use, multiple abuse, as the BLM.

. . .

Now, if you're still with me . . . What should we do about this situation? This is the fun part—this is the part I like.

It's not easy trying to argue that we should do away with cattle ranching. But I have some solutions to overgrazing.

Like cutting down on the number of cattle on public lands.

Of course, range managers will not face up to that. In their eyes, and in the eyes of the livestock associations that they work for, cutting down on the number of cattle is the worst possible solution— an impossible solution. So they propose all kinds of gimmicks. More and more cross fencing. More wells and ponds so that more of the land can be exploited. Or what they call more "intensive" management. These proposals are basically an evasive maneuver by the Forest Service and the BLM to attempt to appease their critics without offending their real bosses in the beef industry.

Surprising as it might seem, there are more cattle on our public lands than there were in the industry's glory years back in the 1880s. There are more cattle now than a century ago, and they are bigger, heavier, greedier, more sluggish, more spongy, water-loving animals by far than the longhorn descendants of the cattle brought to North America by Cortés in 1521. This growth in the number of cattle is made possible not by improvement of the range but simply by more intensive use of it.

I suggest that, in order to improve the range, we open a hunting season on cattle. I realize that domestic beef cattle will not make very sporting prey at first. Because, like all domesticated animals (including most humans), beef cattle are slow and stupid and awkward. But, if hunted regularly, the breed will improve. Furthermore, as the number of cattle is reduced, other and far more valuable, useful, beautiful, interesting animals will return and will increase.

Let me explain this theory by wish fantasy fulfillment. Suppose, by some miracle of Hollywood or inheritance or good luck, I should acquire a respectable-size working cattle outfit, what would

I do with it? Well, I'm happy to tell you, first I'd get rid of all the stinking, filthy cattle. Every single one. Shoot them all. Give the meat to the Indians or the Mormons. Get rid of the cattle. And I'd stock the place with real animals, real game, real protein. I mean, with buffalo. I mean with pronghorn antelope. And bighorn sheep. And elk. And prairie elk. And moose. Down in the Southwest, with peccary and wild boar. And other animals—just for decoration—like eagles. We need more eagles. And wolves. We need more wolves. Mountain lions and bear. Especially, of course, grizzly bear. Down in the desert, I would stock every water tank, every water hole, every stock pond with alligators. Or a desert crocodile.

You may note that I have said nothing much about coyotes or deer. Coyotes seem to be doing all right on their own. They're smarter than their enemies. I've never yet heard of a coyote as dumb as a sheep man. As for deer, especially mule deer, they, too, are surviving—maybe even thriving, as some game and fish departments claim. Though nobody claims there are as many deer now as there were before the cattle industry was introduced to the West.

If you must eat beef, don't hunt for it with a shopping cart in your local supermarket, for God's sake. Go outside for it, into the range. Make your own kill like a hunter would. You'll be doing yourself and the land and all of us a favor.

It seems to me that the whole essence of this abuse of our Western lands (remember, I'm only talking about the Western beef industry) is based on the old mythology of the cowboy. The myth of the cowboy as a kind of natural nobleman. I'd like to conclude this lecture with a few remarks about this most cherished and fanciful of American fairy tales. Let's talk a little truth for a change, although I realize nobody wants to hear it.

In truth, the cowboy is only a hired hand. A herdsman, who sometimes gets on a horse to do part of his work. Some ranchers are also cowboys; many are not. There is a difference. A rancher is a landowner, first of all. A businessman. Most of them are big-time farmers of the public lands—our property. And as such, these ranchers do not merit any special considerations or special privileges. In fact, there are only about 35,000 of them in the whole American West. That's what, less than the population of Laramie, Wyoming. Most of our Western ranchers have a lot of money, and a lot of power. Partly because they have been here a long time. They've been squatting on our public lands for over a century.

Because they're well established and have been here a long time and have a lot of leisure time, they are politically powerful. Disproportionately powerful, considering their numbers. Cowboys, themselves, are greatly overrated. Consider the nature of their work. Suppose you had to spend most of your working hours sitting on a horse, contemplating the hind end of a cow. How would that affect your imagination? Think what it does to the relatively simple mind of the average peasant boy, raised amid the bawling of calves and cows in the splatter of mud and the stink of shit.

Anyway, next time you see a big, full-spread picture of the Marlboro man, speculate. Let your imagination roam freely. While we're at it, let's look at that guy a little more closely. I hope he's not here tonight. Did you ever see an alleged cowboy with such immaculate shirts? Such clean jeans? Such snowy white hats? His laundry and dry-cleaning bill must be enormous. And who pays for it?

And more. What kind of a man is he, anyhow? Who makes his living pushing cigarettes? He's no better than a dope peddler. Or a pornographer. He's not a man at all, he's a pimp! A pimp for two of the most corrupt industries in America today: tobacco and subsidized public lands beef.

Do cowboys work very hard? Yes, sometimes. At certain times. Most ranchers don't work very hard. They have a lot of leisure time for politics and bellyaching. Anytime you go into a small Western town and you want to find some of the local ranchers, you can usually find them at the nearest drugstore, sitting around all morning drinking coffee, talking about their tax breaks.

Is a cowboy's work socially useful? No.

As I've already pointed out, the subsidized Western range beef is a trivial item in the national economy: 3 or 4 percent. And if all of our 35,000 Western ranchers quit business tomorrow, we'd never miss them. Not in the marketplace. It seems to me that any public school teacher does harder work, more difficult work, more dangerous work, and far more valuable work than any cowboy and/or rancher. And the same thing applies to collectors and to traffic cops. Harder work, tougher work, more necessary work. We need those people in our complicated society. We do not need cowboys or ranchers. We've carried them on our backs long enough—over a century.

A cowboy's work, as you know, is sometimes brutal—even cruel. Often violent. Anyone who's taken part in a gathering, roping, branding, dehorning, castrating, ear notching, wattle clipping, or winching a calf from its mother knows how mean and tough and brutal it can be. And if the cowboy's mind and sensibilities have not been permanently deformed by that kind of work, he'll admit it. Brutal work tends to bring out the brutality in all of us. And that's probably why most cattlemen, as a class (I emphasize this, as a class), tend to hate nature. Hate wildlife. Especially anything they dream might compete with their cattle. They hate the idea, and, most of all, they hate the idea of preserving wilderness. Most of them.

"This Abbey," the cowboys and their lovers will say, "this Abbey is a wimp. A chickenhearted sentimentalist with no feel for the hard realities of practical life."

Especially critical of my attitude will be the Easterners and Midwesterners newly arrived here from their cabin cruisers in Key West, or their rustic lodges in upper Michigan. All of our nouveau Westerners with their hobby ranches, their pickup trucks with the gun racks, their pointy-toed boots with the undershot heels, their gigantic comical hats. And, of course, their pet horses.

This type of transplanted Westerner is what I like to call the instant redneck.

Now, to the critics who might accuse me of wimpery, sentimentality, I'd like to say this in reply. I respect real men. I admire true manliness. But I despise arrogance and brutality and bullies. What is a real man anyway? A real man, I would say, is quiet. He's not a loudmouth like me. A real man is quiet, thoughtful, strong, courageous, resourceful, and he is also kind, considerate, and loving. A real man is a gentle man, though not necessarily a gentleman. Or, in short, a real man has the same virtues as a real woman.

I believe that it is a writer's duty to speak the truth, especially unpopular truth. Especially truth that offends the powerful. It is a writer's obligation, I believe, to be a critic of the society he lives in. If the independent freelance writer will not speak the truth to us and for us, then who will? Do we get the truth from politicians? Do we get the truth from chambers of commerce? Do we get the truth from the bureaucrats of government? From the Cattlemen's Association? From *Time* or *Newsweek* or CBS or ABC or NBC? Do we get the truth from the TV evangelists of commercial religion? Do we even get much truth from science and scientists?

Well, we get some. But not enough. It seems to me that the majority of scientists are specialized technicians. Most of them long ago sold their souls to commerce, to industry, to government, or war. Therefore, I repeat, it is the writer's duty to speak truth—you notice I carefully don't attempt to describe or define truth, however offensive that truth may sometimes be.

I'm going to quote Tolstoy here. In one of his earlier books, Tolstoy said, "The hero of my work, in all his unadorned glory and beauty, is truth."

Truth is always the enemy of power. And power is always the enemy—at least the potential enemy—of truth. Writers who shirk from telling the truth, who simply go with the flow, who pander, for example, to those East Coast literati (my deadly enemies) . . . Writers who do that are merely hacks. Hemingway once said it, and said it good, in respect to power, governmental power: "A writer is like a gypsy. He owes no allegiance to any government. If he's a good writer, he will never like any government he lives under. His hands should be against it, and its hand will always be against him." This from a letter probably got him into all kinds of trouble. He probably died in some labor camp.

In the United States, government means industry. In the Soviet Union, government controls industry. In the United States, industry controls government. That's the essential structural difference between them.

Hemingway knew what he was talking about.

Well, I know I've been unkind, been harsh. But as Johannes Brahms once said when he was leaving a Viennese salon where he had been playing the piano for a bunch of Austrian aristocrats, "If there's anyone here I failed to insult, I apologize."

So let me wind this up with some nice remarks about cowboys and cattle ranchers. They are a mixed lot, like the rest of us. As individuals, they range from the bad to the ordinary to the good. A rancher, after all, is only a farmer on a horse. A cowboy is a hired hand trying to make an honest living. Nothing special. As people they are no better or worse than the average of the rest of us. As persons they are not nearly as bad as the class of which they are a part.

I have no quarrel with these people as fellow humans. All I want to do is get their cows off our public lands. Our property. Let those cowboys and ranchers find some harder way to make a living, like the rest of us have to do. Like me, for example. There's no good reason why we have to subsidize them forever. They've had their free ride. It's time they learned to support themselves. Self-reliance is a good tonic for anybody. Even for a cowboy. Even for a rancher.

Well, let's see, I never did get around to saying much about books or writing or American lit. I'm sorry about that.

In the meantime, I'm going to say good-bye to all you cowboys and cowgirls. I love the legend, too, but keep your sacred cows and your dead horses off of my elk pastures.

◆

Philosopher, essayist, novelist, desert rat, river runner, social critic, and eco-warrior, Edward Abbey is the author of Desert Solitaire, *a classic of environmental writing, and the novel* Monkey Wrench Gang, *which inspired the founding of the radical environmental group Earth First! He died in 1989.*

DANIEL KEMMIS

◆ ◆ ◆ ◆ ◆

THE ART OF THE POSSIBLE
IN THE HOME OF HOPE

My first political memory was an unhappy one. I must have been about five. The memory has the feel of late fall and early evening about it; the kerosene lamps were lit, and we were in the living room, between the coal "heater" and the wood-encased, battery-powered radio, which looked like a little house. My father tuned the radio, then settled in to listen with a neighbor. I was used to the nervous, flighty sounds of Fibber McGee and Molly, or the unearthly laugh of The Shadow, but this was a program I hadn't heard before. My father said something about "the president." I asked him why he was listening to this, and he hushed me up with uncharacteristic sharpness. In the presence of the neighbor, this hurt, but what hurts more, down all these years, is the sense that I failed to understand the gravity of the situation; I didn't know that when the president spoke, I was supposed to pay attention.

I can calculate now that the president was Harry Truman. Over the next few years, I would slowly fill in some of the missing pieces, feeling more than knowing the dimensions of my father's respect, not just for the presidency but for this president who spoke, as his predecessor had, to the plain, straightforward home-liness which was all my father had ever known, all he ever wanted to know. By 1956, at the age of ten, I had become a Farmers Union, FDR Democrat to exactly the same depth of my being that my father and my love for him occupied within me. When Ike beat Adlai Stevenson again that November, I heard about it in the Richey grade school, and during the lunch break I walked away from the school, out into the eastern Montana hills, where I could cry in peace.

I suppose that I cried in part because Adlai Stevenson and my father were a little confused in my mind, and this felt like a defeat for my father. Every once in a while my eight-year-old son bursts into a facetious but cathartic bout of hostility toward the gentleman who defeated me for chief justice of the Montana Supreme Court four years ago. When I remember that November afternoon in 1956, I think I know how he feels. Part of growing up, of course, is acquiring the capacity to distinguish your political friends and foes on a somewhat more objective basis. But most of us probably never escape altogether from those early, purely emotional alignings of our political compasses. In my case, I acquired not just a particular brand of politics through my relationship with my father but a particular attachment to politics itself.

It is politics which is my principal subject here, not my family or myself. To be more exact, my subject is the loss of politics—its diminishing presence as a force, or a value in our midst—and the possibility of its revival. But I am coming to suspect that both its loss and its revival are tied to the health of the family—not family in the abstract but real, concrete, living families. "We begin our public affections in our families," wrote the great British conservative Edmund Burke. "No cold relation is a zealous citizen." The more I have tried to understand what politics means or what it might mean, the more I have found myself agreeing with Burke. Since I know my own "relations" best, I can hunt most easily there for the roots and meaning of my own politics.

My family has passed down from one generation to another a tiny tableau which I realize now is about the intersection of the domestic and the political worlds. My great-great-great-great-grand-father, John Kemys, grew up in what is now Washington County, New York. He fought as a British soldier in the French and Indian War, where he managed to survive the Battle of Quebec. Returning home, he married his red-haired sweetheart, Sarah, and together they established a farm in the shadow of the Adirondacks. John, like most of his neighbors, joined his local militia. When war came with Great Britain, he became a captain and Sarah became the chief farmer of the family. One day, redcoat soldiers appeared at her door, demanding the family pewter to be melted down for British bullets. Sarah, of course, had done her patriotic duty: She had buried the pewter. And now for eight generations we have repeated what Sarah told the British soldiers: "If ye want pewter, seek out Captain John, and he'll give it ye."

Like any old family story, this one binds together in a variety of ways those who are involved with it. All the family members who hear it are bound through pride to Sarah and John. But ties of other kinds come with the story even if they are never spoken of or thought about. The story has survived in part because it is seated, implicitly, in a real, living context. We can only imagine Sarah behaving as she did because she participated in certain practices which sustained her and gave her courage. It was partly the knowledge that all of her neighbors also had their pewter buried which made Sarah feel herself part of a larger effort that gave her own act meaning. So, too, when she threatened the British with mention of Captain John she really meant John and all the other neighbors who were part of his militia unit. Certainly, Sarah was brave, but her courage rested upon the knowledge that the whole neighborhood stood behind her, just as she spoke her defiance on behalf of the entire community. Such stories, then, not only bind families together but, as they are told in various families, also bind us to the communities which have sustained those families.

Because this particular story has survived so many generations of our family, we are bound in gratitude to all those intervening generations for having remembered the story well enough and fondly enough to tell it and retell it to their children. About many of the intervening generations I know almost nothing beyond a few indisputable facts—that they told this story, that they had children . . . and that they were farmers. No one in this entire line was ever anything but a farmer until I and my generation moved to town.

This continuity in itself means that we know more about those generations than we think we know. I can be sure that almost all of what I learned about farming by watching my father and mother had been learned by them in the same way, with many of the more subtle skills reaching back to the Welsh, Scotch-Irish, and Dutch peasants from whom my father and mother descended. I still have my father's "Swede" saw, and still use it occasionally to saw down a limb or an overgrown bush. When my four-year-old son takes the other end and pulls, he learns from the rhythm of the work, from the language of my hand on the other end of the saw, how to keep the pressure of the teeth on the wood. The lesson comes through the saw to him, just as it came to me when my father was at the other end. An assured imagination tells me that this is an unbroken chain of young and old farmers' hands, reaching at least back to the farm of Rhys Kemys, sawing wood with his son on a Welsh farm in the seventeenth century. These and larger lessons a succession of farms provides. Some of them, finally, are political lessons—resulting in the kind of dependability, ingenuity, courage, and loyalty which stories like those of John and Sarah provide. It was the observance of such practices, and the virtues they produce, which led Jefferson to speak of farmers as "the most valuable citizens . . . the most vigorous, the most independent, the most virtuous, . . . tied to their country, and wedded to its liberty and interests, by the most lasting bonds."

I grew up with an absolutely unqualified (and equally unexamined) acceptance of this Jeffersonian view of virtue. "City kids," I knew to a certainty, simply did not have the same moral standards that we brought off the farm. (For many years, the only city kids I knew lived in Richey, a metropolis of some 600 people. But we were convinced that those children who actually lived in town differed markedly [and morally] from the much larger number who, like my brothers and sisters, only came to town to go to school.) Years later, when I actually did move to a city to go to college and acquired in the process some new behaviors my parents could not understand, it was the city which they blamed for my departure from the straight and narrow.

In fact, the city had simply unmoored my sense of politics. I grew up so enamored of all things political that I never doubted that I would study that subject in college and then return home to practice it. But in the city this straight, clear path lost itself in a maze of uncertainties. The world was much bigger and much more complex than it had seemed; how to get any kind of effective grasp on it became more and more of a mystery. As politics came to seem less feasible, Montana and the West appeared increasingly irrelevant to anything that seemed to matter in the world. So I finished college having lost both my attachment to politics and my determination to go back home.

A few years later, suffocated and powerless in the East, I was surprised to hear the West call again, urging me back to open country. Within two years of my return to Montana, I had done what I would not have done in a lifetime in New England: I had run for (and, with the help of Watergate had managed to win) a seat in the Montana legislature, representing a district in Missoula.

Three terms later, I found myself rising to speak on an issue which had set rural and urban legislators at one another's throats. I was an urban legislator; I occupied that pigeonhole as I took the microphone. But I remember taking the trouble, in this particular speech, to invoke my farm boy upbringing, something I apparently had never done before, since at the mention of this fact, a number of faces (the kind with hat marks halfway down the forehead) turned to look at me with the purest astonishment. Just for a moment, there was a remarkable flash of kinship in the gaze of a number of those rural eyes. It could not last, of course—my pigeonhole was too tight for that—but the sense, suddenly, of being considered acceptable because I grew up on a farm has never left me. And it has never quite stopped saddening me.

Those were Jeffersonian eyes; they were Western eyes, the eyes of my father and of all the farmer-fathers before him. There was a passing sadness in them, that I who had once been a farmer too had been lost. My sadness has not passed so quickly nor has it been understood so easily. What I mourned then and mourn now is the declining possibility of politics, of the great, high calling whose honor and nobility had commanded me to respectful silence before the old wood-encased radio one autumn evening.

My pigeonhole was not only that of an urban but also that of a liberal legislator. Of my conservative colleagues, I found myself more and more curious about what moved them to devote their lives to this kind of enterprise. I felt quite certain that their motivations were at least as worthy of respect as mine—yet about these things we could never speak with each other. I could only know their conservatism on its ideological surface, in the slogans which they hurled back in response to the slogans that I served them. Much as I enjoyed the game on that level, there began to emerge a sense of loss. Was this, in fact, the profession, the practice of politics to which I had always felt myself called?

What legislative politics lacked was highlighted most clearly for me by an episode in which it was not lacking. The Senate had passed and sent to the House a bill requiring small children to ride in safety seats in automobiles. The nature of the debate was perfectly predictable. The pickup drivers led the charge. Gun racks belong in pickups—not the long arm of the regulatory bureaucracy. You're going to tell me how to carry my kids around in my own pickup? We liberals, meanwhile, presented our own well-worn litany of reasons for one more set of rules. Here we were, in the midst of politics as usual, with no minds being changed anywhere by anything that was said, and I could feel the old sadness rising again. Then Tom Asay, a Republican from Rosebud County, who had already given one of the most impassioned pickup speeches, asked for permission to speak again. He said that he had been thinking about his newborn grandson, and how proud he was of him, and how terrible he would feel if that boy ever got slammed against the dashboard of a pickup. It seemed to him now like his right to do whatever he wanted in his own outfit wasn't the point so much as the right of that kid to grow up.

After Tom gave that speech, you didn't have to watch the big scoreboard with the green and red lights to know how the vote was going to turn out. I still think of that debate almost every time I strap my own son into a safety seat. What I remember most about it is not the arguments but the fact that somebody actually listened to somebody else, that minds were changed, not by the power of ideological arguments but by reference to something everybody could understand: the way a new grandfather felt about his grandson. The sadness that I had come to feel about politics flowed together from two directions. First, that there were not, within politics itself, more scenes like this one, where people could simply solve problems as decent human beings. Second, and sadder yet, was the recognition that because politics seems so cold and impersonal, most of the people that I like best don't really like politics. They don't consider themselves equipped for it. They know something about what it takes to be a good grandfather, or a good brother or sister, but they rarely have anything like the same sense of full-bodied, engaged competence at citizenship. I had come to feel that until people were as involved in being citizens as they were in being fathers or mothers, or at least cousins, politics would not be what I had thought it was supposed to be.

As Jean-Jacques Rousseau watched nations being born from the wreck and rabble of a worn-out feudalism, he found himself torn between hope and fear for the future of politics. At his most despairing he would declare that "keeping citizens apart has become the first maxim of modern politics." Across the Atlantic to the west, this kind of politics could be fashioned from whole cloth, with no interference from the web of feudal interconnections. The great debates over the drafting and ratification of the Constitution had to do with struggles between large and small states, between slave-holders and opponents to the slave trade, between urban and rural interests. All of those conflicts were present, of course, and show their mark throughout the document. But behind all this seethed a deeper debate, about the nature of politics itself. How should these clashes of interests be dealt with? One option was to address them by bringing people into direct, open dialogue with one another, calling upon the parties to rise occasionally above their particular interests to find a higher common ground. This would be politics of engagement, the very opposite of "keeping citizens apart." The federalist solution, however, rested not upon citizen engagement but a largely mechanical system of checks and balances and mixed forms of government, designed to play competing interests off against one another so that no one interest would ever gain a lasting ascendancy. The public good would emerge not from asking diverse interests to seek common ground in face-to-face engagement with one another but through a mechanical balancing of various factions, each pursuing its own parochial interests.

This was part of the solution, and it still defines most of what we call politics. But America offered one other means for keeping citizens apart, and its influence continues also to shape our politics, especially in the West. It, of course, was the open frontier. As he worried about how to avoid the dreaded "tyranny of the majority," James Madison looked not only to the system of checks and balances but also to open country, into which various interests would expand, always moving farther on and thus never likely to come face to face with one another long enough to form an effective majority. "Extend the sphere," Madison wrote in the *Federalist Papers*, "and you . . . make it less probable that a majority of the whole will . . . discover their own strengths and act in unison with each other." Keeping citizens apart.

Oddly enough, Jefferson looked to the frontier for a very different reason: He sought not to disperse majorities but to preserve a particular majority—agriculture, the one interest which had to remain a majority if democratic culture as Jefferson understood it was to survive. Writing to Madison from Paris, Jefferson expressed his doubts about Madison's impersonal system of checks and balances as the foundation for democratic government. The foundation, he insisted, must be civic virtue. Democratic politics would remain viable "as long as we remain virtuous, and I think we shall be so, as long as agriculture is our principal object, which will be the case, while there remains vacant land in any part of America." Jefferson worried continually about the growth of cities, which he saw as the death trap of civic virtue. He knew that in finite spaces, urban populations grew faster than rural ones. His solution amounted to an astonishing denial of reality. If the frontier was endless, then agriculture could keep growing at least as fast as commerce and industry. In 1785, he had written to John Jay that "we have now lands enough to employ an infinite number of people in their cultivation." An infinite number. If we want to speak of the "myth of the West," we might well begin here with the recognition that, in certain important ways, the West was in its very essence a myth—something it could never be. Even Texas could not be that big.

But it did work for a while. For several decades, the issue of slavery, for example, could be averted by carefully adding as many new slave as free states to the Union. But there had to come a time when the only land left to settle was too dry and cold for cotton and tobacco. As Jefferson's wave of new farmers began to inhabit the more arid lands across the Mississippi, the inevitable tension mounted.

The next thing I know with any certainty about the Kemmis line, after the story of John and Sarah, is that one of their great-grandsons, Thompson, drove stagecoach in "Bloody Kansas" during that state's preview of the nation's civil war. By what stages the intervening generations had moved west we cannot be sure, but surely they did. Thompson had actually moved briefly all the way west, appearing in the California gold fields before returning to Kansas. After the war, he and Jane followed the trail to Oregon but found it both too settled and too wet, so they turned back east and came to rest in the Lower Yellowstone Valley, just outside what would eventually become Sidney, Montana. There they proved up a homestead a few years before Montana (and the Dakotas, Wyoming, and Idaho) joined the Union, marking the end of the old American frontier.

More than a few of the settlers who came into this region in the 1870s and '80s followed very much the path of my great-grandparents. In *Fair Land, Fair Land*, A. B. Guthrie has Dick Summers turning back from Oregon, where he found the air "wet enough and salt enough to pickle pork in," to return to Montana. "Going east he was, going east to find the west," Guthrie writes, describing the journey of many of this region's early white settlers.

If the West was a myth of the infinity into which people could escape from one another, or into which rural virtue could outpace urban corruption, then this turning back upon ourselves might signal something new. In the 1820s, when Americans most fervently believed in "manifest destiny," Hegel sat down to write his history of civilization. Before he got down to the real work, he asked whether America had anything to contribute to that history. His answer, given without hesitation, was that America would not contribute anything substantial to the history of civilization until it developed a genuine civic culture—a real politics—and it would do that "only after the immeasurable space which that country presents to its inhabitants shall have been occupied, and the members of the political body shall have begun to be pressed back on each other." This, of course, was the exact opposite of Jefferson's formula for civic culture. In fact, Hegel disagreed even more pointedly with Jefferson, arguing that cities, not farms, were the root of civic life:

> Only when, as in Europe, the direct increase of agri-
> culturists is checked, will the inhabitants, instead of
> pressing outwards to occupy the fields, press inwards upon
> each other—pursuing town occupation, and trading with
> their fellow-citizens; and so form a compact system of
> civil society, and require an organized state.

When Thompson and Jane came to Lower Yellowstone and began to farm there, they established roots in that valley which endured for four generations. In all of their wanderings, and finally in their settling down, they reflect what Wendell Berry identifies as the two main strains of the white race's peopling of America. "As a people," he says, "wherever we have been, we have never really intended to be." As Berry says, the continent was "discovered by an Italian who was on his way to India," and much of the exploring and even settling was done by people "looking for gold, which was . . . always somewhere farther on." But if Thompson was a part of this history, he and Jane were also examples of what Berry calls the second main theme of the frontier: "the tendency to stay put, to say, 'No farther. This is the place.' " For this couple, and for thousands of others, this region has been "the place." It is out of this simple, enduring fact that the possibility of politics must and will reemerge.

Recently I attended a meeting sponsored by the Missoula Chamber of Commerce. The meeting sought to get business and government leaders to talk openly and honestly about this city—why we live here, what we hope for, how we view the economy, the environment, one another. It was one of those meetings, increasingly common now, where people were urged to take some risks, to try to hear one another, to try to make themselves heard by speaking some simple truths. We survived the usual maelstrom of small groups, sheets of newsprint, colored markers, time spent deciding who will use the markers and who will "give the report." But in the middle of all that, truth was spoken, very clearly, and with unmistakable conviction. The first truth was this: that for almost everyone in the room, this place represented a deeply intentional part of their lives. Insurance agents, tire salesmen, and leaders of environmental groups spoke in almost exactly the same terms about the variety of pressures that they faced to move elsewhere, and about their firm determination to stay here. Over and over, they talked about having found a place where they could feel good about raising a family, and by God, they were going to stay here and raise that family.

The discussion went on to issues of economic growth and environmental regulation, and everyone began falling back into the use of slogans—into politics as usual. But in fact, the earlier discussion is the signal that politics as usual is at an end. We have become accustomed to a brand of politics where we act as if we expected to win, in some decisive sense. Both liberals and conservatives behave as if they thought that if they just did a better job of organizing or getting out the vote or grooming attractive candidates, they could score a decisive victory which would send the opposition packing. But what becomes clear from discussions like the one I just described is that no one is going anywhere. The politics of keeping citizens apart cannot work for long in a place to which large numbers of people with diverse interests are equally committed. The only kind of politics that can work here is a politics of engagement. And it will be in our families, above all, that we will learn the basic skills of that kind of politics.

When my father died, many of his neighbors came by to pay their respects. They talked about what kind of man my father had been, and I heard him praised, over and over, for the way he always kept his counsel, speaking little, but then being carefully listened to when he did speak. Because I loved him, I saw only the virtue in this circumspection. And indeed there was virtue in this circumspection. And indeed there was virtue in his humility, his not needing to hear the sound of his own voice, his capacity to hear everything that others were saying, and then, at least occasionally, to draw a glimmer of wisdom from what he had heard. Here again, as with the way he performed the routine tasks of farming, I always had the sense of standing in a long line of largely silent fathers, setting an example of reserved judgment for their sons to emulate.

But lately I have been required to view that chain of strong, silent men in a different way. My wife, like many another wife these days, has encouraged me (is that the right phrase?) to think of the chain of women living with those silent men, and of what they have suffered as they attempted, and almost always failed, to elicit from the men any glimmer of emotion about anything that ever happened to them. As I find myself wrenched and pried and scraped away from this ancient skein of emotional isolationism, I can at least occasionally justify my recalcitrance by pointing out how deeply rooted in family history the patterns are. But in the end, nothing will do but to learn what none of my ancestors seems to have been required to learn.

I took part in a conversation, not long ago, about what men

and women were learning from each other these days. I asked why there seemed to be so much energy going into this education, and someone responded that she thought that many couples had come to see it as the only alternative to divorce. What staying in these marriages seems to require first of all is learning some new skills of engagement. Women rightfully require of their men that they learn something that they have not known or cared to know about emotional engagement. In many marriages this has become a condition for staying married. The man can either learn or leave. Many, of course, do leave, but more all the time are putting themselves to the painful work of learning to engage. But rarely are the adjustments in these marriages so one-sided. Learning to engage usually means breaking down the roles of rote behaviors which both partners perform. One partner may always have had the role of "paying the emotional rent," but she may have been quite willing to let the other partner take full responsibility for other family tasks. At their worst, these dysfunctional divisions of roles become neurotic, but few marriages are free from some of these problems. Most of the therapeutic responses involve teaching both partners to rely less upon a kind of rote role performance, learning instead to respond creatively to each other and to external circumstances. This is almost always a painful process, because it means giving up what we know and trust—especially our stereotypes about ourselves or our spouses.

Curiously enough, our politics has become dysfunctional in almost exactly the same way. One segment of the political family assumes responsibility for worrying about the health of the environment or about caring for the unfortunate; another part takes responsibility for safety in the streets or for guarding the stability of the economy. Like partners in a dysfunctional marriage, we eventually get to the place where we need the other partner's overemphasis upon one half of the equation; we define ourselves by contrast to that role. We cannot live without the other partner, and we cannot live with them. This is the current state of our politics, as of so many of our marriages.

This dysfunctional state of politics leads increasingly to deadlock and frustration. It was that teeth-gritting frustration which led the Missoula Chamber of Commerce to experiment with asking people to talk to one another about how they felt about living in Missoula. It probably should not surprise us that the people at that meeting spoke about their determination to stay in Missoula much like the way many people seem to be approaching the challenge of staying in marriages. There was the same recognition of the variety of pressures to leave (the city or marriage), and the same tone of determination that this should not happen.

Perhaps it would help if we could think of families, and of cities, as a kind of biological jest. Hegel, always appreciative of cosmic jokes, argued that "the difference between men and women is like that between animals and plants." Nature uses these differences for her own purposes, but she does not necessarily make life easy for humans in the process. The fundamental importance of genetic diversity to the well-being of the species is a perfectly placid abstraction when it appears in biology textbooks, but it becomes very concrete, and very challenging, where it must be lived out—within real households. It is for the sake of the children that the parents must be so different from each other. Yet if the children require this diversity, and add to it, it is also for the sake of the children that the parents are so motivated to find a way to maintain a household— to stay together in the face of the odds.

In this sense, cities are very much like families. At that same Chamber of Commerce meeting, the second theme that emerged from all quarters was an appreciation for what people called the diversity of the place. Almost all seemed to feel an instinctual need to be surrounded by people who were quite different from themselves. But this makes life difficult: We need to live near people whom we do not understand, who consistently do things the wrong way—people who want less growth, or more growth, than we want, the civic equivalent of wanting the window open when I want it closed.

Diversity seems as essential to cities as it is to families. In *The*

Good City, Lawrence Haworth writes, "Because urban life is specialized it is diverse; the person confronts an unprecedented wealth of opportunities to act, to express himself, to develop his potentialities." Haworth addresses the psychological lure of the city, the element of urban life which the people at the Chamber of Commerce gathering alluded to when they spoke of liking to live in the midst of diversity. Jane Jacobs, another student of cities, finds in this urban "wealth of opportunities to act" a bedrock economic fact. Jacobs argues that when economies grow, it is for one reason alone: because a city responds to its own diversity by producing goods which the city and the region surrounding it need. As a result, she argues that the only real economies are those made up of cities and their surrounding rural regions. Neither nations nor states are economies, capable of generating their own growth, their own strength or stability. City regions alone can do this, and they can do it because they carry within themselves their own dynamic of diversity, which is held together in one place, held together by that place, drawing strength from the very differences which make it difficult for the inhabitants to stay together. The image bears some strong similarities to that of a healthy ecosystem, which also occupies an identifiable place and draws strength from a vital diversity which is at the same time a source of tension and conflict. Ecosystems, real economies, and households are all of that nature. The Greeks seem to have had some understanding of all this. Ecosystems and economies carry names derived from the old Greek word *oikos,* which meant "household."

Americans, and especially Westerners, have never understood cities in these terms. Our prevailing view of cities has been the Jeffersonian one—that they were a kind of cancer upon the body politic. The frontier offered above all an escape from cities—an escape into open country—and if cities insisted on following into the open country, they would be made as unwelcome as possible. No one has been as good as Westerners at making cities feel unwelcome on the land. As a consequence, our cities have never been given anything like the political autonomy that would be required to cultivate the natural economic potential which Jacobs sees as being centered, inherently, in cities. The "household" this kind of economy represents consists of rural and urban elements, mutually reinforcing one another. But as Jacobs argues very persuasively, these latent economies are not capable of realizing their potential unless they acquire some attributes of sovereignty—some power to shape the way they inhabit their place. Given the deep Jeffersonian distrust that exists between rural and urban areas, especially in the West, there has never been any prospect of developing this kind of mutual householding. The situation reminds me of nothing so much as the way Emma Goldman, an early-twentieth-century feminist, described the prospects for marriage ever really working:

> Behind every marriage stands the life-long environment
> of the two sexes; an environment so different from each
> other that man and woman must remain strangers. Sep-
> arated by an insurmountable wall of superstition, custom,
> and habit, marriage has not the potentiality of developing
> knowledge of, and respect for, each other, without which
> every union is doomed to failure.

For the past few decades, as the divorce rate has climbed and then climbed higher, it has seemed that this kind of thinking must be correct. At the same time, political participation has headed, just as alarmingly, in the other direction. Now, as the 1988 presidential election draws to a close, we find ourselves in the midst of a vast competition between the two parties to see which can be the most profamily. Little harm will be likely to come of this, but politics as we now know and loathe it has almost no capacity to do anything for families. The real question is whether families, as they back warily away from their own dissolution, as they learn once again the fundamental skills of householding upon which all real politics is built, will in fact build that politics. It is not enough that we acquire those skills in our private lives. There will be no world within which families can thrive until we put those householding skills into practice in public. All of politics rests on those two statements that everyone at the Chamber of Commerce meeting was making: "I am claimed by this place, and by the diversity of human diversity which it presents, and I intend to stay and raise my family here." Yet one further step is needed to turn these sentiments into politics. What we wish or want, we must learn to will. Benjamin Barber puts the matter plainly:

> To render a political judgment is not to exclaim "I prefer" or "I want" or "I choose such and such" but rather to say, "I will a world in which such and such is possible." To decide is thus to will into being a world that the community must experience in common: it is to create a common future, if only for selfish ends.

In families people are learning that they must mutually will the household or it will not exist. Learning this skill of mutual willing is the deepest kind of political education. But there is a point at which the members of a family cannot honestly claim to have willed the well-being of the household unless they are also ready to will into being a larger household within which their family may thrive. That act of will is the beginning of politics. But politics in this sense is not just a way of relating to one another. Like the family household, this politics also has its place. This household was once known as the *polis*—the city-state, from which we derive not only our word for politics but also our best understandings of what politics might be. The city-state was that same "household" consisting of a city and its rural environs which Jane Jacobs argues is the real locus of economies. It is that household which we must learn to nurture, using the same skill and exercising the same will with which we are learning to nurture our families. Taking care of this household is what politics would be.

Last winter I went to visit my mother, who lives alone in the Lower Yellowstone Valley town of Sidney, Montana. Each day I ran a different route through the town where I had gone to high school, reminding myself of whatever it was that needed remembering. One day I ran out of town, into the broad, flat valley of the Yellowstone, down a country road to the Pioneer Cemetery. I stopped when I got there, and went in to the snow-covered graves to visit some of my relations. Thompson and Jane were there. In fact, the cemetery had been part of their homestead, and they had donated this acre or so of good farmland for their neighbors' use. A couple of their sons were there, too, including John, whose homestead had been on the other side of town but still in the valley. And John's son, whom he had taught to saw wood on that farm, my father, was there, too. His farm, where I had grown up, had been out of the valley, out in the dryland, some fifty miles west.

Once I'd caught my breath, I had a little talk with all these fathers of mine. I asked Thompson what he thought of this town of some six thousand people which had grown up so near his homestead. He had gone from Iowa to Kansas, to California, to Oregon, and finally out here, trying to get away from towns, and here was a town that I would run back to in a few minutes. All around me were rich irrigated farms, and I remembered how my father had told about his father, John, working with all the other farmers in the valley to build the Big Ditch, some thirty miles long, which made all this irrigation possible. They had done it with horses, and my father, when he was using the little horse-drawn equivalent of a backhoe—what they called a fresnoe—used to tell me about Grandpa John and his neighbors building the Big Ditch with those little implements. I asked John if he thought you could build up the productivity of the valley that way and not expect to have a town there. He didn't seem to mind the town, but when I asked him if his politics had ever had anything to do with the town, he seemed puzzled. His brother, Walter Kemmis, lying there next to him, had been a state legislator. That was politics. The town could take care of itself.

And the farms, I asked, could they take care of themselves, too? My father had lost his farm, finally, because it was too small and dry to keep us all alive. I reminded him of how he had taught me all about Ezra Taft Benson, who was Eisenhower's secretary of agriculture—had taught me to blame Benson for our misfortunes. For good reason, I'm sure, but I can't help wondering, now, if more of those farms might have survived if they had directed their attention less toward Washington or Helena and more toward Sidney. Did Sidney and its farms ever really understand how they were part of the same household? Do they yet? Did these men, my fathers, ever talk to their wives?

Before I turned back toward town, I talked to my father about the farm—about one tree there that had always haunted me. It was a single cottonwood tree, the only one for miles and miles around. Cottonwoods have two unique characteristics that made the story of this old tree so fascinating to me. They are sexually differentiated; there are male and female trees, and they cannot reproduce without each other. And they are what botanists call phreatophytes, which means that they can only live if they can get their roots down, not just into moisture but into the water table itself. So they live along river bottoms. They were all around me, here in Yellowstone Valley, but to find one way out where we lived was almost unheard of. A seed had to have floated on the wind for fifty or more miles, and it had to have lit on a spot where the water table lay within ten or fifteen feet of the surface. Our old tree had been the result of all those circumstances coming together, but now she stood there, alone, with never any prospect of seeding any new cottonwoods.

My father reminded me that, because he grew up with cottonwoods here in this valley, he knew that there was a water table down near the foot of that tree, and because we always needed water so desperately, he and my older brother had dug a well, by hand, there in her shade. They found the water, all right, but there was too little of it to make a working well. I remembered the muddy bottom of that hole, which my younger brother and I had been sternly warned away from. It occurred to me now that there was so little water because the tree was drinking whatever was available, and I asked my father if he had ever considered sawing her down, but he reminded me of how his father had taught him to make little boats out of cottonwood bark. Having grown up with these trees, he couldn't saw down the only one on his whole farm. I remembered his hands, his pocketknife, showing me how to make those boats. I stood up and trotted back toward my mother's little house in town.

◆

Contrary to all Jeffersonian wisdom, Daniel Kemmis, beginning well enough as a farm boy in eastern Montana, eventually became mayor of Missoula. His career had peaked somewhat earlier, during the period in which, as the officially designated Grey Eminence of the Northern Lights Institute, he wrote this article.

PART IV

TENDING THE LAND

LEE EVANS

♦　♦　♦　♦　♦

INCENSE CEDAR

I stand here gathering silence
into my coat—here and not here,
the way birds cry out all of a sudden,
invisible among the thick branches of a cedar.
　　　　I stand here watching
this cedar that gives more light than shadow,
snow coaxing my eyelids
all the way down.
　　　　Standing here
in all of this brightness, I don't know
whether I'm opening or closing—cedar,
carry me home. When I am a very old woman,
so old I can no longer see you, let me
remember all of this with my body,
the way a branch can drift
for a very long time through the mind.

Lee Evans currently teaches writing at Chuo University in Tokyo, where she writes mainly about surviving the speed of life in that city: trains, concrete, and crush hour crowds (with an occasional plum blossom when she's lucky). She has written a chapbook of poems, The Fisherman's Widow, *published in 1989 as the Merriam-Frontier Award, and her poetry has appeared recently in* Puerto del Sol, The Cream City Review, *and* The Denver Quarterly.

TERRY TEMPEST WILLIAMS

◆ ◆ ◆ ◆ ◆

THE CLAN OF ONE-BREASTED WOMEN

I belong to a Clan of One-breasted Women. My mother, my grand-mothers, and six aunts have all had mastectomies. Seven are dead. The two who survive have just completed rounds of chemotherapy and radiation.

I've had my own problems: two biopsies for breast cancer and a small tumor between my ribs diagnosed as "a borderline malignancy."

This is my family history.

Most statistics tell us breast cancer is genetic, hereditary, with rising percentages attached to fatty diets, childlessness, or becoming pregnant after thirty. What they don't say is living in Utah may be the greatest hazard of all.

We are a Mormon family with roots in Utah since 1847. The word-of-wisdom, a religious doctrine of health, kept the women in my family aligned with good foods: no coffee, no tea, tobacco, or alcohol. For the most part, these women were finished having their babies by the time they were thirty. And only one faced breast cancer before 1960. Traditionally, as a group of people, Mormons have a low rate of cancer.

Is our family a cultural anomaly? The truth is we didn't think about it. Those who did, usually the men, simply said, "bad genes." The women's attitude was stoic. Cancer was part of life. On February 16, 1971, the eve of my mother's surgery, I accidentally picked up the telephone and overheard her ask my grandmother what she could expect.

"Diane, it is one of the most spiritual experiences you will ever encounter."

I quietly put down the receiver. Two days later, my father took my three brothers and me to the hospital to visit her. She met us in the lobby in a wheelchair. No bandages were visible. I'll never forget her radiance, the way she held herself in a purple velvet robe and how she gathered us around her.

"Children, I am fine. I want you to know I felt the arms of God around me."

We believed her. My father cried. Our mother, his wife, was thirty-eight years old.

Two years ago, after my mother's death from cancer, my father and I were having dinner together. He had just returned from St. George, where his construction company was putting in natural gas lines. He spoke of his love for the country, the sandstone landscape, bare-boned and beautiful. He had just finished hiking the Kolob Trail in Zion National Park. We caught up in reminiscing, recalling with fondness our walk up Angel's Landing on his fiftieth birthday and the years our family had vacationed there. This was a remembered landscape where we had been raised.

Over dessert, I shared a recurring dream of mine. I told my father that for years, as long as I could remember, I saw this flash of light in the night in the desert. That this image had so permeated my being, I could not venture south without seeing it again, on the horizon, illuminating buttes and mesas.

"You did see it," he said.

"Saw what?" I asked, a bit tentative.

"The bomb. The cloud. We were driving home from Riverside, California. You were sitting on your mother's lap. She was pregnant. In fact, I remember the date, September 7, 1957. We had just gotten out of the service. We were driving north, past Las Vegas. It was an hour or so before dawn, when this explosion went off. We not only heard it but felt it. I thought the oil tanker in front of us had blown up. We pulled over and suddenly, rising from the desert floor, we saw it clearly, this golden-stemmed cloud, the mushroom. The sky seemed to vibrate with an eerie pink glow. Within a few minutes, a light ash was raining on the car."

I stared at my father. This was new information to me.

"I thought you knew that," he said. "It was a common occurrence in the fifties."

It was at this moment I realized the deceit I had been living under. Children growing up in the American Southwest, drinking contaminated milk, from contaminated cows, even from the contaminated breasts of their mothers, my mother—members, years later, of the Clan of One-breasted Women.

It is a well-known story in the Desert West, "The Day We Bombed Utah."[1] Or perhaps, "The Years We Bombed Utah." Above-ground atomic testing in Nevada took place from January 27, 1951, through July 11, 1962. Not only were the winds blowing north covering "low use segments of the population"[2] with fallout and leaving sheep dead in their tracks, but the climate was right. The United States in the 1950s was red, white, and blue. The Korean War was raging, McCarthyism was rampant. Ike was it, and the Cold War was hot. If you were against nuclear testing, you were for a Communist regime.

Much has been written about this "American nuclear tragedy." Public health was secondary to national security. The atomic energy commissioner, Thomas Murray, said, "Gentlemen, we must not let anything interfere with this series of tests, nothing."[3]

Again and again, the American public was told by its government, in spite of burns, blisters, and nausea, "It has been found that the tests may be conducted with adequate assurance of safety under conditions prevailing at the bombing reservations."[4] Assuaging public fears was simply a matter of public relations. "Your best action," an Atomic Energy Commission booklet read, "is not to be worried about fallout." A news release typical of the times stated, "We find no basis for concluding that harm to any individual has resulted from radioactive fallout."[5]

On August 30, 1979, during Jimmy Carter's presidency, a suit was filed entitled *Irene Allen* v. *the United States of America*. Mrs. Allen was the first to be alphabetically listed with twenty-four test cases, representative of nearly twelve hundred plaintiffs seeking compensation from the U.S. government for cancers caused from nuclear testing in Nevada.

Irene Allen lived in Hurricane, Utah. She was the mother of five children and had been widowed twice. Her first husband with their two oldest boys had watched the tests from the roof of the local high school. He died of leukemia in 1956. Her second husband died of pancreatic cancer in 1978.

In a town meeting conducted by Utah Senator Orrin Hatch, shortly before the suit was filed, Mrs. Allen said, "I am not blaming the government, I want you to know that, Senator Hatch. But I thought if my testimony could help in any way so this wouldn't happen again to any of the generations coming up after us . . . I am really happy to be here this day to bear testimony of this."[6]

God-fearing people. This is just one story in an anthology of thousands.

On May 10, 1984, Judge Bruce S. Jenkins handed down his opinion. Ten of the plaintiffs were awarded damages. It was the first time a federal court had determined that nuclear tests had been the cause of cancers. For the remaining fourteen test cases, the proof of causation was not sufficient. In spite of the split decision, it was considered a landmark ruling.[7] It was not to remain so for long.

In April 1987, the Tenth Circuit Court of Appeals overturned Judge Jenkins's ruling on the ground that the United States was protected from suit by the legal doctrine of sovereign immunity, a centuries' old idea from England in the days of absolute monarchs.[8]

In January 1988, the Supreme Court refused to review the appeals court decision. To our court system, it does not matter whether the U.S. government is immune. "The king can do no wrong."

In Mormon culture, authority is respected, obedience is revered, and independent thinking is not. I was taught as a young girl not to "make waves" or "rock the boat."

"Just let it go," my mother would say. "You know how you feel, that's what counts."

For many years, I did just that—listened, observed, and quietly formed my own opinion within a culture that rarely asked questions because they had all the answers. But one by one, I watched the women in my family die common, heroic deaths. We sat in waiting rooms hoping for good news, always receiving the bad. I cared for them, bathed their scarred bodies and kept their secrets. I watched beautiful women become bald as Cytoxan, cisplatin, and Adriamycin were injected into their veins. I held their foreheads as they vomited green-black bile, and I shot them with morphine when the pain became inhuman. In the end, I witnessed their last, peaceful breaths, becoming a midwife to the rebirth of their souls. But the price of obedience became too high.

The fear and inability to question authority that ultimately killed rural communities in Utah during atmospheric testing of atomic weapons was the same fear I saw being held in my mother's body. Sheep. Dead sheep. The evidence is buried.

I cannot prove that my mother, Diane Dixon Tempest, or my grandmothers, Lettie Romney Dixon and Kathryn Blackett Tempest, along with my aunts, contracted cancer from nuclear fallout in Utah. But I can't prove they didn't.

My father's memory was correct. The September blast we drove through in 1957 was part of Operation Plumbbob, one of the most intensive series of bomb tests to be initiated. The flash of light in the night in the desert I had always thought was a dream developed into a family nightmare. It took fourteen years, from 1957 to 1971, for cancer to show up in my mother—the same time Howard L. Andrews, an authority on radioactive fallout at the National Institutes of Health, says radiation cancer requires to become evident.[9] The more I learn about what it means to be a "downwinder," the more questions I drown in.

What I do know, however, is that as a Mormon woman of the fifth generation of "Latter-day Saints," I must question everything, even if it means losing my faith, even if it means becoming a member of a border tribe among my own people. Tolerating blind obedience in the name of patriotism or religion ultimately takes our lives.

When the Atomic Energy Commission described the country north of the Nevada Test Site as "virtually uninhabited desert terrain," my family were some of the "virtual uninhabitants."

One night, I dreamed women from all over the world circled a blazing fire in the desert. They spoke of change, of how they hold the moon in their bellies and wax and wane with its phases. They mocked the presumption of even-tempered beings and made promises that they would never fear the witch inside themselves. The women danced wildly as sparks broke away from the flames and entered the night sky as stars.

And they sang a song given to them by Shoshone grandmothers:

> Ah ne nah, nah
> nin nah nah—
> Ah ne nah, nah
> nin nah nah—
> Nyaga mutzi
> oh ne nay—
> Nyaga mutzi
> oh ne nay—[10]

The women danced and drummed and sang for weeks, preparing themselves for what was to come. They would reclaim the desert for the sake of their children, for the sake of the land.

A few miles downwind from the fire circle, bombs were being tested. Rabbits felt the tremors. Their soft leather pads on paws and feet recognized the shaking sands while the roots of mesquite and sage were smoldering. Rocks were hot from the inside out, and dust devils hummed unnaturally. And each time there was another nuclear test, ravens watched the desert heave. Stretch marks appeared. The land was losing its muscle.

The women couldn't bear it any longer. They were mothers. They had suffered labor pains but always under the promise of birth. The red hot pains beneath the desert promised death only as each bomb became a stillborn. A contract had been broken between human beings and the land. A new contract was being drawn by the women who understood the fate of the earth as their own.

Under the cover of darkness, ten women slipped under the

barbed-wire fence and entered the contaminated country. They were trespassing. They walked toward the town of Mercury in moonlight taking their cues from coyote, kit fox, antelope, squirrel, and quail. They moved quietly and deliberately through the maze of Joshua trees. When a hint of daylight appeared they rested, drinking tea and sharing their rations of food. The women closed their eyes. The time had come to protest with the heart, that to deny one's genealogy from the earth was to commit treason against one's soul.

At dawn, the women draped themselves in Mylar, wrapping long streamers of silver plastic around their arms to blow in the breeze. They wore clear masks that became the faces of humanity. And when they arrived on the edge of Mercury, they carried all the butterflies of a summer day in their wombs. They paused to allow their courage to settle.

The town which forbids pregnant women and children to enter because of radiation risks to their health was asleep. The women moved through the streets as winged messengers, twirling around each other in slow motion, peeking inside homes and watching the easy sleep of men and women. They were astonished by such stillness and periodically would utter a shrill note or low cry just to verify life.

The residents finally awoke to what appeared as strange apparitions. Some simply stared. Others called authorities, and, in time, the women were apprehended by wary soldiers dressed in desert fatigues. They were taken to a white, square building on the other edge of Mercury. When asked who they were and why they were there, the women replied, "We are mothers and we have come to reclaim the desert for our children."

The soldiers arrested them. As the ten women were blindfolded and handcuffed, they began singing:

You can't forbid us everything
You can't forbid us to think—
You can't forbid us our tears to flow
And you can't stop the songs that we sing.

The women continued to sing louder and louder and louder, until they heard the voices of their sisters moving across the mesa.

> Ah ne nah, nah
> nin nah nah—
> Ah ne nah, nah
> nin nah nah—
> Nyaga mutzi
> oh ne nay
> Nyaga mutzi
> oh ne nay—

"Call for reinforcement," one soldier said.

"We have," interrupted one woman. "We have—and you have no idea of our numbers."

On March 18, 1988, I crossed the line at the Nevada Test Site and was arrested with nine other Utahans for trespassing on military lands. They are still conducting nuclear tests in the desert. Ours was an act of civil disobedience. But as I walked toward the town of Mercury, it was more than a gesture of peace. It was a gesture on behalf of the Clan of One-breasted Women.

As one officer cinched the handcuffs around my wrists, another frisked my body. She found a pen and a pad of paper tucked inside my left boot.

"And these?" she asked sternly.

"Weapons," I replied.

Our eyes met. I smiled. She pulled the leg of my trousers back over my boot.

"Step forward, please," she said as they took my arm.

We were booked under an afternoon sun and bused to To-nopah, Nevada. It was a two-hour ride. This was familiar country to me. The Joshua trees standing their ground had been named by my ancestors, who believed they looked like prophets pointing west to the promised land. These were the same trees that bloomed each spring, flowers appearing like white flames in the Mojave. And I recalled a full moon in May when my mother and I had walked among them, flushing out mourning doves and owls.

The bus stopped short of town. We were released.

The officials thought it was a cruel joke to leave us stranded in the desert with no way to get home. What they didn't realize is that we were home, soul-centered and strong, women who recognized the sweet smell of sage as fuel for our spirits.

1. John G. Fuller, *The Day We Bombed Utah* (New York: New American Library, 1984).

2. Discussion on March 14, 1988, with Carole Gallaher, photographer and author, *Nuclear Towns: The Secret War in the American Southwest* (New York: Doubleday, 1990).

3. Ferenc M. Szasz, "Downwind from the Bomb," *Nevada Historical Society Quarterly*, vol. 30, no. 3 (Fall 1987), p. 185.

4. Philip L. Fradkin, *Fallout* (Tucson: University of Arizona Press, 1989), p. 98.

5. *Ibid.*, p. 109.

6. Town meeting held by Sen. Orrin Hatch in St. George, Utah, April 17, 1979, transcript, pp. 26–28.

7. Fradkin, *Fallout*, p. 228.

8. *U.S.* v. *Allen*, 816 F. 2d 1417 (10th Cir. 1987), cert. denied, 108 Sup. Ct. 694 (1988).

9. Fradkin, *Fallout*, p. 116.

10. This song was sung by the Western Shoshone women as they crossed the line at the Nevada Test Site on March 19, 1988, as part of their Reclaim the Land action. The translation they gave was "Consider the rabbits how gently they walk on the earth. Consider the rabbits how gently they walk on the earth. We remember them. We can walk gently also. We remember them. We can walk gently also."

Terry Tempest Williams is a naturalist-in-residence of the Utah Museum of Natural History. Her books include Refuge—An Unnatural History of Family and Place, Coyote's Canyon, Pieces of White Shell, *and, most recently,* An Unspoken Hunger—Stories from the Field. *She is the recipient of a Lannan Literary Fellowship in nonfiction.*

GARY PAUL NABHAN

◆　◆　◆　◆　◆

ON TUMBLEWEEDS AND DUST

I reckon the Lord put tumbleweed here to show us how the wind blows.

Ramon Adams, *Western Words*

Ask me to choose an image of damage done in the American *deserta*, of our weird ways of covering up those wounds, and I will. I'll draw you a tumbleweed, tumbling along in the wake of Westering man. Ask archaeologists a hundred or a thousand years from now what remains they found in central Arizona after the last drop of water was sucked from the wells, and they'll tell of a White Drifter culture whose only remaining resource was this Russian thistle. I'll wager that even now, these short-lived, seemingly rootless plants tell us a whole lot about those of us who reside in the freewheeling rural West. A man with "roving proclivities," I am told, is called a tumbleweed. But the image also aptly fits entire waves of colonists: ones which were estranged from the land; ones which tried to make it over in an image altogether foreign to it; and ones which left it poorer than the way they found it. Their lives, too, have been impoverished, but they have left us some lovely, haunting images that dress this barrenness in the same way a blues song might celebrate the pain of a love in vain.

At first, it was easy for me to dismiss tumbleweed images in Western folklore as simply romantic notions of an Old West that never really was. Cowboys' kitsch. Plowboys' follies. And yet, paradoxically, tumbleweeds often speak to something larger than that, the culture's first acknowledgment of something gone wrong, a little hubris over all the humus already lost. The tumbling tumbleweed of Western song, story, and legend is a chimerical creature, at first look, pure cliché, at last glance, true beauty in the stark or tragic.

Its image did not finally move me until I moved westward, breaking off my Midwestern roots in the sand dunes along Lake Michigan. On my way to Arizona, I happened upon this story in the Great Sand Dunes, originally told by an elderly woman responding to the mention made of tumbleweeds during a "nature walk":

"I grew up during the Depression, in the Dust Bowl, when the drought and dust storms made it hard for families to get by on their dryland farms and ranches.

"I was just a little girl when it got tough for my family. Times got so bad, the animals my folks had given me for pets had to either be sold or eaten.

"So, since I didn't have any playthings, nor any pets left, my folks put a leash on a tumbleweed for me, and I'd let it trail behind me, bounding along, bouncing along behind me in the dust."

I soon learned that the tumbleweed is not a native but came to America as an imperfection in a dream to remake the country in the image of the Old World. The imperfection grew, while the dream eroded away, and eroded away at the land.

Folklore has it that this weed arrived in the West in 1873, as peasant farmers from the Ukrainian steppes tried to escape their hardships by emigrating across an ocean of water to an ocean of grass—the Dakotas. They had planned to raise flax for making linen shirts, sheets, and blouses, as they had done in their mother country. But an unnoticed contaminant had ridden along in their flaxseed— an impurity, no more than a speck in size, the coiled seed of *Salsola*, ready to strike. Where their iron plowshares ripped at the prairie sod, where they sowed the flaxseed into the dust-laden winds, the Russian thistle seed landed, germinated, and proliferated. In their own language, Ukrainian immigrants called this tagalong wind witch and leap-the-field. Later, ethnic slurs abounded as Russian Mennonites were accused of deliberately introducing the weed as revenge against those American frontiersmen who met them with insults and religious intolerance. As they have done many times before and since, tumbleweed seeds simply used unknowing humans as agents of long-distance dispersal. To paraphrase Wendell Berry about such colonists, they did not know what they were doing because they have never known what they were *un*doing.

Wherever America had been unsettled, this alien weed advanced across the West an average of ten miles a year, occasionally taking large leaps along railroad lines or wagon routes. While unable to survive in undisturbed prairie, a mother tumbleweed in the late nineteenth century could still find plenty of sod-broken homes for its 200,000 seeds. As it proliferated within the sweeping stretch of the West, then known as the Great American Desert, schoolteachers were commanded to show their students the plant and to "teach them to kill it as they would a rattlesnake."

In Arizona in particular, the tumbleweed landed on cow-burnt rangelands, cutover scrublands near wood-devouring mines, and floodplains ruined by beaver trapping, field clearing, and poor irrigation practices. The Pima Indians began to describe it as *votadam shai*, "the rolling brush," a name hardly more than a provisional description of a newcomer on its way through. Mexicans in Arizona called it *chamise*, a term also applied to a half dozen other hardy dwellers of the desert scrub and chaparral. Anglos called it Russian cactus. Throughout the West, whole towns would pick up and leave once this pest became established. At one point, a North Dakota farmer proposed to his legislators that they erect a wire fence across the state to hold back the further spread of tumbleweeds.

I find it ironic that this alien plant first took to American soil in the Dakotas, for it is here that the Mandan, Hidatsa, and Arikara tribes offered immigrants a rich mix of native foods to help them survive. These Missouri River tribes had developed a great number of hardy crop strains and knew of dozens of wild plant foods that could meet their nutritional needs in that harsh, dry climate. One Anglo who did learn native plant lore from these tribes, ethnobotanist Melvin Gilmore, tried to warn Western residents of the potential hazards of exotic plant introductions at the expense of the native flora:

> The country cannot be wholly made over and adjusted to a people of foreign habits and tastes. There are large tracts of land in America whose bounty is wasted because the plants that can be grown on them are not acceptable to our people. This is not because the plants are not useful and desirable but because their useful qualities are not known. . . . The adjustment of American consumption to American conditions of consumption will bring about greater improvement in conditions of life than any other material agency.

I am not the first to notice a fatal correlation here: The spread of Russian thistle across arid America is tied to the failure of immigrants to consider the value of native plants in the areas they were colonizing. The same year in which Gilmore wrote his warning (1919), *Scientific American* recorded how the tumbleweed had recently gained a foothold over much of the West, and how it had been widely adopted, presumably by independent invention, as a trivial pursuit of the region's youngsters: "Children in the Dakotas, Montana, Colorado, Idaho, and Utah find the tumbleweed a splendid late-fall playfellow. Two big weeds are harnessed to a string, and in front of a wind they go hurtling down the streets 'driven' by shrieking, happy boys and girls. At other times, the weed becomes a kite, attached to a long cord dangling from a fishpole."

But I should not leave you with the impression that the tumbleweed is always playful; at times, there can be something palpably terrible about it.

On a windy, wintry day my first year in Arizona, I witnessed an occurrence which made me shudder with fear. Hitchhiking between Dewey and Prescott, I watched as a tidal wave of tumbleweeds suddenly spilled onto the highway, the frontal wall of them towering eight feet tall. They descended upon a handful of passing cars and pickups, totally engulfing those vehicles. A few of the drivers panicked and veered off the road into gulleys, their visibility having been obscured by the froth of stickers and stems rising above their windshields.

The only vehicle which stuck to the road was an old cowboy's pickup. He smashed his way through the roiling mass, obliterating its mass into a scant window of splinters and prickly bracts. In another minute, the road was clear of all debris, as if there was no substance to the tumbleweed terror at all.

The terror, however, lies in the fact that most onlookers would have said that the plants "came out of nowhere." The truth is that not far from the road, the earth had been turned into a nowhere land. *Salsola* stubble covered the manure piles in fallen-down corrals; the pastures where soil, water, and capital grew scarce and failed to "make the desert bloom" a permanent, insipid green, as if painted on. Where chaparral once clothed the hillsides, Russian thistle infected the scars left when real estate developers scalped the vegetal cover, then blundered at making concrete their dreams.

Clearly, tumbleweeds infest the most wounded places. Fields left high and dry by the depletion of groundwater. Roadsides bladed to free passersby of all obstructions. Town sites abandoned as a result of land frauds. Spoils left outside collapsed mine shafts. Cemeteries gone untended as the descendants of the deceased moved on, to seek artificially irrigated, temporarily greener pastures.

Some of the same peoples have wounded place after place, on continent after continent. The Scotch-Irish, for example, are quintessential White Drifters. In Great Britain, they were the Angles and Saxons pushed north by various post-Roman invasions. Between wars, they were relegated to the most marginal lands, and their poor farming practices depleted the soil over several centuries. Historian Bil Gilbert claims that by Elizabethan times, the Scottish lowlands "had been turned into a barren literally tree-less northern desert." They began to move on to Ireland around 1620, as Protestant fodder against the Roman Catholics. There, potato monoculture became their quick fix; they mined the soils already too poor for the production of other crops. By 1715, some Ulster Scots who were dispossessed farm laborers began to emigrate to the New World; they were the lucky ones. Those who remained soon faced overpopulation, pestilence, and famine. Culminating with the Irish Potato Famine, which killed millions, their land abuse forced most of the survivors to flee to America. Again, Bil Gilbert: "Perhaps no other sizeable group of emigrants arrived in North America with less baggage, material or cultural, than did the Scotch-Irish. Because of poverty and insecurity, they brought few folkways."

Once in the New World, they contributed to the deforestation of Pennsylvania and West Virginia, then to that of Kentucky and Tennessee. Stung by the bug of Manifest Destiny, they moved out of the temperate woodlands, to undo the deserts and grasslands. They planted trees where they ought not to be, and cleared pasturelands at great cost to the native flora and fauna.

One of their descendants, Joseph Walker, achieved notoriety as a mountain man, surveyor of the Santa Fe Trail, leader of the wagon train to California, and mining entrepreneur who opened Prescott, Arizona, to gold prospecting in 1863. He opened up Yavapai County to the "unsettlement" of the kind now seen between Prescott and Dewey.

Such ecological damage has most often been done at the hand of marginalized peoples, forced to do the dirty work by the power brokers; they soon moved on rather than having to deal with the full consequences of their actions. They inevitably move on to repeat the same mistakes elsewhere, leaving the tumbleweed seeds they bring with them more disturbed ground to colonize.

Oddly, the fact that the tumbleweed is not native to the West is lost on most people. It is so embedded in Western folklore that many assume it has always been here. Anglos nickname it Nevada barbwire, Canada thistle. It is part of a pathology which West Jackson exposes when he says, "We have colonized the land, but we have not yet begun to *discover* America."

The overriding sentiment among Westerners is that the tumbleweed epitomizes life on all desert lands, not just the artificially desertified ones. When I asked Sons of the Pioneers spokesman Dale Warren what moved his colleague Bob Nolan to write the song

"Tumbling Tumbleweeds," Warren replied, "Bob always loved the desert. He loved Nature. In fact, when he died, he had his ashes flown up in an airplane and spread over the desert."

Nolan, as a student at the University of Arizona in the late 1920s, had been editor of a literary publication called *The Tumbleweed Times*. A poem written for that publication in 1929, "Tumbling Leaves," was rewritten as the song "Tumbling Tumbleweeds" while Nolan worked as a golf caddie at the Bel Air Country Club in the Los Angeles area during the fall of 1932. He first recorded it with the made-for-Hollywood combo called the Sons of the Pioneers in 1934. The song continues to be the hallmark of that Western singing group today, but it has taken on a life apart from the Sons as well. Much the same way Woody Guthrie's "This Land Is Your Land" has entered folk song status within popular American culture, so has Nolan's classic. It is sung around campfires as much as it is blasted over the airwaves. Leonard Slye, who was an original member of the Sons, made it one of his features when he started his movie career as Roy Rogers. Gene Autry, Bing Crosby, Rex Allen, and others have made it a standard in their repertoires, and overall it has been recorded more than two hundred times. The Sons themselves, with or without Roy Rogers, have recorded the song on nine different occasions:

> See them tumbling down,
> Pledging their love to the ground,
> Lonely but free I'll be found,
> Drifting along with the tumbling tumbleweeds.
>
> I'll keep tolling along,
> Deep in my heart is a song,
> Here on the range I belong,
> Drifting along with the tumbling tumbleweeds.

Dale Warren has been one of the Sons since 1951. He vaguely recalls a time when the Sons were invited to Texas as part of a promotional scheme:

"Oh, yes, it was just one of those things, you know. A little town in Texas. . . . They renamed the town Tumbleweed, if I remember. . . . Yeah, we had an engagement there that night, when they gave us these hats—tumbleweeds pressed up and shaped just like cowboy hats . . . the scratchiest thing I ever wore. . . . They had this scheme with the wells, to pack them full of tumbleweeds. It was going to be some kind of experiment, sticking all its tumbleweeds down dried-up oil wells around there. I can't recall the reason for it. . . . Now, I don't know if it ever worked, but you see, tumbleweeds were easy to come by around there, and if you could put them to use . . ."

That is not the only time that tumbleweeds have been part of a promotional scheme. In the late 1970s, the University of Arizona attempted to develop a Tumblelog product to make some use of the millions of Russian thistle plants growing on thousands of acres of abandoned farmlands in southern Arizona. The mechanical harvesters used to collect this biomass would likely disturb the ground enough to guarantee a continuous supply of the weeds. Yet the economic cost of the logs was too high compared with the cost of conventional fuels at the time; the energy used for harvesting and pressing the weeds into logs, for packaging and shipping them to consumers was probably greater than that released by burning the logs. Nevertheless, some rural residents of Arizona thought of the possibility of producing Tumblelogs as their salvation. Ethnohistorian Tom Sheridan recalls going into a small, run-down store in San Simon, Arizona, in an area depressed by the depletion of aquifers and the foreclosure of farms:

> The place looked like a scene out of Walker Evans or Dorothea Lange photos from the Depression days, all that land out of production and all those wells gone dry. But I ran into this man in a store there who raved on and on about how Tumblelogs could turn the place around . . . they had tons of tumbleweeds close by. . . . Tumblelogs were the wave of the future.

Promoters have since given up the ghost: Tumblelogs are no longer regarded as a panacea for the problems of damaged rural lands. But the plants themselves do have a part in the future of the arid West. They can serve as an indicator of the damage we have done, and direct us to places that need healing. Unless we begin to see what we have wounded, and acknowledge what has been lost, we may not take the responsibility to begin restoring the desert so that it can be appreciated by future generations.

Fifteen years ago, I worked for a while on the maintenance crew at the Research Ranch near Elgin, Arizona, a grassland sanctuary where cattle have been removed so that the wild plant and animal community can recover. One day, while pitchforking tumbleweeds out of a corral that was no longer in use, this poem came to me as *spoken word*, as if it had arisen out of the wind and landed in my mouth. Only later did I write it down:

> I work with tumbleweeds and dust,
> Telling people we've come the wrong way.
> This land has never been pictured.
> Get inside the wind, you'll see:
> It moves too fast, it moves too slow.
> You can never keep up with it.
>
> If you're dying to, not just if you'd like to,
> Take on the tone and age of bones,
> Get as hard as them,
> As hard as parched corn,
> While singing,
> "Time and time and time again,
> Time again, we've lost our way."
> Those of us remaining here
> Know that good directions are hard to come by.
> We assume the way Tierra gives,
> What she breathes into us,
> Molds out of clay.
> Like earthenware, Tierra holds us, preserves us,

A bit of her taste rubs off on us.
She gives us a trailing scent to follow.

◆

Dr. Gary Nabhan works for the Arizona-Sonora Desert Museum and Native Seeds/SEARCH. His latest book, coauthored with Steve Trumble, is The Geography of Childhood: Why Children Need Wild Places. *He is a MacArthur Fellow and John Burroughs Medal winner.*

JOHN DANIEL

◆ ◆ ◆ ◆ ◆

CUTTINGS

Sometimes the fallers would be working on a distant slope where we could see them, and when I wasn't wrestling a choker around a log I'd watch them drop the Douglas firs. As a tree toppled and then fell faster, its boughs would sweep back, the whole trunk would flex a little just before it hit the hillside, a flash of wood showing if it broke somewhere. Across the distance the sound came late, and small. The saws sounded like hornets.

The fallers worked in pairs, and they worked slowly. It's a dangerous job—the trees are big, the hills steep. On any one day they never seemed to advance very far against the front of the forest, but they worked slowly and steadily, and day by day they got the job done. They drove the back roads every morning, they laid the big trees down, they bucked them into standard lengths. All across Weyerhaeuser's Northwest empire, they turned the forest into Pick-up Stix.

There are forests on the rainy side of the Cascade Range where the best way you can walk is on the trunks of fallen trees. Some of them are thicker through than you are tall. They make a random pathway through devil's club and thimbleberry, one to another and another, leading you nowhere except to more trunks with upthrust roots, more standing moss-coated stubs and skeletal snags, more big-leaf maples and western hemlocks and tall Douglas firs. The bark of the big trees is pocked and charred, and most of them lean, already beginning their eventual fall. The filtered light is clear and deep. The only sound you hear is the stepping of your feet among ferns and seedling trees that grow out of softening sapwood. And when you climb down from the pathway of trunks, your feet sink into a yielding matrix of moss and needles and rotting wood—trees becoming earth, earth becoming trees, the forest falling and gathering itself, rising from the abundance of its dying.

Up on the landing the steel tower stands a hundred feet tall, a diesel yarder at its base with a reel of heavy cable. When we've set the chokers and scrammed out of the way, the rigging slinger sounds his whistle. The yarder roars, the chokers cinch, and two or three logs start stubbornly up the hill like things alive, plunging and rolling, snagging on stumps and lurching free, dragging and gouging the ground, then dangling in air as they approach the landing where they're deftly dropped in a neat deck for the waiting trucks. Everything goes to the landing—butt cuts ten feet through, mature saw logs, buckskin snags, measly pecker poles, even half-rotted slabs and splintered chunks. Nothing is wasted. The operation scours the hillside, as far as the cables can reach, and by the time we lower the tower and trundle along to a fresh show, only stumps and sticks and boughs are left, patches of sun-struck fern and sorrel, low, raw furrows in the barren ground.

"No, it ain't pretty," a man said to me once, "but it's the only way to harvest these trees. It don't pay to go in there for just a few." We were standing in the rainy morning outside the Weyerhaeuser time shack. His tin hat battered by years in the woods, a lunch pail and steel thermos of coffee in his hands, he spoke those words with a certainty I remember clearly—just as I remember what a good man he was, how he cussed beautifully and told fine stories and was friendly to a green choker setter, how he worked with an impossible appetite that left me panting and cussing unbeautifully behind him. I don't remember what I or someone else said that drew his response, or whether he was answering some doubt he himself had raised. I only recall the authority of his voice, the rain dripping from his tin hat, and the idling crummies waiting to carry us out the muddy roads from camp, out through the stripped hills to another day of work.

The voice that spoke those words is my voice too. It's in all of us—the voice of practicality and common sense, the voice that understands that ugly things are necessary. It's a voice that values getting a hard job done and making an honest living. It has behind it certain assumptions, certain ideas about progress, economy, and standard of living, and it has behind it the evidence of certain numbers, of payrolls and balance sheets, of rotation cycles and board footage. It is not a heartless voice. It has love for wife and children in it, a concern for their future. It has love for the work itself and the way of life that surrounds the work. And it has at least a tinge of regret for the forest, a sense of beauty and a sorrow at the violation of beauty.

I must have nodded, those years ago, when a good man spoke those words. I didn't argue—against his experience and certainty, I had only vague uneasiness. Now, I suppose, I would argue, but I know that arguing wouldn't change his mind, just as I know he wouldn't change mine. As he defined the issue, he saw it truly. Many of us define the issue differently now, and we think we see it truly, and all of us on every side have studies and numbers and ideas to support what we believe. All of us have evidence.

The best evidence, though, is not a number or an idea. The land itself is not a number or an idea, and the land has an argument to make. Turn off the highway, some rainy day in the Northwest, and drive deep into a national forest on the broad gravel roads and the narrow muddy roads. Drive in the rain through one of the great forests of Earth. Drive past the stands that are left, drive past the gentle fields of little trees and big stumps. Pass the yellow machines at rest, the gravel heaps and sections of culvert pipe, the steel drums here and there, a rusting piece of choker in the ditch. Drive until the country steepens around you, until you come to a sheer mountainside stripped of its trees—you will come to it—where puke outs have spewed stone rubble across the road, where perhaps the road itself, its work accomplished, has begun to sag and slide.

Stand in the rainfall, look at the stumps, and try to imagine the forest. Imagine the great trees spiring skyward, imagine the creatures weaving their countless strands of energy into a living, shifting tapestry, from deep in the rooted soil through all the reaches of shaded light to the crowning twig tips with their green cones. The trees are gone. The creatures are gone. And the very genius of these hills, that gathered the rain and changing light of untold seasons, that grew and deepened as it brought forth a green and towering stillness—it too is leaving. It's washing down in gullies to a muddy stream.

◆

John Daniel, author of a collection of essays entitled The Trail Home *and two volumes of poetry,* Common Ground *and* All Things Touched by Wind, *is poetry editor for* Wilderness *magazine. He also wrote "Naming the New One," a poem that appears earlier in this collection.*

WILLIAM DEBUYS

❖ ❖ ❖ ❖ ❖

AERIAL RECONNAISSANCE

I sit near the back of the southwest-bound flight, beside a window. A burly Indian slides in next to me, barely squeezing between the armrests. He wears shades and a black T-shirt with the image of a silicone-chested bar dancer splayed across the front.

"Where you headed?" I ask him.

"Vegas," he says. "To catch the Dead. You?"

"San Diego," I say, leaving it at that, my purpose being still new and not easily explained.

An artificially tanned Anglo with rings on each hand the size of lug nuts takes the aisle seat. For all his bronzing he looks dangerously gray. "I hate takeoffs," he says, fastening his belt, and the gold chain around his neck flashes as he swallows.

"Yah, me, too," says the Indian amiably. He proceeds to describe how he just got out of the service and, taking off from London on the last leg home, the engine outside his window blew up. "Whoa man, good thing they have long runways in England 'cause we used every inch. I was thinking I was gonna die."

His story fails to relax Jewelry-Man, now the color of cement.

The plane fills quickly. Sombreroed tourists disentangle from their bags. A troupe of tall, black athletes in identical earphones and leather jackets fold themselves like mantises into their seats. A baby screams two rows ahead on the right. There is commotion in the back as a clot of polyestered real estate types claims a block of rows, guffawing loudly and fratlike: "Manny, gimme that mag. Looks like it's got dirty pictures." "Shut up, Ferdie, you're bothering the lady in front." "Really, lady, I'm just trying to keep these guys under control. If you don't amuse 'em, they tear up the seats."

A young couple sits in front of me. His eyes are only slightly less doelike than hers. A prim little man in a cheap suit fills out their row. He chatters at the seeming bride even before he settles. "It's just a really great day, isn't it?" he foams, and I think I hear in his smarmy greeting the lulling, sick cadence of an evangelist. I can see the side and back of his head, which is all but hairless, not from baldness but from an excess of barbering. Already he is telling the polite, compliant bride his six reasons why the new year we've just begun is the best in the history of mankind to be alive. One of the six reasons is the miracle of "instant travel," which only twelve people in the world really understand. He's one of them.

We taxi for miles, and the concertgoing Dead Head Puebloan next to me, who introduced himself as Lawrence, says, "Maybe we are driving to Arizona." Jewelry-Man, his face in a migraine wince, never opens his eyes, and the shorn evangelist prattles on: "Know why our opportunities are superior to any others in the history of the world? Because America . . ." Then the roar, acceleration, and up.

Pretty soon Jewelry-Man is feeling better. He gets the flight attendant to bring him a Bloody Mary and asks Lawrence what he plans to do now that he's out of the military. Lawrence says he gave it a lot of thought. When he got home from Europe, he worked on his old V-8, dual-carb Toronado until he got it to crank. Then he rolled on down to Coronado Auto Salvage in Albuquerque. He traded the clunker for $250 and spent the bundle on a set of golf clubs at the Pueblo's pro shop. Golf is pretty much where it's at at the Pueblo, he explains, because tribal members play free on the new course.

Jewelry-Man bypasses the subject of golf nirvana but allows as how he knows something about salvage yards, since he owns three and is on his way to buy a fourth. "Keep your eye on scrap," he says. "It's goin' through the roof." He takes a pull on his swizzle straw. "Scrap is gold."

We descend through smog to Phoenix, over houses in tight rows, over the ruined desert pitted with swimming pools, over gangrenous golf courses sucking their millions of gallons a day, over the blue junkie veins of aqueducts stretching to the horizon.

We land and Lawrence leaves to catch his connection to Vegas. A tall dyed blonde with a silken voice and no wedding ring takes his place. She wears a pink V-necked sweater, soft as peach fuzz, and no one can mistake that the only thing underneath is her own abundant self. As she shrugs and twists to settle in her seat, Jewelry-Man takes heart. By the time we are airborne, he has conquered his nausea and learned that she is a housecleaner from Palm Springs who takes off six weeks at this time every year just to travel. He travels a great deal too, he tells her. He is in the recycling business, a helluva growth industry. "The first million was easier than I thought it would be. The second was easier than that. . . ."

West from Phoenix the desert simplifies and, at this early hour, wears the colors and patterns that mapmakers use for its portrait. Rand McNally tan paints the unclothed plains, and *Geographic* green stipples the woodlands. Each bare mountain and range of hills casts its shadow in relief-map indigo, and lava flows reveal the same disordered swirls, sand dunes the same puffy circles, as one finds on an atlas plate. A sudden intense rectangle, green as rain forest and miles long on the side, betrays the alfalfa farm and well field of some lesser water duke. A full-scale replication of Timbuktu would have contrasted less with the vast enfolding desert, but as feats of transforming the earth go, this exclamatory island of verdure is mere foretaste. On the horizon not far ahead stretches the blue ribbon of the Colorado River and, beyond it, California, land of water kings and emperors.

The color of the formerly great Colorado must not slip by unnoticed: It is a *blue* ribbon, the same baby jumpsuit blue beloved by cartographers for rivers and creeks of all kinds. Its presence here is no less than an epitaph for the natural West. We look down from above and see a river no longer brown, as would befit a stream formerly as silt-laden as any on earth, nor still less red, which is what Juan de Oñate had in mind in 1604 when he called a side stem *Colorado*.

Today, assuredly, the river is blue, and so are the sprawling tepid lakes behind the monumental dams that block its canyons. The water mirrors the cloudless Southwestern sky while houseboaters putt-putt up the side canyons to drink and belch and jet skiers roar across its domesticated surface. Beneath them the earthen harvest of the immense eroding intermountain West settles invisibly, whole deltas in suspended transit behind the great white emboli of the dams, a series of geologic Ellis Islands, where immigrant grains of soil arrive and arrive and arrive, never departing.

The plane now crosses above the Colorado where the river exits its final canyon and pools behind the gleaming colonnaded works of Imperial Dam. Beside it, the self-proclaimed "resort" of Imperial Oasis shines with Airstream aluminum and RV sheet metal of every conceivable color.

Here at Imperial Dam is the end of a river and the beginning of a story.

When I first visited Imperial Dam, I drove up from the south across the Gila River and Yuma Proving Ground. It did not surprise me, crossing a low bridge, that the Gila, a lesser river, had no water. In the Southwest, a river—to be a river—need not carry water, only provide it for irrigation, which the Gila does generously to the ultimate drop. What surprised me was that the Gila had been plowed, a phenomenon that approached Homeric strangeness—like the sea shining red as wine or the great sailor Odysseus marching inland with an oar on his shoulder until he should come to a place where no one knew the oar's purpose. Here, the plowed river, as puzzling to me as an oar to an inland bedouin, may have had more to do in an immediate sense with floodway maintenance than with expiating sin or placating gods, but the sight of it still did not prepare me for misplacing the Colorado.

I knew I was close to the mighty Colorado, after crossing the bestirred desert of the proving ground, when I came to a series of green-water ditches in a marsh where blackbirds trilled. I drove along a short causeway and up a low ridge of sand expecting any second to see the great river of Wyoming, Colorado, and Utah, of the Grand Canyon itself, diminished but vibrant, spread across its plain. But at the top of the sand ridge the road turned south, and I marveled that even here, downstream of so much monumental plumbing, the muscular Colorado still forced highways and human plans to bend. On I drove several miles, ever southward, and saw no river nor any chance to turn west, where the river ought to be. Only slowly did I begin to suspect that the river had not forced the road from its logical path so much as, somehow, it had evaded me. I was traveling alone, a condition in which one entertains thoughts that do not occur in company. Had I crossed the river and missed it? Had I blacked out? Was I even now in a twilight of consciousness? Worse had happened in other times and places, and I had been on the road without rest since Show Low, nearly four hundred miles away.

Anxious to get my bearings, I pulled over where a dirt road met the highway, and there encountered a barrier and a sign proclaiming, "All American Canal, Property of Imperial Irrigation District." I got out of the car and heard the whispering suck of great waters moving fast. A hundred steps forward and I stood at the canal's concrete bank. At my feet ran the brawny, unimpeded flush of the mighty, canyon-carving River of the West.

Centuries of miles since sunrise to reach it, and now I realized that the stagnant marsh where blackbirds trembled with desire was the old main channel of the Colorado—and a mapmaker's lie. Atlases innumerable notwithstanding, the blue line of the Colorado reaches no saltwater outlet in the Gulf of California, nor has it done so meaningfully for decades except during rare periods of "natural disaster" when the raging Gila plays havoc with southern Arizona and spews its floodwaters past the reach of engineers. The base flow of the tamed Colorado flows by way of one aqueduct to Los Angeles and San Diego, by way of another to Phoenix and Tucson. It flows to the farms of greater Yuma by various siphons and canals. And most decisively and definitively it flows westward across the driest, hottest desert in the United States to the Imperial Valley and Salton Sink of southeastern California. It accomplishes this unlikely journey by way of its current main channel, the All American Canal, whose name provides full answer to anyone south of the border naive enough to wonder where the river went.

From the air there is no mystery. The green-water ditch, crowded on either side by a gauze of tamarisk, trickles down toward Yuma and the Mexican line. Terraces of cotton fields and mesquite woodlands shield it on either side from the great dun vastness of the desert. But what draws the eye is the perfect and unnatural geometry, delivered whole from the draftsman's triangle and S-curve, of the blue All American Canal branching gracefully from its lesser parent and arcing sinuously through gravel hills toward unseen destinations.

Our 737 follows. The canal snakes into a wilderness of sand—the Algodones Dunes, once a menace to travelers but today a noisy and ever-ravaged playground for the ORV and dirt bike tribe. The canal contours the shifting slopes under plumes of sand, twisting in long parabolic curves, blue on buff. For a time the waterway roughly parallels Interstate 5, the main highway from Yuma to San Diego, whose engineers—or their lunatic successors—conquered the capriciousness of the landscape by paving a great swath of the dune crest with asphalt, creating a parking lot large enough to be seen from space.

Past this congealed petrochemical rug, the dunes again swirl, and in their midst the canal divides, its smaller portion angling northward toward purple-black mountains, the larger sidling to the border, where it soon runs laser-straight as far as the eye can see. Now a haze lies on the land, a thickening murk of moisture, smoke, and dust, and through it, there emerges an apparition of monumental cultivation, checkerboard lines and quilted greens and yellows on a scale as large as the Texas plains, waist high in cotton, or endless Iowa, buried in corn. It is an agricultural sea capacious enough for as many amber waves of grain as would inundate half of Kansas or the Ukraine, field after field, square and rectangle, fallow and full, Nile green and bile green, ground glass and jade. The twill of crop rows runs here with the sun, there athwart, everywhere at different angles, each a new weave of shadow, dirt, and leaf.

This is the Imperial Valley, where the last waters of the Colorado River feed half a million acres of cropland and, by extension, the people of the United States. In its fields grow dozens of varieties of head lettuce, leaf lettuce, iceberg and romaine, carrots, artichokes, asparagus, beans, beets, broccoli, celery, cilantro, cucumbers, bok choy, eggplants, peppers, cabbages, and kale, collards, and cauliflower. But that's just a start. One must not omit the onions, garlic, parsnips and squash, potatoes and tomatoes, watermelons, muskmelons, honeydews, and cantaloupes, not to mention wheat, barley, sorghum, oil seeds, alfalfa, sweet corn and feed corn, sugar beets, nuts, dates, lemons, oranges, tangerines, and grapefruit, Sudan, Bermuda, and rye grasses, cotton and other fibers, nearly the entire complex of cultigens supporting North American civilization, as well as its animals, who are here represented by roughly a million sheep and feedlot cattle, plus dairy cows, swine, farmed catfish, and enough commercially tended bees to keep the organs of the plants and the air humming. Here, beyond the reach of frost and chill, the growing season is in a state of perpetual motion: disking, planting, irrigating, harvesting, disking, planting, and on again, restlessly and efficiently, thanks to armies of work-starved, brown-skinned pickers and packers, thanks to endless boxcars and truck caravans of fertilizer, pesticide, herbicide, and machinery. And water, *gracias a Dios*, that without which nothing can be, a great continental river delivering the equivalent of lakes, bays, and inland seas, all of it originating in distant lands with different climates, all making possible in this place the environmental semblance—from a seedling's point of view—of forty inches of annual rainfall, where less than five actually come from the sky. (And the farmer hardly welcomes those few natural inches, for they muddy roads, cause ditch banks to slough, and mar the perfection of his absolute control.) The result is the apotheosis of industrial agriculture: Here food is not grown so much as manufactured.

And farther to the north, shining placidly like an oval mirror to the sky, a mirror large enough to reflect the vanity of a powerful and prosperous nation, lies Salton Sea, the vast inland lake that receives the leachate and dross of those fields, just as the fields first receive in the Colorado's water the leachate and dross of countless other fields elsewhere in the quarter-billion-acre watershed. Selenium salts washed from Wyoming end their poisonous travels here, as do the progressively richer effluents of fields and towns in Colorado, Utah, New Mexico, Arizona, and Nevada, to say nothing of the raw sewage that flows north across the international boundary from Mexicali along the misnamed New River—such a spumy, fetid, viral broth as to disable an onlooker's appetite for weeks.

The desert basin beneath this droning jet, half food factory, half sump, is what the intermountain West boils down to—or leaches or evaporates or otherwise reduces to, the verb being variable though the process has never been, the process being as immutable as the law of gravity, which is in fact the only law its acolytes have not refashioned to their purpose.

Gravity decrees that in low places consequences collect, and here is the lowest of the low: poor Salton Sea, foul and maligned, its sometimes wildly fluctuating surface lying over two hundred feet below the level of the nearby Gulf of California and its unseen, toxic, and nacreous bottom still sixty feet deeper than that. This is the place, below in hazy view yet many hours and miles away by rental car and highway, that I have boarded this plane to explore.

I blame the trip on a photograph. The image, black and white, shows an empty, altogether abandoned swimming pool yawning like a gutted melon beneath its useless diving board. A solitary, drought-murdered palm stands guard in the minimal background, and the entire tableau is duplicated by reflection in the accumulated liquid filth at the bottom of the pool. This ruin, I learned, was part of the once-vaunted Salton Bay Yacht Club, chief jewel of a sprawling real estate promotion staged in vacant desert beside the Salton Sea. Its brochures, film clips, and other come-ons, replete with leggy, sun-bronzed models lounging beside this very pool, promised a Palm Springs lifestyle for people of ordinary means. It was to be the land of Summum Bonum—step right up and take a look:

Here's life without work, and golf forever! Year-round sunshine! Fishing, sailing, no urban congestion! Affordable greens fees, plus bingo, drinks, and dancing after dark! Never mind the goosefart stench of the water's edge or an entire river of Mexican sewage flowing up from the south. Never mind that lots were sold from airplanes and tents in a rush to grab the dollars of the guileless. Never mind that the money boys in this and every other development up and down the sea were ready at any second to turn off the irrigation of their make-believe and pull out, leaving yacht clubs, golf courses, and palm trees by the thousands to wither and die in the solar wind. Never mind that they did exactly that, as any fool with half an eye could have seen they would. Never mind, never mind. The train, my friend, is leaving the station. I've got another call. Do you want to get in on the ground floor or not? Buy one homesite for investment and another for yourself! The first will pay for the second. Just get out of the way and watch your money double, triple, quadruple! The future won't wait—I know you and the missus would like to be part of it.

The photograph completes the tale. There in the putrescent liquid at the bottom of the pool you can see what happened when the adman's dreamy appeals to ordinary greed and indolence turned belly-up. Suffice to say that the image of the pool—the sump within the sump at the end of the West—suggested that more rivers than one ended in the Salton Sink. Clearly, the Colorado subsided into nothingness there, but possibly another river did as well, a river of the spirit and of dreams, which are no less a part of the American West. This other river, I thought, might rise from notions, born centuries ago, of free land and westward migration; it might, flowing through time, change character as long rivers do, reflecting not the country from which it departed but the country in which endlessly it arrives and shedding along the way all connection to hoary ideas about labor and fair reward, about building things to last. Perhaps along the way its current might gradually metamorphose into something unknown and unforeseen at the headwaters, an honest-to-god New River, changed by Gold Rush, Hollywood, and postwar defense bonanzas, flowing onward through and past the frozen, face-lift smiles of Palm Springs, where kisses taste like margaritas and golf clubs rattle timelessly, past the diamonds and concha belts and the country clubs that smell faintly of disinfectant, and flowing ever onward down the eastward slope of San Gorgonio Pass, descending past the shacks of migrant crop pickers and unemployed Indians, down to the loneliest of deserts, pressing ever toward the mirage, barely out of reach, of the pool in the sun and the girl by the pool, her beckoning smile as bright as the white linen suit of the master of ceremonies, whose voice in your ear reminds you over and over that this deal, played right, is the only real estate jackpot you'll ever need; and his mesmeric chant sings you onward, palm trees swaying, toward the smiling, long-legged girl, toward the bar at the country club, where faces turn in welcome, toward the quiet house on the cul-de-sac with its wet bar, climate control, and carpets soft as beds, onward toward the promise—*deal again! fifty on black!*—of getting something for nothing, then doubling that.

All this, the photograph seemed to say, lay in the sump within a sump at the end of the West.

The plane has crossed the mountains and now descends toward San Diego. Joan Myers, a photographer I have known for years, will meet me at the airport. It was she who captured the image of the defunct and squalid pool, as well as scores of others no less expressive of corrosion, abuse, and abandonment.

By edict of the pilot, tray tables are put away and seatbacks returned to their full upright positions. Now I can see warships in the harbor. The plane lurches, buffeted by wind. Jewelry-Man now matches the putty color of the paneling of the aircraft. The glamorous housecleaner takes notice, and pity. She covers his white knuckles with elegant fingers and lavender false nails. The stricken junk dealer twitches with pain and pleasure.

In the row ahead the small, prim man still preaches to the seeming bride. I cannot make out his words, only the earnest and unctuous tone, the studied cadence of the televangelist, and I cannot help but picture him in the theater of a new and cavernous Baptist church, the nave not a nave but a soundstage equipped with spotlights, ceiling microphones, and camera boxes all set for Sunday broadcast.

We land and taxi. At last we stop. The prim man stands. "Now please tell me again," he smarms, "what was that pretty name of yours?"

"Joann," the bride replies.

"Now that's a real easy name for me to remember," he says, as though Joann's name were exotic like Svetlana or Clytemnestra.

"That's a real easy name for me to remember," he repeats, and now for the first time I can see his cocker spaniel eyes—earnest and guiltless and, ipso facto, depraved. "Joann is the name of the second girl I ever dated, and I only dated three." He leans forward and in a hushed voice confides, "I married the third."

Who now, that very third, appears smiling at his elbow amid the jostling, disembarking crowd, plump as a life jacket and her hair the same color. And the man goes on, "You know I really enjoyed talking to you and I dearly want to thank you for listening."

"My pleasure," the bride lies hopelessly.

"Well, and you understand these things," the small man says. "Not many do. You say to most people, 'Which will you take, $500,000 cash right here, right now, or a penny a day, doubled at the end, each day for a month?' And nine out of ten will take the cash up front. But how wrong, how shortsighted they are, because—and now you understand this as few people do—because that penny a day, doubled at the end, would be twenty-one million four hundred seventy-four thousand eight hundred thirty-six dollars and forty-six cents by the end of the month, I kid you not. That, Joann, is the power of compounding. Very few people understand it, but let it be your guide and your happiness will grow like the penny."

The small man jerks to attention and nods his head at Joann in a nearly Prussian salute, which he finishes with an actual wink. Then he strains to reach the overhead bin and hauls down a giant leather briefcase that shines like mahogany.

I realize I misjudged him from the start. He's not a huckster for salvation. What this man sells surpasses even that. His product is not mere afterlife but paradise, now, right here—start today, take the pledge, join the program. Give compounding a chance to work its magic, and with the right guide and these easily affordable materials, you too can enter the ranks of the elect.

The line of passengers is moving. Orange-headed wife before

him, the too-shorn, hope-spewing, dollar-down-and-forever-to-pay, all-American dream merchant sallies to the teeming city.

We're in southern California.

◆

William DeBuys's past work includes Enchantments and Exploitation: the Life and Hard Times of a New Mexico Mountain Range *and* River of Traps: a Village Life. *DeBuys is currently at work on a third book, entitled* Salt Dreams: Reflections from the Downstream West, *of which the essay collected here is the first chapter.*

ELLEN MELOY

◆ ◆ ◆ ◆ ◆

COMMUNIQUÉ FROM THE VORTEX
OF GRAVITY SPORTS

On a list of recalled products, Consumer Reports, *September 1990: " '90 Fleetwood Bounder motor home: TV set in overhead cabinet could fall on driver or front passenger."*

The morning sun, already burning an eighty-degree day, tops a cliff cut with fine strata of red rock and broken at its foot by emerald cottonwoods and a silt-gold river. I don a khaki uniform shirt, shorts, ninety-seven-cent hot pink thongs and, clipboard in hand, walk from the trailer to a boat ramp plunked down in nearly a million acres of sparsely inhabited desert. This is an act of courage. Courage to face the violation of isolation rather than the isolation itself, for I savor the remoteness and the rare times I'm alone on this muscular river in southern Utah, a precious ribbon of wild water between reservoirs and the suck holes of industry and agriculture.

Officially, I'm here to have my peace disturbed. Floaters must have a permit to run this stretch of river. During the peak season a ranger checks lottery-drawn launch dates and a short list of gear related to safety and environmental protection. The permit system allows the federal agency in charge to hold numbers of floaters to a maximum of about 10,000 a year, set in 1979, when use increased 250 percent in just three seasons. Each year since, the actual number of people down the river has hovered close to this ceiling, which the agency believes is the river's carrying capacity for a "quality wilderness experience." Socially, if not physically, however, "wilderness experience" seems to have become an illusion if not irrelevant. Right now I'm the volunteer ranger managing both the illusion and the irrelevance.

Most people accept the permit system as a panacea for the explosion in numbers of river runners and the consequences for a fragile riparian corridor. Others find regulation about as painless as an IRS audit. They see the Southwest as a region of federally neutered rivers where a person is no longer free to kill himself in a four-foot rubber ducky pulling an inner tube piled with beans, testosterone, and a small machete. Instead, some geek rangerette at the put-in asks to see his bilge pump.

The boat ramp is swarming with people and vehicles to be shuttled to the take-out. Someone's dog is throwing up what appear to be rabbit parts. I'm approached by a pickup driven by a man waving a spray nozzle and hose hooked to a large barrel of allegedly lethal chemicals. He's from county weed control, he says. Have I seen the loathsome pepperweed? Not a leaf, I lie.

Cheerfully I sign the permit of the outfitter who specializes in theme river trips—stress management seminars, outings for crystal fondlers or fingernail technicians from East Jesus, New Jersey, overcoming, at last, their irrational fear of Nature. Today's load is priests troubled by lapsed faith—pale, anxious, overweight fellows in the early stages of heatstroke. I also check gear and answer questions about bugs, snakes, scorpions, camps, rapids, and Indians (one side of the river is reservation land). Do I live here full-time? they ask. No, I respond, except for an occasional shift at the put-in, I'm on the river eight days out of sixteen, six months a year. Would I please call their mother in Provo to tell her they forgot to turn off the oven? Am I afraid of being alone when the ax murderer shows up? Did Ed Abbey live in that trailer over there?

Some rafts look as if they barely survived World War II. Others are outfitted with turbodynamic chrome-plated throw lines, heat-welded vinyl dry bags, cargo nets spun from the fibers of dew-fed arachnids from Borneo, horseshoes, volleyball sets, sauna tents, coffin-size coolers stuffed with sushi, a small fleet of squirt boats, whining packs of androgynous progeny who prefer to be at home fulfilling their needs electronically. All of this gear is color-coordinated with SPF 14 sunscreen and owned by business majors in Styrofoam pith helmets and Lycra body gloves, in which they were placed at birth. Once loaded their boats are pieces of personal architecture, stunning but nevertheless stuck on the sandbar six feet out from the boat ramp after a dramatic send-off.

Two commercial boatmen with platinum-blond buzz haircuts, Arnold Schwarzenegger bodies, neon green bicycle shorts, matching tank tops, and Day-Glo pink, insect-shaped sunglasses with lenses as luminescent as an Alaskan oil spill stand beside their rafts, arms folded across entirely hairless pectorals. Neither speaks; all communication consists of barely perceptible bicep movements. (This mute surfer look is new. The boatmen of a previous generation looked like anorexic ferrets—beards, missing teeth, a dagger on the life vest, ear-shattering, maniacal laughs as they slipped down the tongues of the wildest rapids.) "Trade you this clipboard for your sunglasses," I sweetly offer one of the Arnolds. His right bicep pops in boredom.

When check-ins are completed, I trudge wearily to the trailer, passing a group still in sleeping bags inside a crumbling log cabin, the remains of a ranch built nearly a hundred years ago. The doorway is strewn with beer cans; empty vodka bottles are perched on the end of each hand-hewn log. Unless it's raining and rangers take pity, people are discouraged from camping in this fragile ruin, so I reprimand them gently. "Good morning!" I say in my most sunshiny voice. "Sleep well? Did you check your scrotums for black widow spiders?"

At the trailer a radio dispatch alerts me to ten thousand gallons of crude oil spilled in a tributary upriver and headed my way. Also awaiting me is an extremely animated man whose shorts are unzipped. So absorbed is he in his mission, he neither notices nor cares that he is exposing his underwear (turquoise bikinis) to a federal agent.

He is from Germany and seeks the cactus, he says, a claret cup cactus. He pronounces it "cactoose" but speaks English well, with a charming mix of words. "I am engineer but botanical by hobby," he explains. His colleagues in Germany told him he would find claret cups in this area, but "these botany friends are so secret and convenient, so much pride, they do not tell me exactly where are the cactus." Right. Let's begin with the 400,000 acres on my left.

I explain that claret cup grow downriver but take him for a walk atop the mesas to admire the prickly pear cactoose. He worries about traveling on the reservation side of the river. "It is wonderful to talk to Indians?" he asks apprehensively. Yes indeed, I say. His fine blond hair stands on end, his eyes are as blue as the sky. How lovely to be lost in the American desert in search of a claret cup.

Day's end. I've sent today's recreational flotsam down the river. I've "applied the minimal bureaucratic constraints associated with rationing a scarce resource," as the manuals say, and I've melted into the greasewood, leaving everyone to float ranger free into his or her wilderness illusion. I've advanced German-American friendship, I've communicated with a bicep, and I've fended off a deadly assault by herbicides. Yet I'm much too weenie to be a ranger. Soon it will require a different breed: rangers trained in negative campsite-encounter negotiation, field liposuction, and the delicate art of chaperoning tasteful social events in exotic outdoor backdrops. After a day like this, I long to buy the Uranium Motel two counties south of here. No one will come there, I shriek desperately to myself, its name is like a leper.

Coyotes throw their songs from rim to rim across the river, and the breeze carries the heavy scent of heat on greasewood and salt cedar. Lizards chew quietly on my melon plants. I stroll down to the boat ramp, hoping to watch the nighthawks that feed there at dusk. Instead I find a small party of floaters—tomorrow's permittees, an excellence management seminar from Boulder, Colorado. These totally excellent people are standing in a circle, holding hands and wearing funny pointed hats. I won't ask to see their permit. I'm sure they have one.

◆

Ellen Meloy is the author of Raven's Exile: A Season on the Green River. Harper's, Outside, *and other journals have published her peculiar stories about aimless wanderings in her native West. Her work appeared in the anthology* Montana Spaces, *and she frequently contributes cartoons and essays to* Northern Lights. *She lives in Montana and southern Utah.*

DONALD SNOW

◆ ◆ ◆ ◆ ◆

ECOCIDE

*Very often the child comes into life after a struggle, and
we don't realize that he needs consolation and the arms
of a mother. We give him medication, hospitals, and high
technology instead. And we think it is good for the child—
only because we had the same experience years ago and
think it is usual.*

—Alice Miller

*The technological society will go on, turning its railroads
into space colonies, but it is doomed by its own success,
for if you live like an empire, you die like one. All of the
little peoples, whether Irish or Hopi, can only watch Tribe
and Empire play it out to the end.*

—William Irwin Thompson

Opening day, 4:00 A.M. The coffee perks in a cheap aluminum pot
on the Millers' gas range. John Miller and his boy Jimmy are still
pulling wool pants over their long johns when we arrive. The dogs,
a pair of winter-pelted beagles, are awake out back in the dark,
climbing up the wire mesh walls of their kennel like monkeys. They
know better than to howl right now. It's early spring, not autumn,
but John might take them anyway.

John and Jimmy aren't talking much, but they aren't the ones
who got up at 2:30. They live near the Seldom Seen Valley Mine,
up here in this dramatic oak and hickory country crisscrossed with
deer trails and river gorges. Their little house stands on a steep
hillside, well-tended and nicely dug in, snug on April mornings like

this one while the coffee brews and the anticipation builds to a deafening crescendo in a boy's ears. The mine where John works is less than a mile away. When the sky lightens, you can see the black hole of the portal from Jimmy's bedroom window—that maw of dread his dad disappears into five days a week. Just like my dad. But not this morning.

We have another job to do. We have to drive a dozen more miles yet, then climb down into the frothy gorge of Chest Creek and stake out a stretch to fish before some overwhelming tangle of bobber casters beats us to it. The coffee better hurry up, because by 5:00 we'll have missed our biggest chance of the season.

The opening of trout season in western Pennsylvania was not to be confused with actual fishing, at least not as we knew it in the West. Still, it was a fine pursuit which had to do as much with beating fishermen as it did with fooling fish. The streams were all stocked, and in those days nobody dreamed of catch-and-release fishing any more than he would hope to shoot and release grouse. The little lady back home was supposed to act pleased when The Men returned with fat creels all amess in brook trout. Television and magazines projected this pleasant little drama of the wild, and somehow we believed it. Since we knew the Millers, and the Millers knew the hot creeks, we were assured of many reeking creels.

Chest Creek was special because it was hard to reach and harder to fish. In April it ran full from snowmelt and the engorged springs that fed it from the ridge tops of the Alleghenies. It was known to be a pure stream, salvaged somehow from the acid mine drainage that had killed so many brooks and rivers nearby, and it carried its own population of tough, native trout who somehow managed to hang on despite the annual onslaughts of pale hatchery turkeys and their pale, turkeylike pursuers. I knew about these matters only vaguely, trusting my father and honest men like John Miller to know where to go. For hunters and anglers like us, disappointment and despoliation lurked around every bend. Look, it was 1961, before the protectors had emerged.

We parked on a ridge top along a skinny, potholed highway

that ran mostly coal trucks. We rigged up in the dark, set the dogs free, and started the scramble by flashlight down the steep, half-mile-long hillside. Jimmy and I surged on ahead with the dogs while our fathers, both nursing hangovers, trudged along behind.

I never had a lot to say to Jimmy Miller, preferring to admire him as an older boy and a good athlete, a starting guard on the Hastings Junior High basketball team. We both listened to the men for clues, but in the taciturn conversations between two miners we found ourselves virtually combing words with our ears. Characters in Hemingway seemed like blabbermouths by comparison with our fathers.

The season opened officially at daylight, so we had to wait along the banks, stamping our horrid rubber boots to stay warm and turning our hoods and collars up against a chilling sleet. John passed the thermos around, but he liked coffee bituminous black while I preferred great gobs of milk and sugar in my mother's weak brew.

I had a thing about rocks in the middle of streams then. I loved wading out to them, the big flat ones especially, and fishing all sides of the rocks. In my mind's eye I could see myself out there, a dark statue in the mist of a gray river, catching fish after fish as I slowly wheeled a clockwork 360 with my rod. The rock in the middle made me a fishing hero, a solitary legend in my own mind.

As soon as the sky began to lighten, we four split up. Jimmy took off downstream with the dogs, and if I knew Jimmy he'd fish three miles of creek before lunch. The two men disappeared into the upstream brush, leaving me to a nice flat rock hole in a wide stretch. I waded out and took my perch on the rock. So far, so good; no other anglers had crossed our trail.

I baited up with Christmas red salmon eggs, the caviar of the angling proletariat, and pinched on a pair of BB shot with my teeth. The men had said Chest Creek was stocked several weeks ago, leaving the trout with plenty of time to acclimate. By now they should have been nicely ensconced in the little niches that occurred everywhere along this tumbling stream. I began tossing in my baits with the confidence of a slam-dunk artist at an eight-foot hoop, but no strikes came. I kept casting and drifting, jigging and twitching as the slate gray water gradually differentiated from the air and I could see little beads of ice forming on my line. Still no strikes. This was not right. As the sky paled, I fished both sides of the rock, above it into a grand, broad hole, and below it where the two fast spills came together in a gentle feed-line V. Nothing. When the light finally rose enough to penetrate the water, I had my answer.

Every few minutes a trout flashed past near the surface, belly-up or spinning in the fish's slow, disoriented dance of death. At first I thought I was seeing old birch leaves tumble past, but then as the light rose I stopped fishing and started counting. By lunch, when we had all converged at our starting place, I had counted over two hundred dead or dying fish. John Miller's face was too ashen to be just cold. No one had caught a damn thing except the dogs, whose coats were flush with burrs. We spent a long time crawling up the hill after lunch and appeared at home a half day early. My dad said, "It's getting to where you don't want to go outside."

A few days later, the sports page in the Johnstown *Tribune-Democrat* carried the news in a well-hidden brief. Chest Creek had fallen victim to a spill of mine drainage in the headwaters. The fish and game people feared it would wipe out the trout for decades unless the source could be abated. There was no mention of the company responsible for this disaster. Meanwhile, anglers were advised to fish elsewhere. No one expressed outrage or even sadness over the death of Chest Creek. The editorial writer for the paper never mentioned it. Since no one else, including my father, said anything about it, I didn't either. I went to school those first weeks of trout season, and on weekends we found other creeks to fish. We stopped seeing the Millers.

We lived on a street of duplexes in a neighborhood where all the streets were named after trees. Joann Rice and her two daughters lived behind the wall of our half, numbered 529 Oak. Joann was the only divorcee I knew as a child; everyone on the block talked about her, not realizing that her life was the shape of things to come. Her brother Leonard Kaiser trapped animals in Africa and South

America and sold them to zoos all over the world. When Leonard pulled up in his plum-colored Lark, children would dash down to Joann's hoping he'd have his spider monkey Cheetah, or Shasta, the great cougar, on a leash. Leonard wore khaki shirts with epaulets and meant it.

The Dumeyers filled the duplex on the other side, but no one flocked when a Dumeyer pulled up. They were horticulturists, the only family around who had no use for a lawn. The elder Dumeyer, grandfather to three children about my age, had converted his and his son's yards into one enormous garden. A grape arbor spanned the brick patio just behind the houses; the rest of the garden was a riot of vegetable plants and flowers, as neatly kept as the rooms throughout the Dumeyer family duplex. Old Dudley's wife was already dead when we moved in next door, but photographs and memories of her seemed to linger palpably in the old man's house and garden. He kept apples in his cellar and learned to bake the pies she loved. If a boy was good enough, crotchety old Dudley might notice and take him down to the cellar, redolent with that cidery smell, for a crisp Northern Spy.

World War II was only ten years past when we moved into 529, and the Dumeyers, though American-born, maintained Old World views. They were visited some summers by relatives from Germany and Austria, and on many hot evenings in July the alley out back where we played was filled with the guttural ring of German mixed with chopped English. A gregarious family, they seemed to take in the whole neighborhood with their uncanny reach of hospitality, but there remained one ritual which Dudley performed in silent penance and into which no one was ever invited.

At the end of our block stood a synagogue left over from the days when our Hornerstown neighborhood had been mostly Jewish. No Jews lived anywhere near now, but the synagogue remained a place of worship. It was an antique building with running water but no automatic furnace. On winter mornings, when everyone but the milkman still slept, old Dudley would don his snow boots and trudge up the street to stoke the synagogue furnace with coal. During the week he kept the pipes from breaking, and on days of worship he would stoke the fire with an extra load of coal so that the building would be warm when the worshipers arrived. For these favors he accepted nothing and never spoke of his devotion. Every Sunday he attended services at the new Lutheran church on the corner of Goldie and Ash.

Goldie Street ended at Messenger, where the electric trolley ran. The trick was to invent an excuse designed to cover at least two hours away from home on a summer morning, and head across the tracks and over the riverbank below the lumberyard. You didn't want to do this a lot, though, because what you found when you visited the Conemaugh River was not the imagined primeval world of Leonard Kaiser but the stuff of nightmares.

Steel and coal built Johnstown, and steel and coal killed the two rivers that came together at a place downtown called the Point. No one seemed dismayed at that fact, either. Stony Creek and the Conemaugh, after all, were responsible for the floods that savaged this little city every few decades beginning in 1889. By the time we moved to town it was hard to tell who was showering revenge upon whom.

Thirty years later I had to visit again, the way landless people ache to feel roots and thus must visit. I thought about Chest Creek as I drove a rented car down the swirling pike into the Conemaugh River gorge, and when I saw the river and knew it had not changed, I felt my gut tighten with rage. It was no wonder Chest Creek died without a fight: For generations these people had watched the deaths of rivers. In hindsight, I saw that the wonder was not the lack of struggle, but the fact that Chest Creek had even made the news.

I walked the neighborhood again and saw that the Dumeyers had stopped gardening long ago and the gardens were planted back into useless lawn. The synagogue now stood empty and dark with its windows smashed. Numinous as this walk was through the cramped streets of my rootless childhood, I could not bring myself to walk down to the river to look over its steep, beveled concrete banks—those engineering marvels which the residents were told would stop floods "forever" but did not.

A month later, home again and stunned by my little adventure,

I woke up in the middle of a Monday night and wrote this into my journal:

And there we were, stunned at age five, sliding on our dungareed butts down the long, comical, concrete banks of the Conemaugh River, a river in form now only, a river biologically only in its distant past, about which we had not a single guess, not a gram of data, and we slid and slid, careless about getting back up and comprehending nothing except the joy and freedom of the slide. We were our own wild men then, and that was our moment neverending.

When we reached the bottom we found a new world, and a slippery one. The river's ancient rocks were done with their sighing now. They lay covered with a thick ocher skin, and they lay silent, the life in them plunged into something like a rock's unconscious. They were slippery, and we slipped, falling on our butts made white from the concrete slide, and now our butts were filthy yellow and we were suddenly slimy as salamanders. We had slid from a living world into a world of death, and when we thought to leave it was too late for us already. We stank of that death. It was on our hands and bodies and in the fibers of our clothes, and it would never wash out any more than those rocks would ever be cleansed again. We turned a few rocks, looking out of instinct for the living things children look for. We found nothing but slime beneath slime, all yellow, all as dead as dead can be, yet the river moved strangely as if still alive, the way living rivers move, past and past and beyond.

When we judged it time to crawl out, we faced the ordeal none of us had considered. We had to climb back up the concrete chutes, along the seams of our undoing, but now we carried the oily skins same as the rocks. We could not wipe the rubber soles of our sneakers smooth enough to grip the concrete slabs, so we found that we could not crawl straight up but had to traverse at a low angle, stopping to rest on the seams between the giant plates and holding on to whatever fibrous, tough weeds those were, planted in the cracks by God. We must have been climbing the south-facing bank, because I remember the waves of toaster heat radiating from the concrete, and the way the dry snap of the air above the cement seemed to magnify the stench we carried up from the river like other boys somewhere might carry fish.

I was the littlest on this expedition, and I remember stopping once far behind the others, my knuckles skinned and bleeding as I passed the midpoint, stopping in near panic and visualizing my tiny body rolling headlong back down the hot concrete slope and landing with a sick yellow splash in that river. I remember the moment when I quit fighting back the tears and just allowed them to fall, and the way they washed my face, and the taste of them mixed with the taste of that slime we brought up from the river. Then the anger I felt with myself and the others for leading me here, the anger that came in the realization that I did not have to come here, and never would again no matter who pushed me. I ran the rest of the way, not looking back or even thinking about it. I ran until my feet hit the level top, and the others were sitting up there waiting for me calmly, and they laughed in my tear-streaked face.

It was a biological river only in its past, and far away in that. Imagining it with fish and crawdads, and hellgrammites scampering beneath safe rocks, and mayflies landing and taking off from the surfaces of its long, willowy slicks is like imagining the universe of time traced by the faint light of a supernova. Someone suggests it took that light several million years to reach our eyes, and we are crushed. Someone suggests the Conemaugh River here at this junction with Stony Creek was once a place of villages and prosperity borrowed from the water and forest, a place where insects lived in the cool air above the river and no one had ever thought of concrete, and we are transported. Our feeling comes out like a soft hand to touch the river if we can, and we want to follow it and follow it, wading up its flow a million miles, upstream and into the clouds and clouds before those into the fossil clouds of the Conemaugh River, into the cool air above it back up in those distant, blue mountains, back into that haze we came from when our lips uttered wild thought, different songs, and we could feel. The feeling of all the world wrote out our faces then. And no one laughed into them when we emerged from any ordeal.

In the Yellowstone fire summer, the summer of 1988, watching hundreds of river miles in Montana heat up and then dry up in a drought which many believe was deepened through human agency, I went back again and again to my faded images of Chest Creek. I quit fishing by the middle of June, powdered my waders, and hung my rods above the workbench. When Montana's rivers can no longer be fished, we're fresh out of elsewheres. As I sat out the summer pecking at my keyboard and watching the sun pound our flowers into colorful, crisp raisinets, I wondered if those Chest Creek trout sought out shade or sunlight, cool or warm water, as they began to die. I wondered how it might be for us, facing similar circumstances, trapped in an atmosphere of poison. Like dedicated smokers, we have been warned but the warning has not altered our lives.

Writing in a June 1987 issue of *The New Yorker*, Barry Commoner asked a provocative question about environmental protection. He wondered, nearly two decades following Earth Day, what progress had been made in the national fight against water and air pollution. His answer, based upon extensive research into Environmental Protection Agency data, is most disturbing.

"The regulations mandated by the Clean Water Act," he writes, "and more than a hundred billion dollars spent to meet them, have failed to improve water quality in most rivers. The relatively few locations that have improved are more than canceled out by the locations that have deteriorated." Commoner bases this alarming contention on data for the five standard parameters which measure water pollution: fecal coliform, dissolved oxygen, nitrate, phosphorus, and suspended sediments. Surveys of four hundred locations on American rivers between 1972 and 1981 revealed no improvement at four-fifths of the sites. Lakes fared even worse: Only 2 percent of the total lake acreage surveyed for water quality showed any improvement at all over a ten-year period. Meanwhile, groundwater, which provides 50 percent of America's drinking water, has steadily and alarmingly deteriorated nationwide. The principal culprits are fertilizers, which leach into aquifers from Maine to California.

Air pollution improvements fared little better. Ozone and carbon monoxide decreased by about 15 percent between 1975 and 1985, but then leveled off. Carbon monoxide has recently begun to increase once again.

While sulfur dioxide emissions declined by 19 percent during the same period, most of the improvement had occurred by 1981. Levels now seem to remain constant despite conclusive evidence that acid rain has killed thousands of acres of American and Canadian forests, not to mention its effects in other countries. A 19 percent reduction clearly is not good enough.

The other contributor to acid rain, nitrogen oxide, has actually *increased* by 4 percent since passage of the Clean Air Act, and with the increase have come elevated levels of nitrates as a contributor to acid rain. Commoner concludes that "as the sulfur content of [acid] precipitation declined by 27 percent between 1964 and 1981 the nitrate content increased by 137 percent." The principal sources: coal-fired boilers and automobiles.

Commoner is careful to point out that America's dismal record at pollution control is not merely a failure of technology, yet an abiding faith in technology has played a major role in this national tragedy. In nearly every instance where pollution *control* technol-

233

ogies are applied as add-ons to existing sources—baghouses, scrubbers, catalytic converters—the reductions in pollutants have been negligible. Control technologies seem to maintain, not improve, the status quo. The real gains, Commoner writes, have come with source elimination, and these, few as they are, have been dramatic. He points to some impressive examples: The removal of lead from gasoline caused an 86 percent reduction in airborne lead emissions and a 37 percent decrease in lead levels in human blood over a ten-year period. The elimination of DDT, at least in the United States, caused levels to drop precipitously in the bodies of eagles, peregrines, and other raptors whose eggs were being decimated by the chemical. And the amounts of strontium 90 detected in milk and children's bones dropped to negligible traces once the United States and Soviet Union agreed to halt atmospheric testing of nuclear weapons.

Since the appearance of Commoner's startling essay, the worldwide debate over environmental pollution has shifted suddenly and dramatically. The discovery of the rapid deterioration of planetary ozone above Antarctica surprised even the scientific doomsayers. The summer of '88 prompted editorialists all over the world to begin speculating about the dawning of a new age of global warming, when agriculture and coastal zones may begin a steady and perhaps irreversible decline, threatening the very foundations of human survival. Lester Brown of the Worldwatch Institute observed that the 1980s were the first decade on record when worldwide food production no longer kept pace with consumption. Paul and Anne Ehrlich's prediction that rain forest destruction will trigger the loss of 20 percent of the earth's remaining plant and animal species by the turn of the century has led to widespread speculation about the abilities of industry to synthesize products formerly derived from "exotic" species, as if the rain forests existed only to serve civilization like some weird pharmaceutical laboratories. By the mid-1990s, people in every region of the country were expressing puzzlement, and not a little anxiety, over the bizarre mood swings of the weather. From the scorching summer of '88 to the polar opposite winter of '94, people were beginning to realize for themselves what scientists have been saying for two decades: global warming implies not just more heat, but climate shifts, with consequences that will be hard to predict. The margin of habitability may be growing dangerously slim.

Barry Commoner attributes the failure to curb pollution to a failure of political will, and he faults the national environmental community for "taking the soft political path" in an effort to compromise and appear reasonable in the face of impending disaster. The reformers have joined the conspiracy of inaction, he charges, and their own publications and announcements declare their reckless duplicity, apparently in an effort to recruit supporters under the illusion of progress which these groups have helped to shepherd along. Interestingly, Commoner's favorite *piñata* is the Conservation Foundation, whose former president, William Reilly, was then the administrator of EPA. The foundation's annual "State of the Environment" reports have routinely portrayed the 1970s and the '80s as decades of great progress; Commoner grouses that "[these reports] nearly match Ronald Reagan's optimism about the course of environmental improvement." But the facts, he says, prove otherwise.

Commoner's solution is plain enough, no matter how ludicrous it appears to nearly everyone. He says that the government must intervene forcefully in the development of "technologies of production" and stop leaving critical decisions about human environmental health to closed boardrooms full of *laissez-faire* marketeers. The intervention must include a willingness to declare certain technologies unacceptable. Thus, if fertilizer nitrates, which pollute groundwater, cannot be controlled—and they cannot—the government should ban them. If the petrochemical industry has become "the major threat to environmental quality"—because only about 1 percent of its profuse toxic waste is destroyed, the rest routinely being injected into aquifers—the chemical industry ought simply to be eliminated through government action.

Barry Commoner envisions an America without plastic but with a government capable of shutting down entire industries in the name of environmental protection. Lest this suggestion seem too radical to take seriously, we should ponder what is perhaps an even more outrageous notion: Lewis Mumford's vision of American cities devoid of automobiles, which he maintained had degraded our lives worse than anything else on the planet.

Commoner's analysis arrested me when I read it years ago, but I have never been comfortable with placing the blame on a simple failure of political will. There seems to be something much deeper going on here—something that reaches into patterns ingrained in our culture. How could it be that after all we have learned in the last generation about nature, pollution, and the environment, we continue to commit ecocide without seeming even to notice?

Deep Ecologists see the roots of the growing environmental crisis in our gradual abandonment of a more "primitive" state of consciousness in which people almost universally regarded nature as sacred. Their argument suggests that even had the technological means been available, people of such consciousness would have refrained from ecocide. Their spiritual orientation would have made it unthinkable. Modern, industrial consciousness, descended from the ideas of Descartes, Kant, and Newton and cheered along by modern religions—which sold away their ties to "primitive" practices of self-actualization while substituting a vision of totalitarian monotheism—did not hesitate over qualms about a sacred order in nature. After this particular fall from grace, whole societies could move toward a view of "the environment" as a joint supply depot and dump. Ecocide became normal, a simple trade-off for prosperity, and not even a particularly unfortunate tradeoff, since in an urban-industrial society, hardly anyone has any real contact with "nature," anyway. Those who decried ecocide seemed to show signs of "neo-tribalism," which in the midst of a capitalist industrial society is surely mental illness. Doubts would begin to emerge only when people came to realize that ecocide also meant suicide, that the technologies which brought us to this point probably could not save us.

Many Deep Ecologists thus view environmental recovery as coterminous with spiritual recovery, and those who can lead us back onto the path of recovery are essentially shamans who will help us rename and reclaim the sacred.

To a Deep Ecologist, the notion of simply enforcing greater

political will to defeat pollution is little more than pouring kerosene on the conflagration. It was the centralization of politics and the economy that got us into this mess in the first place, and we aren't about to get out of it simply by increasing the grip of centralized control. People don't need merely to be protected from industrial processes that harm them; they need new opportunities to dissociate themselves from industrial processes altogether. The harder path by far—to use Commoner's metaphor—is the path of cultural and spiritual realignment.

It's fascinating to me that during my lifetime that very path has led thousands of spiritual pilgrims into the nation's interior. This is perhaps the least understood imperative driving the late-twentieth-century "resettling" of the American West: the quest for a spiritual life, which in modern terms probably means the opportunity to link together livelihood, personal growth, and the appreciation of wild nature. As a sociological phenomenon, this new movement into the interior has the interesting feature of rekindling one of the East's oldest myths about the West, the myth of the "safety valve." Long in the domain of Western historians, the notion of the West-as-safety-valve may be worth looking at again:

Eastern capitalists, fearing the rise of organized labor in the nineteenth century, sought to disarm working class protest by selling the West. They advertised the West as a place of limitless horizon, limitless land, limitless possibilities for growth. Anyone disaffected with life or livelihood, anyone given to complaining, was encouraged to march West, take up the plow, "grow up with the country." To wit: the West was a great place to send troublemakers. To sweeten the dream, the promoters tried to convince the crushing proletariat, including the agricultural peasantry, if they were interested, that the West was no Great American Desert, but rather a burgeoning garden where, miraculously, "rain followed the plow." A few scientists claimed to have the data to prove it.

Today, the seekers still come, wave upon wave of them, only this time they carry very different dreams. To them, the New West is not a place of limitless *economic* opportunity, but of *spiritual* opportunity. Indeed, most realize that they face financial peril in places like Montana, Idaho, or New Mexico, but they come anyway, in the hope that they will reclaim the spiritual center of their lives. How? By living near wilderness; by floating wild rivers and hiking the backcountry; by feeling the living presence of grizzly bears and mountain lions, moose and wolves and elk—species that do not adapt well to urbanity; by skiing and cycling and paddling—the outdoor, physical challenges that reclaim the body, that bring the ecstasy of childhood back into the adult frame. And not to forget society, it is also critically important to the West's spiritual newcomers to be surrounded by others of their kind. In Missoula, Montana, and a few dozen other towns around the West—microcenters of intellectual life—the local newspapers are full of stories you just don't see elsewhere—stories about bears and logging, watershed protection and wilderness designation, "green" economics and the industry we have come to call "recreation," even as we miss the obvious play on words.

The West is now all about the re-creation of the American character through the claiming of both self and place, and in the American style it is not always a pleasing sight. In the early years of the conservation movement, there were societies of wealthy men who loved to dress up in buckskins and commune with nature by killing animals. They would rush off to week-long pup tent revivals in the Adirondacks and wallow in what they took for "nativism." Their spiritual progeny have now come West. They are severe white men with serious firepower; they are the chest-thumping deadly nimrods, who, having realized that most of the trophy animals were long ago shot out of Montana and Colorado, now visit sprawling private game farms where for a fee they can kill animals that would have made Boone and Crockett giddy. But alongside these sad hormonal throwbacks are thousands of others who don't need to kill in order to reclaim their sense of place, who have traveled to the interior to make a new start, to try to live more simply, to pay attention to nature, culture, and community. Though they are copious users of technology, they are not convinced that technology will save anything or anyone. They are increasingly skeptical that enhancing the powers of a centralized government can heal the land.

As irritated as I get with population growth and shopping malls, with crowded roads and rivers, with backcountry trails pounded to rocks and dust by mountain bikes, the HIV of mountain travel, with the suburbanization of the once-rural West, I have great empathy for the part of it all that is spiritual pilgrimage. I am a pilgrim, too.

As I have spent my adult years simultaneously fleeing and revisiting the ruins of nature I grew up in, I naturally travel again and again to the scenes and mindscapes of childhood, the only time in our lives when we seem to live in eternity. For many years I saw the ruined countryside and streams of my boyhood as something distinct and apart from the rest of my experience growing up. It did not occur to me, for example, that the drunks who vomited on the creaky wooden steps of the Hyde Hotel and Tavern near where I lived as an adolescent had anything at all to do with the ruining of the West Branch of the Susquehanna River which flowed below. There was nature sickened by what people had poured into it, and there were drunks sickened by what they had poured into themselves, and although both were tragic, I saw no way to connect them. Certainly, I saw no common source of this toxicity.

When I saw the blind cruelty of men afield, heaving carp or suckers they'd caught up onto the banks of decent rivers to die painfully in the sun, or when I saw them crushing the heads of wounded game animals with shotgun butts or boot heels, I turned away, afraid to face what I was seeing and desperately afraid of feeling, as I had been taught to fear feeling and had learned my lessons well. We hunted or fished the next place, moving on as the animals died away, somehow savoring the killing of the very things which brought us our greatest sense of the joy in living.

Having digested that much, it was easy next to enter into the silent sickness of ecological devastation, the failure to cry or object in any way when ecocide occurred, and with that failure came a clear and abrupt separation of the self from the observed, and that is the well-worn gateway into hell. It was for children and weaklings to be touched by ecocide, or beatings, or drunken abuse. Living in a steel town whose high school colors were black and blue, I was so quickly not a child.

When I went away to college and joined up with the bewhiskered crews who saw themselves as ecological campus warriors, I made sure to contribute my share to keeping the debate firmly from the neck up. Self-righteousness works best cerebrally, because it is the poor body, not the extravagant mind, that delivers most of the doubts. Trained as I was to obey, I could not doubt the methods or claims of our leaders, and my own blindness fed itself as I remained convinced that I had artfully broken every old pattern of my own upbringing and had liberated myself through an education I had not paid for.

I would have agreed with Commoner then: it is the business of the good guys to rout the bad guys, using whatever coercion is necessary and taking no hostages. And I would have agreed with the Deep Ecologists, too: Our harmony with the planet must lie somewhere in the past, someplace out where the faint drumbeats can be heard at a twilight we barely remember.

Only recently have I begun to see something else.

Down in the deepest core of the ubiquitous abuse and self-degradation we learn as infants lies the failure to accept responsibility, and it is that, not merely the cycle of abuse, which is passed on from generation to generation, from small businesses to large ones, from dreamers of the rules to the rulers themselves. The self, always a child, is the final refuge, but before we reach down to it, to bend long enough to see that clear, terrifying, loving reflection in our own polluted river, we can rush through a lifetime of correcting and confronting others.

We want someone else to manage the planet. We want the security of legislation to protect us. We have even learned to delegate clean-up to a string of government agencies, knowing all the while that they are bound to be the most impotent actors around—a group of cowardly lions who are reduced to whimpering when a little girl slaps their nose. We know deep in our hearts that our agents of government can be no more responsible than we are for the havoc wrought by technology and consumption. Our laws and our new agencies are mostly expressions of hope. As Barry Commoner tells us, the best we can expect of them so far is that they help us hold the line.

What the lives of many New Westerners seem to be saying is that there must be another way. It will be the defense of place, not merely the promulgation of abstract statutes and ever more abstract responses to statutes, that will bring about the healing. And as the healing comes, we will be its first reflections. Only when self and place have merged will we protect nature as diligently as we protect ourselves.

As I write this, the Exxon *Valdez* slowly breaks to pieces in Alaska's Prince William Sound. It has hit a reef and dumped a quarter of a million barrels of crude oil into one of the richest marine environments on earth. There is much more oil left in the hold, and the local fishermen, pessimistic to begin with, are expecting most of it to pour out, as well.

The media have already dubbed this an "accident" and "the worst oil spill in U.S. history." It has immediately taken on the tones of a major political and media event, the environmental nature of it, of course, playing second fiddle. For instance, ABC television is much more interested in what it means for George Bush's plan to drill the North Slope than what it means for salmon.

One of the first acts of the National Transportation Safety Board in investigating this catastrophe was to call for drug-testing of the tanker crew. Now today as the oil and the news reports spread, Exxon executives have suddenly gone mute, refusing to release statements until the NTSB can conduct an investigation. This, of course, is a legal maneuver; the company wants to create a united front as its best hope of building an unassailable defense against the charges of an oil-crazy population who will "demand answers" and hope somehow to assign blame. It should be easy; the five-hour emergency response time promised by Exxon when they were permitted to ship oil from the port of Valdez has now swelled to ninety-six hours with no effective reponse. The captain of the Valdez has a long record of DUIs. On the night of the crash he had illegally turned the ship over to his third mate and retired early to his cabin.

A lot of citizens will count the ruination of Prince William Sound as another of those inevitabilities—the price we pay, once again, for our blind consumption of the planet's past productivity. Nearly all of us will remain powerless and silent in resignation while attorneys file briefs and invoices. If you accept that seals are alive and therefore have souls, this could easily remind you of Bhopal.

In Japan, executives who found themselves in Exxon's position may very well maintain responsibility through the close of the investigation, then resign in shame and dishonor. They may disappear from public sight, perhaps following some code of religion as a kind of penance, doing hard, menial work along the way as they contemplated what it is in themselves that could have allowed such an atrocity to occur. The self-exiled executives may or may not ever return to corporate life; after all, they may find exile, simplicity, and self-examination to be much more satisfying and productive than any triumphs they could achieve through corporate control.

In my neighborhood, when I was five, there was an old man named Dumeyer, a German-American who spoke the language of his ancestors and attended a Christian church nearby. Every morning in winter he rose early to trudge up Oak Street in his heavy boots so that he could stoke the furnace of the synagogue with coal. He accepted nothing for this, neither money nor praise. You would have had to have lived next door to him, as we did, even to know what he chose as his morning work.

◆

One of two editors of Northern Lights *magazine, Don Snow was born in the mining camp of Hiawatha in Utah. He is an outdoors enthusiast and the father of a ten-year-old daughter named Tenly.*

BILL VAUGHN

◆　◆　◆　◆　◆

NOTES FROM THE SQUALOR ZONE

Less than a day after we moved into Dark Acres our red heeler crossed the cordon sanitaire dividing our place from the neighbor's, and beat up a chicken. By the time I rushed to the scene of the crime, Radish had fled into a barley field and the chicken was lurching around like the survivor of a farm implement demolition derby. The bird was bloodied and dazed but seemed to be functioning—as much as these genetically jerry-rigged dead ends could ever be said to function. No one in the trailer responded to my knock, so I left a note, collected my chagrined and penitent dog, and drove into town.

When I pulled off the county road that evening the Bunker brothers were waiting in my drive. One of them—Luke, I would soon learn—was cradling the chicken. Brother Rick looked on, arms folded.

"Yer dawg done bit off Pecker's butt hole," Luke announced. We all stared at Radish, who sampled the air apprehensively and, refusing to meet our gaze, slunk off on some trumped up canine excuse.

Pecker clucked.

"Geez, I, I'm really sorry about this," I stammered. "But I had to get to work this morning and the chicken seemed okay. What do you mean, bit off its butt hole?"

Luke hoisted the bird so we could examine its business end, which indeed looked gnawed. "He cain't hold in his turds no more."

"Is that important to a chicken?" I asked.

"It is to this one." Luke sniffed, a little haughtily, I thought. "Pecker is a *fightin'* chicken."

I noticed then that the eyes of the Bunker brothers were of a blue so washed the color resembled water which had only been *shown* the sky. And one of Rick's eyes was wobbling around, independent of its mate. Luke was wearing his flannel Kmart pajamas backward, and his shoes didn't match. I found out later through the neighborhood gossip that the Bunkers were from Arkansas or Missouri, and that they were raising several little boys in that rusty trailer across our dirt road without the benefit of a woman's touch. The children were the get of either two different moms or one mom with a drug problem who ran off. According to my source, the paternity was equally unclear.

"Well, look," I said, "if your chicken dies I'll buy you another." I deeply regretted this offer as soon as it escaped.

Rick's face lit up as if he'd found a Mickey Mantle rookie card in his mattress. "Pecker is a hundred-dollar chicken."

Since I'd already lost control of the situation, and it was my first confrontation with neighbors I expected to spend my golden years around, I didn't argue. Radish, as it turned out, had learned his lesson—he would never violate the chicken line again.

And Pecker would live to fight another day.

They say you can't go home again, but that's never stopped me from trying. The instant Century 21 showed us Dark Acres I knew my circle was complete. Here was an empire of knapweed-infested pastures, hideously tangled cottonwood breaks, and fetid sloughs packed with tires, tin cans, and rotten timbers bordered by a polluted river, a cattle ranch, and exactly the sort of squalid rural disarray I associate with my joyously chaotic childhood. Although the agent referred to the swamps as "wetlands" and offered the imperious raccoon we glimpsed dog-paddling in one as evidence of the "abundant wildlife" on the place, he refused to make eye contact. I already knew that Dark Acres languished in the shadow of Black Mountain all winter and that river fogs blocked what sun there was from October to April and that the pulp mill upwind routinely smote the air with olfactory events rivaling the result of force-feeding black beans and bratwurst to a coast-to-coast busload of Delta Sigma Phis.

I fell in love.

Mosquitoes were swirling through a warm drizzle when I made the agent an offer. Kitty, my wife, looked alarmed, as if I might actually be serious about this. When she saw that it was for real her hand went to her head; I figured she'd been bit. But the price was right. And we were desperate.

In truth, we'd been evicted, and had been living for some weeks in our second-story office downtown, paying ransom to a deaf woman and her belligerent bowling ball of a husband to stable our horses, taking Radish for walks on the roofs of the business district, and waking with the sweats at dawn when the first city trucks rattled our windows with their bellicose deliveries to the retailers on the street below. The utility company that owned the thousand acres where we'd rented a house and corrals had decided it was time to cash in on the Western population boom. I called the place Ranchito Maloso—Small, Bad Ranch—and sometimes pretended to be the current major dude in a long lineage of stern but fair dons who were stewards of the land and gods to the campesinos. However, the pastures and hillsides we had ridden across for years were now destined for the subdivider's block. Neither the don nor the good-intentioned patriots in the Valley of the Liberals where city jammed this doomed parcel against the mountains would be able to flex enough vote-muscle to save it.

Our pastoral cul-de-sac in the valley was, I see now, only a Super 8 on a road trip that began and ended in the same place. My true destination was a psychic theme park where I could again live in the simplicity, grace, anarchy, and kick-ass good times of my motherless and intermittently fatherless Huckleberry Finn youth along the backwaters of the Missouri. If I could just find this luminous geography again, maybe I could shuck the anger and wounded pride that seem to taint most adult lives like a fungus.

Everyone called the unzoned sprawl of shacks, hopeless farms, junk-yards, stock car tracks, and river bars where I'd grown up Rat Flats.

My father bought a house and three acres there for $6,000 in 1952 with a down payment he got from the air force for a sheet metal mishap in a bomber factory resulting in the loss of the last joint on his left pinkie. The house had once been the largest turkey coop in the county. It was, however, cool in the summer and warm in the winter, and there were many convenient ways in and out during the middle of the night. It's now surrounded by bankers' homes, cabin cruiser docks, and prissy little Rodeo Ranchettes sporting thorough-bred fencing and the silliest of all lawn ornaments, the white ceramic jockey.

The Rat Flats of my imagination and the Dark Acres of my reality are in fact part of the same Big-Dog-and-Trailer belt that surrounds most cities of any size in the West. Or call it the Squalor Zone—it lies like an unsavory sediment between the last residential neighborhoods of the metropolis with their safe houses, streetlamps, and curbs, and the true country of cattle, sheep, wheat, timber, and wilderness. The Squalor Zone, of course, is a suburb of sorts. Most of us commute to town for our livelihoods, it is true. But unlike in the suburbs of Ozzie and Harriet, the lingua franca out here is the wild and domestic animals that wander all through our hapless lives. Without them the freeholders would have absolutely nothing to talk to one another about.

Ranchito Maloso was the last taint of the Squalor Zone in the Valley of the Liberals. For years I had enjoyed the redolent sense of decay in the wind-battered barn, the collapsed fences, and the rodeo grounds whose topsoil had blown away exposing a hoof-punishing glacial scree. Although the six-bedroom show-off houses of rich California fugitives stared at our shack from their hillsides and creek-front vistas, on our thousand acres the jungle was taking over. Sway-backed plugs abandoned years before reached high into the feral orchards for the wormy McIntoshes that still ripened there. Unnat-urally brazen coyotes lapped at the irrigation water leaking from Ranchito's original pine conduits and, in broad daylight, cried for our dogs to join them in a run. A flock of brilliant, vulgar ravens accompanied by what appeared to be their pet chickadees flapped slowly from one end of the ranch to the other all day in a narcotic corvine dance that I began to interpret as a sign of unpleasant things to come.

In truth I was relieved to see Ranchito Maloso fade in my rearview mirror. Living there, my nerves had begun to frazzle. Maybe it was the increasing sense of being prodded from all sides, or because I had no real control over the deteriorating political conditions governing its fate, or maybe that fungus had finally whipped everything else into submission.

I even lost patience with the harmless neighborhood eccentrics who were beginning to stake an even stronger emotional claim to Ranchito Maloso than we could. There was a city councilman who liked to strip off his shirt and sit lotus-style in the wheat grass, screaming in that primal way apparently intended to persuade even timid men that he must be kicked in the teeth. There was a deranged white-haired Coventry gentleman who patrolled the fields with an oak walking stick and a hearty swagger, ferociously maintaining his English common law right to trespass as long as he wasn't harming anything, while the coven of mismatched dogs that accompanied him terrorized the pasture horses and assassinated all the ground vermin they could catch. And there was a jogger whose Afghans went berserk every evening in our corrals, snapping at our enraged equines while their mistress, wrapped in periwinkle Lycra, shrieked "Gretchen! Ambrosia! Courtney! Come!" This spectacle was usually followed by the promenade of the wealthiest man in the state, a self-made gazillionnaire who strode by our shack flanked by two body-guards and a lapdog so badly planned it resembled a muskrat that had been processed in a commercial dryer. This man, who bore an uncanny likeness to Muammar Qaddafi, had enraged the valley by erecting a Berlin Wall of spruce planks on the border between Ranchito Maloso and his estate to prevent pedestrians and joggers on the ranch road from peering across the creek into his nouveau riche domain.

Stabled in a confusion of outbuildings near our shack were some expensive horses whose owners had moved beyond eccentric. There was an Appaloosa mare named Booster, whose master fancied himself a circus man. He stood on her back while she struggled to make circles, her peripheral vision scanning the vicinity for something painful on which to deposit this witless drool. There was a pair of Arabians owned by the Girl Shrinks—dour psychologists specializing in substance abuse and sex therapy who barked orders to the other equestrians at Ranchito Maloso as if we were patients confined to the grounds. To me, their horses seemed neurotic in unnamed ways, as if they'd been trained according to the principles of Jung, Skinner, or k. d. lang.

I stopped smoking and started drinking. Occasionally in the winter when the traffic on the ranch road petered out I would start up an old pickup named The Kenny, put it in compound, and head off in the direction of the wilderness. After a ways I would open the driver's door and climb back into the bed while the truck chugged merrily along. Then, as if I were making a command performance on Booster, I would step up onto the roof and stand there, allowing the sharp mountain air and the astringent starlight to treat my disease.

Once I even thought: Maybe the Girl Shrinks could help.

I went over the edge the day I buried Slick. Fifteen years old, he'd been ailing for some time with the maladies only ancient dogs suffer. His back legs had stopped working, for one thing. We moved him from place to place with the Dog-o-Matic, a belt we invented that went around his belly and attached to a handle we could use to lift his butt off the floor. Radish was then a puppy fond of sitting on Slick's head, and latching onto his tongue and pulling it out as far as it would go. I selfishly refused to part with my old pal, who had shared so much of my adult life, but eventually I could no longer endure the harsh glare of people walking by who saw this decrepit, rummy-eyed warrior panting in the yard.

His heart was so strong it took two heavy doses to still its beat. When Slick died at last, quietly in my arms, the vet rose and with deft consideration walked soundlessly out the door. I had adopted Slick as a yearling when his addled mistress broke off with me and, as a final parry, threatened to put him in the pound. A springer-Labrador cross, he was as true and fine as a dog can be, and I mourned his death two weeks before it happened. It is said that when you point, an intelligent dog will look where you're pointing; a stupid one will look at your finger. Slick was a dog of such sweet disposition that when I pointed he looked in my face. Kitty and I, both weeping, wrapped him in his favorite blue blanket, removed his collar so we'd have something of his to touch, and laid him to rest in the flower garden grave I had dug. Then I got real drunk.

At midnight I staggered to the garden with a flashlight to say good-bye again. When the light lit his grave it wasn't marigolds I saw there but a flash of blue and the wide-eyed visage of old Slick himself. I screamed and fell back. Jesus H. Christ, I had buried him alive! I cried out for Kitty, who came running. As usual, she grasped the truth right away. "No, no, honey, it was Radish," she soothed. "Look, see his claw marks in the dirt? Radish missed Slick, that's all. Radish dug him up." When she managed to convince me that what she said was right, I let her put me to bed and deal with the grave. The next morning Slick was back in the earth, covered with rocks to keep our confused puppy at bay. After I could bring myself to think about him again I composed an obituary and sent it to people whose dogs Slick had fought, and to friends who had marveled at his enormous capacity for food. A favorite story was how the missing Slick was finally located one night by his howling from a Dempsey Dumpster. He had managed to jump into the thing, and had eaten his way through the offal to the bottom, where, too bloated to move, he simply laid down and called for help. We later buried a canister next to Slick's grave containing the ashes of a brindle cat named Laverne. A neighbor's pet when we lived in town, this was the only feline friend he ever made, and it seemed right that they should sleep together forever.

Just before we moved I was given an opportunity to make a final gesture in defense of what Ranchito Maloso had once been. On my last tour of the place I came upon a welter of party garbage dumped in a borrow pit. Judging by the contents—Big Mac Styrofoams, Coke and beer cans, cigarette butts, and movie stubs—I guessed teenagers on a road trip. There was also a Domino's Pizza carton on which was written the buyer's name and address. I immediately packaged this trash in a big box along with some astoundingly rancid food products found during cleaning in the back of our fridge, addressed it, pasted on a magazine tear sheet that said, "You May Already Be a Winner," and mailed it first class from the university post office. The note I included began: "Dear Dick Head— Since everyone knows your momma eats kitty litter we figured she might go for some of this." Then I angrily disassembled our corrals by ramming into them with The Kenny, and drove the posts and rails to our rented storage garage near the airport. Since these corrals were the last major item left to store, I was free at last to ponder what our next move might be.

The long and winding road from ground zero in the city to Dark Acres is marked first by paint, and later by blood. As you leave urban life behind, the roadkill on this two-lane blacktop changes from the random impetuous squirrel to an accelerating slaughter of rodents, reptiles, cats, and dogs and finally to skunks, pheasants, whitetails, and the occasional cow. People in the Squalor Zone just don't see nothin' wrong with lettin' critters run. Packs of collared dogs lope in the ditches on sex missions about which we can only guess. Although no one believes me, I once witnessed two bald eagles squabbling over a freshly whacked poodle. Horses commonly escape from their pens and pastures and, tossing their heads, trot down the asphalt in that giddy, stiff-jointed way, forcing frightened motorists onto the shoulders.

The smells change, too, as you travel this road. First there's the complicated mélange of car exhaust and fried food mixed with the cloy of Dumpsters. Farther out, winter and summer, stinging banks of wood and diesel smoke roll in waves across the blighted land. When you reach Dark Acres the inevitable sulfurs from the pulp mill blend with a fecund fishy rot from the river and powerful stenches from the Burn of the Day. Because this low-income precinct of trailers, shacks, and shabby modular homes is far enough from town to make those who enforce the civilizing influences of zoning and health regulations less than eager to drive out and do their duty, the denizens feel free to torch whatever they like, whenever they like. One day it might be the garbage pit behind the trailer, a discarded mattress, or a wrecked '69 Bonneville. Another day all the underbrush on their five-acre stake. Or for the best pyrotechnics: a pile of used tires, which hiss and snap and send fierce black funnels spiraling toward God. For sheer stink, however, nothing can match a week's supply of dirty Pampers smoldering in an oil barrel. Sometimes I close my eyes and breathe deeply of these smells, letting them conjure up pictures of the anarchy and incompetence in those parts of the third world I have seen. They make me feel good in the same way that ne'er-do-wells everywhere are pacified by watching disaster movies. That is, despite their wealth, fame, and power even the shakers and movers are surely marching in the direction of zero.

Except for an occasional silence so interstellar it lets you hear the course of your own blood through its tunnels, Dark Acres can be as noisy as town. First, there's a constant hum from the pulp mill that pauses only once a year when the boilers are shut down for maintenance. Then there's the whine of chain saws as the residents put up their stove wood or "clear" their land for pasture. And since Dark Acres is under one edge of the airport's landing pattern, the rumble of very close passenger engines rattles us a dozen times a day. From the north comes the firecracker pop of the trap and skeet club. And across the river behind the first ridge is a rifle range issuing a steady fusillade of small arms fire day and, lately, night. Although we've grown used to this Sarajevo serenade, Radish spent the first month huddled against our legs, and the horses paced their corrals like neurotics in a zoo. Now it takes extraordinary firepower to get our attention. I have heard buffalo guns over there, dynamite and the firing of clip after clip from some automatic rifle such as an Uzi. In and out of hunting season, however, it's the gunplay on our own lane that still makes us jump. We've laid bets on whether a particular gaggle of geese or flock of ducks will escape the Squalor Zone without being fired upon. The shotgun blasts and random cracks from .22s are commonplace enough to make me wonder: Must my neighbors poach to live, do they relish the illusion of self-sufficiency created by stealing from the common weal, or do they just like the noise?

At sunset, if the clouds have lifted, the mountains will occlude the sun, producing a glow that infuses the zone with a lilac cathedral light. It's then that you can see the Manx cats bent over holes in the grain fields, still and intent like little Jesuits at prayer. This is also when the whitetail move skittishly from foraging in these fields to the river and the brushy shelters they cram into all winter to preserve their body heat. They pause at the barbed wire, ears cocked; the adults jump over, the adolescents crawl through.

On our first voyages of discovery in these floodplains Radish and I came upon many little platforms twenty feet up in the canopy. They looked like tree houses for dwarves, but bow hunters had built them. Some of them were old and rotten, maybe indicating one of those father-to-son rites involving dark talk about manhood, whiskey, and manual transmissions. When I stumbled on the first dead buck, a broken arrow in its shoulder, I felt bad for his suffering, but in the end these herds wouldn't be degraded much by his loss. Besides, the scavengers needed to eat, too. After we found the second one that season and then a third, I wasn't so sanguine. Either these hunters were just lazy or incredibly bad shots or maybe bow hunting is just a bad way to hunt. My mind got made up when I found another one of these venison pincushions last season not a hundred yards from the house. And then I found a game path through the purple willow along the river that had been decorated with little red ribbons. Bow hunters call this "marking the blood trail," knowing that an injured animal will always hide itself along familiar routes while it waits to bleed to death. Hunters call this sport.

This last dead whitetail was incontrovertible evidence of the sort of trespassing we could no longer tolerate. The next day I bought a dozen bright red-and-white No Hunting or Trespassing signs at the office supply and mounted them from horseback on conspicuous trees. We had debated blanketing our horses with colors that made them look like fugitives from Rajneeshpuram but in the end simply turned them out into the back pastures, crossing our fingers and hoping our signs would save their hides from the killer monkeys above. But it was without surprise when I walked back one day during bow season to bring in the horses and happened to glance up into the larch on which I had nailed a notice. Perched there on a portable steel shelf was a hunter. He was dressed in camouflage fatigues and had smeared his face with camouflage makeup. He wore a camouflage hat and had donned camouflage boots. I admired his zeal.

"I see you," I called out in a singsong.

"What?" he whispered.

"I said, 'Get your goddamn ass out of my tree.' "

"What?"

"Here's the deal, dick head," I explained. "I'm going to the house for my chain saw, and if you're here when I get back I'm going to cut you down."

"Is this place posted now?" The innocence he feigned was energetic, I had to admit.

I tapped on my sign. "Do you read?"

When I got back with the saw my newest bestest friend was gone, and so was his perch.

A week after the attack on Pecker I crossed the chicken line with a six-pack of Mexican beer. I was greeted in the yard by three young boys. Although they'd just disembarked the bus after a long day at school, their clothes were impeccably clean and pressed. They knew who I was. "My name's Lefty," the smallest one announced in a voice that sounded like the Captain of the Lollipop Brigade. "But you can call me Foghorn."

The Bunker brothers emerged from the trailer, and we sat down in the yard to drink one while the boys changed clothes and set out on their chores.

After a while Luke belched loudly and put down his beer. "Think it's true what they say about beaners?"

"What's that?" I asked.

"That they piss in this stuff before they send it north?"

I drank again and thought for a second. "Yes. How's Pecker?"

"Fine. Want to see him?"

I followed them to the lot behind the trailer, and there indeed was the famous victim, in a large cage of his own. A dozen or so other fowl pecked at the floors of their cages as well, or wandered around loose. Although I wouldn't have a clue about what to look for in a fightin' chicken, these birds didn't seem all that tough.

"We been breedin' for two years now," Luke explained.

"What are you breeding for?" I asked.

He squinted at me through those washed-out eyes like I was soliciting for the Junior League. "For meanness."

"Huh. How do you do it?"

"Well, at first we just let 'em all go around and fuck anyone they wanted, but now we're real see-lective. Only Pecker, Cop, and Randy get to. They're the meanest."

I nodded. "You know, I don't think cockfighting is legal in this state."

They looked horrified. "It ain't?"

Finally, by noon on Labor Day the thermometer hit ninety for the first time that summer. I spent the morning working on an earth retainer I called the Whining Wall, built from bulbous river rocks. My long labor of love on this project was a big joke on the lane, but when it was done someday I would have a stone wall—these doubters wouldn't.

Later, Radish and I found a perfect log, pushed out on it into one of the sloughs, and coasted around aimlessly in exactly the same way I coasted around my slough when I was a kid. Water weeds reached up from the bed six feet down, and tiny black leeches attached themselves to my ankles before I splashed them away. Then, after a ride on Timer and the China Horse, our snappish, inseparable little quarter horse mares, Kitty and I grabbed our inner tubes and went off to the river.

Downstream from Dark Acres lies a long, skinny island owned by the state. When runoff in the spring floods this secret place, only the tops of the willows stand above the rush, flapping in the current as if waving for help. When the flood recedes, it leaves the island shiny with sand as scrubbed as anything found on the Sea of Cortés. In our alcove fringed by river brush, our wet legs frosted with sand, we felt as isolated from America as if we'd been put down on Mars. That is, until a Boeing shattered our seamless blue roof right over-head, the roar of its engines kicking up ripples and startling birds into flight. Radish winced and ran to sit between us, where I calmed him with an explanation of his exceptional canine value. As the plane passed with its gawking load of New Jersey chiropractors and Akron politicians, I shielded my eyes with my arm, a silly and involuntary habit developed after I read about frozen shitballs from one of these carriers raining down on the rubes below.

Exploring the island after another swim we came across one of those animal murder mysteries that once occupied whole weeks of my time when I was searching Rat Flats for adventure. There in the sand was the corpse of a black Nubian goat, and lying close by, the equally desiccated carcass of a great horned owl. Radish sniffed them carefully and looked at me to see if they were okay to eat. What had happened here? Had these beasts washed up on the island in separate events? Was the owl killed by something when it swooped down to scavenge the goat? Could the owl have killed the goat, then in turn been killed by something else? Why didn't the something else settle down for a nice big meal of goat and owl? Were these victims of a mad poisoner? Whew, where was Columbo when you needed him? We also found three headless dolls, a four-hundred-foot span of heavy industrial cable, a huge rock so perfectly squared it looked as if it had been quarried by a stonecutter, and four yellow rubber ducks.

I woke up at three that night with a sunburn and went for aspirin. I was alarmed to hear the faint strains of some tune floating from the river on the hot, heavy air. I got Radish, told Kitty to go back to sleep, and set off to find out what was going on. Our only neighbors on the river side of Dark Acres had moved into the Squalor Zone the same week we did. Although we'd never met them, and had heard not a peep from their digs in four years, we knew some-thing about them from the manner of their arrival. On the first day they graced their forty acres on the bluff with a trailer, of course; the second day there were two trailers; the third day two trailers, a propane tank, and a doghouse; the fourth day two trailers, a doghouse, a propane tank, and a corral with eight horses; the fifth day all this plus a fenced enclosure containing a dozen wrecked cars; on the sixth day there were two trailers, a doghouse, a propane tank, a corral with eight horses, a dozen wrecked cars, and a milk tanker stuck in the mud.

The music was much louder when we got to the river. It was "In My Room" by the Beach Boys, blaring from speakers set up by the trailers across the water. I sat down on the bank to listen, trying to extract the most out of the last good day of what had been a short, stingy summer. I could see wavering shadows thrown against the yard trees by a bonfire. There was a lot of good-natured whooping as well, and the growl of a truck being gunned. I just had to smile. Down below me the mossy water slid past on its way to the opposite ocean from the one that accepts the Missouri, but the sounds and smells and sights of Dark Acres on this close and starless night felt just like home.

•

Bill Vaughn designs books and advertising and is golfing the Lewis and Clark trail.

PART V

RITUALS

PAUL ZARZYSKI

◆ ◆ ◆ ◆ ◆

STAIRCASE

For Joe Podgurski

How can lovers of buckers lament
a favorite bronc down
and dying on timberline range
we glass for elk—meadow
he's pawed to a raw circle
around him like mool. What can we say
under this scant angle of Montana
half moon, when we wish the whole
universe would grieve
for one rodeo star, throwing all
his heart into each roll
and futile lunge for all fours—
first stand he learned
as a colt, gravity pulling less
against him.
    Like two helpless sailors
marooned with age and mourning
a familiar orca beached
in the storm's debris, we crutch
our feeble human frames
beneath the horse's weight and heave
each time he tries. The Rockies return
our holler in a salvo of shouts,
grandstand uproar

we hope will spring him
to his feet. We pack-in water, last-meal
grain and pellets. No way can we swallow easy
looking into the white of a single eye
sinking, giving in to red. No way
hunters can repent—can we take back the metal,
aimed or stray, sent through flesh.
   Riflefire
across this big-game state
echoes reports of 44 wars
from guerrilla worlds, the unarmed falling
fair prey as varmint, as target,
when killing comes
nonchalant. What's one shot more—mercy
or otherwise—one more animal soul
to this planetful of procreating shots
and souls?
   Yearlings gallop a kettledrum
roll along the rim. What I can say
in light of this violent world, I hold
silent: Staircase, number 12,
bucker who broke my partner's neck in '78
who flung me off 3 times
to hometown fans, I wanted this
life of ours—love for what hurt us most—
to last a full, eternal, 8 seconds more.

*Paul Zarzyski, a former bareback bronc rider, now works full
time writing and reciting poetry in both the literati and* lariati
*(Have Poems—Will Travel) arenas. He's published two collec-
tions,* The Make-Up of Ice *and* Roughstock Sonnets, *the latter
a collaboration with Western photographer Barbara Van Cleve.
Although he holds the title "The One and Only Polish-Hobo-
Rodeo-Poet of Flat Creek, Montana" (so far), his genuine claim
to fame is having studied with Richard Hugo.*

JIM HARRISON

◆　◆　◆　◆　◆

NESTING IN AIR

I think it was Santayana who noted that all people seem to have a secret religion hidden beneath, perhaps surrounding, their more public worship. Our consciousness paints our world. The obvious fact that there is no actual connection between our senses and the world around us is troubling indeed. The fact that the discomfort is there whether or not you wish to take responsibility for your perceptions is also troubling. With ten thousand rituals I paint time and mortality, not only to make them endurable but to give them the dimension, splendor, resonance, perhaps beauty, that I sense they deserve.

That said, we may return to earth and discover we like one rock better than another, and sometimes imbue rocks of certain shapes with religious significance. We are not far here from the cross and swastika. Land configurations have always drawn religious interpretations, and the impulse cannot be entirely discounted by the fungoid happenings around Sedona and Taos. We frequently choose to live in a place by inkling, intuition, and our dogs will follow the same process in choosing their best spots on our places.

I awake as a mammal, and it usually takes some time before I remember that I am a college graduate or a writer. "With all its eyes the creature world beholds the open," said Rilke. As my consciousness begins its paint job I frequently, but not always, go outside and bow to the six directions, mindful of the ironies involved. I don't mind if the gesture would appear absurd to someone else as I eventually have to die all by myself. After coffee I often do zazen for a while because most of what we think about never has happened, and probably won't. This culture-oriented brain foment is a part of consciousness I like to skip. I also say my own version of the Lord's Prayer just to cover the bases, as it were.

Of course bowing and prayer, even the verbless prayer of zazen, are a specific form of consciousness running counter to the time. Our time is a vast and anguished picture show, as have been all other times. Individually, we have always been like that very rare Brazilian bird that nests in air.

In the area of the food I eat, the consciousness and rituals become a tad esoteric, particularly when the food is wild in origin. Some of this I can trace to my youth up in the country. I am dark complected and tended to become chocolate brown in the warmer months. This and the fact that I had been blinded in one eye gave me a somewhat strange appearance. When we chose up sides to play cowboys and indians I always had to be the indian and get killed because of my appearance. I suppose to compensate for this I spent a great deal of time sneaking around in the woods, and still do for that matter. It's just fate, that's all. But what I remember was one afternoon when I was seven and cleaning a pail of bluegills I had caught, I felt bad because there were too many. My Dad misinterpreted my sadness and said, "If you feel so bad just tell them you're sorry." Surely this was an accident more than anything else, though my Dad had given me the works of Ernest Thompson Seton. Fifty years later I am still talking to any fish or game I have killed, or any fish and game I've received as a gift, often because someone else doesn't want the bother. The main part of these conversations (which can become real two-sided depending on mood) involves my imagining the lives, the *otherness* of the creature at hand. Maybe like so many rituals it is simply a gesture to allay fear, dread, guilt, whatever, though just the other day in Arizona I spoke at length to a road-killed roadrunner. I am also at the age where I no longer care if I'm nuts.

There are occasionally spooky aspects to this process. Eating bear meat tends to produce bear dreams. Last fall at a tavern in the Upper Peninsula of Michigan I was given a big chunk off the hindquarters of a black bear. I asked how the bear died, and the hunter said it had stood up with its paws on a deadfall and howled at him. This fact was quite troubling when I was talking to the meat that I certainly couldn't throw away.

RECIPE

Trim off all the fat, which tends to get rank. Cut in inch cubes, flour, brown in lard (the pig is a distant relative). For five pounds of meat I use a half cup of chopped garlic, a half cup of chopped fresh jalapeños, a half cup of ground chimayo chile (other ground chili depending on your taste), a few tablespoons of cumin, a few dried anchos, maybe one chipotle, and a pound of dried posole rather than nixtumal. Cook about three hours in a Dutch oven at 325°. Eat it and dream.

◆

Jim Harrison is a poet and novelist living in northern Michigan. His most recent book is Julip.

GEOFF O'GARA

◆ ◆ ◆ ◆ ◆

AMERICA EATS

When a Frederick Lewis Allen of the twenty-first century sits down to describe social customs of the 1990s, he will no doubt assemble video clips of Roseanne Barr wolfing beer and pretzels, and Robin Leach leering his way through the dining rooms of the rich and famous.

The audience will see TV people hurling one-liners over indifferent food on the TV tables, and whatever scent the viewer retained from reading M. F. K. Fisher's or Jim Harrison's descriptions of food and eating—I'm assuming the twenty-first century still reads—will be quickly deodorized by the flat, cultural fumigant of the tube.

Anyway, historians fifty years hence will have little interest in the way people eat, because food is less and less shaped by where we live, nor does it much shape how we live. The trillionth Big Mac doesn't tell us much about anybody.

We are luckier when we look in the other direction, back toward the supper tables of a few generations ago. Even then distinct regional styles of cooking and dining were slipping, thanks to refrigeration and the automobile. But our luck is in the way we view that past, because looking back at the 1930s we must rely mostly on words, and the imagination is allowed to do its imperfect work, taking suggestions from a tongue-in-cheek memoir of chuck wagon cuisine: "The cook, who is a sailor, never learned to cook."

These glimpses of 1930s sensibility, dug from the archives of the Federal Writers Project and the Farm Security Administration at the Library of Congress, have the effect of complicating, instead of simplifying, our understanding of the past. They require interpretation. Memoirs about the way people cooked and ate during the Depression tend toward the particular, instead of the national mean (or should I say mien?) sought by today's commercial mass media.

Nothing of what these essays tell us is any more true than what the Jetsons will see when they watch 1990s reruns, but it is more useful. The written word leaves you rummaging through your own memories, contributing your own embellishments while your senses turn inward. Television, sadly, is louder, brighter, more insistent, and better organized than our experiences and memory, and it asks nothing of us.

A few years ago, I found a fragmented collection of short essays about American eating habits that had been written for a federal agency by indigent writers in the 1930s—layabouts including the young Saul Bellow, Nelson Algren, and Richard Wright. The primary mission of the Federal Writers Project was a series of road guides (which I traveled with and wrote about during the 1980s), but the project also tackled things like a history of grazing, a lexicon of trade jargon, and "America Eats."

"Eats" was a wonderful idea but not easy to execute—and interrupted, in the end, by World War II. Memos among the different state offices of the Writers Project make it clear that everyone liked the idea but no one knew quite how to produce "an account of group eating as an important American social institution."

A memo from the Washington office showed that, then as well as now, the deskbound urbanites knew all about the West: "Mixed tradition but dominated by mining, cattle raising, and lumbering traditions; miners' banquets with champagne and other exotic items were earliest social gatherings; roundup barbecues and big game hunts came next—primarily male feasts; meat always most important part of feasts. . . . Wyoming's sportsmen's riots, mountain oyster feasts (when lambs are docked)."

Indignant memos fluttered back and forth from office to office. Wrote a Mrs. Florence Kerr, in the Works Progress Administration Office in Washington, D.C., to the director of the Writers Project:

"The Mississippi Project is incorrect in its belief that the eastern and northern states uniformly prefer sirloin steak while the South and West insist on T-bone cuts. . . .

"[Beef] Hearts are not popular because housewives do not know how to cook them. . . . This is a confidential report but will be loaned to us for our use for a short period."

Still, a book about how Americans feed themselves was a capital idea. The rituals of nourishment—from how you cook the lutefisk to where the minister sits at the table—tell us plenty about one another. As in most New Deal projects, there was a certain amount of "boondoggling"—silliness and time wasting—but from amid the gray piles of memos we find a few gems about life as it was and never will be again. An essay called "Women Stops the Meat from Breathing" came in from Mississippi. From the Rockies came notes about frying beaver tail, fake champagne, four-hour Basque feasts, and an early rendering of cowboy poetry, "Casey's Table D'Hote."

Throughout the West is the imprint of the old range cook. The things he accomplished under the spur of necessity have been made easier through modern advances and today offer taste sensations that have withstood the test of time. They are preserved in the ranch homes and featured in the romantic atmosphere of the dude ranches. Furthermore, they are godsends to the packer, hunter, fisherman, and Western outdoor man, who must face temporarily the problems of cooking that were everyday occurrences to the old-time cook.

Take son-of-a-bitch in a sack, for instance. That's what they called it before dainty lady dudes in jodhpurs made their appearance. Today, it's somewhat shamefacedly referred to as son-of-a-gun. Nevertheless, despite the change in name, it hasn't lost any of its old-time attraction. It's like the story J. Frank Dobie tells of the cow horse that was named Old Guts in the typically salty and descriptive manner of the cowboy. It seems that he had an internal structure that caused his entrails to rumble and churn when he struck a rough gait. This day, the cowboy was out riding with a particularly insistent governess. She wanted to know the horse's name and the cowboy wanted to change the subject. As usual, the woman won out, but the cowboy softened it up somewhat with characteristic chivalry. He told her the horse was named Old Bowels, but the horse rumbled on just the same. That's the way it is with son-of-a-bitch in a sack and its more substantial companion, son-of-a-bitch stew.

For son-of-a-bitch in a sack you take water, flour, sugar, salt, and baking powder and make a soft dough. Then you add raisins, dried apples, and suet. In the old days this mass was placed in a sack with space enough for apples to swell and dropped in a kettle of boiling water to cook for several hours. Today, it is merely steamed in a steamer. Either way, it's all the same, and when served with a sweet sauce made of water thickened with flour and sweetened with sugar plus a little cinnamon for flavor, it's quite a treat.

Son-of-a-bitch stew is a bit more complicated. This treat comes the evening a beef is butchered. You slice up a good supply of the leaf fat that is found around the stomach and place it in a Dutch oven. About fifteen slices of liver, a half inch thick, is added, along with the sweetbread found near the large intestine. Then the smallest intestine, which is always empty and is called the marrow gut, is sliced into pieces about three inches in length. The kidneys and the butcher stake are then sliced and added. The butcher stake is the thick part of the diaphragm where it fastens to the back. Salt and pepper are added, and it is all stirred together until nicely browned in the hot fat. When the lid comes off a rich odor is released that is a combination of clear, fresh fat mingled with the delicate odor of fried meat.

Among the rare foods of the West, rare because of trapping restrictions, but still a delicacy in the Rocky Mountain area, is fried beaver's tail. In the early days, before conservation, it was much more common.

The tail of the beaver is held over a fire by means of a stick, pincers, or even the hand. When the fat softens, the skin peels off like a banana skin. Any other method is exceedingly difficult because the skin is tough as shoe leather and hard to separate from the flesh by means of a knife.

When the fat is trimmed away, the tail may be rolled in flour and fried. When boiled, it is best pickled in vinegar in a manner similar to preparing pigs' feet.

THE INDIAN POTLATCH

Although customs differed somewhat when it came to feasting among the various tribes, a very common practice was observed in the giving of a potlatch. Fundamentally, the potlatch was a feast, usually given by some Indian of prominence, at which he gave away, along with the food, everything of value he possessed to the friends he had invited. But after giving his all, he in turn could visit any of the guests at a later day, and receive food, clothing, et cetera, in exchange for having had this party to his own potlatch. One historian describes it as a form of Indian insurance.

Idaho Indian potlatches featured deer, salmon, wapato, and camas as foods. The gifts were generally blankets, beads, dogs, et cetera. A northern Indian custom was for the chief giving the potlatch to invite others to bring their own gifts and put them in a common pool. The feasting, dancing, and singing lasted several days.

Disgusting as these orgies might appear at times to whites, historians agree that "through an exaggerated respect for wealth in use, even to breaking or destroying prized possessions, the Indian potlatch was not without its cultural value," so stated the Belgian missionary Father De Smet, in his *Life and Travels Among North American Indians*. The kindly father saw something more than just a wasteful orgy in the native festival and noticed the binding together of kinship groups, and that the potlatch was even used as a medium to repay debts.

The first day of the potlatch was often spent in prayer and passing the calumet or peace pipe around. The Indians prayed for plenty of bison, deer, bighorns (mountain sheep), and mountain goats. While their customs differed greatly in many respects, this potlatch often had as its incentive the recognized need of more food, and might be likened to the fertility rites practiced by natives of distant lands.

The second day of the potlatch was often given over to the medicine men for their shows, with the third and consecutive days going into the heavy feasting and dancing and singing.

TYPICAL BASQUE HOLIDAY MENUS

Before breakfast: a liquor of their own called Anisette
Breakfast (served with wine)
Tortilla de chorizo (Spanish sausage omelet) or Bacalao Frito con Vino (dry codfish seared or toasted on hot coals).
Lunch (served with wine)
Sopa de Pollo (chicken soup)
Ensalada Bejitabales (vegetable salad)
Potaje de Garbanoz (chick peas or chick beans from Mexico)
Lengua en Salsa de Pimento (tongue in red pepper sauce)
Tortilla de Kiskillas (shrimp in omelet)
Callos a la Viscaina (tripe)
Dessert
Compote de Peras con Vino (pears cooked in wine)
Colineta (rum cake or cake made with rum or Sherry wine)
Coffe Completo (coffee royal)
Second lunch (around 4:00 PM)
Chocolate con Churros (fritters)
Morcilas Frilos con Vino o Cervesa (blood sausages with wine or beer)
Dinner
Sopa de Chirlas (clam soup)

Mexcla de Ensalada (mixture of salad: tuna, eggs, lettuce, etc., with vinegar and oil, never mayonnaisse)

Angulas en Aceita (brood of eel, imported)

Arroz con Pollo (Spanish rice with chicken)

Calamares Rellenos en Su Tinta (stuffed squid or ink fish; a special Christmas dish)

Chuletas de Ternera con Pimentos Morrenes (veal cutlets in pimento sauce)

Patas de Cerdero en Salada de Chili (pigs' feet in chili sauce)

Caracoles (snails)

Polo (chicken)

Dessert

Salada de Nueces (nut dessert)

Flam casero (Basque custard)

Turron nougat (almond paste cookies shaped like rabbits or other animals, or even snakes)

Coffee Complete (Coffee Royal rest of night with dancing and singing)

The Basque dinner starts about 8:00 P.M. and lasts four hours, with an extra one thrown in for coffee drinking. They eat slowly because they believe in lots of loud, joyous conversation. They are by nature a happy people.

CASEY'S TABLE D'HOTE

Oh, them days on Red Hoss Mountain, when the skies
    wuz fair 'nd blue,
When the money flowed like likker, 'nd the folks wuz
    brave 'nd true!
When the nights wuz crisp 'nd balmy, 'nd the camp
    wuz all astir,
With the joints all throwed wide open 'nd no sheriff to
    demur!

Oh, them times on Red Hoss Mountain in the Rockies
   fur away,—
There's no sich place nor times like them as I kin find
   to-day!
What though the camp bez busted? I seem to see it
   still
A-lyin', like it loved it, on that big 'nd 'warty hill;
And I feel a sort of yearnin' 'nd a chockin' in my
   throat
When I think of Red Hoss Mountain 'nd of Casey's
   tabble dote!

Wal, yes; it's true I struck it rich, but that don't cut a
   show
When one is old 'nd feeble 'nd it's nigh his time to go;
The money that he's got in bonds or carries to invest
Don't figger with a codger who has lived a life out
   West;
Us old chaps like to set around, away from folks 'nd
   noise,
'Nd think about the sights we seen and things we done
   when boys;
The which is why I love to set 'nd think of them old
   days
When all us Western fellers got the Colorado craze,—
And that is why I love to set around all day 'nd gloat
On thoughts of Red Hoss Mountain 'nd of Casey's
   tabble dote.

This Casey wuz an Irishman, —you'd know it by his
   name
And by the facial features appertainin' to the same.
He'd lived in many places 'nd had done a thousand
   things,
From the noble art of actin' to the work of dealin'
   kings,

But, somehow, had n't caught on; so, driftin' with the
    rest,
He drifted for a fortune to the undeveloped West,
And he come to Red Hoss Mountain, when the little
    camp wuz new,
When the money flowed like likker, 'nd the folks wuz
    brave 'nd true;
And, havin' been a stewart on a Mississippi boat,
He opened up a caffy 'nd he run a tabble dote.

The bar wuz long 'nd rangy, with a mirror on the
    shelf,
'Nd a pistol, so that Casey, when required, could help
    himself;
Down underneath there wuz a row of bottled beer 'nd
    wine,
'Nd a kag of Burbun Whiskey of the run of '59;
Upon the walls wuz pictures of hosses 'nd of girls,—
Not much on dress, perhaps, but strong on records 'nd
    on curls!
The which had been identified with Casey in the
    past,—
The hosses 'nd the girls, I mean, —and both was
    mighty fast!
But all these fine attractions wuz of precious little note
By the side of what wuz offered at Casey's tabble dote.

There wuz half-a-dozen tables altogether in the place,
And the tax you had to pay upon your vittles wuz a
    shame
To patronize a robber, which this Casey wuz the same!
They said a case was robbery to tax for ary meal;
But Casey tended strictly to his biz, 'nd let 'em squeal;
And presently the boardin'-houses all began to bust,
While Casey kept on sawin' wood 'nd layin' in the
    dust;

And oncet a trav'lin editor from Denver City wrote
A piece back to his paper, puffin' Casey's tabble dote.

A tabble dote is different from orderin' aller cart;
In one case you git all there is, int' other, only part!
And Casey's tabble dote began in French, —as all
    begin,—
And Casey's ended with the same, which is to say,
    with "vin";
But in between wuz every kind of reptile, bird, 'nd
    beast,
The same like you can git in high-toned restauraws
    down east;
'Nd windin' up wuz cake or pie, with coffee demy
    tass,
Or, sometimes, floatin' Ireland in a soothin' kind of
    sass
That left a sort of pleasant ticklin' in a feller's throat,
'Nd made him hanker after more of Casey's tabble
    dote.

The very recollection of them puddin's 'nd them pies
Brings a yearnin' to my buzzum 'nd the water to my
    eyes;
'Nd seems like cookin' nowadays ain't what it used to
    be
In camp on Red Hoss Mountain in that year of '63;
But, maybe, it is better, 'nd maybe, I'm to blame,—
I'd like to be a-livin' in the mountains jest the same—
I'd like to live that life again when skies wuz fair 'nd
    blue,
When things wuz run wide open 'nd men wuz brave
    'nd true;
When brawny arms the flinty ribs of Red Hoss
    Mountain smote
For wherewithal to pay the price of Casey's tabble dote.

274

And you, O cherished brother, a-sleepin' 'way out
    West,
With Red Hoss Mountain huggin' you close to its
    lovin' breast,—
Oh, do you dream in your last sleep of how we used
    to do,
O' how we worked our little claims together, me 'nd
    you?
Why, when I saw you last a smile wuz restin' on your
    face,
Like you wuz glad to sleep forever in that lonely place;
And so you wuz, 'nd I'd be, too, if I wuz sleepin' so.
But, bein' how a brother's love ain't for the world to
    know,
Whenever I've this heartache 'nd this chockin' in my
    throat,
I lay it all to thinkin' of Casey's tabble dote.

A delicacy not to be found on any restaurant menu is smoked native or brook trout. Preparation of this *chef-d'-oeuvre* assumes an ample supply (from fifty to two hundred pounds) of freshly caught trout, since the time and labor required in the operations would not warrant dealing with a picayune quantity. The place should be in the mountains where plenty of the right variety of willow for smoking may be secured—almost any lake will do. The next step is to build a conical tepee or wickiup of stout green boughs, covered with leaves. Then, from the nearby marshes or shores of the lake, loads of young willows are brought by canoe to the improvised smokehouse. When the fish have been suspended inside the structure, a subdued smoky fire of willow twigs is maintained for twenty-four hours—a task requiring energy, patience, and an optimism that is justified by the results. After the smoked trout are dressed with butter in a hot pan and cooked over glowing camp coals, the gourmand has only to take the final step and eat as heartily as he likes, while the rest of the catch can be conveniently shipped from the mountains to his home.

. . .

Mountain oysters, a seasonal by-product of sheepshearing, are now established in respectable circles as lamb fries. The prairie oyster, on the other hand, is even today eaten by a more limited number of gourmets, with the initiation no less timorous than that of their predecessors whose food was less a matter of choice. Cooked at branding fires, it is a product of the branding of calves. The prairie oysters are taken back to the ranch kitchens by devotees to their flavor, and their cooking is wholly a man's affair, from which most women are quite agreeable to banishing themselves.

After branding, it is the duty of the attending cowboy to turn each bull calf into a baby beef steer—the accomplishment of a certain dexterity and a razor-sharp knife. As the "oysters" are removed, they are tossed *over the fence* into a bucket and kept until the last calf is branded and the last bull calf is "altered."

At length the branding man climbs out of the corral, followed by the roper and flanker, all sweat streaked and grimy. As one, the three approach the bucket, a lusty hunger lighting their eyes. Then, as devotees to an exotic cult, each bends over and retrieves two oysters. These are tossed into the simmering bed of coals remaining from the branding fire.

The tidbits roasted, they are recovered by a sharpened stick, then split and salted. As soon as they are cool enough, they are eaten slowly, with the reverence of epicures seasoned by wild tastes. If, as is usually the case, the roper and flanker are from another ranch, the remaining oysters are divided equally. These will form the pièce de résistance of a stag dinner, when the female contingent of the household remembers, or is reminded, that she really must go over and have supper with her mother.

During the great days of Leadville, champagne was *the* drink. The miners and day laborers might guzzle beer and "red eye" whiskey as much as they wished, but the Carbonate Kings must splurge with "the drink of princes." Naturally, the supply of imported champagne was limited, so a shrewd Denver businessman hit upon a method of supplying the mining barons with an endless supply. He worked out a recipe for a "cider" composed of malt, brown sugar, and water, which he put up in old champagne bottles picked up in Leadville and Denver alleys and sold at exorbitant prices to the nouveaux riches, whose untrained palates never detected the difference.

Doc Rickert, who lives in Little Boulder Bain, and who blazed trails all over western Wyoming when he was a pioneer in the Forest Service, is an authority when it comes to fish chowder cooked in a Dutch oven. According to his instructions, you first dig a hole about two and one-half feet deep and thirty inches across. Build a timber fire in it. Let this burn for two hours, replenishing it with fuel now and then.

In the meantime, put bacon in a Dutch oven, then a layer of trout. If the fish are large, cut them up and split them in two. Next spread a layer of raw Irish potato, cubed, and then a layer of sliced onion. On top of that place another layer of fish, and repeat the layers in order until the vessel is filled. Add a small slice of salt pork. Cover the whole with water, and place over an open fire. Bring to a boil, then set off. As soon as the fire in the hole has become a mass of coals, shovel the coal out, except a layer of about three inches. Then add a cup of cold water to the chowder to check a sudden boil, place the lid on the Dutch oven, and lower the oven upon the bed of coals. Then bank the remaining coals on top and all around the oven. Cover with dirt and tramp down firmly. At the end of twenty-four hours, open the hole with care to prevent the ashes from getting into the oven. Lift up the lid, and a perfect concoction will be found.

Although the prairie dog (*Cynomys ludovicianus*) lives on the same diet as the rabbit, and the meat is similar in consistency, the name has, in a great measure, prevented the use of the animal for food. In the late 1890s Morace Quinby, a rancher of the Rampart Range foothill country north of Pueblo, conceived the brilliant idea of killing prairie dogs and shipping the dressed bodies to eastern markets as "mountain squirrels." Others adopted Quinby's idea, and during the next three years "mountain squirrel" was a prominent item on the menus of swank New York and Philadelphia hotels. Finally a buyer from one of these establishments came to Colorado to contract for increased shipments of "squirrel" meat and discovered what the ranchers were doing; fear of publicity kept the matter quiet, and no prosecution was brought, but no more "mountain squirrels" graced eastern tables.

♦

Geoffrey O'Gara is a producer for Wyoming Public Television and the author of A Long Road Home. *He is currently completing a book about Wyoming's Wind River Valley.*

MARK SPRAGG

◆ ◆ ◆ ◆ ◆

IN PRAISE OF HORSES

When I was a boy my father had horses, over a hundred of them, some of them rank, and I sat them well. He believed that horses were to use and that boys were nothing if not used and that by putting me with horses he was tending to some grand plan of economy.

When we did not have them in the mountains, packed with foodstuffs, duffels, or dudes, we worked them at the ranch. In the kidney-warm manure cake of the corrals, in the ridden to dust round corral. They milled, roiling like a vast pod of smallish whales, multicolored, snorting at their handicapped buoyancy, rolling their eyes white at me, a boy who had come to straddle their hearts.

I walked among them clumsily, not much used to walking, having spent so many hours attached to them. They moved away from me, parting, and in my wake would re-adhere into a whole of watchfulness. It was my job to remind them of the union of man and horse, to ride them, to ride the younger ones again and again until they became convinced that I was part of them and other men a part of me.

In the evenings I turned them out of the corrals and hazed them upstream in a tight valley and left them to fan and separate and feed. They grazed the rifts and slant of the young mountain range, their shod hooves striking sparks from the granite in the night, their senses sparked keenly to the dangers of the night.

In the mornings, before four in the morning, I gathered them, riding in the dark, hearing the bells put around the necks of the leaders of the different clans of this tribe of horses separate like the parts of a simple chord, spread wide, sounding in resonance their prehistoric energies. I brought them together thundering through downfall, scree, and fast water, impossibly up and down the steep and careless landscape, back to the corrals, where I would spend the day reviving their marriage to me.

I was a boy, and I believed deeply in the sightedness of horses. I believed that there was nothing that they did not witness. I believed that to have a horse between my legs, to extend my pulse and blood and energy to theirs enhanced my vision. Made of me a seer. I believed them to be the dappled, sorrel, roan, bay, black pupils in the eyes of God.

I worried over my love of them, I wondered at our connectedness. I looked for hazard through their eyes. I scented the earth and the wind that swirled across the earth with their wide nostrils. I felt the gravity in river water against my legs and stomach, my hooves skating for balance on the round and moss-covered rocks of streambeds. I nibbled at the world with their blunt, soft lips. I felt them drowsy between my legs, enraged, frightened, straining in their solid work. I felt the rare ones reach exhaustion and reach past it to drain a last reservoir of spirit, dammed with horse pride, and when it was drained I felt them reach again and use its muddy bottom to fuel themselves, and once sat a horse that trembled and staggered and had no more to give. An animal who had come to the bedrock of himself. He fell, and I fell with him. I held his head on my knees and laid the side of my face against his flat forehead and wept and whispered to him that my life was draining into his and that I knew it was not enough. And yet, I emptied myself into him. I prayed aloud for the strength to lift and carry him to safety. The night blurred our peripheries and brought us close to death, and still I chanted my whispered prayers for union. In early light we got to our feet and cautiously through the trees to home, where I vowed never to extend my stamina past my adolescent strength.

On days out of the mountains, at midday, with the sun hotly at me, I would slump in the shade close to the noise and smell of them and reconstruct a fantasy that made me happy. In this midday dream I was on a horse, on the back of a mixed blood, a mutt gently broken to saddle, unshod, a feral and unfettered thing; a horse with the heart of a flowering herb, windblown and glad to bloom at the peripheries of husbandry. I was a boy who rode wildly in his dreams. Startled when I woke from them that my body was so little haired, held upright by two thin legs.

In the afternoons I rode the colts. The young ones who could be counted on to rupture into the air and to earth again, and again, twisting, grunting, screaming in their rage, bent on divorce from me. And when exhausted, finding me still part of them, would stand quivering, sweating their hot, sweet scent to further foment my intoxication with them. I took no pride in riding them down. It was simply the use we made of one another, and I felt smaller for their loss of recklessness.

A dozen times each summer, in the hot late part of the summer, I would ride a dark, sun-sleeked horse to a meadow above the ranch. A long, tight valley bordered by timber and bare rock mountain, the home of a smooth stream lost from view in the waist-deep grass and late wildflowers. Beside this stream I would strip us of clothes, saddle, boots, bridle and remount cleanly, my naked heels against naked ribs, my buttocks clenched on the warm, haired spine, and ride stiffly into the water.

On the short, straight stretches the animal walked warily, as though on the skulls of mice, belly-deep in the water, its hooves sucking at the graveled bottom. And in the bends, the water squeezed into a thick emerald green against green banks overhung with green grass we would have to swim. I would grip the tuft of hair at the nape of its mane and rise toward the sun, slowly towed as the animal momentarily fell away from me, cooling in the water, lightly connected by our heat only. Connected more vastly by a sense of movement past the heat that we could make.

At night my dreams had more grandeur than those I could muster in the sun. At night I lived on the back of a horse and fasted. I lay along its back, my mouth open in the rain, collecting water and ozone. I slept draped forward on its neck, my arms hanging to the sides of its neck in loose embrace, my hands clenching in my sleep to grasp and hold the vision that grazed beneath me. I breathed into the coarse, dark mane, my lungs filled with the salted taste of horses.

In my sleep before dawn I would stand on its rump and urinate and afterward scream my naked, gaunt presence into the vault of the black, night sky, unsilhouetted; leaked into the lightless ether.

And in my dream I would ride this horse, oddly, often a pinto, dark-eyed, dark-nostriled, dark-stockinged with one white hoof, front left, slightly softer than the darker three, striking the earth in a tone a third lower, making music as it ran.

And I would know, sitting upright on this horse, my arms held high and wide, that when a horse is hot and lathered and running toward the curve of the earth all four feet, regardless of color, leave the ground at once and that in those suspended moments relaxed from effort the rider and ridden are afforded, for that instant, and the next and the next after that, the sight of God.

I am a boy no longer. I am a man now who works away from horses, who lives in a common blindness, seeing with his eyes only. But a man with a remembered glimpse of sightedness. And it is horses that I have to thank.

◆

Mark Spragg writes essays, screenplays, and poems from Wyoming, and if the wind did not blow, would have a greater body of work. As it is, he saves what he can, occasionally drives to South Dakota and Nebraska to retrieve what he can, and is careful to write on only one side of the paper so that what escapes him will be useful to others. There is much that escapes him.

JEANNE DIXON

◆ ◆ ◆ ◆ ◆

RIVER GIRLS

They were late this spring because of the cold. But every year when school lets out and the weather warms up, those pale young girls with stringy brown hair or blond, freckles maybe, their cotton-blend dresses hanging straight to the knee, those country girls with lunch box and thermos—Donna, Ardella, Delphina, and Joyce, and Tootie (if she's not too grown-up), dark-eyed Debbie, tall, shy Johanna with her braces and glasses—all those see-through girls the boys never notice, shed school clothes like snakeskins and take to the rivers on horseback.

Donna rides a pinto, a stocky black and white. Ardella has a common bay, Delphina a blaze-faced sorrel. Tootie's horse is part Belgian, black as soot at midnight. He pulled a loaded stone boat to victory in a pulling match at the Hamilton Creamery Picnic one year, "broke his wind" doing so, and was sold to a canner for dog food. Tootie's dad bought him back. "A darn good kid's horse," her dad said. "Slow and steady. Can't get him out of a trot." The man could not have guessed what wild currents the old horse would swim, what heights he would scramble to, how he'd pace like a hound to the hunt through the quivering light of the river lands.

Appaloosa, buckskin, mouse gray—they gather speed at the first scent of river water. And all the dogs for a mile around hear the clatter of hooves on the graveled lanes and bark to get out and go with them—fat black Labs that slept through the winter by the heater stove, water spaniels, springers, a wirehaired fox terrier, two red dachshunds, Babs (the postmistress's old Pomeranian with bulging eyes), Donna's German shepherd and its pup, Ardella's black poodle, Tootie's three-legged Airedale that got caught in a trap set for wolves. Ranchers' dogs, too, will run with the river girls. No master's voice can hold them.

The girls take shortcuts down to the Clark Fork, to the Musselshell, to the Yellowstone, Flathead, Whitefish, Blackfoot, Stillwater, Tongue. Montana rivers belong to the river girls. They don't care what they have to do to claim them. They will rip fence posts straight out of the ground, hold the barbed strands flat so the yelping, galloping horde can jump over. Landowners shoot at them—rock salt, buckshot—but no one can hit them. River girls will do what they want to do. Not even their mothers can stop them.

Tootie and her bunch belong to the Flathead. They tear across fields that used to hold steers or alfalfa, now contain trailer-house occupants. They ride at full gallop over new-seeded lawns, topple tubs of petunias, scatter trailer-house cats and trailer-house children in their rush to get down to the river. A trailer-house woman shakes a fist at them. "I know where you're going, you bad, bad girls! I know what you're up to!" But river girls are already gone, down through the buckbrush and feathery grasses, down through the silver-dimed aspens, down to the willows that shelter them, to the cottonwood trees that love them.

Fishermen don't love them.

Fishing the Flathead, Dutch Anderson and his slow-witted son heard the yelps of the dogs, the whinny and splashing of horses. Dutch dropped his fish pole and tackle, turned for home, and ran. Ever slow, the boy waited on the riverbank, astonished in place, as the girls came swimming through the thick green shade. River girls speak softly of this, how the boy reached out to catch them, how he shouted a foul obscenity at them, how Ruth Ann on Dark Hunter scooped up river water and threw it at the boy's face. Dutch and his wife still search the river lands, looking for him. All they've ever found is a mountain ash twisted in the shape of a fisherman, fishline ingrown in the bark of its branches.

Ruth Ann isn't with them anymore. She became a cheerleader, and Joyce has heard that she's gone all the way with three different members of the Flathead Braves. (Ardella *will* not believe this,

Delphina swears it is true!) Tootie will be the next to leave, though she would never say so. Her breasts have grown to the size of the small green apples on the tree by the homesteader's falling-down cabin. She's unbraided her hair and has combed it out in a kinky mass of marshgold or tansy. The last day of school, Pinky MacHarris asked if she'd go out with him when he got his new car, and she said no, not in ten million years.

She leads the way to the place they will go. She jumps the black Belgian from a white clay bank and into the river. The others follow. Smoothly as carousel horses, the sorrel, the pinto, the buckskin, the bay, go up and down, their legs reaching out underwater, drawing together, galloping underwater as they gallop on land, heads thrust out, ears forward, nostrils red with effort. The dogs form a V-shaped flotilla behind them: the Airedale, the spaniels, the brave little Pom—its fur fluffed out like dandelion puff keeps it afloat. Sun slants across the surface of the water like fire, white fire, flaming around them, subliming them all into gold.

This is what they are up to:

They swim to an island in the middle of the Flathead. They will come ashore on gravel banks or sandbars, sand thick with river mint and hoptoads. And they will turn the horses inward, follow a streambed through wolf willow, wild blue iris, pink roses, through sumac implicit—poison or true. The mothering trees watch over them. They are going to the Place of the Dragon.

They tether their horses to thin green saplings, and they run through the river sand to the edge of the deep blue pool edged in snake-grass and water lilies. All together, the girls will jump in, climb out, jump in. They dive for gold flakes at the bottom of the pool, gold that will always avoid their grasp. Showers of gold rise up around them until they are swimming through clouds of shimmering gold, suspended in water as clear as the vapors of heaven. They weave garlands for their necks, they sing what river girls sing. And they talk, they talk about the time when they will have bosoms, and will walk like Madonna, and sleep in the arms of the boys from their school. But they *won't* have babies, on this they're agreed. No matter how the boys bug them, they won't give in.

Think how the forest has fallen to silence. The smallest of

leaves will not tremble. Tootie is chosen this year, so she stands up, steps up to the edge of the pool. She dusts the sand off one shoulder and thigh, hipless, her long legs coltish and dancing. She glances back at the others, at the horses on their tethers, at the dogs beneath the trees, then she calls out across the pool and into the shadows of the cottonwood grove, and waits for the echoing answer.

"Dragon?"

. . . dragon, dragon, dragon . . .

"Are you home?"

. . . home, home, home . . .

The horses stand in the shade, hooves cocked, eyes closed. Even the dogs are quiet, hardly panting, hidden in the tall green grasses and rushes, waiting in the green leaves of willows.

"Tell me, Dragon, who will I love?"

. . . love, love, love . . .

Tootie gasps and covers her mouth with her hands.

Debbie whispers, "Don't be scared, go *on*, ask the question!"

Tootie calls out to the darkness moving through the trees. "Dragon, will anyone love me?"

. . . me, me, me . . .

"Dragon, will I marry?"

. . . marry, marry, marry . . .

At this, the girl falls over backward, laughing and laughing on the river sand. The river girls fall down beside her. They tease her and tickle her. They rub her breasts and her belly with willow leaves. They struggle to hold her, then let her go. She flees.

The girls chase after her, shrieking through the river brush, and the dogs jump up—the dachshunds, the Airedale, the German shepherd and its pup are barking and chasing her, too. The girls free the old Belgian from its tether, drop the halter rope, have to chase it through the undergrowth, weaving through the trees. They catch the old horse and lead him to the pool, lead him in. They climb on his back, bring him irises and roses to twine in his forelock and mane, white daisies for his tail, water lilies—both pink and white—and they want him to know how they love him, how they cherish him, how they're going to miss him, the big, black brute.

By the end of summer the Belgian will be put out to pasture, but only for the winter. He will always belong to the river girls—if not Tootie, to someone else, maybe Alice Starbuck, or Daphne Winters out on Fox Farm Road, maybe Kim or Cara will ride him next summer, maybe Starla.

Sometimes we see them on their run to the rivers, or watch them walk their horses across a high trestle—careful, setting each hoof down just so across the cross ties—or hear the yelping of the dogs late at night, sight the girls beneath the moon in autumn gardens, working their changes, doing what river girls do.

◆

Jeanne Dixon lives in the Rattlesnake Valley just north of Missoula. Her roots in Montana go back several generations and include homesteaders and cavalry men, district judges, farmers, and ranchers. When she was a river girl, she rode a bay quarter horse named Gypsy Melody, or an old rodeo horse whose ringbone disappeared at the call of the river each spring when he became Man-of-War. "River Girls" appeared in The Pushcart Prize *collection, XVI for 1991–1992.*

JEANNE DIXON

◆ ◆ ◆ ◆ ◆

BLUE WALTZ WITH COYOTES

Before my brother was born, Dad promised that if I didn't like the baby we could throw him to the coyotes. I didn't like him. Billy Lee was always wet, he smelled bad, and he got more than his share of attention. By the time he was four he hadn't improved. He still didn't talk. "He don't have to talk," Mom said. "He rolls those big brown eyes of his, and wraps you 'round his finger." Not me, he didn't. I held out for coyotes.

My dad had gone back on his word to the point that when we were ready to move away from the Two Medicine (where we had *plenty* of coyotes, coyotes that left bloody and mutilated sheep carcasses littered across the plains) and moved to a ranch near Columbia Falls, loading all our household belongings into an old '36 Dodge truck with a cattle rack to contain everything, Billy Lee went along.

And I didn't like him any better on the west side than I had on the eastern slope of the mountains. We still had plenty of coyotes. "Nope," Dad said, hunkering down and stroking his chin, the way he did when he had bad news to deliver, "you're growing up. Eight years old is too old to keep fretting about a little brother. Try to get along . . . find something else to occupy your mind."

Most of that summer I didn't have time to think about coyotes; I had to help Mom and neighbor women cook for farm crews. I pumped hundreds of buckets of water to carry to the house, hauled in that many armloads of firewood for the black iron Monarch. I caught fryers, chopped their heads off, scalded them, plucked them, drew them; the women fried them in sizzling fat in black iron skillets.

Heat swamped us: meat roasting, baking, stewing; vegetables at the boil; biscuits baking, or white bread, corn bread. And desserts: ice cream to crank in the maker, berries to pick for pies; cakes, gingerbread, cinnamon rolls, strudel rising in the swelter. Tempers flared. Big Anna Anderson, with her baby-fine hair, spattered glasses, and ragged apron always complaining. Bossy Krissi Olmstead, always scolding: "Whad ya go an' do it *that* way for? I told ya, and told ya . . . for gosh sakes!" She'd grab the peeler out of my hand, make potato peels fly like a January blizzard through the hot, unbearable steam of the kitchen. If we opened the door, flies swarmed in. Clouds of flies attacked us, biting our necks, arms, faces. They clamped themselves to our sticky skin like carpet.

While I worked in the kitchen, Billy Lee played in the shade with his dump trucks, or took his nap, or rode into town with Dad to pick up parts for the mower. At the end of haying, Anna Anderson gave him a nickel for being so good. She gave my mother and the other women each a big bottle of Blue Waltz perfume from Woolworth's, a heady concoction of floral scents blended with musk, possibly, or civet. It came in a thick bottle of deepest blue, a gold cap, glass wand and stopper. Mom said she didn't particularly care for it, that I was welcome to hers; but Anna's leaving me out the way she did stirred up hurt feelings. I thought long and deep about coyotes.

Up in the piney bluffs behind the woods where the aluminum plant would go in one day, coyotes yapped and howled. We had to put the chickens in at night, drive the lambs back into the shed. We found fresh tracks around the farm, but the coyotes seemed content to thrive on what they hunted in the red rock ledges, for they never bothered our stock. The day I got left out of the big perfume giveaway, I decided I'd go and bother them—Billy Lee included.

While Mom and Dad slept on a blanket under the tree, I told Billy Lee we could play a new game: Party. First we would have to dress up. I doused us both with Blue Waltz, then led him up the ladder to a storage place across from the haymow in the barn. In the musty dark, among spiders, mice, secret packets of dynamite, binder twine, tire chains rusting in a corner, *Rangeland Romance* (with pictures of grown-ups hugging and kissing), we hauled Mom's old rag bag from under a horse collar, opened it up. Long-legged underwear, an Oriental parasol, ostrich plume hat, a Queen Victoria bustled gown, strings of beads, corsets with stays, a whirl-away cape of yellow silk, lace-net petticoats that rustled when we held them up to study them. Billy Lee stuck an enormous brassiere on top of his head. It flopped over his ears like two huge cones. He tied it under his chin.

We laughed.

He skinnied out of his overalls, shirt, shoes, socks. Out of the wealth we had to choose from, he chose a gray shantung dress that looked like Anna Anderson, a multilayered lace-net petticoat over the dress, laddered silk stockings up his arms like long gloves, a string of glass beads that swung to his middle.

I pulled the Queen Victoria velvet over my jeans, pulled a floppy boned corset over the dress, donned the ostrich plume hat, and tied the yellow silk cape around my neck for final effect. We chose high-heeled pumps, mine with jeweled buckles, his with bows. Reeking of mothballs and the floral perfume, we climbed down the ladder, rung by rung. "Careful," I warned him, sweetly, "don't you fall," and we went through the barn, out the back where the cows came in, out into the long summer twilight. Sky and grass had turned the same shade of yellow as the cape on my shoulders. Yellow coulees rose around us, leading us away from the house, out toward the gully, the alkali plain, the long, dark shadow of the mountain. Coyotes. We lifted our skirts over cow pies, dragged them through harsh yellow grass, into the cool yellow wind.

I yapped, three quick barks, a long howl.

A coyote answered.

Billy Lee yapped.

We both yapped.

The breeze grew stronger, cooler, as we moved up the coulee. It caught our veils and billowed our skirts, rattled corset stays and beads, tugged at the yellow cape as we stumbled along in our awkward shoes. Billy Lee tripped and fell; the brassiere flopped one cone over his face. I laughed, loud. He got up, stickers in his foot, looked about to cry, laughed instead. We both shrieked with false laughter, and over the top of a coulee, looking down at us, we saw the silhouette of a coyote. He had drawn his lips back to fangs, he peered down at us through yellow slit eyes, and his sleek body looked rigid as a black paper cutout. My skin, lungs, guts turned to ice. "Come on," I said to Billy Lee, taking his stocking-clad arm, "he won't hurt us."

The coyote disappeared, and the earth cooled in the yellow wind. Billy Lee and I proceeded up the coulee, over the stony ridge, down into a boulder-strewn gully and an ancient streambed. Shadows stirred in the grass, a pheasant flew up, beating the air, squawking. Billy Lee stopped, turned to me. I said, "It's okay, everything's fine." And a coyote sprang out from behind a rock. It flew straight up into the air, jaws open, teeth flashing. It came down in the tussocks of grass, tail between its legs, yipping, yapping. Two more appeared on the ridgeline—the three dashed away. We were close, I thought, to what we had come for.

Down in the gully no air stirred.

Shades of unspeakable vicious things slid across the ground in big, black shapes. Yellow sky turned a yellow-gray; I took Billy Lee's stockinged hand. "Let's dance," I said, shrill with the knowledge of what I was doing. "Like grown-ups," I said.

He bowed deeply, cones flapping at his ears. I curtsied in my velvet, ostrich plume, my stays. Another coyote sprang up, up into the yellow air, all four legs splayed. It yapped, landed in the grass, bounded off, and we chased it. Three others came down from the ridge at the far end of the gully. They raced along in the twilight, a single swath of gray silk, their feet skimming the ground, nose to tail, attached like a single fur neckpiece women wore in those days to the movies, silent.

Billy Lee and I ducked behind a rock. As the line of coyotes rushed past us, we jumped out at them, yipping and barking. They whirled so fast their tails curved around them, and they sprang straight up, barking like our imitation of them. They laughed, chuckled, howled. We chased after them, our skirts held high, my yellow silk flaring out in the falling light. Billy Lee's petticoats lofting about him like sails. He tripped and fell.

One of the coyotes ran back to him.

"No!" I shouted, as if to a dog. "No, go away!"

The coyote pushed the fallen Billy Lee with her nose. Billy Lee got up. The coyote waited, patient, ears twitching forward and back like a mother dog with her pup. She lay down on the grass in front of him, head flat to the ground, ears down, tail swaying gently in the grass. "She likes you," I said. "She does, she really does like you."

Billy Lee put his feet back into the high-heeled pumps with bows, and he did a pirouette in his foolish dress. The coyote danced away, looked back over her shoulder, woofed, trotted ahead, stopped and looked back. She wanted us to go with her, and we went.

Once out of the gully, we danced on an alkali plain in moonlight, the white-poison ground baked hard as a dance floor. Reeking with perfume, we bowed to the coyotes, curtsied. We took hands and whirled around in an allemande-left, a do-si-do, in our too-big shoes, our silks and our plumes. We honored our corners, the watching coyotes, and we danced in the darkening winds as the wild creatures danced with us, coyotes darting in and out, weaving a mystery of wilderness, and easing the hatreds, the violence, all those hard forbidden thoughts that plague us—eased them as wild things always ease heartache.

♦

At present, Jeanne Dixon is working on a collection of short stories and essays. In addition to writing, she likes to garden and take long walks in the mountains with the dogs while her cat stays at home sniffing the flowers.

ELLEN MELOY

◆　◆　◆　◆　◆

PASSION PIT

They now lie half-collapsed at the edge of many Western towns in a dismal landscape of trash and weeds, an automotive Stonehenge. The River Vu Drive-in Theater in Green River, Utah, is disintegrating just east of town, waist-high in globemallow, which in the spring blankets the once carefully sculpted rows of humps in a sea of orange blossoms, nearly obliterating the tiny projection and ticket booths. The booths are built with smooth rectangles of brick, each hand-painted red, yellow, green, turquoise, or black, in no discernible pattern. The glassless windows tunnel the desert wind. Lizards scurry around the two remaining speaker posts, and pieces of scaffold have fallen behind the screen, pushing it forward in a *Poseidon Adventure* tilt. On one side of the green and pink marquee, stripped to the sockets of its neon, the word *melon* beckons tourists to a nearby fruit stand.

The Sunset, El Rancho, Prairie, Go West. The names hinted a decadent exoticism in the peculiar calligraphy of pop culture; *gh* was particularly disposable—the Twilite, Starlite, Sky Hi—and left room for neon accents, seductively flashing lightning bolts, star bursts, and blinking arrows.

Many drive-ins have disappeared under the tarmac of encroaching communities or changing real estate markets. But the survivors cater to the curious persistence of customs that have changed little since the first drive-in opened in Camden, New Jersey, in 1933.

The movie should be really lousy.

Cruise in slowly at dusk.

High-center your car on one of the humps.

The tinnier the sound system, the better. Clint Eastwood should sound as if he's speaking from the bottom of an algae-choked swimming pool. Better still, speakers that don't work at all.

Necking. Even after fifty years, bucket seats, the sexual revolution, and the Playboy channel, drive-ins are still "passion pits." Deter snoopers by parking far from the snack bar. Steam up those windows. Rock that Volvo.

The end of the automobile era brought the end of the drive-in. A pickup straddling two slots sideways, the back filled with pillows, lawn chairs, binoculars, Walkmen, and rhubarb pie, becomes the jet set of the Starlite Drive-in in Hamilton, Montana. Then up cruises a gargantuan RV. They back into a slot, open the rear window, and watch the movie while lying in bed.

Outsiders used to comment in Big Timber, Montana, "Too bad your drive-in burned down." To which locals responded, "It hasn't."

The ticket booth was an abandoned car parked at the entrance. The ticket seller sat at the passenger window and checked each carload—missing, of course, the three people suffocating in the trunk. Nonneckers raced to the only two speakers that worked. The town kids' Fords and Chevys easily high-centered on the humps. Amid the knapweed in the front row were two old car seats reserved for the night's four walk-in patrons.

The screen blew down often. Big Timber rivaled nearby Livingston as the Windiest Place in America. For a while, several large sections in the upper left corner disappeared completely, and remained that way. On a given night, planting Doris Day with a dreamy, quiver-lipped, out-of-focus Hollywood kiss, a large chunk of Rock Hudson's head floated off toward Billings, lost in the starry void of the Big Sky.

◆

Ellen Meloy, author of the essay "Communiqué from the Vortex of Gravity Sports," which appeared earlier in this collection, is the author of Raven's Exile: A Season on the Green River.

SHERYL NOETHE

◆　◆　◆　◆　◆

RINGFINGER

I was having lunch
with some ranchers.
I noticed no one was wearing a ring.
Louie, on my left, connected
with a live battery beneath the hood
of a truck once
and took his off forever.
Guy on my right jumped lightly
from a beam and hung himself,
ringfinger, to a nail,
full weight, three feet from the ground.
Man across the table had butcher's hands,
color of raw meat,
knuckles the size of walnuts.
One finger doesn't move at all.
"Ya reach into the machinery," he says, "and bang!"

Then I tell them how my ring
caught me up in a marriage
where I hung, afraid to fall,
for years.

Felt it deep up into my armpit, he said.

When it happened
we thought the ring
would tear our hearts out.

Sheryl Noethe came to the West from the schools of New York City to work in Salmon, Idaho, and marry a firefighter in Missoula, Montana, making Highway 93 her home.

She has had two collections of poetry published and runs the Mad Hatter reading series at the Missoula Museum of the Arts.

She is raising two bossy spaniels at the feet of Mt. Jumbo and has frequent and uninvited close encounters with the skunks that come to visit her yard.

JUDY BLUNT

◆ ◆ ◆ ◆ ◆

BREAKING CLEAN

I rarely go back to the ranch where I was born or to the neighboring land where I bore the fourth generation of a cattle dynasty. My people live where hardpan and sagebrush flats give way to the Missouri River Breaks, a country so harsh and wild and distant that it must grow its own replacements, as it grows its own food, or it will die. Hereford cattle grow slick and mean foraging along the cutbanks for greasewood shoots and buffalo grass. A two-hour trip over gumbo roads will take you to the lone main street of the nearest small town.

"Get tough," my father snapped in irritation as I dragged my feet at the edge of a two-acre potato field. He gave me a gunnysack and started me down the rows pulling the tough fanweed that towered over the potato plants. I was learning then the necessary lessons of weeds and seeds and blisters. My favorite story as a child was of how I fainted in the garden when I was eight. My mother had to pry my fingers from around the handle of the hoe, she said, and she also said I was stupid not to wear a hat in the sun. But she was proud. My granddad hooted with glee when he heard about it.

"She's a hell of a little worker," he said, shaking his head. I was a hell of a little worker from that day forward, and I learned to wear a hat.

I am sometimes amazed at my own children, their incredulous outrage if they are required to do the dishes twice in one week, their tender self-absorption with minor bumps and bruises. As a mom, I've had to teach myself to croon over thorn scratches, admire bloody baby teeth, and sponge the dirt from scraped shins. But in my mind, my mother's voice and that of her mother still compete for expression. "Oh for Christ's sake, you aren't hurt!" they're saying, and for a moment I struggle. For a moment I want to tell this new generation about my little brother calmly spitting out a palm full of tooth chips and wading back in to grab the biggest calf in the branding pen. I want to tell them how tough I was, falling asleep at the table with hands too sore to hold a fork, or about their grandmother, who cut off three fingers on the blades of a sickle mower and finished the field before she came in to get help. For a moment I'm terrified I'll slip and tell them to get tough.

Like my parents and grandparents, I was born and trained to live there. I could rope and ride and jockey a John Deere swather as well as my brothers, but being female, I also learned to bake bread and can vegetables and reserve my opinion when the men were talking. When a bachelor neighbor twice my age began courting me when I was sixteen, my parents were proud and hopeful. He and his father ran a good, tight spread with over a thousand head of cattle. They held a thirty-thousand-acre lease. They drove new Chevy pickups.

After supper one spring evening, my mother and I stood in the kitchen. She held her back stiff as her hands shot like pistons into the mound of bread dough on the counter. I stood tough beside her. On the porch, Jack had presented my father with a bottle of whiskey and was asking Dad's permission to marry me. I wanted her to grab my cold hand and tell me how to run. I wanted her to smooth the crumpled letter from the garbage can and read the praise of my high school principal. I wanted her to tell me what I could be.

She rounded the bread neatly and efficiently and began smoothing lard over the top, intent on her fingers as they tidied the loaves.

"He's a good man," she said finally.

. . .

In the seventh grade this year, my daughter has caught up with the culture shock and completed her transition from horse to bicycle, from boot-cut Levi's to acid-washed jeans. She delights me with her discoveries. Knowing little of slumber parties, roller skates, or packs of giggling girls, sometimes I'm more her peer than her parent. She writes, too; long, sentimental stories about lost puppies that find homes and loving two-parent families with adventurous daughters. Her characters are usually right back where they started, rescued and happy by the end of the story. She watches television now.

"Do you hate Daddy?" she asked once, from the depths of a divorced child's sadness.

"Your daddy," I replied, "is a good man."

In the manner of good ranchmen, my father and Jack squatted on their haunches on the porch facing each other. The whiskey bottle rested on the floor between them. Jack's good white shirt was buttoned painfully around his neck. Dad had pushed his Stetson back, and a white band of skin glowed above his dark face, smooth and strangely delicate. When I moved to the doorway, their conversation was shifting from weather and cattle to marriage. As Dad tilted back heavily on one heel to drink from the neck of the bottle, Jack looked down and began to plot our life with one finger in the dust on the floor.

"I been meaning to stop by . . . ," Jack said to the toe of his boot. He looked up to catch Dad's eye. Dad nodded and looked away.

"You figured a spot yet?" He spoke deliberately, weighing each word. Like all the big ranches out there, Jack's place had been pieced together from old homesteads and small farms turned back to grass.

"Morgan place has good buildings," Jack replied, holding Dad's gaze for a moment. He shifted the bottle to his lips and passed it back to Dad.

"Fair grass on the north end, but the meadows need work," Dad challenged. Jack shifted slightly to the left, glancing to the west through the screen door. The setting sun was balanced on the blue tips of the pines in the distance. He worked at the stiffness of his collar, leaving gray smudges of dust along his throat. Settling back, he spoke with a touch of defiance.

"If a person worked it right . . ." Then his eyes found his boots again. He held his head rigid, waiting.

Dad smoothed one hand along his jaw as if in deep thought, and the two men squatted silently for several minutes. Then Dad drew a long breath and blew it out.

"Old Morgan used to get three cuttings on a rain year," he said at last. Jack's head rose, and he met my father's steady look.

"A person could make a go of it," he said, and Dad nodded slightly. I moved against the doorjamb. It was darker now, and the light from the kitchen threw my shadow across to the floorboards between them. My silhouette was long and thin, barely touching their boots on either side.

"A person could make a go of it," Jack repeated softly. Dad's shoulders lifted slightly and dropped in mock defeat. He placed a hand on each knee and pushed himself up, Jack rising beside him, and they shook hands, grinning. Twisting suddenly, Dad reached down and grabbed the whiskey. He held it high in a toast, then leaned forward and tapped Jack's chest with the neck of the bottle.

"And you, you cocky son of a bitch! Don't you try planting anything too early, understand?" They were still laughing when they entered the kitchen.

I talk to my father twice a year now, on Christmas and Father's Day. We talk about the yearling weights and the rain, or the lack of rain. My parents lost a daughter when I moved away, but they will have Jack forever. He is closer to them in spirit than I am in blood, and shares their bewilderment and anger at my rejection of their life. As the ultimate betrayal, I have taken Jack's sons, interrupting the perfect rites of passage. The move was hardest on the boys, for here they are only boys. At the ranch they were men in training, and they mourn this loss of prestige.

"I used to drive tractor for my dad," my eldest son relates to his friends now, and they scoff. "You're only eleven years old," they laugh, and he is frustrated to bitter tears. He will go back, that one. He will have to. But he will return an outsider, and his father knows this. The first son of the clan to cross the county line and survive will find it easier to leave a second time if he has to. If he spends his life there, he will still have memories of symphonies and tennis shoes and basketball. If he marries and has children, he will raise them knowing that, at least technically, boys can cry.

I stuck with the bargain sealed on my parents' porch for over twelve years, although my faith in martyrdom as a way of life dwindled. I collected children and stress-related disorders the way some of the women collected dress patterns and ceramic owls. It was hard to shine when all the good things had already been done. Dorothy crocheted tissue covers and made lampshades from Styrofoam egg cartons. Pearle looped thick, horrible rugs from rags and denim scraps. Helen gardened a half acre of land and raised two hundred turkeys in her spare time. And everyone attended the monthly meetings of the Near and Far Club to answer roll call with her favorite new recipe.

These were the successful ranchwomen who moved from barn to kitchen to field with patient, tireless steps. I kept up with the cycles of crops and seasons and moons, and I did it all well. I excelled. But I couldn't sleep. I quit eating. It wasn't enough.

I saved for three years and bought my typewriter from the Sears, Roebuck catalog. I typed the first line while the cardboard carton lay around it in pieces. I wrote in a cold sweat on long strips of freezer paper that emerged from the keys thick and rich with ink. At first I only wrote at night when the children and Jack slept, emptying myself onto the paper until I could lie down. Then I began writing during the day, when the men were working in the fields. The children ran brown and wild and happy. The garden gave birth and died with rotting produce fat under its vines. The community buzzed. Dorothy offered to teach me how to crochet.

One day Jack's father, furious because lunch for the hay crew was late, took my warm, green typewriter to the shop and killed it with a sledgehammer.

A prescribed distance of beige plush separated us. On a TV monitor nearby, zigzag lines distorted our images. Jack's face looked lean and hard. My face showed fear and exhaustion. The years were all there in black and white. Mike, our marriage counselor, stood behind the video camera adjusting the sound level. We were learning to communicate, Jack and I. We each held a sweaty slip of paper with a list of priority topics we had prepared for this day. Our job was to discuss them on camera. Next week we would watch our debate and learn what areas needed improvement. We talked by turns, neither allowed to interrupt the other, for three minutes on each topic.

Jack was indignant, bewildered by my topics. I, on the other hand, could have written his list myself. Somewhere in a dusty file drawer is a film of an emaciated, haggard woman hesitantly describing her needs and dreams to a tight-jawed man who twists his knuckles and shakes his head because he wants to interrupt her, and he can't. His expression shows that he doesn't know this woman; she's something he never bargained for. When it's over, they are both shaking and glad to get away.

"Jack," Mike once asked, "how often do you tell your wife you love her?"

"Oh, I've told her that before," he replied cautiously. I cut into the conversation from my corner of the ring.

"You only told me you love me once, and that was the day we were married," I said.

"Well," Jack said, injured and defensive, "I never took it back, did I?"

The break, when it came, was so swift and clean that I sometimes dream I went walking in the coulee behind the ranch house and emerged on the far side of the mountains. It's different here—not easier, but different. And it's enough.

◆

Judy Blunt spent her first thirty years in a Montana ranching community, leaving to enter the University of Montana in 1986. She received her Master of Fine Arts degree in 1994. Her book of poems, Not Quite Stone, *received the 1992 Merriam Frontier Award, and a collection of essays is forthcoming. She and her three children have reinvented the wheel, and now make their home in Missoula, Montana.*

SIMON J. ORTIZ

• ◆ ◆ ◆ ◆

THE PATRIOT AND THE EXILES

In the middle of March a Navajo helicopter gunner
arrived at the Albuquerque airport home from the war.
Balloons, raised flags, flying banners, yellow ribbons.
Television cameras, newspaper reporters, photographers.
All eager and anxious to hear a hero's brave story.
And family, friends, all having always loved him,
happy to see their son, brother, uncle, and father
returned safely home to be with them again.

After flying 9,000 miles, suddenly having to face
newspeople professionally interested in him for now
and willing to believe anything a hero should say,
he said he was embarrassed by all the showy fanfare.
And his joyful kin, tearfully holding tightly to him
as if afraid they would see him leaving home again.

The Special Operations U.S. Air Force Sergeant said
he mainly spent the war on secret missions at night,
flying special forces forays behind Iraqi lines.
And this is what the balloons and flags were for.
And this is what the newspeople came really for.
And this is what the praise for a patriot is for.

On topics for the television evening broadcast news,
the young Navajo from Gallup would give no details,

saying he was strictly restricted by military rules.
Although present to hear and report almost anything,
the news did not record a partiot's days of glory.
And again the news contrived its own heroic version.

In 1863, after fighting years for their homeland,
a beloved sacred way of life, and their sovereignty,
the Navajos were brutally driven to imprisonment.
Bosque Redondo, a fruitless, desolate unhappy place,
was their fate, surrounded by U.S. Army soldiers.
And having no choice, they begged and cried for home,
a return to freedom in the mountains and canyon lands.

After five years, the U.S. government finally realized
its failure and decided to release the exiled people.
Let go, they walked homeward to their beloved land.
Always faithful to a belief in their Creator Spirit,
which kept them steadfast to their own beloved lives,
these exiles were people who could only be their own.
And no news eagerly heard or told the dreadful story.

After four days of war, the young Navajo was a hero.
After years of exile, the Navajos were not heroes.
And no one waited for them with flags or yellow ribbons.
And no newspeople waited anxiously for their return.

Nevertheless, the people's kin waited for them.
Nevertheless, the people's land welcomed them again.
Nevertheless, the people's love was always there.
Nevertheless, these are the people who are Diné,
truer than patriots to community, culture, and belief
in love among all things and the Creator Spirit.
And these are Diné who would have all gathered
their son home, loving him always, always and again.

Simon Ortiz, poet, short fiction writer, essayist, and storyteller, is the author of Woven Stone, From Sand Creek, The People Shall Continue, *and the upcoming* After and Before the Lightning *and is the editor of the anthology* Speaking for the Generations: Native Essays for the Sake of the People and the Land, *which will be published in the fall of 1995. He wrote the narrative for "Surviving Columbus," a 1992 documentary about the Pueblo Indian struggle for their land, culture, and community broadcast by PBS.*

JUDY BLUNT

◆ ◆ ◆ ◆ ◆

LESSONS IN SILENCE

That first week of school the indoor air was sultry with held-over August heat and farm kids too recently reined in and washed up. I was tall for my age and sat toward the back, looking down a row of raw necks and fresh haircuts. The sound of a pickup on the country road lured us like a bird's song. When it shifted down for the corner, we went along with it, anticipating each rev and crank of gears— some neighbor going to town, checking cattle, returning a borrowed tool somewhere up the road. In the next second a familiar pattern broke and we came to full attention. Instead of swelling, then fading into distance, the noise grew steadily louder. Dust streamed through the open windows as a rust-colored pickup eased around the building to the east side and rattled to a stop by the front steps. The engine cut out, lugged a few times, and was still. Five heads lifted in the sudden quiet; five pairs of eyes fixed on our teacher's desk.

Mrs. Norby licked a gold foil star, tapped it into place, then squared the papers on her desk and rose to attend to this new business. I remember the tiny catch in her posture as she glanced out the window, not a motion or a movement exactly, but a slight drawing in as she smoothed her skirt. At the time I interpreted her sudden freezing as fear, and today, four hundred miles and twenty-seven years away from that moment, I believe my instinct was accurate. There was no reading her face as she left the classroom. I can think of nothing that would have kept the five of us from the front window when the door closed behind her.

My older brother Russ, myself, the twins Guy and Greta, and

a neighbor boy named Stevie made up the student population that year, filling four of the eight grades taught at our rural school. Standing in the shadow of the drapes, we could see outside without being seen. The battered red pickup was not one of ours. The driver's door opened with a stiff pop, and an old man eased slowly from behind the wheel. He stood with a red and black plaid cap in one hand as Mrs. Norby walked down the steps toward him. The cab rocked slightly to the passenger side as a woman got out and made her way around the dented nose of the pickup. At the steps she turned and produced a little boy from the shadow of her skirts, prodding him forward until he stood in front of her.

Mrs. Norby had her back to us, and through the window we could hear her sweet, modulated voice. The man spoke very politely in reply. "We didn't know the school had started," he said. His smile held as many gaps as teeth. The woman said nothing. Mrs. Norby spoke in her lecture voice, at ease now; there was nodding and smiling, a gentle laugh from the man. The boy turned to hide his face when Mrs. Norby bent over to talk to him, but when she straightened and held out her hand, he took it.

When the man raised his arm to put his cap back on, we flushed like grouse and were innocently at work by the time the second cloud of dust cleared and Mrs. Norby entered, towing a small, dark-eyed boy with a mop of black hair. His name was Forest Walker, and he was starting first grade. He lived with his grandparents, who were working for the Longs. These things she told us. The rest we saw in the formal tilt of her head, the blank smile, the way her hands cupped together at waist level. Our company manners appeared on cue. That he was an outsider goes without saying; we had cut our first teeth on one another, and we had never seen him before. But Forest was different in another way. Forest was Indian, and his presence in our world went beyond our experience, beyond our comprehension. We welcomed him to our school politely, as we had been taught to welcome the children of outsiders. But we would have been no less bewildered had we glanced up from our math drills and seen a grove of seedling pine take root in the hardpan outside.

. . .

Forest Walker. Even in the fourth grade I was struck by the irony. We paid attention to names, and there wasn't a forest of note for hundreds of miles. Our community was identified by several layers of place names that signified ownership. The Plains tribes who hunted that prairie had left hammers and arrowheads, tepee rings and medicine stones, but no names. Trappers and immigrant home-steaders had labeled the land as they pushed the Indians west, and by the time of my childhood, those earliest names belonged to the land alone. Carberrey, Whitcombe, Krumweide, Cruikshank—to say them aloud was to conjure a place long separated from a face or a family.

The chunk of short-grass prairie we called Regina had been named by French-Canadians who drifted south out of Saskatchewan to trap beaver along the Missouri. The first homesteaders inherited a legacy of French place names that roll across the tongue like music, black-bottom draws and treacherous creeks and drainages identified by hisses and coos. The actual places seemed unrelated to the black letters and blue lines on the official Bureau of Land Management maps. We had little use for maps. Any rancher who wanted to see his land picked up a piece and rubbed it between his fingers. But the maps with their foreign spellings—Beauchamp, Fourchette, Peigneux, DuBuis—drew a solid line between insiders, who knew the history of the land, and outsiders, who only knew maps and could not say the passwords. We all had out favorite stories.

"Had a guy up here yesterday, government feller, asks me directions to Regina," a neighbor might say. We'd all grin and lean forward. The name *Regina* applied to some 2,500 square miles, but on the maps it appeared as a little gray circle, just like a town. "I tell him he's looking at it, but he ain't buying any of that. So we get to jawing and pretty soon he goes for his map and there she is." Here he'd pause and lift his eyebrows and hands in one gesture of innocence. "So hell, I give him directions."

Strangers who were rude or adamant enough about the little gray circle on the map were sent there, to the Regina Post Office.

The best part of the story was imagining the driver's face when he pulled into our mail carrier's barnyard. A big official sign was nailed to the front of an old converted chicken house where Jake and Edie sorted the mail on Saturdays. The flag that waved over the Regina Post Office could have covered it like a pup tent.

We measured the wealth of our knowledge against the ignorance of outsiders, and judged ourselves superior. We pulled cars out of potholes, fed lost hunters at our kitchen table, sold gas from the big drums we kept behind the shop, and for the most part, we did so graciously. We could afford to be kind. But social or political upheaval going on outside seldom intruded, and families who managed to tuck themselves into a fold of flatland and hang on seldom went looking for something else to worry about. Their priorities were immediate—wind and heat and hoppers in summer, wind and snow and blizzards in winter. Our isolation was real. The nearest town lay an hour's drive north when the roads were good. To the south, the land plunged into rugged breaks and badlands, then dropped abruptly into a mile-wide stretch of water the maps called Fort Peck Lake. We still called it the Missouri River. In late summer a double row of dead cottonwoods reared out of the water where the original channel had been, and we could point to the site of submerged homesteads, name the families flooded out when the dam went in in the thirties. Halfway between the river and town, my parents bullied a hundred acres of winter wheat away from the silver sage and buffalo grass, and grazed cattle on the rest.

Our fences marched straight down the section lines, regiments of cedar posts and barbed wire strung so tight it hummed in a strong wind. The corners were square and braced to meet the bordering fields of neighbors just like us. Our families had homesteaded, broken ground, and survived into the third generation, and we shared a set of beliefs so basic that they were seldom spoken aloud. I remember them as adages: Hard work is the measure of a man; A barn will build a house, but a house won't build a barn; Good fences make good neighbors; That which belongs to everyone belongs to no one. "This is no country for fools," my granddad said, and these truths were what separated fools from survivors. They were the only explanation I was ever given for the way we lived.

. . .

Mrs. Norby left Forest squirming in front of the class while she and one of the boys fetched a small desk from the teacherage storeroom. A great deal more energy than necessary went into the shoving and arranging of desks to make room for the new one, and a haze of dust had silted down around us by the time the sharp snap of our teacher's fingers cut through the ruckus and settled us into them. Throughout the process, Forest remained where she had left him, staring back at us with eyes so dark I could not see the pupils. I heard my sister's quick gasp and the teacher's weary voice in the same instant, "Oh, Forest!" A wet spot had appeared on the front of his jeans and a puddle spread slowly along the uneven floor toward the first row of desks.

Mrs. Norby handled this second disruption with cool efficiency, but there was an edge to her movements, and we dove back into our books without being told. She rummaged through the box of castoffs we wore for art projects and came up with a pair of bright cotton pedal pushers and a large safety pin. These she handed to my brother Russ with instructions. Most of us had been in Forest's predicament at one time or another, and remembered our own drawers draped across the oil stove or flapping on the barbed-wire fence outside. Russ took the little boy's hand with awkward gentleness and led him away to the outhouse. They were gone a long time. Mrs. Norby had finished mopping up and was back to grading papers, but she kept glancing at the door, clearly exasperated. Forest finally returned, still wearing his wet jeans, and went straight to his desk. From the doorway Russ met the teacher's raised eyebrows with a small shrug, empty-handed.

At recess, Russ withdrew into his grown-up persona and refused to tell us what had gone on in the outhouse. It was none of our business, he chided, and with his moral superiority established, he dropped the subject and organized a game of Annie High Over. He was thirteen and full of adolescent wisdom, infuriating. Later in the week we sat around the kitchen table after school, munching slabs of fresh bread we had buttered and sprinkled with brown sugar. Guy had captured our attention with stories of Forest. They had been paired up for a project, and Guy basked in the glory of inside knowledge.

"I had to show him everything," Guy bragged. "He didn't know nothing."

"Anything," Mom corrected him absently from the sink.

"I asked him stuff, but he don't know how to talk."

"Doesn't," Mom said, sliding more bread from the oven. Russ chewed and frowned at his little brother. Until moments ago, he had been the silent expert. "Can too," he said. In the two days Forest had spent at South First Creek, we had not heard him say one word. He would nod or shake his head, he would follow directions to get this or fetch that, but he had not spoken.

"I suppose *you* would know," Guy said, rolling his eyes. Russ responded to the challenge, telling us about the first day, the walk to the outhouse, Forest's stubborn refusal to be talked into the orange pedal pushers. He would not undress himself.

"Then I thought maybe he was just bashful, so I gave him the pants and told him I'd wait outside," Russ said. Within seconds, Forest had pushed open the outhouse door and was walking toward the schoolhouse. Russ made a hasty search for the dry pants. Forest had thrown them down the toilet hole.

"So what did he say?" I asked eagerly, caught up in this drama. Russ picked up his half-eaten bread.

"He said *no*," Russ replied. "When I tried to help him with the button on his pants." He chewed thoughtfully. "He meant it, too. He's tough."

Forest wet his pants on a regular basis, and we came to prefer his damp, earthy smell to the reek of bayberry Mrs. Norby left on her after-the-fact rampages around the room with a can of Glade. She never asked, and to my knowledge, no one told her the fate of the orange pedal pushers, but after the first day, Forest wore his wet pants unchallenged.

To her credit, Mrs. Norby never gave up on Forest, although his lessons soon resembled a series of skirmishes. She always began cheerfully enough, settling us to work by ourselves then calling him up to her big desk, where they would spend until recess working on the big alphabet cards. Our first-grade year, we all measured our progress and accomplishment by the growing row of cards, memorized and thumbtacked to the wall above the blackboard. We adored them. On each card the stout, black lines of upper- and lowercase letters were incorporated into a picture and a story. The letter C, I remember, was a profile of a mouth line with teeth; the sound of Mr. C coughing was the sound of the letter C. Lowercase *f* was the tail of a frightened cat. Mr. D was a soldier, and when he stood straight and beat his round drum it went *duh-duh-duh*.

The first time Forest spoke, Mrs. Norby killed our reaction with one remarkably vicious look, perhaps afraid that we would frighten him back to silence. But Forest loved the stories, and his soft, surprisingly deep voice became background music for our own lessons. He learned the cards quickly, repeating the sounds, grandly embellishing the stories unless Mrs. Norby stopped him, and she must have expected him to take the next leap as effortlessly as we had. But he did not. He saw nothing in the shapes and sounds of the phonics cards that connected to the words written in a book. Mrs. Norby persisted like a trainer with a jump-shy colt, putting him through his paces, around the cards faster and faster, gaining momentum, and then the book would appear and Forest would brace his feet and skid to a stop.

Against her decades of experience he had only endurance and a calm, sad stare that he seldom directed at the words she pointed out. After a few days he would have the words of Dick's or Jane's or Sally's exploits memorized and matched to the pictures on each page. Mrs. Norby would open to a page, he would look at it closely for a few seconds and then begin reciting the story that went with the pictures, sometimes adding bits from previous pages and, often as not, reading with his eyes focused on his fingers as they twiddled with a paper clip or a bit of paper. When her voice grew clipped and brittle, he waited her out. Forest did not think in ABCs; for him the story was all.

. . .

From my position as third-row observer, I found Forest's academic failures neither surprising nor disappointing. Looking back, I can see it was his inability to read that kept him alive in my mind. From the first days I had attempted to find the mythical Red Man in Forest, and he had failed me on every other front. We had studied Plains tribes in social studies. We had read the books, and when TV came to the country we were devoted to shows like *Wagon Train* and *Rawhide*. The Indians we admired had no use for reading; they wore buckskin leggings and medicine pouches on leather thongs around their necks. They had eagle feathers and long braids; they danced and hunted and collected scalps. Forest showed little promise of living up to this exciting potential.

Greta and I were more given to fantasy than the boys, and we were the worst. It became a game. Every morning we all hung our coats and placed our lunch boxes in the hallway near the communal water crock. Every morning either Greta or I would ask permission to get a drink, using the few out-of-sight seconds to lift the catch on his lunch box or pat down the pockets of his jacket. His jacket held no crude weapons. His bologna sandwich was as boring as our own bologna sandwiches. No pemmican. No buffalo jerky. Obviously, we knew more about being Indian than Forest did.

My brothers, sister, and I spent our childhood summers playing at myth. We made bows and arrows from green willow and cotton string and bounded barefoot through the creek bottoms, communicating with gestures and grunts like Tonto did on *The Lone Ranger*. We had horses and could ride like cowboys, but my sister and I rebelled at the discipline of saddles and rules. We rode naked to the waist, hell-bent through the meadows on a palomino mare and a black, half-Shetland pony. We turned them out to pasture in late fall with heart-shaped bald spots where our butts had worn through the hair on their backs.

We had no bridge between make-believe and the reality of children like Forest. We knew our land and its people, every pore, every pothole, and every heartache of a close, contained world.

From that knowledge came identity and security. But we had only the vaguest sense of our place in the larger world. The Fort Belknap Reservation that lies twenty-five overland miles from my parents' ranch is no more real in my memory than New York City. What I knew about this place I learned indirectly—jokes overheard, fragments of conversation, phrases that slipped into dialogue sideways, in reference to other whites. Shiftless as a reservation buck. Stank like an Indian camp. Drunk-squaw mean. Wild as, lazy as, dirty as. Racial slurs discounted as harmless because they did not refer to anyone we knew. The people we knew were ranchers, neighbors who lived like we did. Indians were dark and dangerous and different. They got in bar fights and car wrecks; they hung around the Rez and took government handouts; they did not make good hired men. They were like the man we saw behind the rodeo arena pouring his horse a big feed of commodity oatmeal, U.S. GOVERNMENT stamped right on the sack. There was, my father said through clenched teeth, no goddamned excuse for that, no goddamned excuse in the world.

Forest and his grandparents were gone before Christmas. I never knew where they went or why they left. I suppose the extra desk got retired to the storeroom, but I don't remember that, either. What I do remember from that time is the lingering sense of nobility I felt for being kind to him. Tolerance was a gift I could have chosen not to give. I knew Forest would never belong to our school or to our community, just as I knew it wasn't proper to talk about it. These were things I knew without knowing why, things I learned as a child listening with half an ear to all that was said, and most intently to all that was not said. I remember the silence most of all.

The trip to Havre is in my honor, my first trip to the dentist. He pulls four baby teeth to make room for the new ones sprouting through my gums at odd angles, and there is blood. When we leave the dentist's office I make it to the parking lot, then vomit all I have swallowed and feel better. Breakfast happened before dawn, before dressing in our nicest clothes, before our three-hour drive. My father hands me a clean handkerchief to hold against my mouth and drives through downtown Havre in search of an inexpensive cafe. Afraid that misery is catching, my brothers and sisters crowd against the far side of the backseat. Under the stained hankie my cheeks feel heavy and pliant, like wet clay. My father swears at the traffic, a white-knuckle driver unaccustomed to stoplights, and I close my eyes to shut it out.

The cafe we pull up to is small but not crowded, and my stomach wakes to the perfume of hamburgers and french fries, a treat so rare that we could count their every appearance in our short lives, each event of "eating out." But when the food comes I am stunned to find a bowl of chicken soup set on the place mat in front of me, the kind my mother makes when she's too busy to cook. I stir noodles up from the bottom of the bowl and sulk, while the others take turns squeezing ketchup over hamburgers and fighting over split orders of fries. Even driven by hunger, I can't keep the soup from leaking through my numb lips, and when life becomes too unfair to stand, I slide to the floor under the table and begin to cry. My father drags me out by one arm and sends me to sit in the car until I can straighten up.

Outside, I lean against the bumper in pure defiance of direct orders. But the day is too warm and the wait too long. My attention wanders to the bench just outside the cafe door, where an Indian woman sits holding a baby. I'm drawn to babies, and this one is a black-eyed beauty, her fat belly peeking out of a crocheted sweater, just big enough to sit upright on the old woman's knee. The woman sees me edging closer and smiles. "You like babies?" she asks, and I nod, my tongue still too thick to trust with words.

The woman is dressed in layers of bright color, wide skirts that brush the ground, a man's flannel shirt buttoned to the neck, and a shawl that falls from her shoulders and drapes in folds around the baby. Thick gray braids coil at the nape of her neck. She bends her face near the baby's and clicks her tongue, tickling at the chubby brown chin, and the baby dissolves into giggles, her eyes fastened on the grandmother's face. The babies I have seen are next to bald, but this one has thick black hair standing up all over her head. I'm getting up the nerve to touch that hair when the cafe door opens and I leap back, scrambling toward our car, expecting my father. I turn, hand on the door handle, and an old man stands next to the woman and the baby. They are all looking at me, surprised.

The man hands the woman a wrapped hamburger and a paper cup of milk and walks back into the cafe. She lets the baby suck on the edge of the cup while she chews the sandwich, her lips disappearing with the motion of her jaw. She sets the cup aside, and I freeze against the car in wonder as she dips into her mouth with two fingers and pops a bit of chewed food into the baby's open mouth. The little girl works over the mashed hamburger, and they rock gently on the bench, each gumming her own bite until it's swallowed. After a sip of milk, the baby leans forward comically, eyebrows arched, mouth and eyes round, ready for more. My own stomach shivers, squeamish, thrilled, but the process is done so gently that I can't be horrified. I watch the wonderful shuffle of food from mouth to fingers to baby, the easy sway between bites, until I'm full to bursting with news.

Back inside the cafe, I ignore the cold soup and dance against my mother's arm, conscious of slurring as I tell the story of what I've seen. Her nose wrinkles, and her voice drops to a whisper as she hushes me.

"Did you talk to her?" she asks. Her voice is too flat and even, a trap I can't quite read. I nod, ready to work my lips and tongue around an explanation, but her hand snakes out and grabs my ear before I can speak, twisting it, her knuckles pressing against my swollen cheek. Her eyes lock mine into full attention.

"You were told to get in the car." She says nothing else but continues to glare, giving my ear another jerk for emphasis. Stunned, I walk with underwater steps out the door, straight without looking to the car, and curl up on the backseat, heat thumping in my stomach.

It's a long ride home that night, late and dark, and the backseat is a crush of packages and sleeping children. My mouth has been awake for hours, throbbing. In the front seat my mother tells my story of the Indian woman feeding the baby. My father says, "Jeezus Christ." My mother says it would be our luck if I caught something.

317

I hear it in their voices, and my belly fills with anger and shame. The old woman tricked me. On the outside nothing is what it seems, and I long for my own bed, the quilt my mother sewed from wool scraps and old coats, the comfort of a sure thing. My father drives automatically now, slowing for ruts and cattle guards, banking the gentle curves of the county road. Lonesome Coulee. Jackson's Corner. Taylor Hill. I press one cheek against the cool of the window and close my eyes, drifting with the motion of the car. Almost home. I can tell where we are by the feel.

◆

Judy Blunt, who is also the author of the essay "Breaking Clean" in this collection, lives in Missoula, Montana.

TEX GARRY

◆ ◆ ◆ ◆ ◆

SHARKEY

In 1927, while prohibition was still in effect nationwide, a bill was introduced into the Wyoming legislature to try to duplicate it as a state law, making whiskey distilling a state felony offense. It went by the nickname of the Still Bill.

Milward Simpson, lawyer, legislator, U.S. senator, and governor tells a story about the bill.

During the House debate I said the bill was so poorly written that, if it were passed, any lawyer could get an acquittal. To prove my point, I said that if I couldn't get someone acquitted who was indicted under that law, I wouldn't charge a fee.

The press gave that argument a lot of play, but the bill passed, the legislature adjourned, and we went home.

We were living in Thermopolis then, and the first person I met when I got off the train was Sharkey Swaine, the biggest bootlegger in that part of the country. "Mil'ard," he says, "did you mean what you told the newspapers 'bout the Still Bill?" I said I did, and Sharkey pulls an indictment out of his coat pocket.

By the grace of God, a fast outfield, and a good jury, I got Sharkey off. Now we'd neither one said anything about my fee ahead of time, so after the trial I just waited a few days and, sure enough, Sharkey came by to see me.

My office was upstairs in the old Klink Building there in Thermopolis. Dr. Owens, a dentist, had the office next to mine. I really needed the fee just then, so when Sharkey asked me what he owed, I figured I'd make a ten-strike. I told him $350, a good deal of money in those days.

Sharkey never batted an eye. He just reached into his pocket and pulled out a real horse-choker roll of bills and started counting it out in fives and tens.

Dr. Owens was working on a woman's teeth there in the next office. About the time Sharkey's count reached 200, Dr. Owens hit a nerve, and that lady let out a scream like a gut-shot panther.

Sharkey never lost count, but he looked up at me as he kept laying bills on the desk and asked, "Is that a lawyer back there, too?"

◆

Tex Garry is a storyteller who digs up old-timers—before they need to be dug up literally—to hear their stories and to keep some of them (the stories?) alive for another generation.

He is generally considered to be the best liar in Wyoming—when the legislature isn't in session.

DAN WHIPPLE

◆　◆　◆　◆　◆

POKER PARLEY

Wild Bill Hickok was shot to death while holding a poker hand consisting of a pair of aces and a pair of eights. Ever since then, that combination of cards has been known as the Dead Man's Hand. Well, I'm sorry about Wild Bill, but a lot worse thing happened to me in the Palace Saloon and Card Room in normally placid downtown Missoula. I held the same hand and lost my last ten dollars to a young, slender guy with a gap where his left front tooth should have been. I was certain that my two pair were winners, when he turned over a pair of fives in the hole, making him a full house—three fives and two eights—in a game of Montana hold-'em.

I should have known. That guy never bluffs. And when he's got a good hand, he flings his chips onto the table with a short wrist toss, like a Frisbee throw. Don't bet into that wrist.

Some people believe that poker is a game involving luck. In one of W. C. Fields's movies, he is riding a train, shuffling some cards, and trying to get a fellow passenger to play with him to pass the time. The passenger asks, "Is this a game of chance?"

And Fields replies, "Not the way I play it."

Take heed.

Poker is a game of money management. If you are waiting for your luck to turn, or you have to sit in your lucky seat, play crazy eights.

Now it's true that there is an element of chance in poker. But the particles that make up the human body are held in place according to certain laws of probability known as quantum mechanics. You don't call that luck, do you?

Poker is legal in Montana in licensed establishments, which usually turn out to be bars. The bar hires a dealer, buys a felt-covered table, and is granted the privilege of raking about 6 percent of each pot off the top. The dealers, in Missoula at least, are almost all young women, usually students working their way through school. Colleen down at the Palace is a psychology major.

The Palace is a serious poker joint. It seems to be open just about round the clock, and there are plenty of arcane rules and side contests which are unique to the place. For instance, there is a poker tournament every Sunday, and the players who collect the most "points" during the week are permitted to play in it. The points are awarded as follows: one point for an ace high flush; two for a full house; three for four of a kind; four for a straight flush; five for a royal flush and for the high hand of the day. High hand of the day also wins fifty dollars in chips and one ounce of silver.

There's also an odd hand bonus. The last time I was there, the odd hand was king of diamonds, queen of hearts, ten of diamonds, five of spades, and three of diamonds. It's changed every day. The bonus was $495. The odds of that hand turning up on any deal are the same as those for a royal flush in spades—one in 2,598,960.

The Palace also has all the usual rules. Anyone who Mutilates or Tears a Card will buy the Deck—Price $15. No Foul Language or Verbal Abuse Tolerated.

If you play 650,000 hands of poker, you will get one royal flush, 1,300 flushes, and 163 fours of a kind dealt to you as pat hands. So will your opponent. So, the trick is to know when you're going to win and bet accordingly. Conversely, you've got to fold your cards when you don't think you're going to win. Finally, you have to play against players who don't understand these simple rules.

You won't find too many players at the Palace who don't understand the game. In my poker-playing tour of Missoula, I ran into the best players there. I'm told that the *really* best players play at the Oxford, a legendary old bar and cafe on Higgins that used to have a cook who cracked his eggs by throwing them up to the twenty-foot-high ceiling with just enough force to open them but not shatter them. However, I never could get into a game at the Oxford, so I personally don't know if they have the best players or not.

I'd like to say that Montana poker parlors attract a varied and interesting clientele, but I'd be lying. Most of us are somber, serious men—very few women play—who pay close attention to the flow of funds. Nothing will kill a poker game faster than the bar hosting a troupe of exotic male dancers. Most poker players smoke. Heavily.

The most insistent sound at a poker game is the clicking of chips. There are several styles and techniques. Some players hold a large stack of singles and drop them quickly onto the felt covering. Others divide their large stack into two smaller stacks and shuffle them together one-handed. Some merely take a large stack, divide it in two, place the bottom half on top of the top half, and then repeat the motion until the cards are dealt. The players don't think about this or even know they are doing it.

It is possible to win consistently at poker, but it requires an important addition to the rules mentioned earlier. In order to win, you have to play against players who are going to lose. This is an unfortunate side effect of the game. In 1909, two Missouri assemblymen introduced a bill into the state legislature to control and license poker players to prevent "millions of dollars lost annually by incompetent and foolish persons who do not know the value of a poker hand."

◆

Dan Whipple is the worst poker player to darken the tables of the Palace Hotel and Card Room in many a year. He is now an editor with the Casper Star Tribune *in Casper, Wyoming.*

STEPHEN VOYNICK

◆ ◆ ◆ ◆ ◆

THE CLOSING OF WESTERN HARDWARE

The half dozen old-timers, stooped and gray, each a former Depression-era miner, stood across the street from Western Hardware arguing quietly about the year it had opened. No one was sure, because Western Hardware had been doing business years before the oldest of them had been born.

Although none had been around for the opening, they were here for the closing. The big red AUCTION sign had hung in the window for six weeks. Now, cars and pickups from six states lined the streets, and an impatient crowd of buyers waited for the doors to open one final time.

The austere, two-floor brick building had been built at the height of the silver boom a century ago. Western Hardware (it was never called just "Western" or "the hardware store") was a pure hardware emporium, not only by merchandise but by smell, sight, and sound. At the front door, street smells yielded abruptly to those of packing sawdust, coal oil, and the strangely pleasing and comfortable fragrance of machine oil. The sounds, mostly those of metal on metal, spoke of business, purpose, and knowledge: the delicate clatter of nails falling into the brass scoop of a hanging balance; the grating whine of an ace blade against the grindstone; the heavy thud of machine bolts on a wooden counter; the clear, bell-like jingle of the big, ornate cash registers.

Most memorable was the appearance of Western Hardware. The hundred-foot-long main floor was heated with three big, black, potbellied coal stoves. The walls were the work of master carpenters—bins, drawers, cabinets, shelves, display cases, and counters, all fashioned from richly colored redwood and, beneath an omni-present film of machine oil, gleaming like polished mahogany. High overhead, four trophy elk and mule deer heads lent a warm, friendly, almost lodgelike atmosphere to Western Hardware.

Most of the awesome inventory consisted of mining tools and supplies, but even the most specialized needs of carpenters, me-chanics, metalworkers, electricians, blacksmiths, and plumbers were stocked. Accounting for that huge, rapidly moving inventory of everything from three-sixteenth-inch galvanized lock washers to 250-pound shoeing anvils to cases of du Pont dynamite was a full-time job for three green-visored stock clerks.

Yet Western Hardware was a model of almost military order and neatness that was both operationally efficient and aesthetically pleasing. Hammers were precisely arranged by size, quality, and purpose, proceeding logically from the delicate finishing hammers of the woodworkers to the eight-pound mine sledges and finally to the big mauls and wood splitters the lumberjacks used. In kegs and bins, tacks and tiny wire nails grew visibly into brads, then into tenpenny nails, and finally into heavy railroad and timber spikes. Wired to the front of over a thousand small redwood drawers was a specimen of the contents. The highest drawers were fully twelve feet above the floor, yet easily and quickly reached by movable, track-mounted redwood ladders.

Western Hardware was more than just a store. Men went there to learn current metal prices, who was sluicing gold in the gulches, who was building what. Or if a man was building something himself, and maybe having a little trouble, there was always someone at Western Hardware who could straighten him out. Western Hardware provided more than hardware; if you needed a few pointers on how to use it, well, you got that, too. And sometimes, when it was blowing in a mountain blizzard outside, the clerks would put out some coffee and crackers by the stoves.

Western Hardware had changed little by the 1950s. The coal stoves had given way to central heating and the cold light of long fluorescent lamps replaced the warm, yellow glow from the original rows of softball-size, 250-watt incandescent bulbs. The elk and deer heads, a bit tattered now, still guarded the du Pont dynamite display, the four-foot-high nest of factory-greased gold pans, the cased mineral collection, and the dozens of cracked and faded photographs of mining's glorious yesterdays.

But beyond the big front windows, the world was changing. Only a handful of mines were still working back in the hills, and the new interstate highway being surveyed would pass twenty miles north of the town.

One of the old-timers remembered a Winchester thirty-thirty he had bought from Western Hardware back in '56. The trigger pull was tight, and he brought it back to Teddy Lane, the head clerk. After a few pulls of the trigger, Lane placed the Winchester on the worn, oil-soaked redwood counter and disassembled the firing mechanism. Locking the gear in a sixty-year-old vise, Lane filed down a bit of the cam surface, polished it with some emery cloth, oiled everything, and reassembled the piece. Fifteen minutes later, the miner was approvingly dry-firing the Winchester at the dusty six-point elk head. "Back then," the old miner recalled, "you didn't have guarantees and warranties in four languages and an address in Hong Kong to get something fixed. Old Teddy Lane would look at you and say, 'If it don't work, bring it back and we'll make it work.' "

By the 1960s, Western Hardware and the few remaining hardware stores like it were in trouble. Hardware merchandising was now in the domain of franchises and chains that benefited through volume buying and aggressive advertising and promotion, and retail sales and near-wholesale prices. They had names like Coast to Coast, True Value, and Ace, and they offered a new kind of hardware. Home plumbing supplies, for example, came in kits of pastel-colored PVC pipe, snap-on plastic fittings, nylon washers, and tubes of sealant, all antiseptically packaged in heat-shrunk plastic. It seemed only the old-timers wanted—or knew how to use—the copper pipe, cast-iron or bronze fittings, solder, and blowtorches that gathered dust on the shelves of Western Hardware. In 1975 the inevitable happened. The old Woolworth's five-and-dime store down the street from Western Hardware was vacated, and the new occupant was a

Coast to Coast outlet. Most of the old-timers wouldn't even walk in the front door. Sure, there was a modest selection of basic tools and traditional hardware items, but there was far more in the kitchen utensils, toys, fishing gear, sewing supplies, and electrical appliances. A lot of the new people in town, the young ones who skied in the winter and pedaled bicycles in the summer, however, found Coast to Coast to be convenient shopping. They looked through the windows of Western Hardware at the dusty elk heads but rarely went in.

When Coast to Coast moved in, Teddy Lane had worked at Western Hardware nearly half a century, the last three decades as head clerk. Old Teddy still had profound—some called it mystical—mental comprehension of every item in that still-voluminous inventory. More important, he knew how, where, and when to use every tool, every piece of hardware. And he knew what to tactfully suggest when a customer didn't really need what he thought he did. If a man had a cracked impeller flange from a forty-year-old water pump, the old-timers knew there was no sense in going to Coast to Coast, that they didn't have the part, couldn't fix it, and weren't about to order it. "Take that to Western Hardware and show it to Teddy Lane," they'd say. "He'll fix you up some way or other."

The trouble was there were few forty-year-old water pumps left to fix. Everything seemed to be changing now, even the few people who walked in the front door. "They'd take some pictures of the front, then stare in the window. Finally they'd come in. Wouldn't say anything, just stand there and stare.

"Then they'd ask me if this was a museum or a real hardware store, and I'd tell 'em, 'It's a real hardware store.' Then they'd walk around real quiet, whisperin' like they were in a church, then click away with their Instamatics at the gold pans or the dynamite display, maybe the nail kegs. Some would smile real sheepishlike and ask if they could take a picture of me. Then they'd thank me an' be gone."

Teddy Lane was soon gone, too, retiring in 1976. Somehow, Western Hardware, now a place of dust, solitude, and memories, stayed open until 1983, when the last owner died. Two years later, on a crisp high country October morning, the old-timers gathered to watch the last business that would ever be transacted at Western Hardware. While buyers from six states made their bids, the old-timers, still uncertain what year Western Hardware really did open, talked about hammers and drill steels and dynamite, about Teddy Lane, and about the crackers and coffee when it was blowin' a mountain blizzard.

Like Teddy told 'em, it was a *real* hardware store.

◆

Stephen Voynick has worked as a marine salvage diver in South America and the Caribbean, and as a hardrock miner in the uranium, molybdenum, and copper mines of Wyoming, Colorado, and Arizona. He has been a full-time freelance writer since 1982, from his home in Leadville, Colorado. He is a contributing editor for Rock and Gem *and he writes regularly for other national magazines about gems and minerals, mining, Western history, and applied technology. Voynick has published seven books, including* The Making of a Hardrock Miner, Leadville: A Miner's Epic, Colorado Gold, *and* Colorado Rockhounding.

PART VI

SOLACE

SANDRA ALCOSSER

◆ ◆ ◆ ◆ ◆

APPROACHING AUGUST

Night takes on its own elegance.
The catenary curve of snakes,
the breathing, pentagonal-shaped
flowers, the shadblow pliant
and black with berries. Orion
rises in the east, over
fat green gardens, over all meanness
is forgiven.

We canoe the river
in the amethyst hour before dark.
Two billion beats to each heart.
Two passengers fish, two paddle
past the chalk caves, the banks
of aster, the floodplains dense
with whitetail and beaver.

We are lost near midnight, a moonless
summer evening, midseason in our senses,
midlife. The sky overhead like glitter ice.
The water round swollen cottonwoods
pulls like tresses and torn paper.

Today I had a letter from France.
"What a truly civilized nation," my friend wrote

as she drank her morning coffee with thick cream in a country
cafe near Avignon. "To my right
a man in a black tuxedo sips raspberry liqueur
and soda."

And here on the same latitude we lie back at dawn
in the caving bank of the Bitterroot.
A shadow slips through the silver grasses.
And then a moth.
And then the moon.

◆

*Sandra Alcosser is Professor of Poetry, Fiction, and Feminist
Poetics at San Diego State University. In 1993–94, Alcosser
was a Visiting Writer at the University of Michigan, Ann Arbor.
Her poems have appeared in* The American Poetry Review, The
New Yorker, The Paris Review, Poetry, The Yale Review, *and
many anthologies, including* Women Poets from Antiquity to
Now. *A 1993–94 Montana Arts Fellow in Poetry, she is also
a recipient of two NEA fellowships, a San Diego Artist Fellowship, a Pushcart Prize, the PEN syndicated Fiction Award, and
the American Scholar's Mary Elinore Smith Poetry Prize. Alcosser started the MFA Program in Creative Writing at San
Diego State University. She is currently collaborating on a fine
arts book,* White Pelicans and River Silt. *Her second book of
poems,* A Fish to Feed All Hungers, *was selected by James Tate
as the Associated Writing Programs' Award Series Winner in
Poetry.*

*Alcosser grew up in Indiana, was educated at Purdue
University, and received an MFA from the University of Mon-
tana, where she studied with Richard Hugo. She considers the
Bitterroot Mountains of western Montana her home.*

LESLIE RYAN

◆ ◆ ◆ ◆ ◆

THE CLEARING IN THE CLEARING

I remember the first time I realized women were afraid to go outside alone. It wasn't more than a year ago. I was studying, as was my habit on weekends, in the Rattlesnake Wilderness Area in western Montana. The peaks raise a topographic tempest against the urban island Missoula, and the shelves just below ridgeline make a long-sighted camp in clear weather. It was clear weather that day. Down below, glacier lily leaves stitched up through the earth, delivering themselves to sunshine or grouse gullets with the certainty of a good faith.

Long about Christmas in Montana, you start thinking that nothing will make it through the season of blasting winds or the inescapable prison of ice and snow, unless that thing is made out of rock; or bone, sinew, teeth, and rock; or rock and oily fur and will, unfathomable will-to-live. When the wind rips car doors from their hinges, and chickadees plunge headlong and frozen from the pines, pictures come into your head: cold-frenzied monsters screaming in the blizzard winds, battling to the death over a carcass scrap on a bloodied cornice. Soon it is clear that all is lost but the rock and ice, and life is sterile as planks under the cold.

But then you're walking where the snow's melted out and wind-sheared limbs hang like relief in the ones that made it through. Meltwater crinkles all around in the duff, and needles spark the way fireflies burrow and flash in the short rye down south, and all of a sudden there it is, like something imagined, like a fairy light in the marsh. As delicate as if they were formed of ash or web or mist—

three white petals whorling on the green. One breath of yours might dissolve them, waves of translucence bending on a leafy shore. You think of glass cubes by the thousands in palatial museums, knowing that not one protects a treasure more rare than the trillium unfolding here beneath the precarious branch, in the path of paw and hoof, in the fragrance of ready soil. They call it wake-robin, as if its fragile tenacity opens the eyes of all creatures. You kneel more intimately and inhabit, for a while, unlikelihood.

That's the kind of day it was the first time I learned women were afraid to be alone outside, one of those toasting-to-the-trillium days. Lounging on the ridgeline shelf midday, I was reading an article about wildness and wilderness. The author, Stephen Trimble, wondered why more women didn't write natural history essays. He concluded, "The only explanation women have given me is that they fear being alone in the landscape . . . they feel vulnerable, they feel danger—not from the land, but from men. They fear violence and never quite forget about its most disturbing expression: rape."

Then and there I followed my bare hand down to my bare knee and looked down past my bare chest and stomach to the place where my bare bottom was taking a pine needle tattoo, and I said out loud, "Well, I'll be." Why I'd felt safe and happy there for so many weekends with the sun tightening my skin and the ants navigating my appendages, why it had never before occurred to me to be afraid, I don't know.

Then I realized that the travel habits which have always felt sensible to me might appear fearful to others or might be gender-specific. Even for short weekends in the Rattlesnake, I leave an itinerary with a friend. At the trailhead, I wait to strike out until there are no men coming or going, and if I meet a man on the main stretch and he speaks, I outright lie: I say a friend is waiting up the way or fabricate a story about a peak far from my intended path. As soon as it's feasible, I take to the ridge, where voices and footsteps are audible from a distance and the periphery widens. I carry water so there will be no need to recross a trail for replenishment during my stay, and when night falls I turn in, not desiring a telling rim of light around me in the dark.

.   .   .

Am I afraid I'll be raped in the forest? I was raped once before (not in Montana, not in the woods), and I was actually glad I was only raped, if my other option was being raped and killed. The wilderness author calls rape a "disturbing expression" of violence. What "disturbs" me most about rape is how it undermines trust—it scrapes out the place where what's simple and crucial about love might be made, so that even the most tender touch retains tinges of the criminal. For me, alone on those trillium days, the Rattlesnake was as sweet as a first, chosen touch might have been. I felt safe out there. I guess I thought crazy people were only in the cities, not in the woods.

That was what I thought then. Now I know better.

Have you seen that movie, *Silence of the Lambs?* I told myself I'd never watch it, but then at Christmas I was back in Virginia. My brothers were there. We hadn't seen one another for a year, and though they knew I wouldn't be there long, they wanted to watch *Silence of the Lambs* for the third time anyway. We'd been drinking some beers out by the Dumpster, and I said, "OK. I'll watch. But when the scary part comes, warn me, and I'll close my eyes."

It doesn't work that way.

Closing your eyes does not work.

Except for the fact that she worked for the government, I identified with Jodie Foster. She was the star of the movie. As an orphan child, she moved from West Virginia to Montana. In Montana her heart got broken by something she witnessed: the slaughter of the spring lambs, who, for all practical purposes—after Christ— symbolize the innocent. After that, she directed her life toward silencing the screams of the lambs, figuratively speaking, not by killing them but by protecting them. Closed eyes didn't work for Jodie Foster, because the lamb sounds still found her ears. The same thing happened to me watching that movie. It didn't matter that my eyes were closed. Reality still moved in.

You might say that a movie about lambs and serial killers is not reality. I'd say you're wrong.

Even though there are two thousand miles of pavement laid out between Virginia and Montana, I haven't slept outside since that movie. I saw it at Christmas, three months ago. I slept outside pretty often right up until then, even after having read the wilderness author on rape. There's not much I like better than sleeping out, especially on frozen nights when the stars recede so relentlessly that they seem to be sucking the warmth right out of your lungs. In an all-night, mouth-to-mouth exchange with absolute zero, you can get to feeling as sad and real as the one warm spot in the universe. One night before leaving for Christmas, I remember sleeping out in the yard of the cabin, with the big spruce towering above the stars, and the Pleiades floating on one high, up-curving branch. Essential ornament, they were, as lucid eyes are jewels in a face.

But that was before.

Now when it's time to go outside, I arm myself. A black cylinder of pressurized cayenne pepper hangs around my neck on nylon cord. Cayenne will temporarily blind and asphyxiate anyone within twelve feet of me. The soles of my Red Wings were born to imprint the genitalia of criminals. My pocketknife necklace won't lock well enough for punctures, but a big blade compensates for it, ready in pocket. Both knives stay sharp as sin. When it's necessary to go outside for firewood, I move like someone lunging through a canyon thicket, vulnerable parts protected by a swarm of strategies. That's when I feel good. When I feel bad, I beg the fire or go cold.

I wasn't always scared like this. Two years back, in the second week of a solo hike in the desert, I chose a three-day fasting and resting site in the labyrinthine canyon. I hadn't seen people for eight days, and the one dirt road within miles had ruts deep as cradles and a centerline of waist-high sunflowers, so I figured the canyon was remote. On the first night there, about twenty yards from camp, I was peering under ledges for shelter when I came upon an unearthed human skull. Strips of leathery scalp hung off it like bandages. The drying brain would have thudded around inside if I had shaken it. Cigarette butts, gum wrappers, saddle hardware, and the protruding tail of a blanket shroud littered the grave. The rest of the body was still under. In a nose thumb at postmodern causal relativism, I had earlier made a rule that everything during this three-day period happened for a reason, and that, come flood or fire, leaving the canyon was not permitted. So I stayed with the dead one for three days and then lingered an extra day because both lupine and arrow-leaf balsamroot were coming into bloom.

If we were dealing with a simple serial killer here, I'd be afraid, but not like this.

In *Silence of the Lambs*, two of the three main characters are serial killers. Jodie Foster plays an FBI trainee who is sent by her boss to enlist the help of one (imprisoned) killer in obtaining a psychological profile of another—a man who's still at large. The unknown killer on the loose is referred to as Buffalo Bill; he has killed and skinned at least five young women. The killer in jail, Dr. Hannibal Lecter, is a curious, cannibalistic psychiatrist with a high IQ, a fellow who recently ate the face of an emergency room nurse.

Another serial killer hangs around the edges of this movie, but he's not in it. He glows in his own special limelight; his name is Jeffrey Dahmer. He's the real-life man who recently murdered, raped, and dismembered at least fifteen people; he often ate parts of the bodies. All three killers have something in common, something more than just gender.

It seems important to say at this point that I get the creeps just typing these names onto a page. It's like the way people write Gd because saying the word might actually bring them into direct contact with a power which is utterly other. Completely alien. One night my mom was walking home from doing her laundry in Virginia, walking a path behind her apartment complex. A man stepped out from behind a tree and aimed a gun at her head. He said, "Give me your money." She only had three dollars in her purse. She said, "No." Later she recalled that in the instant between her reply and the impact of the gun butt on her skull, she had realized, "His way of thinking is completely alien to me." I wanted to agree, and to add that, in fact, her way of responding was alien to me, but her bandaged head and black eyes silenced me.

Creative energy exemplifies one form of incomprehensible power; destructive energy, another. Most of us can differentiate vaguely between natural and unnatural creation or destruction. I'd categorize Mom's experience with the wallet man as unnaturally destructive. In her book *The Sexual Politics of Meat*, Carol Adams outlines a psychological mechanism by which sexual violence might be linked to butchering, and I think it may suggest some common ground between lesser and greater criminals. She says,

> I see a cycle of objectification, fragmentation, and consumption. Objectification permits an oppressor to view another being as an object. The oppressor then violates this being by object-like treatment (the rape of women denies women freedom to say no; the butchering of animals converts animals from living, breathing beings into dead objects). This process allows fragmentation, or brutal dismemberment, and finally consumption. Consumption is the fulfillment of oppression, the annihilation of will, of separate identity.

Adams also suggests that a linguistic masking process of euphemistic renaming attends this cycle.

Killing lambs is as all-Montanan as improving nature through clear-cuts, as patriotic and commendable as poisoning wolves. If you've been raised raising animals just to kill them later, the idea doesn't seem so alien. If you've lived your entire life thinking the forest exists solely in order for us to use it, clear-cuts aren't that disturbing. And if you believe human animals, too, exist only as resources, turning a boy into a sex zombie by drilling holes into his head and filling them with acid doesn't present much of a problem.

I once worked for a billionaire who financed genetic engineering on beef cattle in the rain forest. The rule for genetically encoding those cattle is this: The more stupid and obedient they are, the better, as long as they're still alive. I've seen cows wander into box canyons in blizzards, and they would've died there if they hadn't been rounded up by diligent neighbors; the brain-drilled boy strayed naked into the street, but he was returned by police officers to Dahmer's apartment. The only difference, aside from a minor species distinction, is that Dahmer's utilitarianism exceeds even that of the most pragmatic billionaire: A dead unbutchered cow is useless, whereas Dahmer had good sex with his corpses before cutting them up.

The boy was not white. It used to be that white people actually thought of "nonwhites" the way we now think of cows, or trees, or wolves, or more specifically, a combination of all three: Negroes, for example, were property to be used for material gain; you kept them cut down to size, and if they got too wild or interfered with your profits, you shot them. In his book *My Bondage and My Freedom*, the former slave Frederick Douglass describes a meeting with slave-traders. "After taunting us, they subjected us one by one to an examination, with a view to ascertain our value: feeling our arms and legs, shaking us by the shoulders to see if we were sound. . . ." It was normal at the time for traders to stand slaves naked on the auction block, inspect their teeth and genitals, and put prices on them. Douglass says, "The first work of slavery is to mar and deface those characteristics of its victims which distinguish men from things, and persons from property." But that was a hundred years ago, that shameful time, when people treated other human beings as if they were mere resources to be used for the material, psychological, or physical benefit of the oppressor. A long time ago; so sorry, black people. When I was growing up in Virginia in the 1970s, many of my friends were black. Someone passed a note around the sixth grade, and it said, "Leslie Ryan is a nigger lover," and all the white sixth graders signed, to show that it was true. A long time ago.

In the movie, Buffalo Bill kidnaps a new victim just after Jodie is put on the case. The girl is a senator's daughter. She hasn't done anything wrong except to walk from her car to her apartment without weapons or men. The killer watches her from behind a bush with special heat-sensitive glasses that allow him to see her in the dark; she appears green as money through his shades. She can't see him. The camera flashes to the girl passing a parked moving van in the lot; a man with a broken arm awkwardly tries to shove an unwieldy couch into the vehicle. The girl offers to help. The man motions for her to get inside the truck and pull. Once she's in, he slams the couch in fast, pinning her against the inside wall of the truck. Trust.

In the meantime, Jodie has learned some interesting things. First, she has seen extracted from deep within the throat of each of this killer's victims a shiny moth pupa, like a pointy nut. Second, she learns from a twisted conversation with Hannibal (the imprisoned killer) that murderous crime begins with coveting something you see every day. "What does Billy do?" Hannibal whispers to Jodie through the bars of his maximum-security cage. Before she has a chance to reply, he answers himself, drawing out the last syllable of the word in a lengthy hiss: "He covets."

The dictionary defines *covet* as if it were a property-related phenomenon: "to desire inordinately without due regard to the rights of others; to desire wrongfully; to covet another's property." In the case of Buffalo Bill, then, what can this mean? No one owns these girls—women ceased being property even longer ago than African-Americans did.

Hannibal has let on to Jodie that Buffalo Bill might be a person who hates his own identity. Maybe he is a man who wants to become a woman. The pupae suggest metamorphosis. Buffalo Bill has harvested two diamond-shaped slices of skin from the lower back and buttocks of every girl he culls. Why?

The best analogy I can find comes from a time in my childhood when I was traveling a Virginia highway with my dad. When the car swerved, we saw a deer's body lying in the road—headless. It looked like someone had butchered him with a saw. I remember my dad saying, "I can't drive with you wailing like a madwoman." Whoever sliced the head off that deer did it for a reason, perhaps thinking the burly antlers could help transform him into something he was not.

I have some mule deer antlers on my shelf at home. They're bony and smooth, like the skeleton of an arch. I found them lying in a dry wash in the Great Basin desert. I took them because I thought they were beautiful. Am I wrong to believe that it's ethically justifiable to pick antlers up off the ground and keep them inside for a while? In some sense, these antlers are objects to me. I use them for my aesthetic enjoyment, and to be honest, I have never considered whether or not it matters to them. It means that I find this arrangement acceptable.

Losing his antlers is, for a buck, a natural part of the process of living. Having them wrenched from his body before it's naturally time by someone who is driven to kill by desire instead of need is not. Losing her virginity is, for a girl, a natural part of the process of living. Having two men forcibly extract it from her when she's too young to even know how babies are made is not. At least it didn't feel natural to me.

You might agree that when two grown men pin an eleven-year-old girl on the underlayment in an unfinished house, strip off her clothes, and fuck her, ethical complications arise. For the girl, for women, for society at large. But for the men? The first man stuffs his hairy hand in her mouth. He says, as if they've been playing doctor, "This won't hurt a bit." The other realizes this child presents no problem, concludes that he just has to wait his turn, and climbs the rafters for an aerial view. He yells, "Robbie likes virgins!"

To these men, a virgin is not a young being with value— however inchoate—of her own. She is a tunnel-thing, a sweet-toperforate barrier between their being who they are and their feeling like something better, or at least, for a moment after ejaculation, something less desirous. We don't make people into objects when we like or respect them; we do it when we covet, when we desire something inordinately without regard to the rights of others. Even if the girl is still technically her parents' property until she reaches the age of eighteen, what's coveted is not her parents'. In this case, the men violate the girl's own rights: her right to her body, her right to live a life of a certain quality, and her future right to feel trust or tenderness with other human beings. She may be glad she was raped instead of raped and killed. It does not follow that the deed is acceptable.

At the next point in the movie, the senator's daughter would willingly give some fingers just to get raped instead of culled. She's been in the pit for days. Everyone agrees that the senator is a very intelligent woman because when she goes on television to plead for her daughter's life, she repeats the girl's name—Katherine—along with the phrase "my little girl." Jodie says, "The senator's smart. If Buffalo Bill thinks of Katherine as a person rather than an object, it'll be harder for him to tear her up." But like most of the senators we petition with letters about the inherent value of wilderness, Buffalo Bill is tuned out, so the mother's desperate plea falls on deaf ears.

By now, the FBI think they have located their killer when they find the slayer's address on a list of rejected sex-change operation applicants. Jodie is way offtrack, they think. They don't pay close attention to Hannibal's tip that crime begins with coveting something you see every day. When Jodie calls her FBI superiors from the hometown of Buffalo Bill's first victim, a seamstress, they dismiss her. She has called to tell them what she's discovered in the murdered woman's closet: a blue and white dress with two diamond-shaped inserts decorating the lower back. Jodie realizes that Buffalo Bill has nothing against the girls he murders; it's just that their bodies hold a resource he desires: human skin, to make a metamorphic shroud, a cocoon of female flesh.

This is what I consider to be the scariest scene in the movie, the only scene where we see Buffalo Bill dealing directly with the living girl. The camera cuts to hairy hands with painted fingernails feeding leathery skin through a sewing machine. Wails and pleas, like echoes in a tunnel, punctuate the heavy-metal rock emanating from a record player. The damp, rock-walled basement is an empire of metamorphosis. Shining garments of fur and feather hang here and there; tilted configurations of bare planks rest against the dungeonlike walls, suggesting darkened adjoining cells. We see Buffalo Bill for the first time without his special glasses; he's decked out like a blond bombshell. He hums his way over to the edge of the well and places a white container in a basket. The basket is attached to the end of a long rope, and when he lowers it into the well, we see the girl in her filthy clothes begging him to spare her. She's soaking wet.

His rouged and plastered face hangs over the rim of the pit; from the girl's perspective it fills the horizon, looming and foreshortened. The man chimes (as if he's reciting an advertising jingle), "It rubs the lotion on its skin, or else it gets the hose again."

In 1907, the Forest Service's "Use Book" declared that the national forests exist for the "homebuilder's special welfare." Once I wrote a paper about the number of trees who have been slaughtered as a result of our blindness to their own purposes in living. The professor commented that the word *who* is reserved for living beings (i.e., humans); for objects, we use "it, that or which."

"It rubs the lotion on its skin, or else it gets the hose again."

The girl pleads in a broken voice, "Please let me go. I want to see my mommy. Please let me see my mommy."

Buffalo Bill winces at the word *mommy*. His voice grows more strained, louder, as if to drown out her words. "It rubs the lotion on its skin and then it places the lotion in the basket," he states firmly, with tense control.

In an article called "The Auction and Sales of Slaves, Horses, and other Cattle," an 1857 Virginia journal states that "the flesh of ordinary niggers is hardly worth $7.00 a pound, the odds being the difference as to toughness. Human flesh, when it is young and tender, is worth about $10.00 a pound. Young women weighing, say 130 pounds are fetching $1,750. This is a fair price a pound: their flesh is tender again."

"Please," she wails, "I want to go home. I want to see—"

"It places the lotion in the basket!" The face turns away tightly.

The purpose of Katherine, like that of the "niggers and other cattle," is use. Timber and meat are euphemistic side effects of use (or slaughter), like the dressy material from the body of the "thing" in the pit. Carol Adams writes, "We see ourselves as eating 'meat': hamburger, sirloins, and filet mignon, rather than the 43 pigs, 3 lambs, 11 cows, 4 calves, 1,107 chickens, 45 turkeys, and 861 fishes that the average American eats in a lifetime." Gifford Pinchot, the figurative king of the Forest Service for the last hundred years, declared in 1906, "The primary purpose of the Forest Reserves is use."

Katherine continues sobbing, "Please, mister, what about my mom—"

Eyes clamped and teeth clenched, the painted face bellows, *"Put the fucking lotion in the basket!"*

What we ask of—or take from—the deer, the tree, or the senator's daughter is not the fallen antler, the fruit, or the shed fingernails, but the body—the life—itself. It's the difference between the bad man asking Mom for her wallet and asking for her neck. Mom has a right to her neck. In a sense, it's her property; it's certainly her life.

You might contend that slicing the neck off someone's mother is not the same as killing, for example, a Pacific yew. Standing in line the other day, I saw on the cover of the *Weekly World News* that a bizarrely attenuated, giraffe-necked woman "may have cure for cancer in her neck!" The Pacific yew will be flayed and dissected in order to get cancer cures, even though it's three hundred years old. In fact, at least one cancer-afflicted Montanan has stated she believes that the Pacific yew exists only in order to be killed for its medicine. Well then, why not the giraffe-woman's neck? Buffalo

Bill, the cancerous Montanan, and Jeffrey Dahmer don't stand too far apart: Sharing the same fundamental beliefs, they just have some species-related fine points to smooth out. A common, covetous psychological process of objectification, denial, transgression, and justification sets the ethical standards of all three.

How can I know the motivations of cancer victims, logging executives, slaveholders, wolf poisoners, or serial killers, you might ask, if I'm not one? I know because I am.

Last year I was teaching wilderness survival in the desert of southern Idaho. We'd been out only five days or so when we came upon some deep pools in a high-banked stream. The tail end of sunset was slipping up over the basalt canyon walls, and circles grew like smoke rings on the surface of the water. Fish. We'd hiked a good ten miles that day in the late summer heat, and daytime fire danger meant we'd had nothing to eat, since all our food required cooking. We were not starving. We were hungry, but we each had plenty of lentils to see us through.

The other instructor cut a willow stick, made a fly of deer hair, and tied a hook onto the end of the string. A true high desert with little water, this land was "looked after" by the Bureau of Land Management, so cattle had decimated the vegetation on either side of the stream. Consequently, the insects which usually fell from the brush into these pools were absent. Again and again, trout took the fly. These fish were not only hungry; they may have been starving.

My friend pulled five good-size trout from one pool; six was his limit. He said, "You want to try?" After thirteen months of teaching survival under a barrage of students who could not understand why other groups got to kill and we never could, I decided it was time to see what killing was all about. Staying low to the ground, I plucked the string out onto the pool. A fish struck immediately. I jerked it out of the water, wrenching and arching, and it flew through the air on the tautness of the lifting line. It flapped its colors dusty between a scrub sage and a cow pie as I pounded its convulsions to a halt with a digging stick.

Down where the cattle had done their flattening work on the creek, I inserted the small blade of my pocketknife into the fish's anus and pulled it up the belly. The skin split easily under the sharp metal. The guts constricted in the desiccated desert air. My friend would eat head and guts in his fish soup, and I would toast the bones on a stone by the fire. The liver shone with a healthy mucus, wine dark and uniform.

Then I saw a grainy prong, like baby corn, running almost the length of the gut cavity, and a blast of realization washed over my face: eggs. This fish was not an "it" but a "she." Moments earlier, she had been going about her life in her own way, when suddenly she was confronted with a power utterly other, completely alien. In the water, she had flickered like a shadow, entwined with the reflections of the few willow branches above; an instant later, the watery pattern changed, diminished, as her creative potential was wrested from her by force. The trout had trusted, as a wary Virginia bass seldom does, that when nature provided her with the stuff of life, the stuff would not be directly attached to her death.

As I plotted to remove her from all she knew and to take from her all she had, I wore some evolutionarily privileged glasses: I could see and anticipate her, but she couldn't see me. Still, I would never understand her and her dense wetness, her innocence. Someone once told a story about a shark who gorged himself on the refuse of civilization. He was found with a swing set and some Volkswagen axles in his belly. But here in the core of this fish was no more than she needed: a compact grasshopper (partially digested), two water boatmen, some brown muck, and a pebble—a diary of the sincerity of her experience.

I am thankful that I saw the integrity of nature in the guts of a female fish who was ripe with the future of her kind. I am sorry I killed her to do so. So sorry, black people. At his trial, Jeffrey Dahmer apologized to the families of the boys he raped, killed, and dismembered. "I'm sorry," he said. "I was sick." But the jury decided he was not sick. Something about what he did, their verdict implied, was not insane.

The fish kill showed me that the process of objectification and violation which had seemed completely alien to my mother is, indeed, a part of me. Hannibal-the-face-eater proved right about the criminal process, and from survival to lunacy it's just a matter of degree. From our position as twentieth-century Americans, a population so extreme in our habits that we have become either unable or unwilling to differentiate between need and desire, the place where humans might behave with ecological sanity or ethical consideration is obscured by a shroud of greed and delusion, like stars by city haze. We can't see the place, we can't remember it, we can't imagine it. We certainly don't operate there. When and if we ever do, we can discuss the ethical implications of subsistence; at present, our luxury approaches lunacy. The trout's cooked flesh, which I so inordinately desired, tasted decadently rich in the desert night, but I do not believe my pleasure in it was greater than her own reasons for living in the way she did, however unintelligible the glyph of a fish's purpose will remain to a confused species like us.

Jodie's not confused, though; she follows her intuition. She ends up on the doorstep of a small suburban house in the seamstress's hometown at the same time the FBI bomb squads surround a different address in a distant city; the FBI chief and Jodie are knocking simultaneously on their respective doors. When the chief and his hundred armed reinforcements get no answer at their door, they finally storm the house, bursting into a bare living room. It's deserted—no one home for years. Hundreds of miles away, a well-manicured but thick hand opens the door to Jodie—alone. She questions the homeowner ingenuously; and when a large, dark moth lands on the table before her, Jodie draws her gun and aims at the individual who she knows must be Buffalo Bill. He disappears into the basement with his own gun in hand.

Katherine wails from her trap as Jodie pursues the murderer into the labyrinth of planked-up rooms adjoining the metamorphic chamber. Somewhere inside, he waits. In the dark, stultified habitat preferred by moths, he dons the green glasses that enable him to see. For several moments we see through his eyes. Jodie, completely

347

blind, stumbles from room to room. He's following her silently; she's feeling her way, she's falling, she's grabbing onto plywood and rebar, doorjambs and cobwebs. Once, her green outline brushes so close to Buffalo Bill that he can almost reach out and touch her hair. Finally she hits a wall, a dead end, and she presses back in a blind sit against the wall, knowing what the next moment must hold, seeing nothing. Buffalo Bill stops approaching; through his eyes we see his dark gun rising toward Jodie's listening green head; we hear only the click of his hammer cocking, and *blam*.

In the next frame we see a body slumped in a corner, dead. The click of the hammer against Jodie's open ears had guided her aim.

There is a bill in Congress now which will release two-thirds of Montana's remaining roadless lands to the Forest Service, an action which is analogous to placing our children in Buffalo Bill's day-care center. It means those forests are as good as dead. It means almost 100 percent of the "suitable timber" in this 4 million acres will be chopped down. "It" was the killer's name for the incarcerated and doomed being in the pit; likewise, "suitable timber" is the Forest Service's name for the places where plants, animals, soils, water, sun, insects, minerals, and air (just to name a few) support one another in an ageless enactment of natural creation and destruction. The final remaining ecosystems capable of supporting a wide spectrum of nonhuman large mammals and sustaining biodiversity will soon be fragmented, packaged, and consumed.

Well, what about wilderness? you ask. The way it's currently interpreted, *wilderness* is what's left over when you take out all the places where diverse life-forms can survive. The joke around here is that *wilderness* means "rock and ice." Except it's not funny, and it's not a joke. The more delicate wills to live who may not survive a winter on the blasting, icy cornice transpire now in peril. We convert their damp, shady homes into our bland planks. We render their lives dust, memory, and finally, naught.

A separate wilderness designation was created for public lands when we realized we could no longer trust the Forest Service with them: The Forest Service covets the bodies of trees and gorges itself on the life of the forest, hacking "it" to pieces under the disguise of euphemistic lies like "habitat enhancement" and "timber quotas."

However, if the analogy between Wilderness and Katherine—the Pit Girl—were to have been played out in the movie, the FBI chief and Buffalo Bill would have been one and the same criminal. If he who is appointed, paid, and lawfully entitled to protect the forest or the girl and to oversee her just treatment, if he himself is a covetous murderer, who can we trust? The woods are no longer safe unto themselves or safe for us. They are controlled, used, flayed, dismembered, and finally "preserved" (like Dahmer's pickled genitalia) by mad institutions that exercise, without restraint, the covetous impulses that exist in all of us, extending them to the lunatic extreme of unspeakable crime.

And even if policy were changed so drastically that the forest were only being raped and not killed, the quality of life for rape survivors would remain an issue. The coyote who chews off his foot to escape the trap, the girl who crookedly rejoices that her life goes on—are these the only options they deserve: either get raped or get raped and killed?

At her FBI initiation party after the big case, Jodie gets a phone call. It's Hannibal, calling to ask if the lambs in her head have stopped screaming. Having escaped from a maximum-security prison using the cartridge from a ball-point pen, the ingenious cannibal is now on the loose. But both the viewer and Jodie know that he will not come after her. When Hannibal gave Jodie clues about Buffalo Bill's psychology, he did so only in exchange for information about her past and her purposes. He has taken the time to learn about her in their sessions together, and he admires her sincerity and courage. It's understood that the denial of inherent value which attends an entirely resource-oriented categorization of individuals or their habitats and which facilitates ultimate consumption is fundamentally incompatible with respect. Hannibal respects Jodie; hence, he can't violate and consume her. Between them there exists, twisted as it is, a kind of trust.

· · ·

I met someone once, years after the first men. His eyes were old somehow, and in them I recognized an almost ancestral honesty. The clarity of his vision polished our words and movements as if from within; it shaped them like light, and the air between us flowed palpable and heightened as water.

In the cool wakefulness of his presence, the mystery of re-membering, of meeting amid all this, rose on me like dew. I re-membered things I had loved as a child: the snail's spiraled hut, the moss, the gray-green wind before a storm. Two things I'd known then came back: how the sun extends its tether of light and warmth across the vacant lapse and the world rolls in that touch like a grassy animal, and how wonder reaches a cusp in its rising where experience cascades from it like bright water.

In the steadiness of his eyes I remembered one childhood dusk, running in the woods alone, practicing after the Indians. Suddenly a single lady's slipper, endangered in those parts, materialized in my path, standing out from the gray-brown mat of decaying leaves. Pink, the blossom billowed out like a silk jug filled with weightless water. In the way that the chambers of a heart curve, it curved in upon itself, and even though I knew it had come from the secret condensed dormancy of the flower world and I from the expansive frenzy of the human realm, I felt as if we had surprised each other by meeting there and that we stood seeing each other for the first time, each still open from the peace of our recent solitude, wondering at one another in the forest dusk.

One night that soul fell asleep with his head in my lap as we watched the fish arching and curling in their tank, big as a coffin, beyond the candles. For a long time I smoothed his hair and watched him breathe, his breath so at home in this world that I thought it might go on forever like the rolling Earth, yet fleeting and fragile as ash. I felt something lunge in my chest, and I was seized by the longing to enfold him, to protect him, like a child, from what would come.

This fear crumbles and grows into many sides; it breaks and

rejoins. I still fear that he will be denied and diminished, refuted and ignored by family and strangers and friends. I fear he will be betrayed and lose faith. I fear he will fade and disperse in this world like an echo, that he will be annihilated entirely. And I know all this will come to pass.

This friend is gone now. Perhaps the flowing loss carried him away. Whenever he and I neared the precipitous edge of trust, tears staved me off lest we'd plunge into an impossible hope.

The crazy men creep the woods with their drills, saws, lies, wheels, and other weapons. The lunatics in charge of protecting the forest beings violate them with a covetous calculus that reduces life to numbers and fractures ethical limits in 'an algebra of infinite permission. But for me tonight, alone by the dying fire while the entire sparkling dome of inaccessible night arches over these ceilings, what's most sad is the broken trust that paves the refuge of natural awe.

In my mind, I crouch again at the bank of a crayfish-filled creek at dusk, gathering water. Nocturnal desert sounds peal against the ascending edge of evening, and something compels me to look up. On the high rim of the canyon, a solitary deer stands stark against the diminishing sunset. His antlers cup the last light. My heart simultaneously opens and deflates beneath his presence. It opens for the simple loveliness and unlikeliness of the physical world, and for the deer's quietly coming through miles of desert to this place, where he will finally drink. It deflates under the knowledge that even as he does so, the highway, the profit, and the loss advance inexorably toward him.

Something—chance, fate, grace—has allowed me to witness the poignant calm of desert and glen; in this sense, I am blessed. But I have a sad understanding of the future that the deer and crayfish do not. Gone are the first joys of sheer surprise and reverence which gave this place a solace where even death came lovely in its rightness. The celebratory curve of a snail's shell and the loping ecstasy of trillium in bloom are trailed so closely by disrespect and destruction that the wilderness experience has become one of crying through an impossibly hopeful smile. Under the shroud of perpetual progress, in this relentlessly transformed place which we desired with such fury and into which we have finally hemmed ourselves, to cherish is to know the end, and each kiss says good-bye.

◆

Leslie Ryan is a student-teacher of Environmental Studies at the University of Montana. She also teaches backcountry college courses for the University of California's Sierra Institute.

LESLIE RYAN

◆ ◆ ◆ ◆ ◆

THE OTHER SIDE OF FIRE

I have heard it said that storytelling starts with the body and ends with the body. That's what gives stories the ability to snag the mind by its ankles from behind and land it facedown in something: life if the story's good, blandness if it's not.

But as a woman I worry about this. For most women, the body, like the story, is not a simple thing. It's a battlefield where lies and truths about power go at it. A woman's mind might wander from skirt to skirt in that smoky place like a dislocated child, looking for some gounded legs to stand by, or on, for years. The woman might end up knowing herself only as a casualty, or recognizing herself only by her scars. While there may be some truth in such an identity, it is only a partial truth, and a potentially destructive one.

I want a different story.

I never thought much about fire until a few years ago, when I began teaching survival in the Great Basin desert of southern Idaho. I worked in a wilderness therapy program for troubled youth. The idea was that direct contact with the natural world could help these kids gain a more healthy sense of identity and empowerment.

Some of the teenagers who ended up walking around the desert like hunter-gatherers had been court-ordered to do so. A few of the boys arrived in cuffs, with their hair shaved down to the rind on one side and left to seed on the other. On their forearms they displayed homemade logos of heavy-metal rock bands, scratched in with sewing needles and flooded with blue fountain pen ink. They wore the tales of their crimes like dog tags, and we called these narratives war stories.

But most of the boys didn't come that way. In spite of a few shocking tales, the boys' toughness hung on them uncomfortably. The manic energy they used in comparing transgressions made me smile, because beneath it they seemed to writhe like grubs set down in unfamiliar terrain, glistening and blinded by their recent emergence from childhood but as yet unsure of how to burrow into the next phase.

The girls came to the desert differently. Their fear wasn't just a thing to guess at beneath layers of toughness and tattoos; it was as evident as the black lace panties and see-through underwire brassieres they wore for twenty-one days of rigorous hiking. Their stories, shared in secret with the other girls, were less war stories than love stories—or, more specifically, sex stories—but they were stories of power and identity just the same.

We instructors taught our students how to make backpacks from their blankets and string, how to find water in the desert, how to dig coal beds, how to construct debris huts and other shelters, how to identify and gather wild edibles, and basically how to keep themselves alive in difficult terrain. But the hardest thing we learned out there—the thing that made the students cry in frustration—was how to make fire with sticks.

I have been questioned about the relevance of bow and drill fire making to everyday life, and I have been challenged on the social structuring of wilderness therapy programs, which mostly benefit rich, white children. Wouldn't these kids feel a lot different about survival if they *really* had to do it—if they had to make fires on the floors of their freezing city apartments, rather than in this fabricated desert game?

I can only answer that question from my own experience, with a story that also takes place somewhere between war and love.

. . .

When I was twelve, my younger brothers and I were abandoned for a year or so in an apartment on the south side of Richmond, Virginia. Mom was wherever Dad had left her, probably back in the old house where she had been struggling with mental illness for years. After repeated complaints from our neighbors, who thought we children were being hurt and neglected, the court had ordered our father to remove us from the old house. We relocated on the other side of town, where no nosy neighbors knew us. At first I thought we would all live in the apartment together—four children and our father— and start a new life. But it didn't work that way.

We still don't know where Dad lived during that time. At first it was every few days that he came back, bringing what we needed to survive. Some groceries: Spam, milk, and a case of Bisquick boxes. Then every week he would come. Then there was no pattern, and we couldn't tell when we would see him again.

Before long, the phone got disconnected. The power got shut off. Water too. We were living in a husk of a house with no resources. The dishes in the sink had been crusted for so long they began to flake clean. The toilet hadn't been flushed in what seemed like months. We just kept using it until it began to overflow, and after that we shut the bathroom door and went in the new construction site under a pile of boards. Some of the windows in the apartment were broken out—one from my head, one from my brother's fist, others from things we threw. My brothers were aged ten, eight, and four. We fought.

We also made a pact. If anyone found out we lived alone, Dad had said, they'd break us apart. Mom was too sick to take care of us, so we'd all have to go live with different families, and we'd never see each other again. The four of us had gathered in the kitchen one day by the dry sink, and I scraped the crud from a sharp knife with my teeth. We sliced a blood pact into our hands: Never tell.

The neighbors on the left had evidently abandoned their apartment in a hurry. We went in there a lot at first, eating the food they had left and looking at the bloated fish floating in the tank. There were parts of a broken water bed, some lava lamps, clothing, and a bunch of empty boxes. All their wallpaper was swirled with bright metallic patterns, like our kitchen paper, but patches of it were torn down and left hanging. No one ever came in or out of there, and after the food was gone we stopped going there too, because it was a creepy place.

The neighbors on the right acted like we didn't exist. I think they knew that we had gone into their apartment and stolen food, because they got double bolt locks and began to talk loudly about calling the police if they saw any delinquents around. We saw that we could get caught and separated, so we stopped taking from them.

My brothers learned from an older boy how to steal from stores. They could walk to the 7-Eleven in about half an hour. They stole ready-made food from there, since we had no electricity to cook the Bisquick and everything else was gone. The boys refused to eat Bisquick raw. Mostly they stole small food, for safety. Candy bars were usually the biggest they got from the 7-Eleven, because the clerks could see down the aisle pretty easily. From Safeway, though, they could get more, like peanut butter; it was easier, because the clerks changed more often and didn't expect kids to be stealing. Sometimes they'd get extra for the baby, who couldn't come. I don't know how long this went on. Nine months, maybe a year.

Then one day I found myself standing in the kitchen. It was coming on winter, dusky in the house. A wet wind blew through the broken windows. I lifted my bare feet up and down on the cold kitchen floor. I was staring at the stove, scooping dry Bisquick from the box with crooked fingers. I wanted to turn on the stove. I wanted to wave my hands over the fiery concentric circles of the working heating element. I wanted there to be power in the house.

"I am twelve years old," I said out loud.

Bisquick floated out onto the air as I spoke. In summer I had mixed the Bisquick in a bowl with sprinkler water and eaten it wet like that. Now the sprinkler faucets were off. The boys had shown me where they drank from the creek; the water was oily and bright orange-brown. I wouldn't do it.

"Bisquick should be cooked," I said.

When was the last time he came? I couldn't remember. He might never come back. Could we actually freeze here?

Something about the stove started to infuriate me. It was supposed to give us something.

"Damn thing," I said.

Big and useless. How it made these promises and never kept them. I spit chunks of Bisquick at it, but they were too dry to stick. They fell all over my arms and chest, making a pattern of white, dusty splats.

I pulled the burner control knobs from their sticky prongs and hurled them one by one across the kitchen at the orange metallic wallpaper peeling from the wall. They left the paper dented like bent foil.

I grabbed a big metal spoon from the dish pile and banged on the steel edge of the stove. I wanted sparks. I wanted gouges. It was the cheap kind of spoon, and its bowl just bent back perpendicular.

"Damn you," I said, with the Bisquick on my teeth like plaque.

The baby was four, and he still couldn't talk. He did know to poop in the lumber. I was still getting good grades at school, because I had learned to read at a young age and was placed in the gifted classes, but my brothers were not doing so well: They had missed over a hundred days of school each. We had received a letter about it, addressed to Dad. I had to do something. I surveyed my options.

The only reading we had were old *Scientific Americans* and the other magazines under the mattress where Dad used to sleep. *Scientific Americans* were all men. The mattress ones were all women: *Penthouse* and *Playboy*. Dad liked their articles best. All of us had read them.

I read them again. There were women who had sex with all their best friends, their bosses, delivery people, and pets, with everyone watching everyone else, and it seemed to make things better. "Dear Xavier," they wrote to their friend Xavier, a woman who was pictured only as a pair of red lips with a penis-shaped lipstick going in. They told her all about it.

I read about all the special techniques women could learn to please men, like mouthing unwaxed cucumbers. Men took women to cooked dinner for this, and gave them promotions. They'd provide apartments, heated, for the whole family.

I walked to the bathroom doorway and stood outside. No one ever went in there. Stuff had actually flowed onto the floor. We could smell it all over the house. But the bathroom had the only mirror. I stripped off my pants, shirt, and underwear. I held my breath, opened the door, and climbed onto the sink counter.

In the murky light seeping in from the hall, I looked at my legs in the bathroom mirror. There were three triangles where the light came through, just like Xavier said men liked: one between the ankles, one between the knees, one between the thighs.

A stiffened orange towel lay on the small bathroom counter. I wrapped it around my mouth and nose like a gag so I could breathe. I turned around on the bathroom sink to look at the backs of my legs and butt.

If I swayed my back I looked curvier. I bent down with my butt stuck out and my hands on my knees to get the sideways picture, checking the curve of dim light along my spine and the flatness of my stomach. I was still holding my breath for as long as I could because the towel smelled almost as bad as the bathroom.

I squatted above the sink and looked into my pupils, wide and black above the bristling cloth. I said aloud through the mask, "You have one thing."

I remember a time not long after that stove day when I was being hit by a jealous man. He was nineteen years old; I was twelve. He had six motorcycles, a punching bag, and a seemingly unlimited supply of drugs. I couldn't leave; he was giving me the drugs I sold for money. I wish I could say I sold them for food money, for food I would share with my brothers. This did happen sometimes. But not often. I wasn't a good mother.

What I really wanted was to be someone. What I really wanted was power, and the only way I could get it was to take it from someone who had more than enough. Drugs were the currency that allowed my body to be exchanged for money, and money is a poor person's idea of strength and possibility. So I just clamped my teeth, stood there, and let my friend hit me.

As he got madder, one zigzagged vein began standing and pulsing in his forehead like lightning. He was hot, coiled up red with his fury.

I, on the other hand, felt like a block of ice. Each blow to my head seemed to break off little pieces of my mind; they would go floating up into the corner of the room and stick there like ice chips behind a river rock.

Soon my body was standing alone in the bedroom, being hit.

But not me. He couldn't get at me. I was hovering alongside the brown ceiling stain from the upstairs toilet. I could watch my head lolling around as he cuffed me.

Do whatever you want to my body, you jerk, I said to myself. That's not *me*.

It was the same way having sex with him, and with the other men who, as I see in retrospect, had no business being sexually involved with a twelve-year-old girl. When I was with them, my mind would slip out the back of my head and go look out the window, if there was one.

My mind became more and more a body unto itself—in time, when it left me on the bed, I could feel its dry, bare feet shuffling across the floor. One time it made it all the way to the door, and paused there with its delicate spirit fingers on the knob. When it looked back to say good-bye to my body on the bed, something—compassion, necessity?—made it pop back inside.

After this went on for what seemed to be a long time, I began to worry about my brothers. One night the eleven-year-old and I sat in the living room watching TV (the power was on at the time). We were both stoned, and the vertical hold on the TV didn't work, so we were watching Captain Kirk's head and torso being severed and lifted by a constantly rising black line. My brother told me that some of the men I'd been sleeping with had given the baby pot to smoke while they were smoking, and maybe other drugs, too.

This, I said to myself, is not what I want our lives to be. I quit doing drugs then and didn't allow any of those men in our apartment again. All my friends disappeared.

I made another plan. My body had gotten me into this trouble; my mind would get me out. I had good grades, but they weren't useful yet. In order to be a good mother to these boys I'd need a job.

But I knew that a girl of my social class couldn't get a job; my clothes were embarrassing, my hair greasy, my shoes fake leather with unglued soles that slapped the ground as I walked. I was thirteen. I couldn't work for three years. I did look sixteen already, though; someone might be fooled into hiring me if I had the proper attire. Even if I couldn't get work yet, I reasoned, it was best to steal my wardrobe now, because as long as I was under sixteen, nothing would go on my permanent record and expose us if I did get caught.

I hitchhiked downtown to a fancy department store called Miller and Rhodes. This was before the days of electronic theft devices. I told the salesladies my father had asked me to come look for something nice for my mother—she was about my size, I said— and he'd be back later with me to see what I'd found. In the dressing room, I opened my big Naugahyde purse and stuffed in a gray wool business suit: tailored skirt, vest, and jacket, completely lined. I broke the hanger in half and stuffed it in, too, and left the rest of the clothes there.

From that department I went to lingerie. I picked out a peach-colored Christian Dior teddy, pure silk. It snapped discreetly at the crotch; one hip was cut out and flounced with pleated gauze. I stole that too.

I see now that my faith in my mind was skimpy. My body was still the bottom line for power. I resented the fact, but I was a practical girl. Even if I was lucky enough to get a job with my suit and my grades, I'd need to be high class underneath, too—for my boss, and for the real work that women do.

When I got home, I went up to my room and found my suitcase full of Barbies, which I was ashamed about still having anyway. I had written my name in pen all over the plastic luggage a long time before, in big, curly handwriting with exclamation points and flowers. I took it into my father's closet and dumped the Barbies on the floor, so no boss would see Barbies in my room. I cleaned the little Barbie shoes out of the side pockets, folded the gray suit and the silk teddy into separate piles in the suitcase, and hid the suitcase under my bed.

As time went on, I added to the suitcase with a tan pantsuit, some oxford shirts, a pair of leather sling pumps stolen right off the rack, red lace bikini panties with bows on them and a matching bra, and the sexy kind of nylons that need a garter belt.

Before the suitcase was full, though, my father had come back, apparently to stay. When he came, it was late at night. He had a woman with him.

He called us downstairs one by one to where she sat at the three-legged kitchen table. Most of the lightbulbs were blown out, so only half her face was visible in the dim light from the hall fixture.

The woman was young, twenty-seven or so. She was twenty years younger than my father, but she had three children of her own. By the time I came downstairs to stand rigidly beside the boys, the woman was crying. We were embarrassed by her emotion, and by the way she said she would marry my father and save us.

She did marry him, but she couldn't save us. She could make sure we had shoes and meals and schooling, for which I am grateful. But she couldn't protect us from our father, who was violent and owned her love. She couldn't even protect herself.

The skirts she wore, and the power they signified, offered no refuge to a child. They were too much like the ones I had stolen. All the pretty garments underneath, which were supposed to lead my stepmother somewhere better, actually only dragged her further into my father's control, like bridles and bits. In a landscape of boys and men and lies about power, though, they were the only skirts she and I knew. A year later, when the nine of us lived in a three-bedroom apartment, my own suits and panties still lay tucked in the suitcase under my bed, waiting there like passwords.

There are other lies about power and identity, more subtle

than the ones told by pornography. When I first learned, not long ago, that being abandoned in a house without utilities or food is called child abuse, I smiled. When I learned that a twelve-year-old girl is a child, and a child being molested by anyone—an adult or another child—is called sexual abuse, I grinned. Suddenly I had a strange, different kind of power over the men who had hurt me, and it lay in my scars: If I had been wronged, then I was on the side of the good, and the men were on the side of the evil. Although I might not be stronger, or richer, or better in any other way, I was morally superior to them. And the moral superiority of the victim brings her power.

Like the virtue of victimization, the promise of pornography—that a woman's body is her identity and her source of strength—wasn't entirely wrong. But the way in which both of them *were* wrong, no person would ever teach me. The desert had to do that.

In my midtwenties, I was led to the desert less by a decision of intellect than by a response to blood urgency. Going there was like picking up a baby who's facedown in a puddle.

Through all those years after middle school, my mind and body had stayed as distinct from each other as the wool suits and the garter belts. My mind had helped me get a job and go through college on scholarships. But as time went on it grew more and more controlling, until it became tyrannically disdainful of my body. By the time college ended I was living almost completely in my head: The intellectual jargon of modern philosophy rang in my brain all night like an alarm, and I hardly knew if or why I was alive.

Fortunately, my body had better sense. She spoke up from under the bed, where I'd kept her locked up like a caged animal and had fed her only scraps for years. She said, "Get outside."

I went west, to the desert, to a state where I knew no one and took a job for which I had little preparation other than backpacking.

I've heard the Great Basin described by one survival student as "Nature's Worst." It's sage and basalt country: gray and brown and fairly nondescript at first. The hunting and gathering Paiutes who lived there in early times were disparagingly labeled Diggers, because they ate roots and grubs rather than something charismatic like buffalo.

In the rain, the Great Basin ground, where it's not rock, turns to slimy mud. If you have to walk when it's wet, the mud will grow on your boot soles in bricklike platforms, your quads will cramp with the weight of them, and your ankles will roll above the boot blocks like they're broken. When the sun sucks the moisture out of the mud again, the ground will crack into miles of dusty pieces.

In some places, a six-foot-tall person can lie in the dirt and make dust angels without knocking into anything but basalt gravel and stickers, so people call the desert barren. But the desert isn't barren. It's alive, and it tells the body stories that are true.

When I began teaching survival, wandering for several months through the basalt-pillared canyons and the expansive plateaus of the Great Basin with some blankets, knives, cooking cans, and personal items, I underwent a transformation.

My hands twisted wet bark into cordage, carved fire sticks, and dug holes for coal beds; my fingers and palms hardened into dark, basaltic chunks of flesh. Wind and sun made my hair spiny as the wild wheat we'd gather near old homesteads; the nomadic days chiseled a landscape of calluses and cracks into my feet. My dung shrank like a coyote's, and my breath came slow and reptilian.

I came to know a little about the creatures who passed their lives out there. Snipes would swoop above us at dawn like bats. Grouse would do the unthinkable—eat sagebrush, puke most of it back up in pellets, pass the rest through in slimy wads like black slugs—and live healthy, normal lives in the process. Golden eagles would fly over with their writhing meals—rabbits or snakes—in tow. Overnight, badgers would excavate holes big enough for a twenty-gallon drum; with their bare hands, they'd put a shovel to shame, plowing through cementlike earth in the dark. And the sun ignited both ends of day with what looked like fire; morning and evening never tired of being burned that way.

My mind and body began separating less and less often, mostly because I was learning to survive out there, and doing so did not require that my mind float up in the air and watch bad things happen to my body.

In fact, the desert required just the opposite: In order to survive there, I had to be fully present. When the summer heat seemed intent on vaporizing my scalp as I walked, my senses would tell me where to locate shade. They'd show me which cranny was safe to crouch in during a rainstorm. They'd let me know which plant was wild carrot and which hemlock.

In the desert, a mind that wanders far from the body can land a person in strange territory, far from water or cover. If at any time I stopped listening to my body and to my lived experience, I might get lost. I found myself realizing that power does come from my body after all, but in a very different way.

On the first winter survival trip I led, I met a student who brought some things together for me. Dawn was fourteen years old. Her face was tinged with a solemn and unnerving coldness, like the blush on frost-nipped fruit. On that trip, she was the only other female. For some reason, I wanted her to be the first to make bow-drill fire.

On the trail, Dawn was a quiet girl, and distant. Like so many other students, she triggered in me the sense that something had been lost. I didn't know why she was there.

On day ten of the trip, we awakened to a low dawn in the mouth of a wide canyon. We'd each built a fire the night before in a rock-lined pit, and then buried the coals. Eight hours later, the earth beneath me was still as warm as hands. Four teenagers and another instructor lay around me in their snowy pods, each tight in a sheet of plastic and two blankets. Three boys snored out of time with one another; one had come unhatted. His hair stuck out in a unicorn spike.

Later that day, I was working with Dawn on her bow-drill fire. I had already let the boys quit trying; they were cooking lentils a short distance away. Big sagebrush, seven feet tall, stood around us on an unlikely patch of fertile riparian soil. Twenty degrees, platy sky, preweather stillness. Serviceberries were shriveled on the bush; the wild onions, yampah, and nettles we'd gathered all year had dried to bony stalks and blown away. Loose strands of gray-brown bark ribboned the tall sage; they scraped in a brief breeze.

Dawn knelt on a thin layer of granular snow. Her left hand, blistered and ruddy from carving, cupped a bone hand socket that served as a pivot point for a sage spindle. Dawn worked wood considerately, and her spindle was just right: Like a stout pencil, it was a little longer than her hand and thick as her index finger. She'd sharpened the upper end of the spindle to fit into the hand socket. The lower, blunt end was black from friction.

When the blunt end was newly carved, before it had begun to burn, it had shown the sage's concentric growth rings. The wood grain moved out from them like the linking strands in a spiderweb. I told Dawn I hadn't seen many things prettier than that pattern. She gave me a sideways, suspicious look.

The thong of a half-moon bow girdled Dawn's spindle, and by stroking the bow back and forth with her right hand, Dawn could drill the spindle down into a plank of sage. The friction between this fire board and the spindle would rub off clouds of smoke and charred wood fibers called punk.

The punk would drop down through a pie-shaped notch in the fire board. Hotter and hotter punk would accumulate there, and it would eventually weld itself into a small coal. Then the fire maker would gently lift the coal into a nest of well-rubbed sagebrush bark, and her long, steady breaths would turn it into flame.

Theoretically. But Dawn still stared at her bow-drill set as if she were illiterate in fire, even though she had cut the set herself. Technically, she was fine. Perfect form. I stayed after her about it, keeping her up later than the boys almost every night, trying to figure out what was wrong. Her light hair whipped back and forth above the fire board, her bowing arm cramped tight, and her breath came hard, but each day ended the same: no punk, no fire.

She'd say quietly, "I'll never do it."

None of the other students had made this type of fire yet either. Everyone could make sparks by striking a quartz or flint rock against their carbon steel knife blades, and they got fires at night this way, even Dawn.

But something about bow drill spooked them. It seemed so

old, like magic. There was nothing but their own bodies and the body of the sagebrush twirling together, and the result was fire.

The boys had a bow-drill-related superstition. The one with the unicorn spike, George, would shake a crusty ash cake at Dawn and say, "Dude. You gotta believe."

On day eleven, the group had hiked the usual distance of about seven miles. We made camp near a shallow basalt cave. It was don't get your hair wet weather, but Dawn and I wanted to wash up. We heated two billycans of water on a small fire, grabbed our bandanas, and retreated to the shadowy cave where we could undress away from the boys.

White owl splats looked like paint along the head-high inner ledges of the cave. Dawn and I shifted our cold barefoot weight on the basalt gravel and tried to give each other as much bathing privacy as possible, but then an echoing crack and rush snapped along the walls, and we both jerked to the sound. Rock and ice from a ledge outside.

I saw then in the half light that the girl had a secret. Low on her breastbone, where no one would see, a lattice of rippling white scars ran over Dawn, like someone had thrown a net on her. Unlike the superficial heavy-metal logos the boys flaunted, her grid was a private and permanent statement from herself to herself; white and geometric as a chain-link fence, the pattern was more certainly the sign of her own neat hand than the cramped signature she made on paper.

Later, when I talked to a supervisor on the radio, she said Dawn was cruel at home. She was cruelest to what was most vulnerable: her younger sisters and the pets. Helpless animals called forth a meanness in her, and trapped creatures flipped something inside—she became vicious.

The supervisor also told me a story about Dawn. She had been seeing a bad therapist not long ago.

He had told her this: "Listen. If you can't get along at home, you'll end up on the streets. You'll need food. You'll need shelter. You'll need warmth. And to get those things, you'll need money. You're a fourteen-year-old girl. You have no marketable skill. You have nothing."

I imagined him pausing and scanning her.

"Well," he'd continued, "you do have a nice body. You could use that."

He showed her magazines, how the girls—eleven, twelve, sixteen—had found their pimps and set up their survival strategies.

He was trying to scare her into behaving at home, but when I asked her about it Dawn said, "He didn't tell me anything I didn't already know."

On day twelve, I was leading, so I called a silent hike. I'd woken up in a funk; I wanted some time to think. We had a five-mile jaunt up and down scree slopes, through icy sage, and over frozen coyote turds. I kept turning around to find the group shrinking on the near horizon. Dawn was farthest back, straggling forlornly.

I realized I was stalking the desert like a madwoman, clamping my teeth and pounding my digging stick on rhyolite blocks without noticing every time I had to wait.

I thought of the untold stories that had caused Dawn to carve a grid on her chest and to torment helpless things. I imagined what had compelled her to shut her body in a cage of scars. I read once that two-thirds of all people jailed for abuse have been victims themselves.

There is something pathological about inhabiting victimhood, and about living off its skewed sense of power and identity. It's like being in a high basalt tunnel. It's all right to hang out there for a while, while the actual storm of abuse is occurring; the true victim doesn't have much choice. The high walls are protective, and "moral superiority" offers an overhang of some dignity. But moral superiority itself can become an abusive trap, and there's not much to sustain a person in that place, where the floor is a sharp cushion of dark gravel. Like anger, victimization is a place to move through. The next step is survival.

I don't know what comes after that.

Dawn wasn't moving; she was fenced into one of those partial truths that quickly become lies. The pornographic therapist told her to separate her mind and body and peddle the body part; her role as a victim told her that power lay as much in being scarred as in scarring. Both lies make battlefields of women's bodies; they require that we keep hurting our bodies somehow, because our power and our identities depend on it. But these lies are based on an incomplete assumption: that strength lies only in our having power *over* ourselves or others.

Day thirteen marked Dawn's turn to lead the hike. Overnight, the temperature had dropped from twenty to zero, and the wind shot up over the mesa rims in a wall of velocity. We began walking over a major plateau at sunup, and by midday it was minus fifteen in the wind.

At one point we set our eyes on a big chunk of basalt three miles away, which appeared periodically through the whipping, granular snow. We planned on crouching there for a minute of rest, but when we arrived, the wind crashed around the rock like icy surf. It knifed through the blankets we had wrapped around our sweaters, and when George stopped there to pee, his zipper froze open.

By dusk we had reached a system of shallow caves and overhangs in a sheltered basalt canyon. We made camp there.

Squatting on the ground, chipping away pieces of frozen earth with my digging stick to make a coal bed pit, I realized why I had been so anxious for Dawn to be the first to make bow-drill fire. I'd wanted her to have power over the boys, so she'd believe in herself. But the desert doesn't teach power over. It teaches something else.

Mastery of fire has long symbolized humankind's power over nature, and it's hard to interpret the forms of fire we usually encounter—electric stoves, internal combustion engines, or nuclear warheads—otherwise. It's true that bow-drill fire can be used to teach us power over the land and over one another. But it can also be used to teach us power through, and within.

Standing in front of a dead electric stove is nothing like kneeling beside a smokeless fire board. Regardless of her race or social class, unless the stove girl is a master electrician who can illegally tap into power from a faraway source, she is bodily helpless before the cold metal cube. All she can do is break it apart and throw it around. The stove teaches her that her body can't bring her power, unless she uses it to take power from someone or somewhere else, at the expense of her spirit.

When she's kneeling by her fire board, though, the cold girl is free to choose another identity. In fact, she can identify with the world through the bow-drill set. After all, she chose the tall, dead sage plant, cut the branches from it, and shaped the parts herself. In choosing and shaping her tools, she has created a sense of autonomy. If the tools don't work, there are things she can do about it, with her mind and body together: push down harder, go faster, examine the set, smooth out the parts, try again.

Fire by friction requires something more than turning a knob on a stove. It requires spirit, or at least, in Dawn's case, the belief that mind and body can go safely together in the world. It requires the faith that a woman's power does come from within her body, but not separately from her mind.

Even though a girl feels individually empowered by making friction fire, she never does it entirely alone. As anyone who has tried to make fire from sappy or sodden wood will tell, she makes flame only through her surroundings, by the grace of the fire which exists already in the sage and in the natural world at large.

In some spots in the Great Basin, basalt towers spewed as fire from the recesses of the earth just three thousand years ago. In these spots, fire making seems less individual than collective: It's an invocation of an ever-present, hidden power.

The attentive student comes to tell which plants—like sage, clematis, and cottonwood—are full of fire, and which are not. The fire in her own arms shifts with her physical or psychic state. In this sense, friction fire making enacts mystery and provides a link with a different sense of identity. The woman has power within herself and through her conneciton with the natural world, not power over them.

This was a sense of identity I could never force Dawn to accept. She'd have to choose it herself or find a different one on her own, probably through a long chain of experiences. Her story might end up sounding nothing like mine, or the other girls' love tales, or the boys' war stories.

Dawn's flint and steel fire-making skills were good enough for safety, and she had hiked well in the lead. I wouldn't keep her up bow drilling any later than the others from now on.

After finishing my fire pit, I went and sat beside Dawn under her overhang, out of the wind. She looked small, sitting back on her heels rubbing tinder. I got out the map and measured the day's route with string.

"Fourteen and a half miles, Dawn."

She quit rubbing and looked up. "What?"

"You led fourteen and a half miles without a break."

Dawn stared at me. I heard the irregular sounds of the boys breaking up wood.

After a while she said, "Either it wasn't fourteen and a half miles, or I didn't lead."

We were silent.

"You led fourteen and a half miles without a break," I said again. I cut the string and laid it over the knee of her wool army pants, across the long strands of sagebrush bark tinder, which spread around her like a dress. The Paiute Indians, "Diggers," used to weave their clothes, boots, and blankets from such bark—the same bark they blew into flame.

"You must be tired," I said. "You can skip bow-drill tonight."

Dawn's camp stayed quiet until after dark. I was about to go check on her when the sound of grinding fire sticks echoed out from under her ledge. I sat for a while wondering whether or not she'd want company for this attempt.

After a few minutes the good smell of sage smoke traveled out toward my camp. I was on my feet heading toward Dawn's spot when I heard the bow drill stop and saw a glowing pile of punk moving slowly through the air on her knife blade.

The cherry coal disappeared into the dark tinder. She lifted the bundle to blow. The tinder nest began to glow orange, and its dim light revealed Dawn's uptilted face as she sent her breath through the fibers.

I walked up just as the bundle took flame. The fire lit the ceiling of her overhang for the first time, and she still held the bundle aloft. But she wasn't watching the fire; she was looking up. Chiseled into the rock overhead was a petroglyph, left by the Paiutes or the Shoshone: a series of concentric half circles like a sunset, or like half the pattern of a pebble thrown in water. Dawn didn't smile, but I saw the reflection of the fire in her eyes.

◆

Also the author of "The Clearing in the Clearing," the essay that preceded this one, Leslie Ryan lives in Montana.

DOUG PEACOCK

◆ ◆ ◆ ◆ ◆

THE WIND RIVERS

Maybe what I needed was a long infusion of solitary living. I didn't seem much good around people. The snows were melting in the high country. The bears had emerged from their winter dens. The geese had long ago flown north. If anything, I was behind schedule according to the timetable I felt in my bones. Something was drawing me north, back into the land of the road map. I packed all my gear and said good-bye. I piled into the blue Jeep and headed toward the northern Rockies.

    I traveled north slowly, killing time since there was still snow in the mountains. It was May 1968. I had been out of Vietnam for less than three months and could not see much change in either myself or the country. In the war zone, events unfolded with sudden violence, and from there you got pushed along by the instincts and the mechanics of survival. Except for the undeniable reality that someone or something was trying to kill your ass, you had no idea what was going on. You hardly ever knew who or where the enemy was. Sniper fire came out of the forest, automatic weapons fire from the tree line, and rockets and mortars invisibly out of the night.

    This confusion followed me back home. From Arizona, I headed north toward the Wind River mountains of Wyoming. I made weekly forays into town for gas and supplies but never lingered in "syphilization." For the next five months, my contact with the human race was limited to "Filler up" and "Gimme a beer." I avoided women without thinking about it. My primal instincts were intact, but there was no way I wanted to get close to anyone. Later, when I sat back and thought about it, I realized I had spent two and one-half years of unconscious celibacy in partial compensation for manslaughter. The applicable phrase, I read later, was "walking wounded."

Sometimes I ran out of money and had to call my dad, who kept my bucks for me. I was in rural Utah heading for the Wind River Range when the cash ran out. One daybreak I stopped at a phone booth by a deserted gas station to call Dad and have him wire me gas money. I got the operator, who told me to deposit $2.10, a quarter more than I had. She was not pleased. I asked her to wait while I went into my backpack, where I carried change for such emergencies. By the time I got back, the line was dead. I dialed O and got the same operator, who was still put out. The phone did not return coins, so I deposited $2.10 again, all the coins I had in the world just then. I heard the coins fall, and then the phone went dead again. I redialed the operator, who said the phone did not return money but that I could have a check for four dollars mailed to my home.

I hung up. Outside the spring wind rattled the booth. Down the highway I could see the steeple of a Mormon church: definitely Indian country. I dug around in the back of the Jeep and pulled out the twelve-gauge and a box of double aught. The first double blast caught the telephone and tore it off the bracket on the wall of the booth. I reloaded, backed off, and fired another salvo; the force of the buckshot cut the metal corners, and the phone booth slumped over onto the ground. I blasted the phone again from six feet. I grabbed the jerry can off the Jeep and poured half the gas on what was left of the phone. I flipped a match onto it. Through my rearview mirror I could see the black smoke rise.

I reached Wyoming in late May and spent another month watching the snow line retreat up the mountains, fishing the Popo Agie and camping out in the foothills near the Wind River Reservation. Just as summer reached the valleys, spring came to the mountains. I got ready for a long expedition into the high country, carefully packing my backpack, sorting out food and cold weather gear.

I drove the Jeep up a faint muddy track leading high into the range and left it parked in a grove of pines. I shouldered the big pack full of heavy, inexpensive gear, and headed up the trail.

The Wind River area of northwest Wyoming was considered one of the wildest spots left in the Lower Forty-eight. In 1968 the only topographical map I could find was the old Fremont version made in 1906. The area was so rugged that the surveyors had to guess at much of the country. They missed lakes and valleys and even had rivers running the wrong way, all of which let me imagine I was going somewhere unexplored and uncharted. It did not bother me that I did not know where I was going.

The first day out the weather held, and I hiked about a dozen miles, not bad considering that I had been wading through miles of creek bottom flooded by beaver dams. I made camp on the shoulder of a plateau that overlooked a long glacial valley running north. Heavy clouds gathered on the southern horizon, but I guessed that the weather would hold through the night. Just in case, I tied an army poncho corner to corner across the top of the hammock in which I would throw my sleeping bag; it was an old jungle arrangement.

The next morning broke gray and cold. Clouds blocked the passes, and the weather looked as if it would get worse. I shouldered the pack and started down the trail toward the head of a long glacial lake with a logjam across its outlet. I would cross the creek there.

By the time I got to the bottom, the clouds were rolling in and the temperature had dropped twenty degrees. I was in for a spring storm sometime that day or the next. I dug out my compass and took a reading. According to the map, that bearing should bring me to the foot of a large lake by nightfall.

By later afternoon, a wet snow had begun to fall. I slogged along through sparse timber and outcroppings of granite. By early evening a couple of inches of slush lay on the ground. I kept on the compass bearing, aiming for the large lake, which lay not more than a mile or two away. I was wet, tired of bushwhacking, and eager to set up for the night. Just at dark I stopped at an outcrop.

Through the trees I could make out the slate gray surface of a large glacial lake. The wind had picked up and was blowing snowflakes into my face. It was snowing hard. I quickly put up a small mountain tent and unrolled my sleeping bag inside. I got out of my wet clothes and put on a pair of black pajama bottoms and a dry T-shirt and crawled into the sleeping bag, listening to the sound of the blizzard slapping against the tent.

I was thirsty and remembered that I had forgotten to fill my canteen. I looked out the tent flap. All I could see was the first ten feet of swirling snow. "What the hell, it will only take a minute." I stumbled down the rocky ledges toward the lake, which was probably a couple of hundred feet away. The cold wind and snow stung my arms. I pushed through a fringe of fir trees and stepped to the shore, watching the whirling snow disappear into the grayness of the mountain lake. I squatted and filled the canteen. I screwed the cap back on and turned toward my tent, shivering slightly in the cold air. I followed my tracks in the snow back through the trees. When I got to the first ledge the tracks disappeared; the blowing snow had covered them up. I could see for only a couple of feet. I did not know where my tent was.

I told myself to calm down. The tent had to be within a hundred yards or so; it was up on a bluff above the lake. Although I was almost naked, it was not dangerously cold. Dressed as I was, I might freeze if exposed to the elements for an entire night, but I still had lots of time. Methodically I began going back and forth across a series of gentle ledges, upon one of which my tent was pitched. It was so dark by then that I could barely see my feet through the falling snow. I forced myself to go ten more feet up the slope and started a new traverse.

I kept at it for about half an hour. By then I was truly cold and wanted to give up. Suddenly I tripped, falling flat on my face in the snow. I felt a guy line. I had fallen over my tent in the dark. My fingers were numb, and I clawed at the tent flap. I crawled in the entrance and stripped off my wet, frozen clothing. I zipped the sleeping bag up over my ears and pulled a woolen cap out of my clothing bag. My mind emptied, and the war marched in.

. . .

We stumbled across the tunnel complex an hour before dark. A five-hundred-pound bomb had landed almost on top of it, and a twenty-meter section had caved in. Otherwise we never would have spotted it. Charlie dug these things all over the place. We knew there were a shitload of hidden trenches under every one of these bombed-out villages in the Song Cai Valley, but we never looked for them or messed with them except sometimes to toss a grenade into an open hole or bunker. This time was different. Apparently part of this collapsed tunnel ran on another fifty meters right into the grove of trees in which we had planned on bivouacking. We were going to set up a perimeter around that little palm-covered knoll and spend the night there. The tunnel made us nervous.

The marines had bombed the hell out of the place a week earlier. Our patrol of two Americans and twenty-three Vietnamese CIDG was attached to a grunt company from Da Nang, which was all that was left of a bigger operation that had swept through there four days earlier. There had been some intense fighting during the first two days. The point company took thirteen casualties in three firefights that lasted less than two minutes each. A day later, two grunts stepped on trip-wire mines, one of them big enough to blow the marine's foot off.

By the time we got there things had cooled down. The last marines had been airlifted back to Da Nang, leaving us behind. We were assigned to do a body count. There was me, Irwin the weapons sergeant, and a Vietnamese interpreter, in addition to the twenty-three CIDGs. We were supposed to mop up but so far had not found any bodies and had not even been shot at. If things stayed quiet, we would walk back to our A camp at Thuong Duc in the morning. All we had to do was make it through the night.

First, somebody had to check out the tunnel. I would have gotten out of the job if at all possible. But for a bunch of reasons, I could not: It was my turn. I was new there, and I didn't want the CIDGs to think I was scared shitless of going down into that hole—which of course I was.

Unlike most GIs, I like Vietnam—because I had gotten to some of the countryside before the war did. The country was beautiful. I loved the Central Highlands and the people who lived there. But the war had always caught up. By the end, there were places in Vietnam I hated like no other spot on earth. The tunnels were at the top of this list. They were gateways to a special kind of hell.

We dropped a concussion grenade into the collapsed tunnel to clear away any booby traps in the immediate vicinity and open up the hole enough so I could crawl in. I dumped my pack and web gear and got out new batteries for the flashlight. Sam, the Vietnamese interpreter, took my M-16, and I pulled out a Colt .45. It was too big and loud for tunnel work, but it was the only pistol we had with us. I jacked a round into the chamber and stuffed two extra clips in each breast pocket of my fatigues. We stood around for a minute while the CIDGs used their bayonets to open up the entrance to the complex. They held on to my feet while I lowered myself headfirst into the hole, feeling with my arms for the walls of the tunnel. It was about a meter wide. I worked my way forward until my feet were in. I crawled a little farther, until the darkness was complete.

I lay there motionless for about three minutes. All I could hear was my own breathing. I carried two standard army flashlights, but I had not turned them on because I wanted my eyes to adjust and I did not know who or what was down here. One had a red plastic disk covering the bulb for low illumination.

The tunnel reeked. I had to get the job over with quickly. The tunnel was the narrowest one I had ever seen. My heart beat like a generator engine. I crawled forward, feeling my way along in the dark. The dirt shaft was wide enough for my shoulders but too narrow for me to stretch out my elbows. There was no way I could turn around. I couldn't even reach the K-bar knife that I had forgotten to take off my belt and tie around my neck where I could get at it.

I rolled on my side and worked my hand down to the sheath knife and pulled it up to my face, stuffing the Colt into the shoulder holster. With the K-bar in my right hand I swept the blade along the tunnel, feeling for wires and probing the earthen floor for mines.

With my left hand I felt along the side and ceiling. Then I shifted hands to feel along the other wall, listened, moved forward a couple of feet, and repeated the procedure.

After about a hundred feet, the tunnel got a little bigger and turned off thirty degrees to the right. I thought I could feel a little cold air blowing around the corner. It smelled of shit and rancid fish or something else unbelievably putrid. I stopped short of the bend and listened. Nothing. I grabbed the flashlight with the low-illumination red light in my left hand. I had the .45 in my right. I held the light as far away from my head as I could so that my head would not be a target. Then I flipped it on and shot the beam down the tunnel. I eased my head around the corner and looked into the darkness. The faint red light illuminated about fifteen feet of tunnel, and near the end there was a shaft leading down. The doors to shafts or subterranean chambers were often booby-trapped.

As I switched the flashlight off, I glanced at my wristwatch; I had been alone in the tunnel for less than fifteen minutes. It felt like hours.

I inched along the floor to the mouth of the shaft. It was wet, and I slid through a pool of slime that smelled of fresh rat turds. I made it to the shaft. No door or lid covered the opening. I probed with the knife blade round the hole. The stink coming up from the tunnel complex below was so bad I gagged. I felt around. The shaft slanted down for a yard or two and then leveled off. Time was running out. Outside it was getting dark, and we were deep in enemy country.

Below, in the absolute darkness of the tunnel, I started down the shaft. I didn't dare use a flashlight. The shaft bent up toward the level, and I had to arch my back to feel around the bend. My fingertips brushed the earthen ceiling, and I felt a pencil-size twig poking out of the roof of the tunnel. I ran my fingers down the stick to a joint, then out to the end of the bamboo whip, which was sprung back and anchored in a wire hoop with a trip wire running up to the roof and back to the tunnel floor in front of me. I shaded the red light until I found the commo wire stretched across the tunnel. At the end of the bamboo whip just short of the wire hoop was a rusty fishhook, a large treble hook with the points straightened out: a primitive little device designed to impale your eye. I checked for some trick, then grabbed the sprung bamboo and lowered the hook. The booby trap was recent; the whip still had a lot of spring left in it.

I turned the light off. My heart raced and my stomach heaved. I could smell human shit and a trace of *nuoc mam*, the rotten fish sauce the Vietnamese used, but these foul stenches were overwhelmed by something far more powerful.

A couple of yards more and I reached the end of the shaft. It opened up into some kind of chamber. I listened and felt around the doorway for hidden grenades or wired claymore mines. Nothing there. This was as far as I would be going. I was out of time. I listened some more and thought I could hear the faintest sound of breathing. For the first time since crawling into the tunnel, I felt there was someone else down there.

In the darkness I sensed I was in a tiny chamber. There was someone sitting in the far corner. I could feel him. A Vietcong. I thumbed the automatic's safety down to off. The Colt .45 felt inadequate. I was probably outgunned: If he had an AK-47 it would be all over. I froze and listened. There was no sound, but I knew he was there.

Then I was not so sure. Maybe I was hearing things. I started to creep forward across the floor of the chamber. I crawled with the Colt ready, groping for trip wires with my left hand. Suddenly I touched something cold and smooth. My left fingers closed around a bloated human hand.

The darkness exploded. I leaped backward, at the same time firing eight .45 caliber slugs in the direction of what I imagined was the corner. I threw the empty clip across the room and pushed a loaded one into the butt of the automatic. I chambered another round but did not squeeze it off. For a moment I was deaf from the discharge of the heavy pistol in the closed space. Then I could hear myself puking. There was no other sound in the room.

I held the bright flashlight high above my head with the .45 leveled. I slid the switch on, and the light fell on the corner of a chamber high enough to stand in. The corner was right where I thought it was, right where I had emptied the pistol. I lowered the flashlight beam and looked into the face of a dead Vietnamese draped in shreds of what had been black pajamas. The man had been dead for some time.

I scanned the room. There were three more corpses falling out of the sides of the room. They looked as if they had been stuffed hurriedly in holes along the walls and maybe jarred loose by the shock waves from the bombing. The bodies looked small. The ones I could be sure of were men. They had been folded up into little fetal-like bundles, just like the prehistoric Indian burials I had found in Michigan as a teenager. The bodies had been there for several days, but it was hard to tell, since everything rotted quickly in this humid heat. I looked at the bloated hand I had held a minute earlier. It was attached to an arm that stuck out of the wall. The rest of the corpse was covered with dirt.

I felt faint and started to black out, so I flipped off the light, just in case. After a minute, I turned the flashlight back on. I looked across the chamber at the first body, which apparently had slid out of the corner I had imagined a man was sitting in. This corpse also was folded up, but I could still see that his intestines had been rended from a violent wound to his abdomen. I knew now what the smells were.

Off to the left of the dead man another tunnel ran off. That was where the smell of *nuoc mam* seemed to be coming from.

I had to get out. I shook so violently I dropped the flashlight, which went out. I did not try to find it. Instead, I turned and squatted, ready to start back out the shaft. The stooping brought on another dizzy spell, and I might have passed out for a few seconds.

When I got my senses back, I was lying at the entrance to the shaft with my feet still in the burial chamber. I was there long enough to get another strong whiff of fish sauce rising above the stench of death. It was coming from the direction of the other tunnel. Now I could hear the unmistakable sound of soft breathing. Someone was alive just across the room near the mouth of the tunnel. Fifteen feet away. Breathing in the darkness.

We sat there on opposite sides of the temporary burial chamber listening to each other's respiration for what seemed a long time. Whoever was there could have killed me or tried to at any time. But he did not. Maybe the dead were his friends or even his family. He might have been paralyzed by grief or mourning his dead. The war could have been over for him. All I could hear was the regular sound of breathing. He did not move. He just sat there with the dead, and so did I.

Finally I turned into the tunnel and retreated quietly in the dark. I moved as quickly as I could crawl the 150 feet or whatever it was back to the caved-in trench where my comrades waited. It was nearly dark, and everyone was jumpy, anxious to move into a night position. I told them I had not found anything down there, that the tunnel was cold.

In the mountains of the Wind River Range, I lay there in the tent a long time without thinking, letting the blood recirculate. It had been an altogether avoidable close call and uncharacteristically careless of me. What had happened to my concentration, to my survival instincts? This little mishap was one of several times in the previous year that I had mindlessly nearly killed myself. During the last few months I was in Vietnam I had stopped taking careful cover during firefights—I had waltzed around during gun battles like a Sioux ghost dancer, invincible against enemy bullets. I had blamed this more on weariness than on a conscious choice to take chances. But now I was forced to admit that I was truly a danger to myself. The capriciousness of survival, that random slice that separates the living from the dead, seemed like a bad joke.

"The hell with it," I said. "I've got too much to look forward to." No wacko death wish was going to get me. There were too many wild places left to explore. Besides, I liked fishing, wild mushrooms, my own cooking, Mozart, good wine, woods, and women.

I slept until the drip of water on the tent told me that the snow was melting. Around noon, I sat up and rolled out of the bag and into a gray spring day. I crammed my wet gear into the pack and broke camp. Above the lake on the far shore, timbered wedges and rotten talus swept up to unnamed peaks penetrating the glaciers that blanketed the east side of the divide. I followed the big lake to its head, where a creek dumped into the milky glacial waters. I would follow it up to a chain of small lakes, where I wanted to set up a base camp from which I could fish and explore.

The snow had melted by the time I began bushwhacking up the rocky creek bottom. I did not expect more snow, although it could have rained at any time; the weather in the Wind River Range was fickle at best. I picked up a game trail running up the drainage. In the mud there were tracks of deer, elk, and a moose. Overhanging branches slapped me in the face. No matter: I was not in a hurry.

About midafternoon I arrived at another large lake, which, according to the map, stood at the junction of two or more strings of glacial lakes. I decided to go up the longer chain, the one leading into the heart of the mountain range. I circled the shore of the lake and lost the game trail but found the going easy enough. A heavy cloud bank hung on the crest of the range and spilled east over into my chain of lakes. Somewhere off to the west thunder rolled. The sparse lodgepole forest gave way to stunted fir and spruce mixed with five-needle pines, limber, and whitebark, indicating that I was nearing the upper limit of the trees.

Again the rumble of thunder echoed throughout the peaks and basins. I ducked into a clump of trees to wait out the passing storm—a few drops of rain with a dozen cracks of lightning. I reached the end of the lake and climbed up the creek bottom alongside a series of waterfalls. There were signs of beaver along the creek. I circled the marshy area, stopping in the mud where the game trail ran. A fresh set of bear tracks was printed over the older hoof marks of deer and elk.

I dropped my pack and got down on my knees to look at the large pad marks. I had heard that there might be a few grizzlies left in the northern part of these mountains. I found a good front track. The marks of the front claws were close to the toe; the toe prints were separated from one another and on a curved line: a black bear. On a grizzly, the toes touch, in more of a straight line, and the front claws are huge. Just the same, it was a big black bear. I started up the wet trail, anxious to find the next lake before dark.

I came out to the edge of the big lake just at dusk. It was the wildest area I had seen since coming home. In the middle of the mile-long lake stood a tiny, rocky island decorated with a few scrawny trees. One of these trees was on fire. I tensed and looked around. Who had set the fire? No one had, of course. It had been hit by lightning during the afternoon thunderstorm. I took it as a sign: my burning bush.

The small tree smoked away as I dug out my tent and poncho, preparing a shelter next to a large rock where I could put my fire pit. I carefully picked out all the small rocks and pebbles from under the tent. This would be a good camp, my base camp for the next two or three weeks—until my food ran out or I got sick of trout.

I lit a fire of pine, which sputtered and threw sparks and debris into the darkness. I felt the best that I had felt in months. The light of the fire shimmered off the huge quartz monzonite boulder. It must have been stranded after the most recent advance of the glaciers.

I did not want to go to sleep. Instead, I stoked the fire and ran through the fishing I would do the next day. In my mind I fished up the creek I had hiked today, casting a fly into each deep eddy. I started halfway down to the next lake and fished up, roll-casting to avoid the brush, exploring each tail-out and run with a number 12 Royal Coachman. I fished all the way back to camp in my imagination. An hour, maybe two, had passed, and I was exhausted.

It was the wildest country in all of Quang Ngai Province, the long valley south of Song Ha. We left two days after Thanksgiving and marched thirty klicks in four slow days of small but endless skirmishes with local VC units. A giant, iridescent green serpent was sleeping snaked along a horizontal limb ten feet above a foot trail. This viper was fully three times longer than any snake I had ever seen and twice as long as any green reptile that was supposed to live in Vietnam. It had a bulge a third of the distance down its gullet big enough to be a large monkey or barking deer, or a small human. The local

Montagnards of my mobile guerrilla team said the beautiful snake did not have a name in Vietnamese, but if it bit you, you went to sleep. For good. We all had to walk underneath it.

The next morning a fine drizzle dripped through the trees. I kindled a small blaze with the help of a candle. The smoke rose to the lower branches of the lodgepole and hung there like a blanket in the heavy air. This was the day I had planned to look for the big black bear, following his tracks up the drainage maybe into the next basin. Instead, I tied the poncho above the fire and huddled underneath it. I left the fire only long enough to fill my canteens at the lake and catch a few trout for dinner at the outlet of the creek. At least I was where I wanted to be: in one of the blank spots on my map.

I poked at the fire with a stick, glancing up every so often at the game trail, vaguely hoping someone might show up: a beautiful mountaineer with a pack full of kinky hardware or a Shoshone maiden clad in wet doeskins. Come and dry by my fire. Let's build a sweat lodge. A two-hour fantasy of girl bums followed. The fire had burned out. It was what the grunts in Nam called an ass trance.

Five days later I was still waiting for the rain to stop. Each day I squatted around the campfire squinting into the smoke until mid-afternoon, when I walked to the creek to catch a dinner. I had no complaint with the diet or the solitude, only the lack of activity. I ached for a chance to explore the hidden lakes and basins. By the seventh day I was thoroughly bored. The drizzle continued, never really raining and never stopping for more than a few minutes. Far off to the east I could see the clouds breaking up. The weather there had to be part of a local pattern, with heavy clouds hanging around the crest of the range. At this rate, the rain might last all summer.

I did not have real rain gear, so I wrapped myself in a wool sweater and a windbreaker, stuck a bag of waterproof matches in my pocket, strapped on my Ruger .357, and stepped out into the light rain. A faint game trail led around the rocky edge of the lake and along another creek that tumbled down from the lake above. According to the map it was only a mile to the big cirque at the head of the drainage. Above that, there would be impenetrable cliffs and narrow passes filled with snow.

The rocky game trail dropped down to the creek and paralleled a marshy strip of beaver meadow. In the mud were the day-old tracks of the black bear. I knelt on the trail and measured the bear's rear track with my fingers. The front print was there too, faint but unmistakable. The rain had washed most of the other tracks away; what was left looked as if a human had walked there barefoot. It seemed clear that the bear was headed up the drainage. Maybe he had not liked the smell of my campfire.

A black bear might raid your camp but otherwise presents little danger to human beings. It was too bad that no more grizzlies were left in there. They had been shot out decades ago or poisoned with the predacide 1080. Even a place as big and wild as this had proved too small for them. Grizzlies have enormous ranges: A male in country like this needs two or three hundred square miles; a female, half of that. In the spring, the big bears ranged from the mountains into ranch country and invariably got blown away.

I found a spruce tree tall enough that I could sit under it. It kept most of the rain off me. I waited, my thoughts drifting. Memories of the war came back, pushing other thoughts out of my mind. I sat with my back up against the tree listening to the rain and letting Vietnam sweep over me.

During the Christmas truce of 1967, Dinh Hun caught four slugs from an AK-47 through his right thigh, fired into him by NVA walking down a foot trail as Hun lay at his listening post only two meters away. Nobody knew how it started. All of a sudden the NVA were running down the trail toward the coastal cities spraying the darkness with their submachine guns.

I was waiting for Hun at the medical bunker when they brought him back on a stretcher. Hun had become my best yard friend, and for a minute I thought I was going to lose this big Hre with the quick smile and four gold teeth. The bullets had shattered Hun's femur, and I was afraid the bone fragments would chew up the femoral artery. I gave him a quarter grain of morphine, and we worked him into a Striker frame. Hun cried out in pain when I started putting traction on the half-ring splint. I couldn't stand to see him in that kind of agony, so I shot him up again with another half dose of morphine—a bit more than I should have. That was about all we could do for him.

I called Duc Pho for a medevac, though the odds of getting a dust-off out here in the middle of the night with clouds all the way down to the ground were about nothing. The night was black, the ceiling zero, and visibility through the fog was the length of your arm.

But the helicopter crews came anyway, flying up the Tra Na River to Bato on Christmas Eve of 1967, a night as dark as they got. They flew up the middle of the river with the skids almost touching it, flying in slow motion with their landing lights shining through the gloom before them all the way to Bato. What a target they made! Every inch of the trip was Indian country. They didn't have to come. The WIA was only a Montagnard irregular. I couldn't imagine anyone being so goddamned brave, though I could tell the pilot did not think it was a big deal. Maybe it was just Christmas.

Later, the wind picked up, driving rain through my light windbreaker. Chilled, I moved up the animal trail along the creek, finding more prints of the black bear. I struggled up a steep grade over a lip of bedrock and found myself looking out over a large lake filling a mountain cirque. Above me everything was in a cloud. The wind whipped the rain into squalls and froze it into sleet. I was cold but wanted to try the lake waters with my fly rod before I left.

I stuck the pack rod together with numb fingers, then quickly tied on a brown-hackled wet fly—one of my dad's experimental patterns—which I cast between gusts of wind. Immediately, I was struck by a fifteen-inch golden trout. I reeled it in fast, too cold to think of sport. I released the fish, a fat golden showing a trace of hybridization with rainbow. I tried another fly: nothing doing. I tied the scraggly brown hackle back onto the line and threw it out into

uld

ore I had time to retrieve the brown nymph, I was hit
n even larger fish. I forgot about the cold, and I played
d-and-a-half fish for a few minutes before I let it go. This
n the best trout fishing I had yet seen up here. This high
must be loaded with game, I thought. In addition to the black
, I had seen signs of lots of deer and elk on the way up. But
t was for another day: I was cold and it was sleeting. I wanted to
op down out of this cloud and build a fire. My fingers were no
longer functioning.

Several soggy days later I was on my way out, beaten down by
the unceasing rain. Toward evening I stepped out into the meadow
next to which my Jeep was parked. I dumped my pack on the hood
and inspected the damage that the curious range cattle had done.
They had stomped a ring in the duff around it and chewed off its
plastic directional signals. The Jeep started right up and lurched
down the rutted Forest Service trail, finally joining a graded ranch
road. I hit U.S. 287 and turned back toward Lander to gas up and
buy a few supplies—including a jug of tequila.

The sun had set behind the peaks, and the wind was blasting
the Jeep with fifty-mile-an-hour gusts as I drove up a muddy logging
road toward Union Pass. Just at dark, I pulled off a series of Jeep
trails and side roads left behind by the messy logging operation and
parked in a grove of open timber. Using the far side of the Jeep as
a windbreak, I staked down the edge of the poncho and guyed it off
against the wind. I unrolled the sleeping bag, pushing it under the
poncho, and lit a fire a few feet downwind in a hole I dug with my
entrenching tool. I sat by the fire and pulled heavily on the bottle.
The sparks shot off into the night.

Sometime around 3:00 A.M. I sat bolt upright in the chilly
silence. The wind had died down and the stars were out. I shivered
and eased into the sleeping bag, hoping to warm up. My face felt
as though someone had taken a hammer to it—that hangover peculiar to drinking half a bottle of tequila. I groped in my pack for
some aspirin, took out two, then thought again and took four. I was
restless and awake, ready to move on, another side effect of the
tequila. Despite the headache, I was aware that I was after some-

thing—that this trip was part of a larger quest of some kind. I wo
move north.

My immediate problem was not to pull another lost tent a
I needed to quit pushing things. I wanted to find a place where th
weather was better. What I had in mind was the Yellowstone Plateau
and the Absaroka Range. That country had magic. Maybe I would
even see a grizzly.

◆

Doug Peacock lives in Tucson, Arizona, with his family. His
books include The Grizzly Years: In Search of the American
Wilderness *and* Baja!

C. L. RAWLINS

◆ ◆ ◆ ◆ ◆

THE MEADOW AT THE CORNER
OF YOUR EYE

I could tell you about a place, though it might be better for it to stay secret. If you wakened there, you would hear a light wind, brushing downslope like a hand on a bare shoulder. The wind moans through rocky fingers along the ridge, combs the grass, lifts the skirt of a grove, silvers the dark water of the lake.

Then it stops. In the calm, a bird calls, is answered, calls again. The stream treads a staircase of boulders. At the corner of your eye, a doe and fawn step into the meadow and lower their heads. Where?

There's a yearning that can be expressed as a place more simply than as a feeling: for beauty, rest, purity, transfiguration. It is easier to think of it as unknown. A knowing love is difficult, like a marriage that persists despite boredom, bitterness, and grief. It can be easier to see love's essence in the face of a stranger, passion in a body you've never touched.

It can be like this with the land. There is a strange resemblance between national parks and brothels: One pays to gain entry, to witness something set apart from daily life. There is likewise a correspondence between a love affair and a wilderness hike: the urge to move beyond accustomed bounds.

Most of us live in cities. Nature, as we define it, is where we go on vacation. Wilderness is what our lives are not: noble, quiet, unhurried. At home, our immediate worlds are defined by exclusion. We are irritable beasts, and wish to keep out the sales representatives, the nosy relatives, the stray dogs, the tomato hornworms, the dandelions, the starlings. We go backpacking to get away from the content of our lives, to forget what we've become. For most of us, wilderness excludes more than it contains. We love the wilderness and hate the neighbors.

Generalized loves can be deceptions. One might claim to teach out of a regard for the young while treating one's students with cruelty. The students become, with their awkwardness and failings, an impediment to the higher purpose of education.

A man with a grand, vague love for women might be unsatisfied by individuals. He might discard them almost without regret—one for her impatience when tired, one for the appendectomy scar on her otherwise perfect belly—as imperfect versions of his dream.

One might also claim to love the land—aaah Wilderness!—but treat most of it as a doormat, a factory, or just a boring drive.

Out on my fieldwork, measuring air pollution in a designated wilderness, I read trail registers. There are one-word reviews: "Awesome," "Unreal," "Radical," "Perfect," usually with exclamation points lined up to shove. There are also complaints. Those who commute complain about the lines of packhorses. Those who flew out bemoan contrails and sonic booms. Those who hug the main trails are angry because the main trails are crowded.

"We did not feel," read one note, "that we had a high-quality wilderness experience as we were led to expect from the information we received. The weather was bad and there were too many mosquitoes."

The irony is awesome, unreal, radical, perfect. In June a year ago, I went up with my partner, Jim, to scout the snowpack for a sampling trip. Our truck stalled at the trailhead. The campground was still snowed in. We postholed up the trail, looked around, and decided to chance it in a few days, with snowshoes. We left the truck and walked back, high above the valley on a road between melting drifts. After an hour, we were passed by a silver van. The driver stopped, and we asked for a ride to town. "I'm going to the campground," he said.

We told him that it was under a yard of snow. He turned around and we got in. His poodle snarled at Jim. "You could camp by the overlook," I said, thinking he could watch the sunset over a nine-mile glacial lake and sleep in his van. He stopped, surveyed it from the pavement, and pulled back onto the road. "Too open," he said.

He told us he was on a vacation from his executive job in Connecticut, seeing the West for the first time. Jim, a native Coloradan, asked him where he'd been. He gave a litany of places, the Grand Canyon, Mesa Verde, Canyonlands, Flaming Gorge. Each was followed by a dismissal: too cold, got a speeding ticket, smelly toilets, too desolate. In the pauses, the poodle snarled.

"Where are you headed?"

"Jackson Hole, the Tetons, Yellowstone, Glacier: all the places worth seeing." At our backs, pines hid the Continental Divide, a rank of granite peaks above thirteen thousand feet. I suggested camping on the big lake, where a campground held spacious rest rooms. He glanced down. "Probably too windy," he said.

He let us off in town two hours before dark, then drove away. He would end up, I thought, in Jackson Hole in a motel, watching the news. The best I could hope for was this: that he would return home feeling lucky not to live in any of the spots he visited. He would never find a place to fit his vision, which narrowed the further it was pursued.

Contempt for what is close corrodes the heart; it can't be escaped. The vision of a perfect love is a remedy for lovelessness. The vision of a perfect landscape is a drug. Only having abandoned the physical world can we love "wilderness" more than any real place.

So, wilderness is about as far from life as we can make it. We'd rather it was over the horizon, so we can fight for it without kicking our bankers and our brokers and our bosses in the shins. So we won't have to alter our ways. So that we can lie to ourselves, that in spite of what we do, someplace, somewhere, is safe.

When I show slides of my backcountry work to conservation groups in cities, their eagerness to embrace my life as an ideal makes me sad. It's work, not a crusade. I measure air pollution, year-round, in a remote range of mountains: a sad fact in itself. It's a place I've begun to know, an obligation that I owe. I don't like being made a fantasy.

I started thinking about this years ago, re-reading one of my favorite books, *The Monkey Wrench Gang*. Abbey made the villain a greedy, rural, Mormon bishop, based on Calvin Black, a man I had met in Blanding, Utah. The excitement took place in the remotest boondocks. What began to amaze me was that the conflict was so completely projected into a rural landscape, onto a sparse population of Mormons and rednecks, when the problem of environmental rape had mostly, as far as I could see, to do with cities and their staggering wants.

In 1985, I talked to Abbey at Arches, where he was the guest of honor at a party for a tenth-anniversary edition of the book. It was dark. There was a fire. Ken and Jane Sleight were frying steaks in a huge, black pan. Stiles, the ranger, was flipping out over the jam of cars locked in the group-camp loop, snarling at Spurs, who had sent out the invitations. Spurs growled back, gesturing with a right hand that clutched a foaming beer, then with a left that gripped a plastic dinosaur.

I'm tall and lanky. I had a can of beer. In the dark, four or five persons stopped to ask if I was Ed Abbey. "No," I said. "I'm looking for him too." I found him in the shadow of a Triple-A Springbar tent, looking mournfully toward the fire.

I echoed his posture, talking about nothing for a while, then asked, "How come you didn't set the book in New York City? You hate New York. Why didn't they blow up the Chase Manhattan Bank? Or Washington. What about Congress? Go for the heart. Limping Jesus Christ!" There was a lot of free beer at the party. Ed had kidney stones, so he wasn't drinking. I didn't have kidney stones.

"Because the cities are dead."

I didn't know how to reply. I was a range rider then, in Wyoming. I'd been offered a Stegner Fellowship at Stanford. Abbey was a Stegner fellow years before.

"I'm going to Stanford next fall," I said. "Bright people, good conversation. No cows."

"May God have mercy on your soul," he said. "Don't forget to cut the deck."

Five years later, I came to Arches to read his elegy. Wilderness is a strange word, like truth. I think too of Emily Dickinson. Hiking down a canyon in southern Utah with her collected poems, I read such gems as this:

> Had I not seen the sun
> I could have borne the shade;
> But light a newer wilderness
> My wilderness has made.

And this:

> But when all space has been beheld
> And all dominion shown,
> The smallest human heart's extent
> Reduces it to none.

What we've been fighting for isn't places but our souls. Wilderness is a fragment, a green ghost at the edge of sight. The land itself is large and various, full of complications, hard to encompass with mere mind. When we set aside a wilderness, we draw a boundary in our thought, divorce it from the scrape of daily life. Only the most acculturated Indians can talk of "wilderness" with conviction. Mostly, they talk about their home places, the fields and nearby hills, the windy grass, the sacred lake from which real water can be dipped. Love is a tangle of sense and memory, hard to sort out, harder still to condense into a neat declarative sentence.

Wallace Stegner said it well: The marriage of people to a place may be close and considerate, and it may be hardly more than sanctioned rape.

How is such a marriage made? It takes time, generations, and more than time. No one is married to a place who has not gotten a mouthful of food from it, picked or grown or hunted down. It is easy to buy and sell ground when you've never known its taste, singular and certain, never taken the hard brown nipple between your lips, rolled your tiny fists against the mountain breast, warmed to the flow of earth's own milk, rough and rich. Nothing could be further from the ideal. You eat from it. In the end, it eats you.

We've driven out our hearth gods, chased the elementals from hedge and gate, purged our lives of modest spirits: a voice in the fire under the kettle, a shadow in the arch of the door, a breath in the grass. Like wilderness, our heaven is remote. Only the dead can travel so far. It is strange to us, that the living realm touches the sacred one, that the fit is so close.

But wilderness is out of reach, a place we can't inhabit. Footsteps alone make it less than sacred, less than wild. So we strain to hold it separate, to border it with laws, to keep it clean and out of reach.

What to worship, now? Under the altars of old churches lie the bones of saints, locked in reliquaries, jeweled and dead. Held apart, they yearn for the soil's kiss, for saturation, for the soft release. They long for dissolution, for the dark return. And the stones of the cathedrals long to fall, to travel in a streambed, to wash up, sandy, on a shore.

I could tell you about a place, but you know it well. The telling will not penetrate its peace. You see the blue, blue mountains, or the sea of windy grass, or the breaking waves that curl along the black rock point. The earth turns, one, regardless, mixing its waters in the sea. There is no wilderness but in our minds. The undiscovered country is not wilderness but a change of heart. Above, below, around, air circulates and water runs, the clouds rise up and shed their rain and snow. And, somewhere, lawless animals cross boundaries without a blink.

◆

C. L. Rawlins was born in Wyoming, where he's cowboyed, campjacked, guided, built log fences and bridges, and hydrologized. In 1989, a risky, innovative study of air and water pollution in the Bridger Wilderness won the USFS National Primitive Skills Award. His poetry, essays, fiction, and book reviews have appeared in jounals from The North American Review *to* The Redneck Review *and are widely anthologized. A 1993 book,* Sky's Witness: A Year in the Wind River Range, *will be reissued in trade paperback this year. In progress are* In Gravity National Park *(poems) and another eclectic book set in the Wyoming peaks.*

ABOUT THE EDITORS

Deb Clow is co-editor and designer of *Northern Lights* magazine in Missoula, Montana. She shares her home in the Rattlesnake Valley with her beautiful eight-year-old daughter, Catherine, five cats, and an eclectic and wild garden. Her passions include eating glacier lilies under a slip of the new moon, listening for red-tailed hawks, and taking naps.

◆

Don Snow is also co-editor at *Northern Lights* magazine. He is a Utah native, born in the mining camp of Hiawatha; an outdoors enthusiast; and the father of a ten-year-old daughter named Tenly. In addition to two books—*Inside the Environmental Movement*, and *Voices from the Environmental Movement*—his essays and articles have appeared in *Sierra*, *The Utne Reader*, *Orion*, *Environmental Law*, and *Gray's Sporting Journal*. Among his civic involvements, he serves as a trustee of both the Montana Community Foundation and the Montana Consensus Council. He still fishes Montana's rivers when there's water in them.

NONFICTION/ANTHOLOGY

In this astonishing collection, forty of the West's finest writers examine the layered realities of their home territory and show how they reflect and magnify the dreams of America at large. They consider the West as landscape and as history; as a country haunted by the ghosts of Wounded Knee and tainted by atomic fall-out, yet offering a profound solace; as the setting for great experiments in freedom, individualism, and equality and for outrageous acts of greed and violence; as the place where America located and then lost its innocence.

Contributors include: **Gretel Ehrlich,** on Western space and trying to contain it. **Jim Harrison,** dreaming of bears and serving up a recipe for bear stew. **Linda Hogan,** with a meditation on water. **Marilynne Robinson,** on the myth of the West. **Richard Manning,** on Norman Maclean and the meaning of fire. **Jeanne Dixon,** with memories of a Western girlhood.

By turns celebratory and tough-minded, wry and elegiac, large-spirited and deeply personal, *Northern Lights* presents the best writers in the West today, at their most eloquent, perceptive and provocative.

A VINTAGE ORIGINAL

U.S. **$13.00**

Can. **$17.95**

Design by Susan Mitchell

Photography by Elizabeth Grell

51300>

9 780679 755425

ISBN 0-679-75542-X